D1706851

HISTORY

The Gordon Highlanders, 92nd Regiment of Foot, 1794–1994

Amalgamated into the Highlanders with the Camerons and Seaforth. Winston Churchill, when a war correspondent in the Boer War in 1900, described the Gay Gordons as the 'Finest regiment in the World'. At Waterloo, 1815, the Gordons charged with the Scots Greys handing onto their stirrups. The regiment won honours in the West Indies, Afghanistan, the Boer War, WWI, WWII, Egypt and the Sudan. World War I: actions at Le Cateau, Ypres I, II, III, the Somme, Neuve Chapelle, Loos, Arras, Cambrai – lost 1,000 officers and 28,000 men, 65 battle honours and 4 VCs. World War II: St Valery, El Alamein, Sicily, Italy, Kohima, Impal, Rangoon, Normandy, Low Countries, Crossing of the Rhine – sacrificed 2500. Since 1945: Malaya, Cyprus, Kenya, Borneo, Northern Ireland. Recruitment originally from the north-east of Scotland. Now the Grampian and Highland regions.

Motto: Bydand (Stand fast).

The Argyll & Sutherland Highlanders, 91st/93rd Regiment of Foot (Princess Louise's), 1794–1999

The regiments amalgamated in 1881. Battle honours in every campaign from Corunna to Cambrai, Alma to Alamein. The 93rd at Balaclava held a Russian cavalry charge, winning the unique battle honour of the 'Thin Red Line'. At Lucknow during the Indian Mutiny, 7 VCs in a day's fighting. Again living up to being the most Highland of the Highland Corps. Reismeid Chataich – Regiment of the Cat. World War I: 27 battalions fought with great distinction on the Western Front and Middle East. World War II: 9 battalions fought in North Africa, Crete, Eritrea, Abyssinia, Italy, France, Germany and Malaya. Since 1945, for 25 years, the 1st battalion became a household word. The Argylls are the most operational unit in the British Forces serving in Palestine, Hong Kong, Korea, Cyprus, Suez, British Guyana, Singapore, Borneo, Aden, Northern Ireland, and recently, Bosnia and Iraq, 1991 and 2004. Recruitment: the counties of Argyll, Renfrew, Dumbarton,

Stirling, Clakmannan and Kinross. Stirling Castle is the regimental headquarters.

Motto: Sans Peur Ne Oblivicaris (Dinna Fear We Winnae Forget).

The Glasgow Police

Was formed in 1886. They were mainly recruited from the Highlands and the north of Scotland where big men in every sense of the word are produced. Glasgow city has always been renowned for its toughness, likewise their police where the Glaswegian hold very dear to their way of thinking. A large proportion of the police came from the Scots Guards. The Glasgow Police Pipe Band have been world champions on innumerable occasions. The Glasgow police sports is an international event at all levels. The author has yet to meet a finer body of men or women.

Motto: Semper Vigilo (Always Viglant).

The Kenya Police

Came into being in 1887 when the Sultan of Zanzibar, Khalifa bin Said, invited the British Government to provide protection for his domains both on the island and the coastal strip, and also to protect the caravan routes between Mombassa and Uganda. This was a paramilitary operation. The Uganda Railway again had mainly Punjabi police recruiting in north-west India looked after the pacification process into Kenya. Explorers, missionaries, military and settlers were the order of early development, hostile tribes, man-eating lions. To be successful in this environment required adventuresome officers to match the raw courage of the African Askari so a traditional relationship sprang up and was to hold, through tribal conflicts and normal police duties all were given the benefit of Salus Populi – remained loyal to their calling. They bore the major part of the insurrection with an expertise of the highest order as the decorations awarded surpassed any other organisation. On the Northern Frontier Province numerous deeds of valour are still performed. Possibly one of the most efficient British colonial Police Forces due to the input from all the others.

Motto: Utumishi Kwa Watu Wote (Serve the People); originally, Salus Populi.

The Tasmania Police

Formed in the 1800s, provided a service to the people of that delightful Apple Isle, mainly in the cities of Hobart and Launceston and in the magnificent rural areas of that state.

The Royal Papua New Guinea Constabulary 1888

The topographical background of PNG has dictated and penetrated into every aspect in this paradise land. Germany held the north known as New Guinea and Australia the south, Papua. When the two police forces inaugurated to control this beautiful rugged land of mountains, islands, plains and vast rivers. In 1914, Australia took over the whole region.

In 1939, the prefix 'Royal' was conferred in recognition for excellent service in the fields of exploration and pacification in remote, primitive areas. 1942 saw the Japanese invasion resulting in 61 decorations for bravery. 76 indigenous members and 12 officers lost their lives. Apart from normal incidences of crime, clan fights, civil unrest, urban riots, tax evasion, cargo cults, Pacific Islands Regiment Mutinies the Royal Constabulary has coped at all times. Since independence in 1975, the Bougainville Rebellion has taken its toll. Corrupt politicians and the triads from Kuala Lumpur in the guise of timber importers are gun runners for the PNG Clans; also the OPM in Irian Jaya this has produced huge pressures for the constabulary to bear. The cap badge is the bird of paradise with laurel leaves surmounted by St Edwards' crown.

KHAKI AND BLUE
A Soldier's and Police Officer's Life
1930–2002

KHAKI AND BLUE

A Soldier's and Police Officer's Life
1930–2002

Angus John MacDonald

ATHENA PRESS
LONDON

KHAKI AND BLUE
A Soldier's and Police Officer's Life 1930–2002
Copyright © Angus John MacDonald 2005

ISBN 1 84401 421 5

First Published 2005 by
ATHENA PRESS
Queen's House, 2 Holly Road
Twickenham TW1 4EG
United Kingdom

Printed for Athena Press

To my very dear wife, Ronnie, who has suffered me through my non-formative years – the power behind the throne

Acknowledgements

To my fellow conspirator in undetected crime, Stuart Sykes: a very fine journalist, of Scottish descent and understanding.

To my secretary/managers, slaving in the office, Barbara and Darleen, my thanks.

Angus Mac, 2002
Without apologies
For Auld Lang Syne

Prologue

The author has enjoyed life and at times has lived life to the full, with all its woes and tribulations. In modern parlance, he has had a ball. He would like to share some of his experiences and views of the great people he has been fortunate to meet, and serve with, during his life to date.

Some deserve higher praise, others possibly not so high. It is not his intention to offend or decry the dead or the less fortunate, but to give everyone a taste of life's rich tapestry – which he has been fortunate enough to view at times from an objective point of view, instead of being very much the subject.

The author, you will see, has varied philosophies on life, based on his upbringing and experiences in far-flung lands. While he was in New Zealand and attempting to run a ski-ing/tourist guest house, a number of guests suggested that some of his experiences were worth committing to paper. Here is the result.

For those of that ilk, it should prove an enjoyment. For others, maybe an opening of eyes and minds at least worthy of some consideration. The overall tone is more controversial than contrite.

'Here's tae us wha's like us.'
'Damned few – they're aw' deed.'

Angus John MacDonald
Soldier/Police Officer
2002

Contents

Introduction

At times, characters herein may be a figment of the author's imagination. Any relation to the dead, dying or damned is purely coincidental.

Khaki and Blue represents the predominant colours of the British Commonwealth Armies and Police Forces. The uniform of the Colonial Police had both, when we British had an Empire to be proud of; before our socialist brothers and sisters in their misbegotten idealism gave it away without a fight; aided and abetted by American economic blackmail.

Part One

The Greatest Experience of All

1: Banchory and Back

It took seventeen years of engagement, but at thirty-six, Betsy McBean MacDonald, née Diack, finally married 42-year-old William MacDonald. The officiating minister was their cousin, Paul Booth, the wedding was in upper New York State and the honeymoon at Buffalo near the Niagara Falls, but the newly-weds were Scottish through and through. Both came from the northeast of Scotland, Bill from the fishing village of Whitehills, with Banff and Macduff nearby, and Betsy from the Aberdeen suburb of Bucksburn.

World War I had seen Bill MacDonald serving as a young Chief Engineer in the Mercantile Marine, taking part in the hazardous Archangel and Murmansk convoys – to Russia with love. Bill was lucky: he had been torpedoed, and survived. Usually a human being lasted about three minutes in the Arctic waters; the even more unfortunate were put through the props of their destroyer escorts.

Betsy Diack too did her bit for God, King and Country as a Matron of a London hospital with the Queen Alexandra Military Nursing Service. She was a strong church-goer, and Bill followed on in the Presbyterian Auld Kirk of Scotland. Their politics were Liberal, and like many Scots they believed in the opportunity to earn a living on merit. Both were well educated. Proficient in Latin, Greek, French and German, Betsy could also cope with advanced mathematics, up to calculus standard. She played the piano, sang, danced and acted. Bill had come up the hard way, despite being the son of a fish merchant. He served his time in a blacksmith's shop, shoeing horses, brazing and welding, then moved on to boilermaking, fitting and turning. Proficient in mathematics himself, he attended night school at Robert Gordon's College in the Silver City of Aberdeen to fuel his ambition of going to sea as an engineer. Once there, he rapidly rose from 4th Engineer to Chief Engineer and served in cargo ships of various tonnages on most routes across the world.

In the aftermath of the so-called 'Great War', during which Scottish regiments bled profusely on the Flanders fields where the poppies grow, as well as in the Middle East, Greece, the Dardanelles and Palestine, the impoverished British Isles held out little hope of a worthwhile future for ambitious people. As one of Scotland's most-loved laments would have it, the 'Flowers o' the Forest have been we'ed awa'' once more. And so the engaged couple emigrated to America in 1928. Bill the Engineer commented, 'You cannot teach the Yanks anything.' Betsy the Nursing Sister later gave her own blessing to their new land, summing up the United States by confessing, 'I was never homesick for Scotland but I am now for the States.'

Bill MacDonald became Marine Superintendent for the Royal Canadian Mail on the Canadian Lakes of Superior, Erie, Huron, Michigan and Ontario. Betsy was in private nursing in New York State. Her patients were affluent and loved the strawberry blonde Scots lassie to the extent that she was regularly mentioned in their wills. On arrival in the States, they married and lived happily ever after. They made new and met old friends, toured the country on holidays and had a taste of the good life. They also accumulated worldly goods in the form of their own apartment in West Orange, plus other apartments which they leased. They played the stock market, had a Buick, a Boxer dog and a bank balance to boot. On August 30, 1930, they also had a son.

Naming him Angus John MacDonald, both parents were overjoyed with their good fortune. It was not to last: the Depression suddenly jolted the MacDonalds out of their comfortable existence. Bill went into deep sea trading – San Francisco, the West Coast ports, to Japan and the Far East – and by 1932 it was decided he should remain at sea while Betsy, where possible, sold off their remaining assets. She took their son back to Bonnie Scotland and left him in the care of his two maiden aunts, Mary and Tib Diack, while she returned to the States for the next two years to tidy up the remains of the MacDonald estate. Mary and Tib were both Queen's Nurses operating from Banchory, a village of some 2,500 souls lying eighteen miles south-west of Aberdeen.

Thus, at two-and-a-half, Gus MacDonald was installed with his two aunts in the land of high endeavour, the land of the shining river – in this case the River Dee – and the land of his heart forever, Scotland the Brave. Bonnie Banchory sits on Royal Deeside, so called because Balmoral Castle, summer residence of the Royal Family, is thirty-five miles up the valley between the villages of Braemar and Ballater in one of the most beautiful parts of Scotland. Deeside starts south-west of Aberdeen, known as the Silver City because it is largely built in silver granite from the quarry at Rubislaw Quarry, a select suburb of mansion homes and miniature castles. Aberdeen boasted two University colleges, Marischall with its magnificent architecture, and King's; it was also a large fishing port of the rough North Sea, it had shipbuilding industries and served as the provincial market town where the famous Aberdeen Angus cattle were sold to the world.

Following the River Dee westward you come to the suburb of Cults, then to Beildside with its Royal Golf Course. Next is Peterculter, known simply as Culter, where Rob Roy's massive leap from cliff to bank across the river is commemorated by a statue which has become a tourist landmark. Banchory, a retirement town, enjoys a backdrop of heather-clad hills of up to almost 2,000 feet (600 metres). They had their fair share of game – rabbit, hare, grouse, partridge and deer – and the River Dee had once given up to a local, Dr Crane, a 125 lb salmon. Industrialists and the like came there to fish from around the globe, making Tor-na-coille Hotel their base. Tor-na-Dee Hotel had provided the Maharajahs of India a year-round Scottish hunting, shooting and fishing resort at the turn of the nineteenth century.

The local industry was timber, mainly pine for pit props and building, plus mixed farming. As one went up the Dee Valley the hills gave way to mountains, Lochnagar at 3,500 feet (1,000 metres) being the most popular among climbers. Aboyne, like Braemar, was famous for its Highland Games where the strong men of Scotland with their Commonwealth brothers and American cousins competed in tossing the caber, putting the shot, throwing the hammer and tossing the weight. Cumberland wrestling and the performance of massed pipes and drums from all over the world made for a right royal occasion.

From an early age, the young Gus MacDonald was schooled in the tradition of north-east Scotland, a tradition tied up with family, Church, a work ethic and a sense of responsibility to the community at large. A great influence on his upbringing was Aunt Tib, a fearsome lady with flashing green eyes and golden red hair, which when not in a bun came right down to her ankles. She was what the Scots call a big woman, about 5 foot 10 and built in proportion, who in her younger day had been an outsize model. Tib followed the noble calling of nursing during World War I. She had been Matron of a Military Hospital in London, coping with the horrors faced by badly wounded soldiers, for whom she had a great respect. As time passed she encouraged the young Angus in all things military. One of a family of twelve, she was a regular church-goer like the rest of them.

Tib's father was the stationmaster at Bucksburn. Tib claimed to be a Christian Socialist but later in her life she changed to the Conservatives, claiming the trade unions had gone far enough. Aunt Mary too had been a Matron of a Naval Hospital but was more reserved than Tib. Gus went on the rounds with both when they were involved as Queen's Nurses administering to the sick. They shared the same outlook on life. As Queen's Nurses they had an area of some twelve miles by twelve to cover, which they did first on horseback, then in a horse and trap, on bicycles, motorcycles, and finally in the mid-1930s in a motor car provided for them.

Tib and Mary were a resilient pair of genuine do-gooders. They had brought generations of babies into this world in the most difficult circumstances. Flood or snowstorm rarely stopped them doing their duty. Like Gus's mother, his aunts were well educated. They knew what was required of them and lived accordingly. Both were British to the core, proud of being Scots and of what the Empire stood for, which to them was an independent Commonwealth where their brothers and sisters in the colonies were to be educated and trained for self-rule within that family of nations. A number of their relatives and friends were missionaries all over the world. They were well acquainted with the problems found overseas, and like many Scots they had relatives in the United States.

Those were years of warm summers and cold snowy winters, with all of Scotland's natural beauty on display on Deeside as the seasons passed: the silver Dee with its heavyweight salmon and sea trout, green pines, fir trees and clumps of silver birch, supple branches of larch and leafy beech trees, and the sturdy oak besides. Known today as Grampian, after the mountains, or Eastern Highlands, the country comprised the counties of Aberdeen, Kincardine and Banff, the latter famous for the River Spey. For this is the country where world-famous malt whiskies are distilled from the crystal-clear waters of the mountain burns and the golden barley of the local farms. But it is also Gordon Highlander country. The Regiment had covered itself in glory all over the world, distinguishing itself in the Boer War when Winston Churchill, a journalist at the time, described it as 'the finest Regiment in the world', though the modest Gordons would never make such a claim. The North-East was proud of them, every family having a connection to the Gordon Highlanders.

In summer and autumn there was always, in the background, the drone and skirl of the pipes as territorial companies in every town did their voluntary parades. Deeside provided the 4/7 Gordon Highlanders, a machine gun battalion, Donside – its sister river area – the 5/6 Gordon Highlanders, an anti-aircraft battalion. Several of the male population served with the 1st & 2nd Regular Battalions, Malaya being their overseas stamping ground, along with India's fabled North-West Frontier.

Angus, who between arriving in Scotland and his school enrolment a year and a half later uttered very few words, as the local children teased him about his American accent and clothes, became a pupil at Banchory School in 1934 and went to Infants I under the tutelage of Miss MacFarlane, a most competent teacher. Prior to this, his mother had returned from the States, but his father was still at sea working from the West Coast of America to the Far East. During that same year of 1934 his father, an Engineer Commander in the Royal Naval Reserve, had been recruited by the Japanese as a Guarantee Engineer to perform installations and trial runs of their latest warships in the Inland Sea. His Japanese associates were quite open about the fact that they would take over the Far East, the Philippines, Australia, and

New Zealand – as well as all the other British, Dutch and French possessions in their area of influence – so it was surprising that Pearl Harbor came as a surprise, as did Singapore.

By now the Depression years were beginning to recede, but in their place rumours of a future war with Germany were beginning to circulate, as Hitler expanded his Reich and that country was under arms once more. At school MacDonald was seen as a slightly above-average student, but this almost idyllic country life suddenly changed when Bill MacDonald returned from the Deep Sea and took up a position as Guarantee Engineer for British Auxiliaries in the Glasgow district of Govan in 1937. As they say in that great city, 'When God left Govan...'

Glasgow: the British Empire's second city after London, aptly described in a famous book title as *No Mean City*. Glasgow on the Clyde, where the greatest ships in the world were built with the local coal and steel and sustained by a labour force second to none in great shipyards like John Brown's, Harland & Wolff of Clydebank and Govan. As Billy Connolly has helped audiences all over the world to understand, the shipbuilders worked hard and played likewise. On the five o'clock hooter on a Friday pay night, five thousand men marched into the local pubs for a 'hauf and a hauf' (small whisky and half-pint of beer), the first half-dozen drinks being downed in quick time.

The MacDonald family resided 'Three Up' in a tenement at 221 Langlands Road, Govan, overlooking Elder Park. It was right in the heart of shipbuilding territory, with huge cranes and the freshly laid keels and hulls taking shape to 'the song of the Clyde' – the incessant ding-dong sound of rivets being hammered home, for welding techniques were just over the industrial horizon. It was an exciting time for the laddie from the country, not least of all because the Glasgow system of separate religious schools for 'Proddies' (Protestants) and 'Papes' (Catholics) produced some intriguing situations.

MacDonald duly went to his Protestant school, Elder Park Primary, wearing a MacDonald kilt. On the way home from school the Proddy Dogs versus The Papes was the fun of the day. Though Gus faced the additional taunts of 'Kiltie kiltie cauld bum, three stairs up!', the teasing dried up when the Kiltie in question punched a few noses in retaliation.

The year 1938 brought the Empire Exhibition to Glasgow's Bellahouston Park, with exhibits and people from all over an Empire that spread over a third of the world. All those different people were made very welcome by the open-hearted Glaswegians. Bands played, there was all sorts of dancing and entertainment, both by day and by night. Young MacDonald was taken up to the city and introduced to the shops and sights. You could, for sixpence, buy a tram ticket for a day and travel all around Glasgow: Argyle Street, with its bargain shops such as Lewis's with its modern escalators and its great toy department, full of fascinating Meccano sets and whippy ice cream cones; Buchanan Street with its sophisticated stores of furniture and clothing, jewellery, paintings, and the restaurants wafting out those mouth-watering aromas; Sauchiehall Street with shops, restaurants, bars, dance halls and picture houses – cinemas to the audiences of today. The main thoroughfare, Glasgow's pride, was George Square, containing the Corporation Headquarters, a magnificent feat of neo-Gothic architecture. Young MacDonald was taken on a trip 'doon the watter' (down the river) to Rothesay on a paddle steamer. Another day he was allowed to chalk his initials on the propeller of the Queen Mary, a lot of his father's pals being engineers and leading artisans at John Brown's of Clydebank.

His mother would sometimes take him to the pictures at the Plaza, Govan Cross, where peanuts and raisins were his special treat, Gene Autry and the Lone Ranger his cowboy favourites. And there was roller skating in the streets on asphalt like ice, with the local cop trying to catch and smash you across the ear or plant a large boot in the backside. Young MacDonald joined up with a local gang, six young fellows between the age of eight and thirteen, their occupations hanging lifts on the back of trucks, trains and bus rides until the conductor approached and the desperados dropped off the moving vehicle. Walking over the top of girders on rail and road bridges was another speciality to test the moral fibre.

Every Sunday, of course, he attended church with his parents and enjoyed the rousing old Scottish psalms and hymns, and sometimes even listened to the sermon from the very articulate minister. A walk home in the park, and back to Sunday school in the evening. His mother was a truly religious woman who praised the Lord with her fine contralto voice. Father followed on, more as a social commitment than a call from the Lord. Mac the younger was uncertain but followed in his old man's footsteps.

Sailing 'toy' yachts in the ponds in the various parks around Glasgow was a lot of fun. Some of these so-called toys had the full rigging, properly based on the real article, and the older fellows raced with some very fine home-made craft showing off the skill of true craftsmen. Other weekends brought outings to Millerston Loch, a public pond with rowing boats where Mac Senior taught his offspring to row and scull and gave a few pointers in sailing. His dream was to win the football pools, buy his son a 500-acre farm and himself a seagoing yacht. On the way home, Barlinnie, the local prison where the 'bad boys' were housed, was always pointed out – up in 'Bar' where you sup porridge, another way of saying you were doing time in one of HM's prisons.

As the years rolled on through 1937 to 1939 Gus had acquired a new accent. He could now speak and understand Glaswegian with its south-west lilt, and with it came some understanding of the different levels of social standing, as Scotland reflected the class-ridden society of Great Britain, although Scotland's social structures were different from England's.

By now, of course, war clouds were gathering. Germany under Adolf Hitler had marched into the Sudetenland and annexed Czechoslovakia, and British Prime Minister Neville Chamberlain had gone to Munich to make the agreement that would ensure 'Peace in our time'. But as Britain and France had a treaty to contain Germany, the German invasion of Poland on September 3rd, 1939, meant we were once again at war. For young MacDonald it was an interesting time, putting up with the 'blackout', observing the ARP (air-raid precautions) Wardens on every residential block, building and factory, who ensured the blackout was policed and gave instructions on how to get to the air-raid shelters which sprang up everywhere. MacDonald's school was being evacuated to Dumfriesshire, in Scotland's far south-west, where volunteer families took in the young from the cities. He developed an old-fashioned gumboil at this stage and was held back. Instead of heading for Dumfries, when hale and hearty he was off in the opposite direction: taken by his maiden aunts back to Banchory, in the North-East, to become a 'Loon' – an Aberdeen boy.

1940 saw German victories all over Europe. Young MacDonald returned to his former home with his two maiden aunts, Tib and Mary, both still practising District Nurses who were now approaching retirement. He returned to his Primary School education and his Glaswegian accent was remarked upon both by his fellow pupils and Miss Ross, his teacher. This again was put to right by a few bloody noses, Miss Ross's not among them. The north-eastern attitude was that they were far superior to the Glasgow product, one being industrial and the other mainly farming. The climate too was colder and drier and the sun did shine.

The war years rolled on and the British at last began to sense victory would be theirs. The Battle of El Alamein was the beginning, in October 1942, when General Montgomery defeated General Rommel of the Deutsche Afrika Corps using his 8th Army with some expertise and a better build-up of equipment. The attacking infantry divisions were on the right, the 9th Australian on the left, the 1st New Zealand with the legendary 51st Highland in the centre, comprising the Gordons, Camerons, Seaforth, Black Watch and the Argyll & Sutherland Highlanders. The 51st Highland was the only division to go with Field Marshal Montgomery from El Alamein to Berlin via North Africa, Sicily, Italy and north-west Europe in three campaigns.

Like the rest of the village, Gus was well aware that a price was being paid for victory. The next-door neighbour, Captain Jack Sharpe, Gordon Highlanders, was blinded at El Alamein, and a number of local lads killed and wounded. Now in his first year of secondary schooling, the patriotic Gus wrote a poem in tribute to the soldiers of El Alamein: 'Remember the boys who fought at El Alamein/They were born brave and gallant men', and so on.

Education still followed the old Scottish curriculum with its three streams. In the 'A' stream you were possibly going to achieve a Higher Leaving Certificate and go to university at the end of five or six years' schooling, or a Lower Leaving Certificate after three. The 'B' stream would leave school at thirteen to fourteen and hope for a trade apprenticeship at 16, while 'C' meant a three-year commercial course in typing, shorthand and book-keeping. MacDonald ended up as an 'A' and nurtured ambitions of being an Officer in the Gordon Highlanders. Like most Scottish youths, he played soccer and was soon in the school team as left back.

While rationing made itself felt in the cities, in the country little changed, although the luxuries of life such as bananas and chocolate were non-existent. The black market flourished like a huge barter system. For a couple of years the summer holidays saw MacDonald work at a local sawmill, carrying 'backs' or offcuts of logs from the saw bench. Then he graduated to working with the Forestry Commission, weeding, cleaning, planting, ditching, fencing, brushing, and eventually felling, learning the use and care of the various tools. Working mainly with a team of adults provided a good source of pocket money, for pictures (movies) and smoking as well as sports equipment, especially the Scottish game that was to become a lifelong passion, golf.

Due to the war, October brought a month's holiday, when all school pupils were expected to help out picking potatoes, a task more commonly called the 'tattie howking'. One shilling an hour for an eight-hour day. The job brought them into contact with co-workers in the shape of Italian prisoners of war, who had a real easy life with their fancy-cut uniforms and plastered-down long hairdos. No wonder, they thought, they were held in poor esteem. As wartime lengthened, the village of Banchory saw the gallant Poles, the quiet, determined Norwegians, our Canadian brothers, Indian Regiments of the Old Indian Army from the Punjab, as well as our own Scots: the Black Watch, Gordon Highlanders, Seaforth Highlanders, King's Own Scottish Borderers and Royal Scots Fusiliers.

There were, too, German POWs who looked like real soldiers and were accorded their due respect, and our American cousins – overpaid, oversexed and over here in the popular phrase. In fact a cousin dropped in who was a Captain in the American 8th

Tactical Air Force, wearing a beautiful uniform with a purple silk lining. The KOSB, the Borderers, stayed longest: they were part of the 52nd Lowland Division being trained as mountain troops, climbing and ski-ing with all-white clothing and equipment. When their time came, it was to land in the Walcheren Islands off the Dutch coast in about a metre (3 feett) of water.

The Canadians, who were motorised infantry, were the first to arrive as the CFC (Canadian Forestry Corps) to cut pit props for the coal mines. All of a sudden the poor bastards were changed to shock troops and took part in the Dieppe Raid on the French coast, where they suffered heavy casualties. The Poles and Canadians did best in the romantic stakes among the lassies. The Black Watch gave an impressive display, having just returned from a 'python' — five years' service on the North-West Frontier of India, skirmishing with the wily Pathan tribesmen, who proved completely loyal when fighting the Japanese in Singapore and Burma. The Watch Officers were mounted on horseback for their weekly church parades, representing the pre-war regular army in great style.

MacDonald had the usual sound Scottish education, which was considered to be the best in the English-speaking world. He was a careless student and did not persevere with homework but managed to pass in all subjects, with the exception of Latin, for his Lower Leaving Certificate at fifteen. His Latin master was Jock Key, ex-Captain Gordon Highlanders, WWI, and a teacher of some ability and personality. Jock, a Classics scholar and a true red socialist, had visited China and had a command of Mandarin. He could take in and give out Latin Study in twenty minutes out of the allotted period of forty minutes, then discourse with his students on a variety of subjects. He was not averse to a bit of lechery, having the girls in his classes sit in the front row directly in front of his desk, from which he would pass ribald remarks. MacDonald, a hopeless Latin scholar, was usually dismissed with, 'Stand up, extinguish or distinguish yourself.' He then would ask if he could go to the toilet, the rejoinder being, 'Aye laddie, go and have a smoke.' He was told not to bother returning but instead to have a good game of snooker at Dago's, the local Italian ice cream and coffee shop.

Granny Gray, the ever-popular English, Art and Geography teacher, was overjoyed when her class passed all subjects with an average of 80%. Mac had filched the exam papers from the Rector's study by opening a drawer and re-sealing the sealed envelopes. As his father had advised, 'Son, be honest, but not too honest.' MacDonald charged five shillings a paper and ensured all of the class was compromised. Granny Gray congratulated her finest ever class, and was cheered in return by a sea of grinning faces.

Having collected only a number of subjects in his Higher Leaving Certificate, MacDonald volunteered for his National Service with the British Army. Being a dual-national with an American birth certificate, he did not want to be called up, but chose to volunteer. He felt he had a duty to do, and he was perfectly willing to do it rather than waiting to be press-ganged. While waiting the few months before his military service began, our laddie decided to work at the local gasworks. He started off as a labourer digging for leaking pipes, then painting the two gasometers, and was then promoted to stoker, servicing a bench of a dozen retorts, shovelling in coal and dragging out the embers to be watered down into coke.

His three workmates had recently been demobbed from the services, one from the Scots Greys, Scotland's only cavalry regiment. Sergeant MacRobbie had seen action in the desert and north-west Europe and had been wounded when his tank was hit. The other had been with the Seaforth Highlanders in Madagascar fighting the Vichy French, and had come up against a unit of the French Foreign Legion (*La Légion étrangère*). As he put it, they were 'nae bad sojers'. The third member of the group was a huge man, six foot six in the old money, but so far had escaped doing his bit. He seemed a bit on the wild side by his antics, speech and general disposition, commonly known in the parlance of Scottish infantry as a 'hard case'. In fact he was the victim of an ambush by the local youth: when he was riding his cycle to work through Captain's Wood they had tied a rope across his path, meaning he was catapulted backwards as his bike continued forward. He had the odd abrasion to substantiate the event.

The stoker's role was dirty, heavy work with an element of

danger. The retorts had to be partially opened and a burning rope end exploded the excess gas. The money was double the norm. MacDonald's former schoolmates, especially the girls, did their best to ignore him as he walked home from work. MacDonald enjoyed the work and the companionship, and of course he had built his muscular development up for his Army training. And so, without further ado, a-soldiering he would go.

2: On His Majesty's Service

A Gordon for me, a Gordon for me,
If you're no' a Gordon ye're nae use tae me,
The Black Watch are braw, the Seaforth and a',
But the cockie wee Gordon's the pride o' them a'.

Scottish popular song

In the year of Our Lord AD 1949, Angus John MacDonald was called to the colours for National Service of eighteen months, at that time the norm for a youth of eighteen years to undergo in the service of his country. The Second World War had recently ended, and the United Kingdom of Great Britain and Northern Ireland still had overseas interests in the way of colonies, spoils of previous wars, occupations, explorations and commercial expansion over the centuries. Little did Mac realise how many of them he would end up visiting! He had decided he would do his National Service in the Gordon Highlanders, his county regiment. A romantic despite his dour Scottish face, he had been filled with tales of glory by his favourite maiden aunt, Isabella Diack. She too, had been in the nursing profession; after running a military hospital during World War I, she had a great admiration for the British 'Tommy' and his fortitude. Despite her experience, she believed the profession of arms a noble calling, and encouraged young Gus, who had a reputation in and around the village as a bit of a wild one – despite a somewhat sheltered upbringing with occasional and sometimes regular visits to church.

Gazing absent-mindedly at the Scottish countryside tinged with autumn gold under an endless blue sky, Mac pondered his future as a Gordon Highlander. Should he become a regular soldier, a twenty-two-year man, or just put in a five-year short term? A commission appealed, but he was still a callow youth with no particular brilliance. The glamour of Highland dress, a decoration for gallantry, a broadsword with silver and scarlet hilt: oh yes, it definitely had appeal. His daydreams came to an end with the train pulling into Cawdor Station where he was to meet the transport for Fort George, the training establishment for the Highland Brigade.

Formed for the most part around the period of the Napoleonic Wars, the kilted Scottish Regiments – the Black Watch (Royal Highland Regiment), the Queen's Own Cameron Highlanders, the Seaforth Highlanders, the Argyll & Sutherland Highlanders, the Gordon Highlanders and the Highland Light Infantry – each had their own regimental area for recruitment. The British infantry are a heterogeneous lot, made up largely of romantic misfits. The professional soldier was represented by the unemployable, the lawbreakers and so on, and now there were also conscripted National Servicemen, who made up 70% of new recruits.

On the platform at Cawdor Station stood Corporal Campbellman, a typical old sweat who had not adjusted to civilian life after six years in the Queen's Own Cameron Highlanders during World War II. A survivor of three campaigns with service in the Western Desert, Italy and north-west Europe, Campbellman was 5' 7" with a swarthy complexion that could be ascribed to his excessive drinking habits. He had a paunch to match, piggy little brown eyes which missed little of the world around him, and a 'wee bunnet' pulled well down over the eyes. Despite any impression the onlooker might have formed, Campbellman was a good junior NCO, capable of commanding a 10-man section in action and saving their less experienced lives, while at the same time making his presence felt to the enemy, whoever they might be. The recruits milled round the platform waiting for the veteran corporal, who patiently waited until the train had departed. To no one in particular, the voice from the south-west of Scotland intoned, 'Right, youse people! In the back o' the three-tonner!' – with a jerk of his head in the direction of the Army Bedford truck parked nearby.

Fort George materialised some twenty minutes later. Near Ardersier in Inverness-shire, the fort was begun under General

Wade in more rebellious times in the mid-eighteenth century. Completed in 1769, it was a massive structure in classic military architectural style, with ramparts twenty metres in depth, more than a mile of bastions and emplacements designed to provide a good crossfire. The Bedford truck came to a halt outside the Fort's main gate, the recruits piled out and Cpl Campbellman snapped, 'Fall in in threes!'

The raw newcomers managed the semblance of a squad in three ranks facing the gate.

'Atten-*shun*!' came next, with our worthy corporal pointing up at a huge notice above the gate, surmounted by the Royal Coat of Arms. 'Take Note,' it said. 'Disengage the left eye, bring the tip of the foresight to the centre of the rear aperture, take first pressure on the trigger, squeeze.' This was followed by 'KILL OR BE KILLED' in bolder print. MacDonald thought, 'Christ, this is the Army...'

The squad was marched off with the insistent 'Left-right, left-right' from Corporal Campbellman to the Quartermaster's Store, where bedding was drawn: coir hair mattress and two blankets. Sheets and pyjamas were still a luxury of the future. The following day brought documentation, medical and psychological testing. MacDonald was assigned to an Assaye Squad for potential Cadet Officers. The name 'Assaye' was from a battle in India, some two hundred years before, where the present training battalion, the Highland Light Infantry, had won a battle honour, and with it the right to wear an elephant on their cap badge. The Highland Infantry, sometimes referred to by its members as 'Hell's Last Intake' and by others as 'The Poisoned Dwarfs', were mainly recruited from that *No Mean City* of Glasgow, their Honorary Colonel-in-Chief being HRH The Princess Margaret. Medical and psycho testing weeded out those unfit for the infantry, while the unrecruitable went to a Corps. Both regular enlisted and National Service men received the same indoctrination, the only variation being that the regular was issued with his kilt and accessories.

The medical, a series of 'jabs' (injections and inoculations), made the recruits sick for the next forty-eight hours, their first weekend confined to barracks – as they were for the next ten weeks.

On the second day of life in His Majesty's British Imperial Army a second visit was paid to the Quartermaster's Store for kit to be drawn. Each company had a Quartermaster with the rank of Staff Sergeant, known as 'Colour' in Scottish regiments as one of his extraneous duties on parade was to form part of the Escort to the Colours, the Regimental Colour and Union Flag, Battle Honours being displayed on the Regimental Colour. Kit was drawn with elements missing so that the QM's Staff could charge for the item allegedly lost and its replacement, a custom within a custom considered part of the recruits' indoctrination. 'Hit the pocket' has always had an enlightening effect.

Private Illingworth, a big Yorkshireman of rugby league fame, lounged against the corridor wall adjacent to the QM's Store. Like the majority of Sassenachs in the Highland Brigade, Illingworth had chosen the Black Watch due to the prominence of their cap badge. It took the form of a Red Hackle won at Waterloo, when the Watch dipped their traditional white cockades in the blood of the French cavalry and a Battle Honour was created. The British Army survives on traditions much envied by our American cousins. Down this same corridor marched Drill Sergeant Hugh MacRae, Cameron Highlanders and a Skianach (from the Isle of Skye), 6' 7", a Bisley shot and the No. 1 Musketry Instructor to the Highland Brigade. MacRae was over the 18-stone mark and did not have any superfluous fat, an impressive figure. In fact Gus wondered how the Japs had missed him in the Burma Campaign.

MacRae crashed to a halt next to Illingworth and roared, in his best parade ground voice, 'Laddie, do you know when the Fort was built? For your edification 1693, and it does not need your bloody support. Get up off the bloody wall!'

The date may have been inaccurate, the message most certainly was not.

The Training Battalion was divided up into companies like a serving battalion, with the exception of Support Coy (who support arms such as machine guns, mortars etc.). There was HQ Coy for Admin and Rifle and bayonet wallahs. The day was divided into one-hour parades mainly by bugle calls, commencing with Reveille and ending with Lights Out. A Duty Piper also played his part in conjunction with the Drummer/Bugler.

The idea entertained by his Commonwealth cronies that the British soldier is a lousy shot is an erroneous one. Having been a gamekeeper in civilian life and now Chief Musketry Instructor, Sgt Hugh MacRae was bent on seeing that the wisdom of hitting the bull was not neglected. Every day for one hour the recruits fired .22 rifles in the indoor range under MacRae's supervision, after introductory comments to the effect that 'You laddies couldnae hit a cow's arse wi' a banjo!' He would then demonstrate the 'prone' lying position. His idea of tutelage was to plant his 18-stone weight on the ankles of any awkward recruit in order to emphasise the correct posture. Each hour of the day the venue was changed for a particular training period and each time the corporals and lance corporals would whip into a minor drill period and dish out petty punishments for real or imaginary errors by the recruits. 'Report to my bunk at 6 p.m. for talking on parade' was typical, whereupon the NCO would have an article of equipment such as boots, belt, gaiters, pack or pouch for cleaning, which meant an hour's extra fatigues.

Private Alec Ferguson from Glasgow, a gorilla-like creature who was a bus conductor by occupation, was singled out by L/Cpl Pearman, a typical Black Watch NCO of London extraction, for talking on parade.

'You horrible thing, Ferguson, right, you're talking!'

'No, Corporal.'

'You are now: report to my bunk 6 p.m., get it?'

'Yes, Corporal.'

Alec Ferguson did not take shit from anyone, and was apt to display the fact; he was not shy in thumping any malefactor who got in his way, irrespective of size – a 'hard man', in short.

Fergie reported to the corporal's bunk and was handed a new battledress (tunic and trousers) for pressing, plus shoulder titles and L/Cpl's chevrons and a long-service chevron (three years) to be sewn onto L/Cpl Pearman's uniform. Fergie returned to the Recruit Barracks and threw the uniform into a corner on the floor, demonstrating his normal fluency in profane language, every second word being that earthy expression of sexual connotations in the various tenses. The gist of it was that Recruit Ferguson had no intention of obeying the L/Cpl's illegal order.

But Ferguson did press L/Cpl Pearman's tunic and trousers. A brown burn mark displayed an exact outline of the iron between the shoulders, and the chevrons of rank and service were stitched on the tunic upside-down. The uniform was returned to the corporal's bunk and placed in a cupboard by L/Cpl Pearman, who did not bother to inspect his uniform for the next day's parade but gave a muttered thanks to Ferguson and an indication that he could now 'fall out'.

The following morning at eight came Muster Parade, when the squad was inspected by the lieutenant sergeant and corporal with L/Cpl Pearman bringing up the rear in a brand-new crumpled uniform newly drawn from Q store, and informing Ferguson very quietly that he would 'get' him.

Private Baillie, a coal miner from the Kingdom of Fife, had married shortly before call up and was clearly missing the joys of connubial bliss. Baillie was not going to take the bullshit of Fort George and the training personnel, and he did not escape 'jankers', or being CB – Confined to Barracks with extra drills, plus an hourly report to the Guardroom, where the Duty Officer performed an inspection. About the third week of training, a captain from the Parachute Regiment visited the Fort and gave a spiel about the advantages of the Paras, such as a rise in pay of 2/6d per day, and less bullshit in the shape of spit and polish. Both Baillie and Ferguson volunteered, were accepted and did their time in the 2nd Battalion of the Parachute Regiment.

The British infantryman was not confused by the broad spectrum of weapons or drills to master, but the basics were hammered home relentlessly. The recruits had a degree of skill in the .303 No. 4 (SMLE) rifle and the screw-drive twin-type bayonet, 36 grenade, Sten gun (sub-machine carbine), or Bren gun (light machine gun). The men were posted to a battalion in Europe or the Middle East after ten weeks' Basic; six weeks' Advanced was further handling and firing of weapons, map reading, camouflage, firing and movement of the PIAT (Projectile Infantry Anti-Tank) which put your shoulder out if not held securely due to its mainspring action. Each day, apart from marching in quick or double time, at the end of each period, there was an hourly session by those glamour boys of the Army

Physical Training Corps. These were distinguished, apart from their bulging muscles, by the wasp-like strip of horizontal black and red stripes, long blue sweat pants and black baseball boots and the instructor's whistle. The recruit was introduced to 'milling', in which two recruits had to 'box' for three one-minute rounds, no holds barred, irrespective of size or weight. Any promising idiot was seized upon for the Company Boxing Team, where the PTIs would give the basics and pitch the unsuspecting pugilist into a regular training schedule and excuse him most parades.

Joe Imrie, a heavily-built plumber from Fife, managed to flatten some smaller individuals on three occasions in the 'milling' series and was promoted to the Coy Boxing Team, who were scheduled to fight 'D' Company, a Drafting Company which comprised re-enlisted 'Blues'. On the night of the big occasion, Imrie climbed into the ring for his three 3-minute rounds at heavyweight. Officers' wives, guests, NCOs and wives and the whole training battalion turned out to see the bouts. The bell went for round one and Imrie got into top gear with a rush and a flailing of fists at his 'D' Coy opponent, who ducked, weaved, danced and darted in and out and peppered Imrie with blows from all points of the compass. Throughout the three rounds, Imrie never laid a glove on his almost professional opponent, who did everything but knock him out. Imrie had his eyes opened up, nose cut, lip split and teeth loosened, not to mention the damage to his ribs. So ended Imrie's short boxing career.

Every Saturday morning, the Regimental Sergeant Major came into his own. Friday was pay day and everyone went on a bit of a spree. On the Weekly Battalion Parade, the Battalion formed up by order of companies A, B, C, D and HQ in the Main Square, which was sacrosanct; only trained soldiers were allowed to cross from one side to the other. One particular Saturday saw the parade under the auspices of Warrant Officer 1 Jack Watson, DCM (Distinguished Conduct Medal), won at the Battle of Arnhem when serving with the Paras. Watson was typical of the species 'Rgt Sgt Maj of the 1st Bn HLI'. Built like a bulldog, barrel-chested and bow-legged, he had a Parade Ground voice that could range from a bass bellow to an alto scream. This voice projected the Word of Command, which gave an insight into the

RSM's personality – every RSM should be the Battalion personality. This morning RSM Watson was dissatisfied with the covering-off of 'C' Company and had noticed that the right-hand man, Corporal MacCauley, MC, was slightly out of alignment. MacCauley was an Argyll attached to the HLI for instructional duties. A former Officer who had won the MC at the crossing of the Po in northern Italy in '44, the light machine gun was his forte. A re-enlistment, part of the flotsam and jetsam civvy street had thrown up, MacAuley, a lanky 6' 2", drank too much and was a 'scruffy soldier'. Dressed in the kilt he was more of a scarecrow than a dashing Highlander – not that it bothered him. MacAuley lived in his own world.

'Corporal MacCauley!' roared the RSM, 'move half a pace to your left!' There was no movement. Again the roar: similar response. A painful pause as the Battalion thought, What's up? Then, finally, 'Corporal MacCauley MC!' produced an immediate reply of 'Sir!'

It was part of the bull among the Argylls: all ranks when on parade insisted that any decorations be recognised.

In the middle of the rear rank of 'C' Coy was one Private Kenneth Bourne from Helmsdale, Sutherland, who was to have his wish (little choice) of being a Seaforth Highlander. Bourne was 5' 6", of medium build, with a shock of fiery red hair, the turned-in toes of a hillman, and a former railway fireman. In his Highland tenor voice he would give us his barrack-room rendition of 'I love my wife, I love her dearly', which went on to describe the various parts of her charming anatomy and his ambitions in regard to each. He was not cut out for parade ground drills and was a loathsome sight in the eyes of any NCO. His sloppiness and shuffle did not resemble the desired martial spectacle of a soldier on parade. Bourne, like Cpl MacAuley MC, was suffering from Friday night's hangover. In fact, he was undergoing a spell of number 9s or, in the language of the MO, 'the shits'. Bourne suddenly realised that despite being on parade, he was in urgent need of the toilet. In a timid, almost unheard voice he tried: 'Sir, please sir!'

His Company Sergeant Major took note with a snarl of, 'Stop talking.' The RSM grasped the situation and ordered Bourne to be escorted off the parade ground with a roar of, 'Two men fall in!'

As could be seen by the majority, the luckless Bourne had well and truly filled his pants. Bourne went on to complete two years' National Service and four extra months for various spells in detention (cells), but was to crown his career by winning a Military Medal for bravery in the jungles of Malaya. A real soldier.

MacDonald, who had joined the potential Cadet Officer squad, had by that time tried and failed, being deemed too immature. Others had been weeded out or transferred to more suitable occupations in the various corps. By now Foot Drill and Arms Drill were paramount, the constant twelve hours a day of badgering by NCOs was having the desired effect, and after six weeks the recruits were allowed to wear their tartan patch behind their cap badges. That year the Fort had produced four suicides among the recruits in various forms, hanging or drowning being the 'favourites'. The Moray Firth on the northern ramparts was always available for the poor despondent bastard who did not appreciate what the Army was making of him. MacDonald had soldiered up and, despite having the 'piss taken' over having been a la-di-da Cadet Officer, he got on with the other recruits. In fact he was a favourite with the senior NCOs because of his ability to spit and polish a pair of boots, an effort which took eight hours. Gus MacDonald charged thirty shillings a pair, two bob more than his weekly pay. His fame spread and he was excused parades to 'bull' boots. 7 Pn 'C' Coy 1st Bn HLI Fort George were beginning to look and act like soldiers by the seventh week and were fast approaching the zenith of their careers as parade ground soldiers. In fact their drill movements would have made a Guards Regiment proud.

The Royal Family was in residence at Balmoral, the Scottish retreat on Deeside some fifty miles from the city of Aberdeen. The Highland Brigade provided the Guard when in the Scottish Highlands. Their duties were as Guard of Honour on arrival and departure at Aberdeen station or airport and guard duties at Balmoral Castle, but their main occupation was as beaters at the royal grouse shoot. This being the shooting season, a guard of 96 would come from recruits decked out as fully-fledged Highlanders in Highland Dress of the HLI. Men from each company – A, B, and C – would be drilled by the ex-Scots Guards

Drill Sergeant and the guard weeded out by a process of elimination. They made a magnificent sight: all members of the Guard were between 5' 8" and 5' 9", though NCOs and Officers could be taller, decked out in feather bonnets with white and red plume, green jacket, white buff belt, the red and white MacKenzie kilt of the HLI, with green hose, white spats, black brogues, rifle and nine-inch bayonet, moustached full upper lip, no watches, glasses or rings worn and haircut 'into the wood', all responding to commands like the crack of a whip. Towards the end of the 10-week basic training, HRH Princess Margaret, the Colonel-in-Chief, came to inspect her regiment. The recruits performed as required: only six were injured when they fell asleep on a two-hour wait for HRH to appear and skewered themselves on their bayonets, causing puncture wounds to the right upper arm muscle. A few stitches and a bawling-out for being idle on parade were the order of the day.

A Passing Out Parade saw the end of basic training. Lt-Col Hugh MacKenzie of the HLI dished out the 'Best All Round Recruit' certificate — to Gus MacDonald. Others were 'Best Shot' and so on. Regulars were posted to their regiments on Home Postings, as were the Gordon Highlanders to Berlin, the Camerons to Tripoli. The Black Watch were at Essen (BOAR) and the HLI were the Training Battalion. The remainder, mainly National Servicemen, were allocated to the Seaforths in Malaya, where they were involved in a counter-insurgency campaign against Chinese communists. The Argylls went to Hong Kong on border duties in the New Territories bordering China. Both regular and National Servicemen now entered six weeks' advanced training, concentrating on firing and field-craft, Fire and Movement. After Passing Out, discipline was a little relaxed. The trainees were now allowed 'out' at weekends, but had to be back in barracks at 2359 hrs, or a late pass would have to be applied for to remain whatever number of hours after midnight. Saturday night saw a visit to Inverness, some twelve miles from the Fort. Typically, some got drunk and brawled in the lesser-known pubs and dance halls. On such a night Cpl MacCauley MC, ably aided and abetted by none other than L/Cpl 'Cooshie' Smith, a Londoner with the HLI, decided they would drive a double-decker bus back to the Fort. The real driver and conductor were politely told where to go, which they did by reporting the hijack to the local gendarmerie. Both Cooshie and Mac were pissed out of their little minds. Cooshie drove, Mac collected and pocketed half-fares for services rendered, abandoning their transport some yards from the Guardroom. Both were busted a rank the following week when they appeared on CO's Regimental Orders.

The 'fully trained' soldiers fired their weapons on the range daily. A certain Cameron lieutenant, an ex-ranker who was Range Officer, had the unfortunate habit of taking his collie dog to range practice. He was one of the extremely sarcastic breed who took a delight in messing about any platoon who came under his sway. One cold, wet winter day, Sergeant Tetley had brought the platoon to fire off a few hundred rounds of Bren gun ammo by automatic fire in long bursts, to accustom the trainees to the noise of battle. After a few practices, those on the firing point would be deafened to some extent. As it happened, the lieutenant's dog decided to wander off and, unbeknown to either Sgt Tetley or the Cameron lieutenant, ended up by walking from left to right on the embankment immediately behind the targets. On the command, 'Target to your front at two hundred yards, automatic fire in your time, carry on firing!', ten Bren guns chattered off thirty rounds, all aimed at the poor unfortunate brute, which simply disintegrated. The Markers in the butts trench from which the targets were being operated on all ten targets simultaneously signalled ten bullseyes by the time our fine Cameron even realised what was happening and screamed 'Cease firing!' Despite protests of innocence, all ten received fourteen days' Confined to Barracks, but at least a touch of ruthlessness had been imparted in their short spell in the Army.

So Advanced Training came to an end. The trained soldiers were given fourteen days' Leave Pass before embarking to their Far East postings of Singapore/Malaya and Hong Kong. They returned to Queen's Barracks, Inverness, the regimental depot of the Queen's Own Cameron Highlanders: as the Camerons were in Tripoli, Libya, the barracks was a transit camp with a good assault course consisting of climbing over walls and crawling under nets, a pull or swing by rope, high towers and long drops with a cliff 'death slide', a metal bar in the shape of an inverted 'U' with handles on the rope. By gravity one descends, and speed can be checked by angling the bar. Participants hit the deck running – a test of muscle, fitness and moral fibre. A week at Inverness, and then the draft of Seaforths and Argylls – about 1,800 troops, marines and airmen – entrained and embarked on the RMS *Devonshire* at Liverpool for FARELF (Far East Land Forces) to join for various Far East and Middle East units.

3: Shipping Out

'I'd like to get you
On a slow boat to China…'

Popular song of the Fifties

The adventure of a lifetime had begun. The Argyll & Sutherland Highlanders, the 91st and 93rd of Foot (Princess Louise's) was a Campbell Regiment raised in 1794, the Napoleonic War period, with Stirling Castle as the Regiment HQ. The 93rd Sutherland Highlanders, raised in that shire in 1799, were a *Reismeid Chataich* (Regiment of the Cat) and the most Highland of all Highland Regiments. In 1852, when the SS *Birkenhead* foundered off the West African coast, women and children went to the boats and the draft of the 91st went down with the ship to the hymn 'Abide With Me'. The 93rd's contributions included the Thin Red Line at Balaklava and the Crimean War when they repelled a cavalry charge of Russians, a unique feat by Infantry: hence the red and white chequered patch worn on the shoulders. They also boasted seven Victoria Crosses at the siege of Lucknow in the Indian Mutiny. The regiments were amalgamated in 1881. Their list of Battle Honours ranged from the South African War to the two World Wars. Though the new Jocks did not quite relate these past glories to themselves, they too would soon enjoy the privilege of adding yet another Battle Honour to the Regimental Colours at a place called Pakchon.

Most of the men were eighteen to twenty with a sprinkling of regular recruits and re-enlistments. The troops lived on mess decks and slept in the traditional hammocks. There were routine parades, mess decks and tables to be swabbed and tables and decks to be scoured with the traditional holystone. One hour of PT a day, one hour Regimental History. Inter-unit boxing was encouraged. In the evening, sing-songs in the wet canteens. After ten days out, covering 300–400 nautical miles a day, HMS *Devonshire* berthed at Port Said, Egypt, the land of the Wog. The bum boats came alongside with their merchandise to flog to the troops: cameras, watches, lighters, dirty postcards, Spanish fly, rugs, ornaments, camel stools. Bargaining was keen, the odd Wog being 'thumped' by His Majesty's Ambassadors, who did not always make the time-honoured gestures of the British Soldiery, but matched the Wog in most aspects of cunning and violence. RAP (Regimental Aid Post) did a brisk business in sutures! Once shore leave granted a mass exodus followed as the gallant 1,800 descended on Port Said amidst the cries of sarcastic welcome – 'Hey Jock, you fucking hard case fae Aberdeen' – in a passable Glasgow accent from some woggish pimp who offered his thirteen-year-old sister for a short time for a pound – guaranteed to be a virgin, also a very clean girl. The younger National Servicemen did the normal sight-seeing trips by garri (horse-drawn open coach), or a ride on some flea-bitten camel, while the older Regulars headed straight for the nearest bar to try the local beer, which tasted like kerosene. They inevitably became drunk, and ready to participate in a wee punch-up, full employment thus being guaranteed by the Highlanders for the Royal Corps of Military Police (the Redcaps).

The trooper made her way down the Suez Canal and through the Bitter Lakes to the Red Sea. As the Canal was still under British protection, along its banks were the usual British Army installations and barracks. These prompted derisive catcalls and comments – 'Get your knees brown!' and so on – to what the Far East postings, bound for a 'python' or overseas service, considered Home Postings in MELF (Middle East Land Forces). Most regiments did three overseas and one year in the UK posting before going to Germany BOAR (British Army of the Rhine), or the Middle East or Far East. One could definitely see the world. The Red Sea was a stinker: over 90° Fahrenheit, in which prickly heat made its unwelcome appearance. Relief was to be had by standing in the rain. The cynical strains of 'We're leavin' Khartoum by the light of the moon' could be heard on the mess decks. The Indian Ocean came up, but the trooper did not pay her respects to the barren rocks of Aden, ploughing on in heavy seas to Colombo, Ceylon, (now Sri Lanka), a lovely tropical city with whispering palm trees. By now the troops had found their sea legs and those who hadn't were still, in the colourful phrase, 'honking their proverbial rings'.

Lieutenant 'Jungle Jim' MacArthur appeared in the kilt to take the hourly lecture on Regimental History. He had been a drill corporal at Fort George and had gone up to Lieutenant overnight. 'Jungle Jim' was his own nickname: he was a regular who had seen service in Palestine and had been wounded by the Irgun, the militant right-wing Zionists who in 1946 blew up the King David Hotel in Jerusalem, killing 96 people, mainly British civilians. He had now requested a posting to the Seaforth Highlanders in Malaya. They had an emergency of their own, and were coming closer to it.

Next port of call was Singapore, crossroads to the East. A communist-inspired emergency was in full swing in the jungles of Malaya, the participants being Chinese who had already fought the Japs. The KOYLIs (King's Own Yorkshire Light Infantry) and Seaforths disembarked. Having trained with the Argylls, the latter were given a special send-off by their brother Highlanders. Shore leave was taken and the troops had their first taste of the Far East − 35° Celsius with 100% humidity. A rickshaw ride, a slaking of thirst with Singapore's Tiger lager; some had a look at the Raffles Club, out of bounds except to Commissioned ranks. A few visited the notorious Changi Jail, where some men had relatives as POWs of the 'Happy Jappy'. The 2nd Battalion A & SH, the Silver Button battalion, had given the Japs their first comeuppance when the Jocks dished out their own medicine by a bayonet attack from the rear, proving that the vaunted Nipponese were not invincible after all. Only sixty men of the Battalion marched across the causeway back to Singapore to the strains of 'Heilan' Laddie'. Old Sweats paid their respects to the odd house of ill repute and got roaring drunk to boot, resulting in the inevitable spell in detention cells − or the brig, as it was named at sea.

Days later Hong Kong hove into sight. The young Jocks gave the island and the New Territories the once-over and decided it looked 'nae a bad place' to soldier, as the trooper came alongside near the famous Star Ferry in Kowloon. There were skyscrapers, Douglas Peak, downtown Victoria Island, and the majestic Peninsular Hotel of world renown, which looked a likely spot for the Officers to relax. Colour Sergeant Ginger Coleman was there to greet the draft, numbering about fifty bodies, half regular and half National Servicemen. The 1st Battalion the Argyll & Sutherland Highlanders were 550 strong, with only 10% National Service, which to new NS men was a little awe-inspiring: half of the Regulars had WWII service in places such as Western Europe, North Africa, East Africa, Italy and Germany, and the remainder had been with the Battalion a year previously in Palestine. FSMO (Full Service Marching Order) was the dress of the day, plus a kitbag slung on top of the big pack. Luckily it was February and wintertime in Hong Kong, with a pleasant European summer climate of around 75° Fahrenheit.

The Draft was marched to the train bound for the New Territories, and Colour Sgt Coleman remarked, 'You lot almost look like bloody soldiers, there's hope yet! Do any of you box? If you do, ask for "A" Company.'

The train, on narrow gauge, meandered its way out of Kowloon, over the top of the hill and descended into Tai Po fishing harbour in the New Territories, an area leased from China until 1997. Despite this, a Border Situation was on the brew. Not that the Jocks were unduly concerned: they had had their first sightings of the Yellow Peril, women in pantaloons and blouses in the paddy fields with huge flat straw hats, a pole horizontally on a shoulder, and a four-gallon tin at either end. Fan Ling Station came into sight after an hour. The Draft detrained and clambered into a three-tonner with '62nd' in green and gold, the battalion markings with the shoulder dicing patch, painted above the lorry cab. A bronzed Argyll driver, stripped to the waist, khaki tam-o'-shanter pushed forward over his eyes, looked nonchalantly at the new arrivals and was obviously unimpressed.

The Adjutant, Captain John Slim, was waiting. Slim was a typical Argyll regular Officer, the son of Field Marshal Sir William Slim. Private Illingworth thought, Well, well, a Field Marshal's baton in every knapsack... The welcome speech was along the following lines: 'You are lucky to have come to this

Regiment, by choice or otherwise. This is a regular battalion and we find that some of you young National Servicemen sometimes measure up to our requirements. You will now be posted to your various companies.'

The British Army procedure was not to be compared to the drivel one witnesses on the movies about our American cousins and their Errol Flynn-like exploits. One was here to soldier, and that meant doing what one was told. It never was and never will be a basis for debate. Smudger Smythe, the carter, went to Carrier Platoon of Support Coy. Jim Donald, a salmon coble fisherman from Montrose, went as a driver to HQ Company, former clerk Bill Illingworth went as the same to HQ Coy — the one round peg in a round hole. Angus MacDonald, student, went to HQ Coy as Bread Storeman, so he could continue his studies; the remainder to A, B, C and D Rifle companies. Imrie, who had been a plumber, went to the Assault Pioneers in 'S' Coy. Esson, the paper mill worker from Muggie Moss, Aberdeen, a proud but dozy Gordon, went to 'B' Coy.

The Battalion Camp was Norwegian Farm 1, a collection of six-man tents in company lines cut out of the hillside. The latrines and ablutions were of corrugated iron, cement floor structure which represented the most permanent building such as the Officers', Sergeants' and NAAFI Canteen, Battalion HQs, Coy HQs, and the QM Store. This was a Punishment Battalion: they had come home to Blighty in early '49 for a rest after the Palestine troubles when Britain handed it over to the Jews. They were stationed at Colchester in southern England for nine months before being shipped out to the China Station. However, prior to casting off from Southampton, the Jocks had thrown up a 'black'. Relatives, wives, sweethearts and the usual smattering of local talent had turned out to wave the 'ancient and scruffy Hardnecks' a fond farewell. Of course the boys wanted to kiss the talent goodbye. The Redcaps on gangplank duty had other ideas, and it ended in half a dozen of the Royal Corps being dumped unceremoniously into the drink between ship and wharf. About 300 of the gallant 500 had taken part to some degree by merely going ashore. RSM Paddy Morrison, the pride of the battalion, and a man of letters, an Honours MA, was heard from amidships in his best parade ground voice: 'Highlanders! You have three minutes to get back on board!' A cynical cheer went up, but three minutes later every Jock was back on board. The War Office was disenchanted and so it came to pass one year as a punishment battalion.

Duty Company each day was on fatigues or trench digging of defensive positions, some four miles behind the camp opposite the Chinese mainland border. All training was done after 4 p.m. to 6 a.m. Reveille.

In Hong Kong, working dress was jungle green hat, shorts, socks rolled down over boots, a shovel or pick in the right or left hand as advised. To and from the battalion area to defence positions was done at the double, day in and day out. To the newly-joined soldiery this was a bit of a bloody pain and to the old soldier, insulting. In truth the Battalion was proud of its toughness and its own family form of discipline. The 20–30 mile route march of WWII days had given way to the 'bash' of 3-6-9 at the double (jog). Performed in Battle Order: tin helmet, small pack, ammo pouches, water bottle, entrenching tool, bayonet and rifle. Usually a Physical Training Instructor, in his red and black top and blue strides, was out front dancing about like a bloody fairy with the usual 'left, right, left' patter and 'up, up, up, one, two, three, four' routine. Even he dried up after a time due to the sheer physical exhaustion induced by the subtropical climate. It was deemed necessary for the new Jocks to be among the first home, delirious with exhaustion, which started on the flat main bitumen road, through paddy fields well endowed with human fertiliser, and then up through the Chinese Hills with the jar graves and back to camp. Four in the afternoon, or '1600 hours' saw the end of the bash. The next two hours allowed for the four 'S's: shower, shave, shampoo and shit. Supper, 5 p.m., and into clean kit: a new dress, draw rifle and bayonet and fall in in Drill Order to mount guard from 6 p.m. to 6 a.m., two on and four off, the usual periods of guard. Four on, eight off was agreed to by drawing straws.

The Orderly Officer would mount the various Guards: Prowler Guard, Fire Picket, Ammunition Dump Guard. Those who were not spotlessly turned out, including personal weapon and bayonet, were charged on Orderly Room the next day.

Confined to Barracks with extra drills, which consisted of parading on the hour every hour at Battalion Headquarters in a different dress and inspected. Sweat stains on equipment were not tolerated, dim brasswork a heinous crime despite humidity over 70%. From the Company lines to BHQ could be up to a mile, so the private soldier stood a good chance of being on 'jankers' (CB) for life. Seven days or fourteen CB was the norm for trivial offences. In fact many a frustrated Jock told the Orderly Officer to go and get stuffed, resulting in 28 days' detention in the Battalion Area run by the Regimental Police – the lowest form of animal life, consisting of a platoon of lance corporals and a sergeant. Most of them had done more than their fair share of detention both at Battalion level and downtown in the Corrective Establishment. Poor old Esson, the slow-moving Aberdonian, landed on jankers and did a month instead of a seven-day period. Esson described jankers as a 'Real Fuckin' Bastard', which is merely a summation of a 10-minute swear when asked his opinion by one of his muckers.

Sergeant Danny Mullen, commonly known as the 'Wee Black Man' due to his exceptionally dark suntan on a horselike face with dark flashing eyes that lit up on occasion like glowing coals in the dark, was another typical old sweat: about 5' 9", slightly bow-legged, long arms and big but delicate hands. The Wee Black Man had done time on the Frontier (NW of India) exchanging shots with the wily Pathan hillmen, who in fact were similar in appearance to Danny but a foot taller. According to his 'gongs' Danny had done two 'pythons'. A ribbon with a silver rosette betokened that double service, plus the usual WWII 'fruit salad'. Danny had a delightful turn of phrase in his Glasgow accent. 'See youse bin a corporal in the Depot, MacDonald?'

'Acting,' replied Pte Angus MacDonald.

'All right, Snowball, you cum wi' me.'

Sgt Mullen had organised a Bren gun carrier and was to zero in the company's Bren guns. He told MacDonald to strip and re-assemble all the LMGs and grunted that the Depot had done something after all to the recruit's education. They drove about a couple of miles into the hills above the camp, in the area of the small-bore range.

'A' right, Snowball, see if you can hit one o' these jeely jars,' said Mullen, referring to the Chinese graves on the hillside.

A couple of hours later and a few 'jars' fewer, the Wee Black Man and Snowball returned to camp, well pleased with their contribution to international diplomacy à la Jock!

Private Harry Kelly appeared in 'B' Coy lines. The new arrivals had been with the Coy about 28 days, which would correspond with Kelly's 28 days in detention for a 'simple' drunk. Lt-Col Neil Neilson, known as 'Hooky' due to his beak nose, was not particularly loved by his Jocks, him being a virtual teetotaller with strict Presbyterian views on drunkenness who only imbibed in the Mess with a port or a sherry. CO Hooky dished out 28 days for a simple drunk and if a repeat, 56 days – and 112 days for a third breach. Over 56 days were done downtown in the Correction Establishment, where the staff Sergeants of the corrective branch of the Army reigned supreme. The 'glasshouse' was a place where grown men wept and became bitter and the hard even harder, as Corporal Bob Sweeney would reminisce when he took Pte 'Sailor' Kelly for one of his incarcerations. The 15 cwt truck with escort (2) and accused/prisoner, plus a corporal in charge would roll up at the prison gate, a discreet knock on a small door would ensure that a barred grill hole would open and a voice would demand, 'Who goes there?' The corporal replied that he had a prisoner. The gate would be opened and the party marched in, when someone would scream, 'Double!'

Every movement for inmates was done at the double, including the initial interview, the handover and takeover of documents, right down to the dawn ablutions, including shower. All members of the establishment were sergeants, addressed as 'Staff'. Parades of various natures were carried out on the hour every hour, twelve hours a day, 6 a.m. to 6 p.m., and then another six hours of polishing, burnishing, scrubbing, washing, pressing of kit and equipment – even the bucket for urinating in the cell shone like a mirror inside and out. Compulsory games, Stone Age football with no rules, and regular boxing matches were the normal recreational outlets. Drill was done with wet sand in the packs and ammo pouches. Trenches were dug to bury matchsticks, which had been scraped white with broken glass. Life was not meant to be easy in this particular segment of His Majesty's Imperial British Army. No inmate was known to express any desire to return.

Time marched on and the Battalion moved to Fan Ling near the Royal Hong Kong Golf Club, still under canvas. Border patrols for illegal immigrants coming from China to the Royal Colony were the order of the day. Observation posts on the border, at Sha Tok Kok. Section to Platoon to Company to Battalion attacks were practised night and day. Annual musketry firing application of all weapons, No. 4 .303 rifle, 9mm Sten gun .303 LMG Bren gun, the throwing of the 36 m/s hand grenade. The Battalion had about 75% five-star privates, which meant at least five years' service and qualified to hold the rank of sergeant, an indication as to standards expected of the nucleus of a regular 'peacetime' battalion.

Once a month the Jocks were given a leave pass to go downtown, some thirty miles. The Highland horde would descend upon Kowloon and Victoria, mainly in civilian clothes, which would be uniform to a man: Hawaiian floral shirt and colourful long strides. Before the serious session of drinking was embarked upon, a visit to the local tattooist was in order. In fact every trip to the Big City was a hullabaloo until banned by Battalion Part 1 Orders. For the not-quite-so-wild spirits, a visit to the Roxy, a Kowloon cinema, to enjoy the air conditioning; a supper of steak, eggs and chips at the Soldiers' and Sailors' Club, a visit to the Fleet Club (Navy and Marines); the 9 Dragons pub-cum-dance hall in Kowloon; a bet on the ponies at Happy Valley Racecourse; a rickshaw ride; a 'short time' visit to a brothel for those who felt the urge; and of course, for the would-be hard cases, the inevitable punch-up. The Marines of 41 Commando always obliged. They were considered The Unit in Hong Kong, which the Argylls disputed. Having had their three F's (feed, fight, etc.), the Highlanders would allow themselves to be shepherded back onto their transport by their own Shore Patrols before the beloved Redcaps threw them in cells for the night, which resulted in a 28-day detention. Some of the fights at the Fleet Club resulted in minor injuries, and on one occasion a marine was killed after being hit on the jugular with a broken bottle.

During May, the King's Birthday was to be celebrated by a Divisional March Past by the 40th Infantry Division (Fighting Cock) in downtown Kowloon. The Battalion, in kilt, drab hose and olive green shirts and TOS (tam-o'-shanter), were to march past the Governor of the Colony taking the Salute. The parade formed up in Chatham Road and marched down Nathan Road, Kowloon. The saluting base was at Murray Barracks, opposite the Army Hospital. The top floor housed the delinquents who had been unfortunate enough to 'catch a dose'. As the Battalion gave the 'Eyes Right', cheers went up from the top floor of the hospital and all along the balconies with the incarcerated VD patients waving glengarries with the red and white dicing of the Argylls. The Jocks on parade did their best to hide grins as they paid their respects to the Reviewing Officer and distinguished guests, at least half of them ladies trying to ignore the waves and cheering. The parade complete, the CO gave the Jocks a lecture to the effect that the VD rate in the Battalion was far too high and he would consider giving out punishment, as to 'catch a dose' was a self-inflicted wound.

War games with the Marines were the order of the day. The 41st Commando were to be the Argylls' opposition. Despite the longer and more complicated training for a Royal Marine, the Highlanders scored the most points in the various tactical manoeuvres; assaults causing bodily harm were dished out and received by both sides. At Stanley Fort on the island proper of Hong Kong, a company of Marines presented arms to 'B' Coy of the 1st A & SH, whose Sergeant Major, Wee Banzai Murray, before the Major commanding 'B' Coy could reply in kind, declared, 'Pay no attention to these people, it's only land girls who wear green bonnets where we come from, right turn quick march!'

The Argyll Major apologised, and the Sgt Major later received a 'bollocking'.

All ranks in the overtrained battalion were suffering from heat exhaustion and were stood down for a complete rest period of two weeks on Lan Tau Island, where the weirdos smoked opium imported from the mainland. Several dancing girls appeared to do the troops' 'dhobi' (washing) and render other services. The battalion had spent almost a couple of years in Honkers and the New Territories, digging positions by day, training and general duties by night and downtown generally making a nuisance of themselves. What could be more typical of Scottish Infantry?

4: Korea, Land of the Morning Calm

The Korean War – or 'Police Action', as the UN referred to it – kicked off on 28th June 1950, when North Korea, backed by Russia and China, invaded South Korea, which in turn was being supported by the USA. The Republic of Korea's Army, ROKS, disintegrated in the face of the North Korean onslaught, while the US 24th Division (TARO LEAF) met a similar fate. The North was prepared: they had at least 100 T34 29 ton Russian tanks of proven performance, and about the same number of Yak fighter aircraft, plus self-propelled guns. The North's forces were highly trained and competently Officer-trained in the USSR. The cause of the war was simply Communism versus Capitalism: the North Koreans are still a bloody-minded dictatorship today, fifty years on.

The Republic of Korea's capital, Seoul, soon fell, and within a matter of weeks the Allies were holding a 90-mile perimeter on the Naktong River some fifty miles north of Pusan, the Republic's second city and main port. Britain offered two infantry Battalions from Hong Kong, the 1st Middlesex and the 1st A & SH. The 'Middies' were mainly National Servicemen, the A & SH seasoned Regulars. August saw the Middlesex, on the aircraft carrier HMS *Unicorn*, and the Argylls, on the cruiser HMS *Ceylon*, embarked and farewelled by the 1st KOSB Pipes and Drums. Some three days later, after being escorted by the Australian warships HMAS *Warramunga* and HMAS *Batan*, they arrived at the docks in Pusan, the first reinforcements for the beleaguered Yanks. Private Gus MacDonald, 2 Sec 4 Pn 'B' Company, remembers an American Negro marching band appearing through the mist to welcome the Brits with a great rendering of the 'St Louis Blues' followed by the 'Chicago Tribune March'. Appreciative cat-calls and cheers came from the infantry of the 27th Commonwealth Brigade, whose three nines in a triangle − dial 999 for Police, Fire and Ambulance − had earned them the nickname of 'The Fire Brigade'.

As the Argylls disembarked the Pipes and Drums replied to the Yanks with some of the 'Tunes of Glory': '*Caber Feidh*', 'Heilan' Laddie', 'The Black Bear'. Rumour had it the 3rd Bn Royal Australian Regiment from Kure, Japan, the 16th Field Regiment, Royal New Zealand Artillery, and the 2nd Battalion, Princess Patricia's Canadian Light Infantry, would make up the Brigade. Later of course would come the gentlemen from the 60th Indian Field Hospital (Airborne), mainly Sikhs from the Indian Army Medical Corps, along with No. 2 Squadron South African Air Force, 'The Flying Cheetahs' with their 'Shooting Stars' – a motley crew to form a very famous Brigade under Brigadier Basil Coade.

The Jocks could see right off why the Yanks had not stood their ground as an occupational force: low morale, little discipline and soft from garrison duty, as well as being poorly trained. Within the hour supplies were shipped off and stowed away on a nearby train and they were off to see the 'Wild East Show'. American C Rations were issued and the Jocks thought Christmas had arrived. American equipment was superior to the British: even their C Rations consisted of a 24-hour composite ration, a half-can of fruit, half-can cookies and candy bar, can opener which you could hang on your dog tags (ID discs) around the neck, twenty cigarettes, matches, toilet paper, tin of ham and lima beans and a tin of chicken and veg. You could eat it cold or warm it up.

Morale was high as CO Lt-Col Neil Neilson (Hooky) and their OC Maj Gordon-Ingram (GI), had their pictures taken and were presented with flowers by a group of Korean school girls in national dress. In fact to dampen the spirits of all British Commonwealth troops took a lot of doing. Captain John Penman MC had earlier declared to his brother Officers that he fully intended adding at least another MC for his wife and the regiment. Pride comes easily to a British regiment, mainly due to the tradition, the discipline and the fact that they come from a particular recruitment area, the latter aspect of course being magnified in a Highland regiment based on the Clan system whose very name is revered by all ranks, binding them into a family: The Battalion. Regimental history was treated as a training subject and the recruit was expected to know his origins and traditions. The pipes and drums played their part in this bonding; certain tunes were familiar. Morale is the great achiever.

The Battalion set off upcountry in what might be described as a little wooden train, detraining several hours later to be picked up by American Army transport, with their big Negro drivers displaying infectious smiles, probably thankful that they would not be going all the way to the Front: base wallahs are always full of alarming rumours of what is happening at the 'sharp end'. For the next twenty-four hours, the Jocks were issued with ammo and briefed on the present position. Their Major, GI, himself a Burma boy, told us of the 'Banzai attack', where the enemy surrounded you accompanied by shouts and bugle calls. The drill is stay in your position, defend by bush knife or bayonet plus the normal fire, backed by 36 grenades, and of course not to worry as the Yanks will come and pluck you out by chopper – which the Jocks thought was all very interesting as they looked forward to their first helicopter ride! The 'A' echelon position was in an orchard and naturally the Jocks 'gutsed' themselves on apples, with the inevitable consequence that the 'trots' were enjoyed by all.

The following day their Negro truck drivers materialised to take them to the Front. Some hours later, in the height of summer – 90° Fahrenheit in the shade – accompanied by columns of dust from the dirt roads, they arrived to be met by a huge Negro US Army soldier charging past the convoy, shouting, 'The dear Lord is pickin' 'em up and puttin' 'em down, an Ah'm buggin' to hell outta here!' He was wearing his helmet, so for future reference they were within ten miles of the Line.

They had arrived on the Naktong River section of the Pusan Perimeter. According to General MacArthur, this was as far as the Gooks were going to push us back, come hell or high water. The Battalion took up positions overlooking the Naktong River. The mortar platoon, in support roughly in the middle, was also the machine-gun platoon. 'B' Company happened to be split, and their particular platoon was on a little knob, slightly closer to the Naktong, about a quarter of a mile away from the river itself. The Naktong was exceptionally broad, in parts up to about a mile, and on the other side were the enemy positions – not that they could see them, as there were some pretty steep cliffs and hilly country with paddy fields in the valleys still tinged with all the various shades of green and the rice almost ready for harvesting.

They took over from the US 1st Cavalry Division, who had dug what they call foxholes – one-man trenches – and left a mess of tin cans and other debris which they threw into their foxholes and buried. Then they dug their own slit trenches, a two-man trench (6' x 2' x 4'), in which – in theory – one supports the other. The American thinks his buddy's doing the firing so he keeps his head down, but in actual fact nobody is doing any firing. The first night each individual infantryman was allocated a South Korean policeman from their paramilitary wing. They lasted the first night with us in the slit trench: their breath stank of garlic so they were immediately told where to go! At daylight they withdrew to the reverse slope leaving only a sentry per section on guard. This observation goes on night and day and then at dawn 'Stand To', and again at dusk – time of expected attacks. The South Korean police-cum-comrades had demonstrated their inability to soldier by swinging grenades tied on to the end of the pin. On the odd occasion the grenade had gone off with scraps of shrapnel flying about and wounding at least three of them. They were again told, by the two magic words, exactly where to go…

The next few days were taken up in minor patrol activity all round their position, finding out exactly the topography of the hills where the re-entrants were and sighting fields of fire. A re-entrant (*Shorter Oxford*: 'an inlet, valley, etc., forming a prominent indentation into a landform') is a military term, the opposite of a salient, usually used for a valley leading to a crest or ridge; two ridges sloping upwards either side of a 'vee' gives a point for a patrol to return to, or can make a good ambush position. They also laid barbed wire in front of their position with booby traps and flares mixed. They had to go back to company headquarters and pick up loads of barbed wire. Their platoon sergeant, Hookey Walker, a Welsh Guardsman from Alford in Gordon Highlander country, had seen a fair bit of action both in the Western Desert and then in Italy and north-west Europe. Hookey had a huge red fungus moustache which was the subject of numerous photographs by the Yanks. He was a very upright soldier, the sort of figure expected of a guardsman. Captain John Penman MC had no particular love of any Guards, whom he considered chocolate soldiers, so Hookey was given a hard time.

One day Hookey had gone back to supervise half their platoon collecting 90-pound loads of barbed wire. He seemed to relish the fact that his pack was empty, as were his Bren gun pouches. The party climbed the slopes carrying 10 lb rifles, 100 rounds of ammunition plus 90 lbs of barbed wire on a Korean 'A'-frame, a four-mile climb up and down hills about 200 to 400 feet high, returning to a break in the hill line where they had to cross about 400 yards of paddy – wide open. They had advanced about a third of the way, over a 100 yards or so, when the fun and games started. They came under heavy machine-gun fire, 50-calibre, from the other bank, with the odd bit of tracer. Hookey immediately beat a hasty retreat back the way the rest of us had come through the wet paddy, eventually arriving at their platoon position on the other side. Private Johanssen, who was a lousy soldier famous for his lack of cleanliness, told Hookey that he would blow his brains out if he did not slow down the pace. Now that he had doubled back out of the way, Johanssen was delighted to pass a few more derogatory remarks, when their lieutenant asked us what had happened to the platoon sergeant.

Our lieutenant, Ken MacKellar, a man with seven years' service and senior for a lieutenant, had seen part of the Italian campaign with the 8th Argylls at the crossing of the Po, and also served with the Battalion in Palestine: not a one-pip wonder. Kenny MacKellar decided to take out a sectional patrol, so off he went with his ten men and corporal in charge of the section, the object being to find out what had happened to Sergeant Walker. By this time, of course, Hookey had taken a circuitous route and was well on his way back to the rear of the platoon positions on the knob of the hill. MacKellar, with his patrol, had travelled only a few hundred yards when they came under the same heavy 50-calibre machine-gun fire, and Kenny had both his ankles shattered. Somebody stuck a morphine needle into him: he was more than 'out' and eventually was put on a stretcher. Gus MacDonald was one of the stretcher bearers. The Jocks were most careful not to shake the stretcher, thinking that Kenneth

61

MacKellar was in acute pain. He was in a semi-comatose state and didn't feel a thing — this was their first experience of morphine.

The stretcher bearing lasted for the best part of the next few hours, over the paddy fields to a higher point where observation from the opposite bank was ineffective. The heavens opened in a tropical downpour. The stretcher bearing party numbered ten — a complete section — and those four men on each corner of the stretcher changed over every fifteen minutes, up hill and down dale, slipping in the mud of the paddy fields and crawling up and down hills, a process that lasted a couple of hours. All members of the stretcher bearing party were exhausted on arrival at Coy HQ, where they handed over the wounded lieutenant. That was the last they saw of Kenny MacKellar: his days of soldiering were over.

In all heavy action the stretcher bearing is normally done by the Defence Platoon of HQ Coy, they being the Pipes and Drums and Regimental Police. At platoon level, the stretcher bearer is the Officer's batman. The batmen deserve a mention when in action for they are festooned with all the bits and pieces of equipment belonging to the Officer: map board, binoculars, extra ammunition, bedding... and on top of that the batman humps the stretcher and becomes the platoon medic. This was not yet the day of the paramedic. His highest level would be to stop blood by the use of a tourniquet, or jab in a morphine needle to kill the pain of the wounded man. Rude and crude, but effective. After this minor action, patrol activity across the Naktong River commenced, mainly led by Captain John Penman MC. The patrols were of different types, the Fighting Patrol being anything up to company strength — in other words, you go out looking for trouble and asking for a fight — or right down to the opposite, where a Listening Patrol or Observation Patrol could be anything from a three-man to a ten-man unit. The patrols were mainly made up of volunteers and, obviously, the better swimmers. They'd be dressed in jungle greens, no head-dress and gym shoes, Sten gun, a couple of magazines and maybe one grenade so as not to weigh us down.

Swimming the river was interesting. The current was reasonably strong and you might start at a point anything to a mile up the river and come out at a point a mile downstream, the water being anything up to half a mile to a mile broad at points. When you landed on the other side you blended into the landscape: you would penetrate through a series of small hills and travel maybe a kilometre to two kilometres inland, passing through the enemy lines where possible – and if not, taking up a camouflage spot and sitting observing them, trying to pick out machine gun and mortar positions. One of these patrols afforded the Battalion its first decoration, an American Silver Star. It was led by Captain Neil Buchanan. When he was badly wounded he told his ten-man patrol to abandon him while he took over the Bren gun and gave the patrol covering fire back to the river. Buchanan and his batman were never seen again. A Silver Star seemed an exceptionally cheap price to pay for the life of a gallant Officer and a brave, devoted batman.

The Battalion had had its baptism of fire, spending a few weeks on the Naktong, experiencing mortar fire as well as heavy and medium machine-gun fire, though with not too many casualties. By now the Jocks had become accustomed to living in holes in the ground, and it was an interesting way of life compared to barracks. Patrolling came down to taking the initiative or became an aggressive way of keeping morale up, keeping the troops sharp and active. But the troops taking part in the patrols became quite nervous under the strain, as each patrol had to be carried out very slowly and calculatingly. 'A' Coy had a successful action when they lured a North Korean patrol into a re-entrant and at close quarters wiped them out, showing superior firepower and ambush skills in their concealed position.

The Jocks soon learned the troops opposing them were regular North Korean infantry and, like themselves, professional soldiers: they were still on a crest of a wave after surging down from the North, everything before them falling like dominoes. Their mortar fire was reasonably accurate, as was their machine-gun fire, but their explosives were comparatively weak. If you hit the deck quickly you could be within feet of a mortar bomb explosion and still live to tell the tale without being wounded. The same applied to artillery fire, including some American 105 'drop-shorts'. Machine-gun fire was roughly the same: if you took

cover you could get away with it, though of course there were no
second chances. If somebody said 'Down!', you got down in
double quick time.

They began to get to know and appreciate their American
allies. They provided them with the heavier back-up and support
with 105s and 155 artillery in position some miles behind us. Also
a 4.2 American mortar battery would come up from time to time
and lob off a few bombs – better value than their infantry.
Everyone looked a bit worn, but certainly not worn out, and were
beginning to be issued with some American equipment in the
form of combat boots. Theirs was a suede boot with a rubber sole
and leather anklet, much lighter than the normal British
ammunition boot but not as comfortable. The Brits also had the
combat jacket, a great piece of equipment because it was both
wind- and rain-proof and you could fit various linings. Eventually
they got trousers to match the combat jacket which were superior
to their own issue.

The Battalion was spread over a few miles parallel to the
Naktong River, very thin on the ground and mainly offering
platoon pockets of resistance on company fronts. How to stop a
serious crossing of the river and attack was problematic, but the
Jocks were not particularly concerned. They were well trained,
were fit, were capably led and had a lot of experience in the
Battalion. Boredom was dispelled by activities such as the cleaning
of weapons, a daily bathe and shave irrespective of the weather
conditions, and the constant revetting of positions. Although they
were not a spit and polish outfit, in action if you looked at the
weaponry it was always spotlessly cleaned and lightly oiled, a sign
of real professionalism. The Jocks looked exceptionally lean and
fit, with the light of battle in their eyes. The daily issue of a can or
a couple of cans of beer was welcomed with some disbelief, but
this was normal ration for American units in the Line. They also
began to receive the American Forces newspaper, the *Stars and
Stripes*, almost as a daily news bulletin giving them a good idea
how their little 'Police Action' was going. The Line seemed to
have stabilised: it was being held and the odd counter-attack put
in. The weather was still wet: humid, typical summer conditions
edging into autumn as they approached the end of August. The

feeling throughout the Battalion was one of impatience: they were still looking for this slice of action, of real infantry fighting. It was just around the corner.

Suddenly, about the middle of September, they were pulled out of the Line, jumped into American trucks (GMC 6x6s, magnificent vehicles) and rode off with their Negro drivers. They seemed to do a loop and then followed the Naktong west. Quite a sight – the whole Battalion together again on the move with grinning faces and rude gestures being exchanged between trucks, and the various signpostings done by the American military police, the various remarks and unit numbers on the signposts pointing northwards. So at last the big move was afoot: they were advancing. 'B' Company was leading when they came to a river. All of a sudden, on both banks, they came under fire from a self-propelled rapid-fire artillery piece. It seemed to be able to get off five shots, bang-bang-bang-bang-bang, with almost simultaneous explosions, some on both sides and some in the river. An American Engineer unit had thrown up a pontoon bridge of rubber rafts with a couple of planks, so at least the infantry could get across. They wandered over this ramshackle bridge, rifles slung, doing their best to balance as the spume from shells exploding in the water came up all round. This shelling lasted for about a good ten to fifteen minutes, during which most of the Battalion had crossed in a great show of soldierly discipline: nobody ran, nobody panicked – just a slow, nice, easy, swinging gait, maintaining balance; nobody fell into the river. Carrying on up the road, moving to the right and left as directed, they fanned out into extended formation to go into the attack. And of course as usual, before each attack, the command, 'Fix bayonets!'

Having advanced about half a mile they came to a ridge on both sides of the road, so the Battalion occupied the ridge facing their front. Sergeant Hookey Walker addressed Private Gus MacDonald, saying, 'You're a bloody student, MacDonald. I've got a compass – you take a bearing on that self-propelled gun that was shelling us.'

The sergeant was asked for a map. Maps were unheard-of, so it was explained to their ex-Guards sergeant that to take a bearing without a map was bloody hard. Anyway, a rough bearing was taken and a call for air support put in.

These jets were magnificent, like a fire brigade: within ten minutes of a call there was immediate help; they were brilliant. Soon enough they heard the magic sound of the Americans, pulverising what was believed to be the gun position. They took no more shellfire; it was taken for granted the position had been clobbered. So this was it, the beginning of the real war.

Pusan 29/08/50, 1st Battalion Argyll and Sutherland Highlanders

5: Korea, Hill 282

He either fears his fate too much
Or his deserts are small,
That puts it not unto the touch
To win or lose it all.

James Graham,
1st Marquis of Montrose,
Scottish Captain-General

'This will go down in regimental history. The Gooks will never drive the Argylls off this hill.'

The speaker was Major Kenny Muir VC, 2i/c 1/A & SH, and 'this' was the action on Saturday 23rd September 1950 in which MacDonald came face to face with the enemy. Was there any reason for MacDonald and his fellow-Highlanders to be there, or were they just putting on a show? Was it another Battle Honour, or an inglorious snafu?

After crossing the ramshackle bridge, approximately two miles north, going towards a small town called Sonju, the Middlesex left the road on the right and the Argylls on the left. The Middlesex were immediately in action, taking what is now termed Plum Pudding Hill and Middlesex Hill. It took them two days of almost continuous fighting, suffering a number of casualties. The Argylls were led by 'A' Company. The following day, September 23rd 1950, 'B' and 'C' companies were ordered to take two hill tops identified by their numbers: Hill 282 and Hill 388. Both Companies were to be supported by American 105 field artillery and a troop of American tanks. The advance kicked off about three o'clock in the morning – still dark in hilly, scrubby country, climbing – with both companies in musketry order in extended line.

The advance went well for about the first two hours, both companies advancing steadily. As dawn began to break around five, they halted and fixed bayonets as the crests of both features were now becoming visible. The advance continued quietly until 6 Platoon of 'B' Company stumbled into a North Korean platoon in the middle of breakfast. A firefight immediately developed, the North Koreans taking flight after a few of them had been bayoneted. During the advance, 'B' Coy Corporal Dick Whittington, known as 'Dicky the Whip', had turned round to Private Gus MacDonald and handed him his pay book, saying that he would not be needing it as he would not be coming out of this action. Sadly, his prediction was correct. MacDonald's Company advanced again after the exchange of fire with the North Korean platoon: about one hundred yards to his front he observed a figure in a black cloak, obviously a North Korean Officer. In a state of excitement as his first target presented itself, MacDonald took aim over battle sights, which are a considerably more rough alignment than a normal sighting on his rifle. He was quite satisfied with the result: despite his excitement, his first shot fired in anger scored a hit as the black-cloaked figure shot through the air backwards.

Sporadic firing broke out down the lines of both companies as they advanced. 'C' Company was now moving more to the left to take the feature on 'B' Company's left. There was some considerable firing on the left. 'B' Company continued with a bayonet charge, claiming the odd North Korean. As the Argylls swept forward, 'B' Company — MacDonald's — reached the crest of the feature known as Hill 282 only to discover a small problem. Normal procedure is that having taken the position you advance through and consolidate on the other side, both so that the enemy does not know your exact range and to repel any counter-attack. On Hill 282 this could not be done: there was a cliff face dropping immediately away at the top of the feature to about fifteen or twenty feet. As 'B' Company began digging in along the crest on top of the cliff face, MacDonald heard the odd shot. By now, artillery support from both the American field battery and tanks would have been called for; three-inch mortars and MMG Vickers machine guns should have been firing in support. They were not. It did not happen, as was later discovered, because the trajectory was too steep for tanks, and artillery had been withdrawn. Both companies ended up without the normal support given to infantry. On the left, 'C' Company, having taken their feature, immediately began to dig in but were attacked at once by a force about triple their number. Fierce hand-to-hand fighting began, with picks and shovels used as weapons after ammunition ran out.

While digging in themselves, 'B' Company came under shellfire from a self-propelled gun, directly into the cliff face beneath the Argyll position. High explosives were being used. Medium machine guns of the Battalion were now supporting both companies by indirect fire using a high trajectory, without conspicuous success. Most of this support fire was also landing in the Argyll positions. The phenomenon of the spent round was being experienced: the odd Argyll was being hit, though the round was not penetrating, only bruising. To the front of the 'B' Company position there was slight movement – the odd bush contained a North Korean infantryman. Studying the lie of the land, the odd shot produced a further sudden movement as a hit was scored. The shellfire now switched to air bursts and 'B' Company found themselves rained with shrapnel. Most unpleasant – and the casualty rate was mounting.

MacDonald's section was commanded by Corporal Danny Jenkins, a regular soldier who had seen action in Northern Italy and Palestine. His No. 2 Section of 4 Platoon was on the left flank of the 'B' Company position, MacDonald in the extreme left slit trench. There was a gap of 150 to 200 yards between the two companies, and the 'C' Company feature was 100 foot or so higher up, with a saddle between the two. This eventually led to 'C' Company being surrounded and forced to fight their way out to the rear of the 'B' Company position. Mortar fire kept coming in, most of it very inaccurate, bursting 50 to 100 metres over the position or landing 50 metres in front. The shellfire, though, was beginning to take its toll, especially the air bursts. One Highlander by the name of Buchan had decided he was not scared: to show his defiance he dug his slit trench standing up. Buchan collapsed and MacDonald, who was at the bottom of the slit trench grabbed him: there was blood on his chest in the heart region. Ripping open the shirt, MacDonald saw gleaming pieces of silver-coloured shrapnel, one below and one above the heart.

Funnily enough, it had not pierced the ribcage and was sticking into the flesh and muscle. A field dressing was applied, but as he did so, speaking to the luckless Buchan, he pulled his web belt and found his hands suddenly sink into his abdomen area: the blast, a common phenomenon, had hit Buchan and blown all his entrails out through his back. At this stage Gus MacDonald experienced his first mate KIA (Killed in Action), as Buchan's eyes rolled shut.

MacDonald carried on firing at the odd movement into the advancing North Korean infantry, who were still advancing slowly about 300 metres up the slope. There was a clear field of fire: it was not altogether a one-way street. Both sides were scoring. Artillery fire intensified for the next hour or so, and with it machine-gun fire. More casualties were taken. Two hours' fighting had now passed. It was eight or nine o'clock in the day — a day that was now stinking hot, the sun high, water out, 50% of the ammunition already expended, casualties considerably higher than first thought and mounting fast.

As the time approached eleven o'clock, machine-gun and small-arms fire had not ceased. A frontal assault had not been followed through; both flanks were being turned as fire was beginning to come in from the sides. An encirclement was in progress — they were in a real cowboys and Indians situation! The wounded could not be taken out by stretcher as the hill was too steep, so they were dragged out on ground sheets. About twelve o'clock the 2i/c Bn, Major Kenny Muir, appeared. As the senior major, Muir took command and decided to call for air support. Two air recognition panels were laid out on the reverse slope, iridescent strips about three metres by a metre in bright orange and red, so that the support aircraft could identify friend from foe. Blunder on Hill 282 – or blessing? The air recognition panels were laid out in a gully, and whether the American support aircraft ever saw them is more than debatable; their spotter aircraft also failed in its duty by reporting back the wrong information. What a balls-up! Minutes later came the sound of jet aircraft. MacDonald looked to the skies, did not see any aircraft but certainly heard them coming in, the scream of jet engines getting closer and closer.

A cheer went up from the Argylls, but all of a sudden there

was the chattering of machine guns and the Argylls were under attack from the air. Machine gun and cannon fire pinned the soldiers down. This was the first aircraft. Then the second aircraft let off its rockets, possibly two from each wing. Rockets are demoralising weapons: the *whoosh* as you hear them coming in and then a tremendous explosion, with a huge blast wave throwing bodies several feet in the air. The natural reaction, even for disciplined troops, was to get the hell out of it. Unfortunately some did bale out: they jumped out of the slit trench and ran for it, carrying their weapons. Then the first aircraft came round again. This time it dropped napalm, a mixture of petrol and rubber landing with a soft sound like a soft rugby ball, then a vast sheet of flame as the oxygen is sucked right out with a gushing sound, changing to the sound of rain as boiling hot rubber cascades down – and sticks in a yellowy golden molten mess that burns clothes and flesh.

The hilltop was a blackened, fiery mess. A second dose of machine gun, rocket and napalm was administered and the troops who had bailed out were caught in this seething mass of destruction. MacDonald noticed the aircraft had flown off and breathed more than a sigh of relief. He looked about him into the other slit trenches to see if there was anybody left, but in front of him, twenty-five feet below, a figure appeared out of the smoke and flames. Lance Corporal Danny Fields. Gus shouted down, 'Do you want a rifle?' Danny, in his inimitable Glaswegian, suggested what one could do with one's rifle as both his arms had been severely burned. Next, out of the smoke appeared Donaghue, an ex-military bandsman, one of the gentlemen of the Regiment, who did not have to go to war – the Band in a Highland Regiment is normally left behind to entertain the civilian population. Donaghue had volunteered to take part in the Korean campaign, and now his arms and face were quite severely burned. He nodded that he would go down and lend a hand to Lance Corporal Fields. When he got down there, Danny Fields was not to be found. He was later posted missing, believed killed in action.

The section commander, Corporal Danny Jenkins, had been badly wounded by machine gun fire and also shrapnel. Private Andy MacKelvie, the father of six children, was dead; a reinforcement, a huge Borderer by the name of Paul Pug, had gone 'gaga': an automatic medical discharge was on the way. Not real nice to see a young man reduced to a useless vegetable... So all that remained of 2 Section, 4 Platoon, 'B' Company was Donaghue and Gus MacDonald. Gus gathered up the odd abandoned weapon of the dead and wounded, including the Bren gun, Sten gun and a half-dozen rifles, and wandered off down the hill in search of what remained of his decimated company. The hill was still on fire. Through the smoke haze, 100 feet or so below the crest, he noticed a movement and discovered the remnants of his company – thirty-odd souls.

Major Kenny Muir and Major Alastair Gordon-Ingram held a conference. Some were only slightly wounded, others severely. One was a young lieutenant, the brother of Captain Brownshaw, who had already been lost on a Naktong patrol. His face was intact, and his boots, but the rest of him was slowly cooking to death as he cried, 'Mother, Mother, Mother!' Captain Penman gave the nod to put the Officer out of his agony. The soldiers still present on Hill 282 by mutual accord began to wander back up the hill, bayonets fixed, and took up position along the ridge, mainly due to Captain John Penman's example. There was no discussion: the Jocks knew their duty, as did their gallant Officers.

Back to that question: blunder or blessing in disguise? It was later claimed that the American pilots saw movement on the Argyll's side of the hill; deciding that the Argylls were the enemy, they immediately strafed the remaining half of 'B' Company. Although it created a larger casualty rate, it could be argued that this was a blessing in disguise, as an 800-strong Battalion of North Korean Gooks were storming up the front slope to attack the remaining thirty men of 'B' Company, and had in fact slowly but surely almost completed an encirclement. Major Kenneth Muir at this stage had been severely wounded in the abdominal area by machine-gun fire. That was when he made the historic statement: 'This will go down in regimental history. The Gooks will never drive the Argylls off this hill.'

He and Major Gordon-Ingram continued to fire a two-inch mortar in an exposed position, along with a number of Bren guns and Stens, plus rifle fire, along the crest. 36" and phosphorous grenades were being hurled down the slope at the screaming hoard of North Korean soldiers, who now were also sustaining considerable casualties. The Argylls were now down to about fifteen Jocks, returning fire. The remainder had in some cases been wounded a second time and were out of action. Capt John Penman MC was having a ball with his Bren gun, his loader being Gus MacDonald, who at times when not loading magazines and reloading the gun was heaving 36" grenades down into the screaming mob below. At this stage, Major Kenny Muir died from wounds received, and it was decided to withdraw what remained of 'B' Company in good order by walking very slowly down the hill and returning fire to the flanks in the approved withdrawal pattern – some groups halting, others withdrawing. The principle is that as one 'leg' moves the other 'leg' stands still, and returns or gives covering fire. The wounded were dragged out. The Post Corporal had had his left arm blown off at the shoulder but the limb was still held by his cuff. Luckily for him, the blast had more or less sealed arteries and veins. The 1st Battalion Middlesex Regiment came voluntarily to the Argylls' assistance with direct machine-gun fire to cover the withdrawal. They also came halfway up the hill to help with the wounded evacuation, and ironically Major Kenny Muir came out on an air recognition panel.

The North Koreans did not press home their advantage but seemed to be quite satisfied with retaking the hill crest. Gus MacDonald saw another potential VC winner that day, a young King's Own Scottish Border replacement, on the left flank, holding off the North Koreans by charging towards them and firing his Bren gun from the hip. Last seen out of ammunition, swinging the gun by its muzzle: unfortunately he was never given a mention for his self-sacrifice, as he was a new boy. At the base of the hill, 'A' Company, along with the machine gun and mortar platoons and the Middlesex helpers, were giving covering fire to the withdrawal. 'A' Company position became the rallying area, where the remaining senior NCOs were attempting to put a nominal roll of survivors together. The wounded were then being cared for at the RAP. Corporal Danny Jenkins had lost so much blood he was unrecognisable until pointed out to Gus. Vic Kinnear, another Jock who had trained with MacDonald, had lost a leg and the shattered limb was on the stretcher with him. Vic was in such a state of shock that he did not realise he had lost it. He said his foot felt numb, and could he have a smoke? Another Jock gave his mate a cigarette and when he pulled the cigarette out of his mate's mouth to let him exhale, his lips too came away with the cigarette.

Despite this desperate action, morale remained intact. The Jocks were ready to take part in a counter-attack, to their credit, and voiced their willingness to have another go at the Gooks. As far as Gus MacDonald was concerned, he was there to prove to himself that he was not going to run from the field of battle. He believed he was fighting for the honour of Scotland and then the honour of his regiment, the Argyll and Sutherland Highlanders, who for centuries had served the British cause with distinction and valour. Also possibly because of the streak that runs through quite a number of Scotsmen — they quite liked a fight. 'Can yer fight, Jock?' does not necessarily mean physical fisticuffs alone, it also applies to the process of hard work, morality and spirit. Nevertheless, Gus gave thanks to his God as did all the others that day in the action on Hill 282, now commemorated in a regimental painting.

The Jocks were beginning to realise that the Americans had better equipment, possibly at every level, including weapons. But never once during the campaign was this used as an excuse for non-performance above and beyond the call of duty. The next few days saw the amalgamation of 'B' and 'C' Companies, various members who had been stretcher bearers returning to bring the Company up to half-strength. Within a week, the Gay Gordons arrived, 150 reinforcements who were originally to come out as an independent company, but given the heavy casualty rate were immediately divided up among 'B' and 'C' Companies, bringing them almost back to full strength. The casualty list showed twenty KIA, ninety wounded, one MIA, and approximately twenty-four being used as stretcher bearers. Gus doubted if there were any who came off Hill 282 who were not wounded to some extent. He had fully got his wish. Now he was a soldier.

1st Argyll & Sutherland Highlanders in Trucks, 1950

Wounded 'B' Coy, Hill 282

Major General Frank W Milburn receives citation for Plum Pudding Hill
and Hill 282, December 1950

Major Alastair Gordon-Ingram serving as loader to Major Kenny Muir
VC on Hill 282

6: Korea, October 1950: Street Fighting Men

The Argylls were now ready for what lay around the corner. They were hurried off to the town of Taegu and flown out to Kimpo, a hundred-odd miles to the north-west. They went in 'Boxcars': Sky Masters, twin-fuselage aircraft with a huge box stuck in the middle to take up to about 50–60 troops with their equipment. Flying was a new experience, and morale high. Everybody gorged themselves on rations, as rations meant weight to be carried. So the Jocks normally would eat two days' rations at one sitting, choosing the 'goodies' first, naturally.

Kimpo was one American miracle. An invasion had taken place against all advice at Inchon, the dream-child of General MacArthur. Amphibious landings in the mud, a swamp area with tide variations of up to thirty feet, high tide expectancy of only five hours – and the gamble had paid off. The 1st Marine Division and the 7th Infantry Division had successfully landed along with some ROK support, and with a very minimal casualty level had taken Inchon and Kimpo airport and expanded in a matter of 48 hours – a brilliant engineering feat by our American cousins. They advanced to the capital, Seoul, where they met sporadic to stiff resistance. Now for the advance north…

But both armies had run out of puff, and there was a pause for about a week. The political background was that President Truman was in a dither with MacArthur. The old warhorse was going to cross the 38th parallel, which he did about a week later. And who should lead the advance on the West Coast but the British 27th Commonwealth Infantry Brigade, commanded by Brigadier Basil Coade. The advance was spearheaded each day by the Argylls, the Middies and the Aussies. In typical American cavalry fashion the 8th Army would dash up the road, led by half a dozen tanks in column.

They came to the town of Kaesong, where the 27th Brigade saw action and took the town. There was no stiffening of resistance, just light, sporadic infantry fighting – exchanges of machine-gun fire and small local tank exchanges, going in to clear out snipers and machine-gun nests at the side of the road. It was almost a carnival atmosphere, bashing up the road, but even the ordinary soldier had begun to wonder where the enemy had disappeared to. Had they just taken to the hills? They had – in their thousands. The North Korean Army was changing sides. Out of their North Korean uniforms and into the white of the Korean peasants, big baggy shirt and big baggy trousers, black shoes, dashing down the road waving to the United Nations liberators and immediately volunteering for the South Korean Army.

The push up the West Coast continued regardless until they came to the town of Sariwon, a large railway junction as well as a military training centre, and here resistance immediately stiffened. The Argylls were in the lead. 'A' Company put in a concerted bayonet charge in an orchard to the left side of the road, clearing out three machine-gun nests, and then took the lead and entered the town in rollicking style. It was bigger than expected, and street fighting set in: inching forward house by house, sometimes room by room, deciding to fire round the corner before exposing oneself, 36" and phosphorous grenades being used, or just ducking under the window and bypassing the house. This carried on from mid-afternoon until early evening, when the order was given to consolidate and defensive positions were taken up.

By this time 'B' Company of the Argylls had arrived in the municipal offices in the centre of Sariwon. At one point, in the Lord Mayor's office, Corporal Geordie Hudson came charging through the building in great infantryman style, rifle at the high port, bayonet fixed – and crashed into a barrel of excrement, right up to his waist: a beautiful green colour with a stench to match!! Did he have a beautiful war! None of his section wished to help the bespattered corporal, who was eventually dragged out by a rope and stripped off. 2 Section had taken about half a dozen North Korean prisoners by this stage; some were forced to donate a pair of trousers, a quilted coat, quilted hat, and his own muckers donated socks, underpants, singlet and pullover, much to the amusement of his Section. Corporal Geordie Hudson, all the way from Accrington, Lancashire, was rigged out like a real 'Gook', right down to the red star on his parka cap, and ridiculed shitless!

MacDonald, who had been acting Corporal since Hill 282 in an adviser's role to the person who was taking over the Section, took great amusement in advising Hudson they would not share a groundsheet that night, as he still stank, despite a regimental wash-down in bloody cold water.

6 Platoon, led by the Mortar Platoon Lieutenant Robin Fairie, had gone into the town square. They were greeted by the confused North Korean soldiers as, 'Russkie, Russkie.' The North Koreans were dishing out cap badges and at one stage the opposing sides were even exchanging cigarettes. The word had been passed around to be on the alert for a change in climate. It came when the Argylls suddenly opened up on the unsuspecting North Koreans. Gunfire erupted for about the next five minutes. The Argylls sustained negligible casualties, but the North Koreans were badly mauled, leaving a number of dead in the town square. The Argylls once again hunkered down for the night and the following morning the Battalion, in extended line, did a sweep through to link up with the 3rd Battalion, Royal Australian Regiment, and took a couple of thousand North Korean prisoners. The sweep through the town met with very limited resistance, only the odd exchange of fire taking place. North Korean wounded were taken, and some of the more badly wounded disposed of. Again the Argylls were off to see the Wizard: mounting tanks, trucks and barrelling up the road in true American fashion, meeting little resistance on the way to Pyongyang, the North Korean capital.

This particular type of advance carried on for about a week. Infantry mounted on tanks; as soon as the forward tank came under fire, whether from machine guns or whatever, infantry would dismount, form up on both sides, and sweep forward into the attack supported by the tank. At this stage, they were mainly used as mobile strongpoints, supporting infantry on a very mutual basis. As the infantry advanced, the machine guns of the tank and the tank cannon would give covering fire as called upon for the infantry, and the mopping-up would be done: short, sharp fight, clear the enemy, then back on the tanks. At times MacDonald found it quite hair-raising, but the Battalion had now reached a very efficient level of soldiering and mutual co-operation with all arms. Rumour had it that the 1st US Marine Division, along with the British 41st Commando, Royal Marines, had gone up the East Coast and had landed at Hunan and charged inland in an attempt to capture the huge Chosin reservoirs, which produced the electrical power for the whole of Korea.

They were to take part in some epic battles in this area when the Chinese People's Liberation Army, the PLA, came into the war. The British Royal Marines performed impeccably, as was expected of a fine force second to none, while their American cousins, the 1st Marines, comprising the 7th and 1st Regiments, also gained the respect of their British counterparts. But disaster lay in store: they were outmanoeuvred, outnumbered and winter had taken hold of the campaign. Freezing cold winds came whistling down from Manchuria, with sub-Arctic temperatures, at times 40 below. This was happening on the other, western side of the country, where the 27th Brigade continued to spearhead the advance to the Korean capital of Pyongyang. Rumour now had it that a crack British Brigade, the 29th, was to be added. The rumour had persisted for weeks, so Gus made up his mind to wait and see what a crack infantry brigade looked like. Even before their appearance they were known as the Phantom Brigade, then the Frozen Arsehole: a white circle on a square black background was their Brigade sign.

It was now getting towards mid-November: no snow as yet, but bitter, freezing winds from the north. 27th Brigade continued to lead the 8th Army advance up the West Coast. All companies in the Battalion had small actions with relatively light casualties, clearing hamlets as they barrelled up the main road at a rate of knots, riding on tanks. The tanks were medium Shermans of thirty tons with the usual 50-calibre and 30-calibre Besser machine guns with about a 75m artillery piece mounted. This was part of the American 1st Cavalry Division, which had three Regiments, the 5th, 7th — 'Garry Owen's boys', named after the Irish jig march past — and the 8th. The shoulder patch of the 1st Cavalry was a shield with a yellow background, the black dividing line with a horse's head superimposed on the top part of the shield. To the 27th Brigade, it became known as the Horse and Horse Shit, with some disrespect on the part of the British Commonwealth troops, although their artillery support usually was passable and their tank support likewise. Their infantry was always questionable: when they had the odd discussion with their counterparts they would willingly admit that they would not engage the enemy at less than 400 yards, which of course required considerable expertise from a rifleman. These people obviously did not have such expertise, and when the enemy reached 300 yards from their position, the main line of attack was to 'bug out', i.e. retreat. Even the Jocks realised the American Army had only been trained in attack. They knew little of defence except as a form of taking cover. As far as withdrawal was concerned, they had no conception of how to put an enemy through the grinder, where one leg stands still and the other fires alternately as you withdraw slowly with light casualties but causing severe injury to your opponent. Their idea of using the bayonet was looked upon with horror, whereas in the British Army before any advance in an attacking area was made, the first order that was always given was 'Fix bayonets'. The bayonet to the Americans was more of a can-opener than a weapon.

Their American cousins were ridiculed for their lack of fighting quality. They had equipment – unbelievably good 6x6 GMC trucks, excellent artillery, and average tanks which were not used to any great degree. Their small arms were far superior, although the Brits were loath to admit even to themselves that they were even less well-equipped than their American cousins. The 3rd Battalion, Royal Aussie, were still using the 1914 Lee Enfield Rifle and 18" bayonet. The 1914–18 uniform was also still in use, but all these Aussies were put to good use as witness the various hard-won Australian actions that were to take place. Actions like Kapyong, 60 kilometres north-east of Seoul, in the face of the spring offensive involving almost half a million Chinese troops in April 1951, and Maryang-San in October of that same year, have gone down in history.

As the advance continued towards the north, morale was high: there was a feeling that the war would soon be over. MacArthur had given out to his American troops that everyone would be home by Christmas. They felt they had won a victory at some cost. They got within a few miles of the North Korean capital and were eager to press on. The Argylls were leading the advance when they were ordered to move off the road with their armour and camp down in what appeared to be a potato patch. That night it rained heavily – freezing rain. They did not have time even to dig in but the potato drill lines were deep so there was very little need. They did have shelter from small arms and to some extent from artillery fire. The word went around that they were going to receive a double rum ration in this lashing rain but it never materialised. They were told next morning that the cooks in all their brilliance had used the rum to wash the Dixies in the cookhouse. Bullshit! Some of the base wallahs had drunk the whole issue. They had received the odd ration of rum before; it used to come up in huge jars protected by a heavy straw covering and it was great stuff – Navy, overproof, blow bloody heads off, marvellous. Anyway, they spent the night there in our potato patch and received a most unusual hot meal at the cookhouse thanks to what was called 'Five in One' rations: a box of rations for five, two boxes per ten men per section; British rations at that – excellent, much more sustaining than the American C rations. American C Rations was great gear for tropical weather but when the bite of winter set in, they could not sustain a fighting man for very long.

The next day they were told they would advance and pass through Pyongyang as the 1st Cavalry had taken the North Korean capital during the night. But they discovered in fact that even the 1st US Cavalry had given way to the 'Rocketing ROKS', the 1st Capital Division of the Republic of Korea's army, and it was they who had had the honour of taking Pyongyang. Very light fighting: street fighting is dirty work, both sides take heavy casualties and it is a slow grinding effort, as they had discovered to some extent at Sariwon. The Koreans came out and waved and lined the streets as if they were liberators as they whirled through their city on tanks and American 6x6 trucks. They had great fun watching Sergeant Hookey Walker as apples were thrown into the trucks as a gesture of goodwill: he would immediately throw them out, saying there might be hand grenades among them.

Hookey received his fair share of derision, bristling with rage, his huge flame-coloured red moustache aquiver at being taken so lightly by what he termed 'puppy soldiers'. Some pups!

They began to hear rumours that the Chinese were about to enter the war, and that there were masses of Chinese divisions north of the Yalu River, the border between Manchuria and North Korea. They began to wonder what General MacArthur's intention was. He had gone over the 38th parallel without the consent of his President and Commander-in-Chief and had been admonished for this gung-ho initiative. Was he going to do the same at the Yalu, they wondered? If so, what might the consequences be: WWIII? Here they were, a light skirmishing line, attacking the mighty Chinese Socialist Republic. Or would he revert to dropping atomic bombs? At this stage, neither Russia nor China had the 'magic' A-bomb. Their thoughts on the subject were limited, like the intelligence they had always received on whom they were attacking. The American attitude was that they were only Gooks, these Asiatic soldiers, not to be considered equals, although they had already demonstrated their military ability and power and gone through Southern Korea like a dose of salts.

They already had a healthy respect for the North Korean soldier. He was highly trained. He was brave. He seized the initiative. He was mobile. He was possibly better equipped for his type of fighting with the Brup gun, which is like a Thompson sub-machine gun. This particular weapon carried about 75 rounds in a drum magazine and when fired made a 'brrrup' sound. Back on that famous Hill 282, Sergeant Paddy O'Sullivan MM was to win a bar to his MM for his brave action in leading an attack in the initial stages: pressing home a bayonet charge, O'Sullivan lead by shouting, 'Get into the bastards!' As it happened he was hit in the stomach by ten rounds of Brup. If it had been the normal Tommy gun or even the 9mm Sten gun ammunition, his days would have been terminated. However, O'Sullivan managed to hold his guts together, and still staggered forward shouting encouragement.

The United States 8th Army had taken the North Korean capital and now advanced north, as usual with their British

Commonwealth allies spearheading the advance just in case they encountered some stiff opposition. Slight opposition was met at a place called Kumchon, brushed aside by tanks and by the normal tank and infantry attack. They then crossed the TaeDong, another typical Korean river: broad, with its depth depending on rainfall. This time there was a bridge that had been blown, so there was some hesitation: should the Yank engineers repair the bridge so they could climb up and go across it, or would they go across in boats, or find another way across by wading or just finding a ford? At this hesitation, 'B' Company, which was leading and only a number of metres from the bridge, came under heavy mortar fire. Normally, troops who come under mortar fire, pinpointed directly on the target and scoring or about to score hits, would run backwards to take cover; but with great presence of mind the whole company ran forward one hundred metres and took cover in a small quarry-like area without receiving a single casualty. They were not just soldiers now, they were Old Soldiers!

Mortar fire was pretty accurate but it took their Northern Korean friends about ten to fifteen minutes before they could start re-sighting. The quarry gave ideal shelter. Their normal long-range artillery, American Mustangs, were shouted up and over they came – all four of them – within a matter of minutes. As the mortar and self-propelled gun positions which were holding up their advance were wiped out, a rather sarcastic cheer went up in admiration of the pilots' support. The whole battalion then moved a mile or so upriver and waded across, while the trucks and tanks found fording places. The Middlesex found boats and paddled their way over – and tally-ho, on to a place called Pakchon, which took us another twenty to thirty miles towards the Yalu River. Here they were to win a Battle Honour.

They certainty deserved a Battle Honour for Hill 282, because there had been exceptionally heavy fighting and they had held their ground. Here they met the 187th Regimental Combat Team of the 82nd Airborne Division, known as the Screaming Eagles, a good outfit. They had been pinned down after making a drop in advance. The Brits were to relieve them. But Johnny Turk of the Turkish Brigade came forward: they too were now getting their fair share of action and they were told to take a village that was holding us up. Johnny Turk bypassed them and they hunkered down for the night, a screen of tanks out in front of their company position. Their American cousins did not like this so they put out sentries in front of the tanks to protect them, which was quite normal. Then the Brits came back and hunkered down in their own little section of dug-outs and scrapes. The tank crews mainly stayed under the tanks, sleeping under the tanks or in them. Under the tank was not the best option, especially if in boggy terrain: the tank would sink several inches during the night with fatal consequences, as some of the unfortunate American crews discovered.

During the night the Turks had put in one of their famous bayonet charges in the defensive position round the village up front and with Turkish thoroughness had wiped out the inhabitants. Men, women, children, dogs, pussy cats – everything that moved received the order of the bayonet. Johnny Turk was a most ruthless fighter both in attack, defence and withdrawal, a great soldier. They were all around the 5' 10" to 6' mark, swarthy, dark, with huge black moustaches, flashing brown eyes and short-cut hair. They had their own style of wearing their uniform, with their greatcoats down to their ankles, the opposite of what the Brits would have done as greatcoats always seemed to impede movement from the knee downwards. As the weather got colder they considered theirs useless except as foot-warmers in slit trenches.

During the night there was a tremendous fireworks display: the whole line had opened up a magnificent artillery barrage. They never discovered the reason why, or what the artillery was supporting. Some idiot in a tank had started firing at an imaginary target and the rest of the tanks had joined in without any orders. The disease had spread to the artillery lines a number of kilometres behind, and they opened up too. This wastage of good ammunition went on for the best part of an hour.

The next day they advanced through the village, now a scene of carnage. The tanks would not go forward unless they had an infantry screen in front. Obliging, of course, with their usual charming remarks to the various tank commanders who were hiding behind their three inches of armoured plate. They advanced through the Turkish Brigade and did a magnificent battalion attack on a hill feature. It was said the Gooks were well dug in, and so they were. There was a dried-up river bed in front of the feature and a road running parallel to it. This was one of the few times they had the pleasure or honour of carrying out a battalion attack in front of their American allies, the 187th RCT (Regimental Combat Team), which is roughly a brigade. The battalion mounted on tanks, they advanced towards the right of the hill they were to take and on a given command the tanks did a left turn, and their guns swung round left. During this piggyback on the tanks their medium and heavy machine guns and three- and 4.2-inch mortars were spraying the area magnificently; the American 105s and 155s were also pumping in the goodies to such an extent that the whole hill seemed to be bouncing in a shimmer of heat and high explosive.

The Americans believed the hill would be clear − nothing could have lived under the sheer weight of explosive being concentrated on it. The hillside was the normal scrub, broken rock country with small oaks and pine trees giving good camouflage. Gus was in the back of his tank, and in the middle of the attack he was handed a Bren gun which had been in the tender care of one Private Ouch, who had also been a military bandsman. Ouch may have been able to tootle the flute but he neglected to clean his Bren gun. All weapons in an infantry section are cleaned at least once a day. Dear old Gus was handed the gun with the accompanying instructions, 'There you are, you're now the Bren gunner,' and said, 'Thank you' – or words to that effect to Corporal Hudson. He then asked Hudson to clear the gun by firing a couple of rounds to make sure the weapon was in working order. He was told 'negative' and Corporal Hudson was told a few negative words in return. MacDonald quickly stripped down the gun in the back of a moving tank, handing out various parts of the weapon to his muckers. Sand was found in the working parts. The gun was inoperable − in the middle of an attack − and of course for the infantry section the main fire power comes from the Bren.

The tanks turned left and went up the hill and took up hull-down positions, which means picking a hollow in the ground where your gun just sticks over the top and rattles off five or six rounds and then stops firing. The PBI (Poor Bloody Infantry) took over again with fixed bayonets but most of the enemy were dead, wounded, or pretty well dazed, so they were dispatched to their heavenly maker. The hill was then taken in half an hour: the troops 'passed through' and consolidated on a knoll on the other side, while the enemy took off into the opposite valley in to the distance. Once again Shooting Stars and Mustang Jets took their dreadful toll, rocketing and machine-gunning and napalming. This was an immaculate attack. It gave the Argylls great pride to have been watched by the 187th RCT − crack US paratroopers − and to have shown them how it was done. If there is such a thing as a happy attack, this was it. For them, no killed, no wounded reported: unbelievable. Such are the fortunes of war.

B Coy Piper

7: Korea, November–December 1950: Wrong Side of the Line

From the first action at Pakchon they then crossed the Chongchon, another broad river, sometimes sluggish, sometimes fast-flowing. They moved out to a place called Chongju. More rumours were now circulating that the Chinese Communists were either over the border or imminent, and it was a huge Chinese Army that was coming. The United Nations troops were still on a high at the rapid advance, although even right down to the rank of private they questioned this American tactic of barrelling up the roads and allowing complete divisions to form in your rear. In fact there were almost as many enemy to the rear as to the front of the UN troops. The British concept was to advance over the hills step by step, clearing the way, securing your supply lines for fuel, ammunition and food, and also to allow your casualties to reach base hospitals. Not their Yankee cousins: they didn't seem to consider such things important but rocketed on like the Rocketing ROKs.

At Chongju they had a contingent of about five members of the press. In the lead tanks there must have been at least one correspondent mounted up with the footsloggers, taking pictures, passing remarks, telling them how they had won the war and what a wonderful bunch of guys they were. And this would be the last battle: MacArthur and his men were going home for Christmas, so it had been declared. At the town of Chongju the column met fire from mortars, snipers, light machine guns, medium and heavy machine guns. This meant clearing the streets, tanks into alley-ways, up side streets, forming up by sections and taking it house by house. The Jocks decided they would burn the town as a celebratory end-of-war gesture; it consisted mainly of wooden structures with a lot of paper instead of glass for windows so that the phosphorus grenades chucked into every building came into their own, and soon the whole town was alight. But unfortunately the wind was not blowing in a favourable direction: the town became enveloped in a heavy brown sickly woody smoke, stifling both defender and attacker. For two hours the attack was pressed home with light casualties. The North Korean defenders were withdrawing rapidly, with no strongpoints holding up the advance. The tanks had now disappeared, as their war correspondents had taken off much earlier in the piece, on the first exchange of fire.

Having reached the centre of the town they decided that resistance appeared to have petered out. The order was given to move out of the town to the right, north-east. 'B' Company came to a quarry and were told to move up the walls. Luckily they were not steep, so it was possible to scramble up and get out over the lip of the quarry. This task was accomplished, 2 section, 4 platoon, of 'B' Company being led by Corporal Geordie Hudson and backed up by Lance Corporal Duffy. Duffy was a Gordon Highlander reinforcement; he had served about six years with the Gordons, had been a cross-country runner and was about to be promoted sergeant but had downgraded from corporal to lance corporal so that he could take part in the Korean Campaign and gain battle experience. On a smaller scale, Duffy was also an exceptionally good lightweight boxer. However, Duffy had never told anybody that he was deaf. Emerging from the quarry, all of a sudden the ground round his feet seemed to erupt as a North Korean machine-gunner did his best to remove him from the face of this earth. The rest of the Section, who had yet to emerge from the quarry, shouted and swore at Duffy, saying, 'Get down, you bastard, you're under fire!' But the indignant Duffy replied, 'Do you know who you buggers are speaking to? I happen to be Lance Corporal Duffy, and watch your bloody language!' Then suddenly Duffy realised that the flak was flying around him.

2 Section carried on and moved off, following the rest of the company and battalion, and moved into the north-east position, high up, to enjoy the sight of the enemy town going up in flames. They dug in slit trenches as a defensive position, expecting a counter-attack to come in. When Sgt Hookey Walker said it might be an idea for somebody to have a recce around the place to see

what was going on, Gus MacDonald decided that would do him. He had heard of the old soldiers of other wars obtaining loot, so it was time to loot and pillage as far as MacDonald was concerned. He had a tatty old bandage tied round the ankle he had injured a few weeks previously and was seen limping off to have a sniff around the place. Of course, Hookey thought MacDonald would be only gone for a few minutes and a few hundred yards, but MacDonald had decided differently and off he wandered, a rifle over his shoulder and a hundred rounds round his waist. He had picked up a tomahawk he thought would be ideal in his search. Losing track of time and distance, he had been steadily wandering into enemy country for about half an hour and had covered about a kilometre. He peered over a garden wall and lo and behold, here it was — the loot. The dear old family were digging up their possessions in the front garden. Suddenly MacDonald realised that two of the gentlemen in the front garden were none other than Korean soldiers with Burp guns. Both were so startled that MacDonald ducked behind the wall, did a couple of zigzags and disappeared among the houses.

He realised he was on the wrong side of the line and decided it was time to make his way back: after all, having helped burn down the town, he would not be the most popular of people in these parts. He was hoping the North Koreans might think he was a Russkie, as he was wearing Russian-style hat with ear flaps, but apart from that no other insignia to show whether he was friend or foe. His uniform, originally an olive-green American combat jacket with trousers, had now been pretty well muddied and faded; with the brown Korean earth pretty well engrained into it, it made him a real motley-looking creature, wandering about North Korea on its own. He paused to take stock of how the Korean houses operate and was interested to observe that most of them were built of mud bricks with wooden floors and mud walls with lattice paper windows; he discovered that they had an ingenious heating system whereby you built a fire at one end of the house and the hot air travelled underneath it and came up through a chimney at the other end in which was the kitchen. In other words, the floors of the house in the winter were always warm and the house likewise. He entered a high school and there on the blackboard was Russian propaganda outlining all the benefits of communism, the North Korean flag, photographs of children marching and soldiers marching and aircraft attacking in this glorious war of liberation.

Ducking and dodging his way past various groups of civilians, he managed to retrace his steps back to his company's position some two or three hours later, and received a bollocking from Hookey Walker, who threatened to put him on a fizzer. Hookey mouthed the magic words about deserting in the face of the enemy being a court-martial offence, then nodded and said, 'Yeah, alright, I'm glad you're back, you bloody young bastard.'

The Argylls had a peaceful night but the Middlesex, way out on the right flank a few kilometres away, had a rip-roaring fight going throughout. You could also hear the chatter of machine guns and the whine of mortar bombs whistling into the 3rd Aussie position. The next day revealed that the Australians had taken several casualties but killed a dozen or more Gooks and wounded a few score.

Winter uniforms were now being issued by the Americans. The Brigade also got Arctic boots, a yellow leather type with huge triangular nails. The troops thought these were the bee's knees but they soon found they were of Norwegian Campaign vintage from 1940, or even WWI. If you attempted to dry the boots out anywhere near a fire, the leather soles cracked within a matter of minutes. The Brigade went back to the regulation British or Aussie boot, which was more serviceable: in the snowpack boot, the foot was encased in rubber and the leg in leather. The boots were issued with large thick fluffy socks, half cotton and half wool. Most who wore them, especially the 3rd RAR, had bad cases of frostbite, losing toes and feet. Down quilts had been taken from houses and you could hear the lice cracking as they died from the severe cold. They were excellent, the same as the Arctic sleeping bag, which was filled with goose down; when wet from frost it would freeze and had to be abandoned. Two-man pup tents arrived, adding marching weight. Imagine a small pack with your mess tins, washing kit, a spare change of socks, cigarettes, writing material, plus a couple of Bren gun magazines tucked in and wrapped around the small pack; two lightweight blankets wrapped up in a groundsheet and poncho cape; and when it got colder, rolled up on your belt at the back would be a sleeping bag, plus rations. For a Rifleman, 100 rounds, small (screwdriver-type) bayonet, water bottle, entrenching tool, a pick or shovel − the latter are good friends of the infantryman and save casualties. If you dig in you are almost safe, if you don't, you're dead. On top of all that you had Bren gun pouches, your two ammunition pouches to the front, two Bren gun magazines each. Any space left? Then add a couple of 36" grenades, plus possibly a machine-gun liner – that is, a belt of machine-gun ammunition for the Vickers medium machine gun that is supporting your platoon – a 3-inch mortar bomb, and you end up carrying about 90 lbs, depending on the disposition required. Clothing consisted of a string vest, a heavy long sleeve woollen singlet, a pair of long johns, an angora shirt, a mountaineering pullover, then a pile waistcoat, a windproof and rainproof combat jacket along with matching trousers, three pairs in all; a pair of gaiters and ammunition boots; on your head a Russian type of ear flap cap or a cap comforter (Beanie), and to top the donkey appearance off, a cowhide three-quarter-length coat without sleeves and secured by toggles at the front − a most picturesque scene which was not appreciated by the infantrymen at all.

The Brits were dependent on their American cousins for transport. Everything the Brigade had was humped on Shanks's Pony, i.e. your feet. Very seldom did they have the pleasure of making an attack or even a defence on what was termed 'Musketry Order': only weapons and ammunition, water bottle, and digging-in tool. By now the steel helmet had been discarded, being too heavy and awkward and unable to keep out bullets or shrapnel.

They heard Johnny Chinaman was coming to war. They were going to withdraw to a pre-arranged line further south, by hoofing it − there were no tanks to ride on, they had disappeared. No trucks to ride on either, so they were marched down the roads and sometimes came off the road and marched through the country on this so-called withdrawal. The Jocks were not happy about withdrawing: they could see no good reason. Why not stand and fight Johnny Chinaman, see how good he was? The attitude was, 'Let's have a bash.' This withdrawal was to last about three weeks, which for an infantryman is a few lifetimes over. They took to the side roads and hill tops looking down into the valleys and, lo and behold, saw the mighty 8th Army, in particular the 2nd Indian Head Division of the US Army, bugging out. What a sight! A complete division of 20,000 men, around 15,000 infantry and hundreds of tanks and artillery. Orders came to hold and fight a delaying action, which was good news: they dug in on the hill tops and on either side of the road and let their American buddies take off to the south.

You might think it would take only a matter of hours to get a Division past a given point. It took a long 48 hours, nose to tail. Yankee Doodle Dandy was in a panic retreat. They were disgusted to see this mighty artillery, armour and weaponry, retreating without firing a single shot in anger, just because it was rumoured Johnny Chink was coming down the road. And he certainly was, running circles round them, attacking from the flanks, attacking from the rear, marching over the country. Lightly equipped, fleet of foot, with no administrative or logistical tail, living off the land – an army of real professional soldiers who had fought the Happy Jappy and the Nationalist Chinese, soldiers with anything up to twelve, twenty years' experience of continuous warfare. They soon respected the Chinese but would have liked to have earned their own by standing and fighting. It was a bitter pill for the Cinderella Brigade. They were ragged and funny but willing to fight.

The withdrawal went on, night and day, marching south. With every day morale dropped with a sullen, frustrated rage. The common feeling was that even if they were to take casualties like Hill 282 all over again, it would be worth it. Possibly honour was beginning to seep away. And then they saw the Yankee tanks having thrown a track and lying there, abandoned. They took weapons off the tanks, food, anything they could lay our hands on. In some cases, they would even blow the barrels for them: jam the barrel, fire the gun, that ruins it, smash the breech block or booby-trap it with grenades. Unbelievable, brand new tanks painted pearly white inside, air-conditioned with all the mod cons. The retreat continued. The intelligence, not only about the enemy but on their own side, was negligible. Their transport consisted of captured Russian trucks which were picked up on the way. These were strictly for any of the wounded, or supplies or ammunition or Battalion Headquarters.

As the Jocks marched, each company had its piper. Spirits were still high. The Americans never understood the discipline of the British Army withdrawing, or their desire to fight, realising as the Brits did that you take fewer casualties fighting than you do running away. Of course you hear the tales of American units being decimated — they were being slaughtered like sheep. And the Rocketing ROKS in the later war in Vietnam were to prove fine soldiers, but in this particular war were mainly a bunch of stupid wee boys.

Freezing cold: rivers were frozen over. Even tanks could go over the ice. The Battalion came to a river about three to four hundred yards wide. The edges appeared to be anything between eight and fifteen feet deep. The Battalion went over: you had to get over the edges quickly because they were not frozen as strongly as the centre. The sound of ice splintering into a thousand cracks beneath your feet. Each Jock had to leave ten to twenty yards to his mucker to cross so as to avoid going through the ice. Ice cracking created an eerie sound, with crazy patterns forming under feet as they shuffled their way in a sort of skate-like step, anticipating going straight through the ice into the freezing water. Experience showed that if you fell through, the ice immediately closed over your head, making it difficult to get out of the water or for any rescuer to get near. At this particular river crossing, they had already marched twenty miles and were tiring. A climb up a mountain feature was next. 'A' and 'B' Companies reached the top several hours later and were preparing to dig in when orders came to saddle up again and move out. Down the other side, as dawn was breaking, the two Companies recrossed the river. A tank had forded the river further up and created a miniature tidal wave under the ice which made for faster cracking. Luck was still on their side. The march continued for the rest of the day. The Battalion had marched non-stop for the better part of eighteen hours. Exhaustion was setting in.

Equipment was being dropped, a grenade here and there to

start with. If something was too heavy for somebody to carry it was passed up and down the section, and then the Section Commander would make a decision whether it was worth holding on to. Picks went first, dumped with some reverence. Picks were very precious tools of their trade. Ammunition likewise. The Jocks always carried extra ammunition. A sprinkling of snow had started. Halts for five minutes every hour, then a ten-minute rest. The Jocks were falling asleep, exhausted, just lying in the road, as soon as they were given the signal to halt. No comfortable spot: men were just collapsing in a heap and going to sleep. There was the odd American tank withdrawing, but the bodies asleep in the roadway did not get up and move out the way: the tank would have to go around them. The latest was that they were going to hold a line, so they took up defensive positions and dug in. Digging in in frozen ground: light a fire to try and thaw the ground out. Sometimes it was frozen six inches down, sometimes a foot down, like solid concrete. This was back-breaking work: between marching every time you took up a defensive position. Thanks to their expertise with pick and shovel going through solid rock, working on the lines of cleavage, they could go down three foot in an hour, two men working flat out.

The Battalion had become all muscle and bone, like greyhounds. Their health to this stage was not impaired: they were exceptionally fit but beginning to tire as the days dragged on in this weary, sad, disgusting withdrawal. Sometimes the odd American transport would come and pick them up, especially if doing an about-turn, racing up and taking up a defensive position to allow some American unit to bail out to the south. They were no longer popular heroes, they were expendable cannon fodder – nothing new for infantry.

Eventually they returned to Pakchon and were told that friends from 187 RCT, the 82nd Airborne Division, were again in trouble: would the Argylls come and bail them out? This time it was a slightly different area from the previous hill attack. It was open paddy. One particular day they had been issued with American army greatcoats. Most refused issue as they were more of a hindrance than a help. The American Army greatcoats had huge golden buttons with the American eagle on. Unusually, the

American greatcoat was of no better quality than the British, but the huge golden buttons were intriguing. It was certainly something to aim at, which they found amusing.

Anyway, they were to do a battalion advance, so they spread out in extended line. The paddy fields had dried up, or were frozen with the paddy stubble sticking through. Paddy fields are arranged so that water can go from one paddy to another by opening a sluice, creating a bank which gave good cover. American Airborne were in their foxholes, a poor American concept. The Battalion advanced through the American positions at the High Port, taking a bit of light and medium machine-gun fire. You could hear the zip of the bullets flying past. Amazingly nobody was collecting them, and every hundred yards or so a signal was given to halt. Everyone would halt, almost like a parade-ground movement, drop down on one knee, invariably behind the bank of the paddy field so roughly only your head and part shoulders were showing, offering a small target. By now they had estimated their machine gun friend was firing from about a kilometre away. Spasmodic fire was sweeping the paddy at about waist height from time to time. The American tank support appeared, to much delight. They took up positions and joined the attacking line: this was going to be great stuff! But at one stage they refused to go forward unless infantry gave them support. The odd mortar bomb was now coming into it. It was only a matter of time before their Gook friends – or Chinese, whoever they were – got the exact range. This was no time to hang about.

Captain John Penman, MC and bar, climbed up on the back of a tank and rapped on the lid. The tank commander appeared. Penman rammed the muzzle of his revolver into the lughole of his American equivalent, the captain of the tank squadron, and told him in no uncertain terms that he was about to have his head blown off if he did not advance and provide supporting fire. Likewise, Lance Corporal Duffy had clambered up on the turret and the NCO tank commander emerged. Duffy explained what was required. The tank commander was unsure, so Duffy got hold of the 50-calibre and fired a few bursts. The 50-calibre did not have tracer so the direction of the outgoing was not picked up. Luckily this tank also had a Beeser mounted on the turret and it had a mixture of ordinary ball and tracer, so Duffy, with the tank commander's permission, got on to the Beeser and gave a few bursts in the exact direction of the opposition. A beautiful sight to see, the red tracer pinpointing an enemy position. The other tanks began to open up; some of them came out of their hatches and got the 50-calibre going plus the Beeser; others managed to ram up the old 55/75mm shell and started going forward, and the over and unders of the white phosphorus – you fire one over far too far, fire one under far too short and then you put a high explosive in the middle and you have the target.

The tanks began to creep forward and to the clanking noise they made it all started to happen. A weird sound, the clank of a tank! Infantry caught in their sights have a bazooka handy to take the tankie out, again problematic, especially for the infantryman. Tanks have impaired vision in the closed-down mode when they batten down all their hatches: they are looking out of periscopes, little slits, reliant on the radio communication between each tank for directions. Not an infantryman's dream. There is a difference – the tankie is behind his three inches of armour, but in a tank battle, when he meets anti-tank gun fire, he is a rat in the trap. When it gets serious, you can imagine a shell ricocheting around inside a tank and the damage it does, taking out three or four of the crew. Their wounds are never anything less than horrific. The infantryman does not like this claustrophobic feeling of being battened down for action. At least they can claw the dirt and go deeper down and creep about and they have great observation; and to ferret out an infantryman is very difficult if the man is skilled and you can only aim at his head and shoulders. Anything over a hundred yards, and it's a difficult shot, especially when camouflaged – you cannot detect his presence at all. So infantry has its compensations and insurances provided there is skill displayed. If not you are back to cannon fodder value.

In this action, 'A' Company received light casualties, but they knew if they kept up these skirmishing attacks the figures would mount up. The Argylls appreciated this advance, one of the pipers playing the regimental tunes. Private Donaghue was trying on his new American greatcoat, standing up to do so, and various members of his Section were beseeching his Maker for him to get down and take cover; but no, Donaghue was absolutely engrossed in these beautiful golden buttons. Not only had he taken off his equipment and put on this new greatcoat, he had buttoned it up to the neck in true General MacArthur style with all these gold buttons to the front – and then put on his equipment, making sure everything was exactly in place. Despite the shouts of 'For Christ's sake get your head down!' he totally ignored the advice, and with it the zip-zip and the crack-crack of fire spattering around him. Donaghue was an unpredictable soldier, brave and full of initiative one day, not so brave and with considerably less initiative the next. This was one of his brave days. Was he totally oblivious, or was he getting bomb-happy? They had not come yet to the Blighty stage where some boys used to stick their hand or foot in the air and say, 'Come on, God, give me one in the foot so I can go home and get the hell out of this!'

The outside of a North Korean and Chinese Safe Conduct Pass

The inside of a North Korean and Chinese Safe Conduct Pass

Al Jolson Bridge, Han River 1951

8: The Korean Hills

Because these green hills are not Highland hills,
Nor the island hills, They're not my land's hills,
And fair as these green foreign hills may be,
They are not the hills of home.

Retreat march, 'The Green Hills Of Tyrol'

Morale had dropped due to the constant withdrawing and not being able to challenge the Chinese. In fact they now realised that the 8th Army was retreating without token resistance. They recrossed all the main rivers going South, bringing back thoughts of earlier actions on the charge North: the Chongchon near Kunuri, the Taedon at Tockon, the Poyong at the North Korean capital, Pyongyang, and finally the Han with the famous 'Al Jolson Bridge', compliments of the US Engineers.

Christmas 1950 had arrived: they were finally pulled out of the line for a rest and were stationed at Ichon to guard Corps Signals HQ from guerrilla attack. The first time out of the Line had been on the way North, about Pakchon, when the 24th Divisional Band entertained them with 'Tico Tico'. It was so bloody cold even then their musical instruments froze up. The Battalion was then given a treat in the form of a Wild West picture. During the shooting scenes the odd shot was fired into the screen to the ironic cheering of the Jocks. This unusual breach of discipline was pointedly ignored by the senior NCOs and Officers. They had also celebrated the American Thanksgiving with turkey, cranberry sauce and all the trimmings, going down into the valley to the cookhouse. On returning up the hill to their positions the whole lot was pretty well frozen, but they 'gutsed' nevertheless. The Yanks certainly knew how to look after their troops: a pity their training and discipline was neglected. The US Marines were the only ones whose attitude commanded British

Commonwealth respect, them and the Airborne.

The Yanks at Corps Signals were most generous, bringing goodies such as cigars, cigarettes and beer, and the Brits swapped theirs, which were more substantial for winter weather. Half a metre of snow was on the ground and most days it was well below freezing. 'B' Company had dug themselves into the walls of a sand quarry and had built hutches with galvanised roofing iron. Each section had a roaring fire at the expense of the civilian population: houses were pulled apart for firewood. Fresh clothing was issued, weapons and ammo checked, but the demi-paradise could not last. The Jocks attended Xmas Church services on a voluntary basis, offered up the prayers of soldiers and enjoyed the generous supply of Communion wine. Even at these services the Yanks managed to get in their usual propaganda about returning North in the New Year. Gus MacDonald had struck up a friendship with a Yank Master Sgt (RSM) with the Signals Outfit, a Pete Thrush from Kane, Pennsylvania, who was a reservist called back to serve his country. Pete seemingly owned a trucking business and invited his new buddy MacDonald to come to the States and come into the firm.

The Battalion soon returned to the line back up in the Hills; the Chinese had come down south of Seoul, the South Korean capital. General Ridgeway had taken over and there was an immediate firming of will and discipline. Affectionately known as 'Iron Tits' due to the grenades he hung from his harness, he was an ex-para from the 82nd US Airborne, one of their better soldiering outfits. So it was decided that the UN would advance systematically over the hills, clearing the enemy as they went. The procedure was to identify the hills being held and the targets, lay on air strikes or artillery, mortar and machine-gun positions plus back-up of tanks, mortars, machine-guns and the finest artillery ever in Korea – the 16th New Zealand Field Artillery with their 25-pounders, a vintage weapon of World War II, but still effective. The Kiwis could jack them up on sandbags and fire them as howitzers; also, more to the Brits' liking, they could put down a creeping barrage, controlled fire landing fifty to one hundred yards in front of an advance by the infantry.

At this stage of the game MacDonald developed acute

laryngitis and suspected double pneumonia. When asked for aspirin, 'Banzai' Murray, 'B' Company's Sgt Maj, decreed that it was for the wounded. When MacDonald reported sick he was bundled off to 60th Indian Field Hospital, a fine parachute unit which had dropped with the 187th Rgt Combat Team (Brigade) of the US 82nd Airborne Division. The Indians were famous for their strong, sweet tea, which was a godsend in the wintry conditions – on average 20 below zero and sometimes 40. Weapons froze and charcoal braziers were kept under them. Engines had to be run every half-hour. From time to time the Jocks would travel piggyback with the tankies, the ideal seat being riding light-guard up front right, where you could doze as there was little movement over the front tracks. The remainder had to cling onto the rear platform over the engine, warm but jerky due to the locking of a track to change directions. MacDonald ended up in Pusan, on the southern coast, via an American Field Hospital. The walking wounded/sick slept on the floor, the litter/stretcher cases had a camp bed. MacDonald came in as walking but for a couple of days lay on the floor as he was more ill than suspected. Eventually a Sgt Orderly got him into bed. The US Nursing Lieutenant attempted to give him a penicillin jab in the backside – unsuccessfully – and had to get the Sergeant to do the trick. She was most upset when the Jock addressed her as 'Sister'. 'I ain't your Goddamn sister, but you can address me as Loo-tenant, soldier.' 'Yes, Ma'am' was the croak! From the hospital to a Yank replacement depot next to witness the overwhelming luxury of Uncle Sam: a real US Army barracks with central heating, beds with blankets and sheets, hot and cold showers, even insect screens although they were in the heart of a freezing winter. Eggs over-easy, sunny side up, how many? Likewise rashers of bacon, unlimited scoff, as many fruit juices or coffees with as much sugar, milk as you could jam in: no wonder this slothful so-called Army couldn't fight. The Quartermaster, called 'Supply', issued just what you wanted. Angus MacDonald ended up with two large kit-bags, US Army pattern, and even then had to jettison some of his goodies, even a Garand rifle and an M1 Carbine with ammunition, tin hat, and US ammo belt with all their great attachments – field dressing, bayonet, aluminium water bottle, entrenching tool, combat boots, even a pair of jump boots. What a Goddamn sharp GI did this Jock make!

A visit downtown to Pusan showed it to be an oriental city out of control: wide-open, including the drains, where anything went. Most of the resident Brigade of base wallahs had concealed handguns. Angus settled for an extremely pointed dagger, made in Japan, as his personal weapon. The place stank and was one huge brothel where military corrective establishments abounded. Luckily the sojourn was cut short and our Angus, having told the authorities he was with the 27th British Commonwealth Brigade, was posted to the 27th Regiment of the 24th US Division. Cutting a long story short, he clambered aboard a truck and headed North, back to the Seoul area where by various hitchhikes he arrived back in his correct Brigade, 'B' Echelon (the Bn Base area), where he got a lift in a British 3-tonner back to his Battalion Headquarters. On the way he found the famous NZ 16th Field Artillery, who were firing support with their 25-pounders jacked up on sandbags in similar gun pits. As the 'sick hero' passed the Kiwi battery he was hit on the head by a blast from the 25-pounders, like being hit with a sandbag on the side of the head. Next after-effect was that the eyesight had changed: excellent long-range vision but almost nil short vision, also a feeling of unreality – really fighting fit to re-join the Battalion.

Battalion Headquarters hove into sight and who should be there to greet his return to the flock but RSM Paddy Boyd, DCM. 'Welcome back, MacDonald of "B" Company!' was the greeting. 'Thank you, Sir,' was the reply. What to do – tell the RSM you were bomb-happy? A good one, even for an Old Soldier. MacDonald thought, Well, this crap will clear up and no-one will be the wiser. 'You will come under my wing, MacDonald, for the next week.' So they took ammo up to the companies who were on top of the ridges (over 1,000 feet). 'This will get your hill legs going, laddie – we will oversee a couple of hundred gook porters. We, the escort, carry liners for the machine-gun section up there.' As decreed, every night for the next week MacDonald went up to the line with the motley band of human mountain goats. The frost was severe enough to crack and explode the smaller twigs on trees so that one night Big Banzai (RSM) was found with his revolver drawn, taking cover behind a tree, much to MacDonald's amusement, which earned an obscene dressing-down for daring to laugh at a distinguished RSM, DCM, making an unforgettable F-up with an imaginary enemy.

Having returned to his Company, MacDonald was welcomed back by being told he should have wrung the sick bit out. He dished out a few bottles of Jap whisky, Santory and Suntory, both about firewater standard. The boys (Argylls) were doing hill clearing and only light casualties were being taken. But it was back-breaking work: advance behind a creeping barrage with mortar and machine gun support, rush the crest, consolidate on top and dig in. Most of the time the ground was frozen solid, the same as cutting through rock without lines of cleavage to work from. On one such hill advance, the Kiwis were giving a good creeping barrage but the drop-shorts had become a barrage behind the advance. MacDonald having at this stage volunteered to get his Section's water from the nearby river-bed, he was seen to walk through the shell-fire and eventually return the same way, much to the amazement of his fellow-Jocks. For some time now he had had to be roused from twelve-hour slumbers with the order of the boot. Some of the NCOs began to suspect all was not well with the laddie. On 'stag' (guard) at night with the Section LMG he would take hours to wake the next relief. After a week, Sergeant Andy Simpson decided that he personally would take MacDonald to the RAP (Rgt Aid Post) to see the Doctor who immediately tagged MacDonald's lapel with the label 'Battle Fatigue'. Next, MacDonald had to be convinced that he had to hand over his rifle and ammo when he had other ideas. Andy Simpson did his fatherly act and MacDonald complied with the MO's orders.

Next he picked up his kit-bags with goodies held at 'B' Echelon and was taken to the 60th Indian Field (IAMC), receiving the customary sweet tea and hospitality. Next day, somewhat hazily, he appeared at some American MASH unit where he proceeded to wander about through operating theatres where the medics were going great guns with amputations, mainly Chinese, so MacDonald thought he was in a Chink prison camp. The following day a Dakota Transport was loading up wounded so he joined the queue; by now he had the American tag of 'Combat Exhaustion' pinned to his other lapel. The flight crew eventually took him on board and off back to Pusan.

There, next day, he was re-assessed by an American Bird Colonel (Full), a medic, in fact a psychiatrist. Mac said he was okay and wished to return to his unit but was told he was being transferred to 29th British General Hospital, Kure, Japan for further treatment. Having flown into Iwakuni Air Base and on by train to Kure, he arrived late at night to be greeted by a Medic Corporal. Acting (unpaid) Corporal MacDonald told the medic that a bed would be no good as he had for the past eight months been sleeping on the ground and his pillow would be his small pack. Although he thought he had a nut on his hands, the medic Corporal allowed MacDonald to sleep on the floor behind the ward door. Next day, after a shower, he was bedded down. One side of the ward was 'skin', including anti-social diseases, the other side very quiet – 'nuts' who were being discharged permanently at a rate of knots. The other 'Bomb Happies' were in the middle, where they played war games, building defensive positions with pillows and mattresses and picking sides for attackers and defenders, all of this accompanied by artificial battle-ground sounds, to the amazement of most of the nursing staff, Lieutenants & Captains of the Queen Alexandra's Military Nursing Service.

After several days this particular 'Bomb Happy' was summoned to the presence of Captain J Flood, the resident 'Trick Cyclist'. Captain Flood asked MacDonald to volunteer for the truth drug pentathol; he was duly told to lie back on the magic couch and relax while he was asked these deep and searching questions:

Q. Have you a marital problem?
A. Sir, I am not married
Q. Have you a financial problem?
A. I have no money. Sir.
Q. Do you have a sex problem?

A. Where I am there are no women. Sir.
Q. Would you like to be a bishop or a colonel?
A. Colonel at the moment. Sir.
Findings:- You are a normal intelligent young man.
Q. Did you see any heavy fighting?
A. I do not know, this is my first war. Sir.

A few days later, having been promised a course of phenobarb, MacDonald was awarded 14 days' convalescent leave. He is still waiting for the phenobarb. It may yet help, but who knows or cares? At this stage toothache prompted a dental visit. The dentist, a Major, demanded a smart salute and proceeded to fill a tooth on the other side of the mouth to the side complained of. Another efficient base wallah. Upon demob some months later, eleven fillings were the order of the day. Thank you. Major Dentist.

Hospital blues were issued to the wounded; as 'Bomb Happy' was in that category he was duly issued with a bright blue jacket and trousers, both at least three or four inches short in the sleeves, and slacks, plus a cheap white shirt and a bright red tie, regulation ammunition boots and self-bought Glengarry to make up this comic picture. Our Heilan' Laddie got rid of the garb and was allowed to visit a second cousin in Tokyo who happened to be William JC Kerr, Gen MacArthur's religious adviser for Japan and the Far East. Kerr, a Yank of Scottish stock, had spent 30-odd years as a missionary in Korea. He lived in the Manetsu Apartments, all very swish, and kindly showed the Scottish soldier over Tokyo, ending up in an Officers' Club. MacDonald was taken for a Dutch Officer and played the part well, considering a reasonably broad Scottish accent. He downed his gratis whiskies with good grace and at a rate of knots, making all the expected noises. But having convinced his missionary relative he would be happier with his own breed, he reverted to the Ebisu Hotel, the Rest and Recuperation centre for British Commonwealth troops. The whole set-up was excellent, right down to a Happy Jappy orchestra playing light classical stuff in the background. Some sophisticate had written out the menu in French so MacDonald had the honour of translating: if unsure, any thought along the line of food would do the job.

A happy, drunken, fornicating time was had by all. The 'team' comprised an Ulster Rifles Sgt, an Ulster Rifles Cpl, an Aussie Signals Sergeant, a Welsh Petty Officer off the hospital ship *Maine* and a Yank Staff Sergeant. MacDonald was the pup. The team decided upon the Ginza, the entertainment area (in the broadest sense) of Tokyo, and entered a dancehall-cum-bar and restaurant; after a few 'taxi dances', where you got round the floor once and paid your partner her fee, you continued to put a nickel in the Nickelodeon for more dancing or other propositions. On the second visit, to liven things up, grenades were rolled across the floor. They had taken the detonators out but still achieved a most spectacular result, the band upsetting music sheets and chairs, screams all round, and the same effect in the restaurant and surrounding area. The 'Snow Drops' (US Military Police) were called in, the Brits plus their US ally were asked to leave and take their amusements elsewhere. They were remiss in their duty on this occasion: there was no punch-up. The merry band appeared on the main Ginza street and MacDonald for the first time in his young life was accosted by a Japanese queer. MacDonald was not sure what was going on until the Ulster Rifles Sergeant gave him some pertinent advice: 'Give him a f...ing kiss, Jock, for Christ's sake!'

After convalescent leave our Highlander returned to Kure to JRHU (Japan Replacement Holding Unit) and Japanese Imperial Guard Barracks, which had excellent accommodation and amenities. Rations were half-Aussie and half-British, as much as one could eat, ice-cream and peaches the favourite, after steak and kidney pie. Bedding issue took the form of five Aussie woollen blankets, immediately traded on the black market to Happy Harry, a Japanese-American who headed up the camp Fire Brigade as well as being the Black Market's number one man. A fellow-Argyll, Anderson from Fife, mucked in with MacDonald and the pair on a weekend pass decided to pay their respects to the devastated city of Hiroshima, not far away. UN and US occupational troops were supposed to travel by train in Allied Coaches, separate from the local population. In Hiroshima they made for one of the local bars, where they proceeded to down the customary few Asaki beers and the odd gulp of local whisky in keeping with Scottish custom. Next the boys decided to board a tram car, which as it transpired was full of Jap females. Despite their partial inebriation the Argylls put on their best face, until out of the blue the tram's electrical box shorted out with a blue flash and loud explosion. The indefatigable Jocks took immediate action by diving under the seats, taking cover in the approved manner, much to the amazement of the female passengers, who burst into spontaneous giggles followed by a polite hand clap all round. The heroes beat a hasty retreat into a cinema where the film was *The Hasty Heart*, a love story involving a Corporal of the Cameron Highlanders who falls in love with his nursing sister with the Burma campaign as background: all very sad, but the two Jocks managed to disrupt the whole theatre by cheering and applauding at the wrong times throughout the film. Next on the list of bloody-mindedness was the return train trip from Hiroshima to Kure, during which they systematically collected the fares and tickets for all passengers in advance of the official Ticket Collector.

Next stop: a replacement camp for Argyll and Middlesex, where the nightly sing-song was led by an Argyll, Spankie MacFarlane, who in his heyday had been a professional boxer. Many years later MacDonald could still hear the strains of 'Maybe it's because I'm a Londoner' led by Spankie, to the pleasure of the Middlesex, a London Regiment. It became more like a ceilidh, as each and every Argyll or Middy passed had to donate to the festivity, and it was all great for morale. MacDonald was recalled to JRHU to face a Regimental Charge of processing illegal arms: a L/Cpl Reservist of the Northumberland Fusiliers employed in the Quartermaster's Store had broken into his kit-bag and found an American Garand rifle and M1 carbine plus ammo. The Presiding Officer was a Lieutenant-Colonel, 8th Hussars, the Senior NCO i/c an RSM of the Seaforth Highlanders. Mac pleaded guilty, explaining that the weapons were for trade on his return to Korea. Here we go: 56 days' Field Punishment with wet sand loaded into your pouches, small pack, doubling up and down hills plus constant drills — a real *bastard*. The Seaforth RSM put in his bit on behalf of his fellow-Highlander and the sentence was reduced to a mere 14 CB (Confined to Barracks), reporting each evening at 6 p.m. to 12 midnight to the main camp's NAAFI Canteen to wash up the dirty dishes and cooking utensils. Not bad, especially as the Japanese girls would not allow their soldier boy to do a hand's turn but made him watch the movie and sup ice cream and peaches.

Spring had arrived with its beautiful, whitish-pink cherry blossom, and with it came the news that the Battalion had been relieved by the 1st King's Own Scottish Borderers and was on its way back to Hong Kong on the USS *Montrose*. All sick, lame and lazy were likewise to return to Honkers aboard HMT *Orwell*. It was the end of April 1951 and the Battalion had been at the sharp end for nine months. In that time every decoration in the British Army, with the exception of the DCM, had been won, including a Victoria Cross. Casualties were 80 dead and 200 wounded, just over 50% − a good average for Infantry. Lieutenants had a 100% casualty rate. Mac wondered if the young pups had even been told: maybe just as well they hadn't. The young regular had performed up to expectations, but some of the older veterans, especially from other regiments, had come in for criticism. They claimed this was a much tougher campaign than Burma, the Western Desert, Italy and north-west Europe. The sprinkling of National Servicemen, mainly in the Rifle Companies, had more than proved their worth as fighting men according to the senior Officers and NCOs, so MacDonald and his like had made the grade and were now accepted at long last as 'of' the Battalion and not merely 'in' it. In fact the 1st Battalion Argyll & Sutherland Highlanders went on to become the most operationally experienced in the British Army for the next 25 years, serving in Palestine, Korea, Cyprus, Suez, Borneo, British Guyana, Aden and Northern Ireland. Major John Penman, MC and bar plus 4 MIDs, who was MacDonald's hero, died in Edinburgh at the age of 35 years, a sad loss to the Regiment he dearly loved and served without reservation so well − a true Argyll & Sutherland hero.

The Argylls were welcomed back to Hong Kong with a dubious accolade in the *South China Post* saying 'It is good to see their ugly faces back in the Colony.' But there were reservations. Within a fortnight Hooky Neilson, the Battalion CO, held a scale 'A' parade (everyone): with all ranks standing at ease he tore strips off the Jocks, NCOs and Officers over the high incidence of anti-social disease within the Battalion. He suggested 98% and said they had only been 'out-poxed' by the 14th Field Artillery, who at times had been their support. MacDonald had only a few months left before he was on the boat with the tartan funnels on his way back to Blighty. Again promoted to Acting (Unpaid) Corporal, he had heard that he was to be posted to the 4/7th Gordons, a machine-gun battalion. Obtaining an interview with his Coy CMDR, Major Ash, he asked to be put on a machine-gun course but was told that it was only for Regulars. MacDonald expressed willingness to revert to Private, which Major Ash accepted, but no course as he felt MacDonald had been a trifle insolent on his application. This was not the first time that a National Serviceman had been put down, bearing in mind it was a regular Battalion, which was unusual for the period. On joining, MacDonald had made sure that in all Coy events including 'bashes', four-, six- or nine-mile runs and musketry application parades, he would come first, second or third out of his Company, Quarter Guards included. Never once was the NS man recognised, although when MacDonald handed in his 1913 kilt and his 1903 sporran, the Sgt Maj passed the remark that he had heard if MacDonald 'signed on' he would be in the Sergeants' Mess and possibly even a Lieutenant by the end of the year.

Wives and families arrived for the 'marrieds' who had been separated for two years and the Battalion returned to peace-time soldiering. MacDonald visited his friends at Ping Shan Police Station, the Morrisons, Bill and Copper, an Aberdeen couple who kindly provided hospitality for most of the Officers of the Battalion. MacDonald kept well in the background, despite attending the odd function dressed up in a penguin suit or Mess Dress of the RHK Police. Luckily he was never caught out. Bill went on to be Deputy Commissioner Malaya and deservedly earned a series of rapid promotions.

During August '51 it was farewell Hong Kong and once again on to a trooper. In Singapore MacDonald renewed acquaintance with men from the KOSB from Korea and the Seaforth, some of whom had won decorations. The KOSB walked straight in to heavy fighting while relieving the Argylls and beat them in the decorations dished out. Bourne from Helmsdale, a Seaforth, had won an MM in the jungles of Malaya fighting the Chinese communist resurrection. It was brilliantly put down thanks to General Templar's tactics, which were put to use again a few years later in Kenya. On the troop deck were the Scottish Jocks, a Section of Marine Commandos, and a large batch of RAF personnel who were treated with considerable disdain by the Jocks. The Troop Deck Officer was a Captain of the Educational Corps, who was left in no doubt as to the lack of respect from the 'hairy-arsed' Jocks. The usual altercations were had with the Military Police at all ports of call and the Wogs of Port Said given the expected run-around.

After weeks at sea the troops came alongside at Liverpool and the Argylls entrained for Stirling Castle, where the remains of the original draft were demobilised. Major J Penman, MC and bar, had a few words: 'MacDonald, you bugger, stand fast when dismissed!' Penman expressed disappointment that MacDonald was quitting the Army as he felt he had a career there. MacDonald said he would try the Police Service before he re-enlisted. Esson, the 'Dozy Gordon', and MacDonald landed at Aberdeen Joint Station, where MacDonald's old man had laid on a Rolls-Royce taxi. They gave Esson a lift to the Wallace Statue bus station, shook paws and went on their merry ways. MacDonald was home in his beloved north-east of Scotland, but found it difficult to settle. He roamed the local hills for days at a time, sleeping out, appreciating the autumnal splendour of Royal Deeside Valley and the beauty of the bonnie purple heather. He was in receipt of the 'dole', which he could hardly believe he was entitled to. Would he take a couple of exams and go to uni, which would take a year? Re-join the Army and hope for a commission? The thought of another war was not a tempting prospect: he had already given thanks to God for his deliverance. The Greatest Experience of All was now over.

Two young veterans, 1951

Part Two

Fighting on a Different Front, 1951–55

9: Back to No Mean City

We have an anchor that keeps the soul
Steadfast and sure while the billows roll
Grounded firm and deep in the Saviour's love.

Glasgow Police Hymn

There is no doubt that the Glasgow Police had a world-wide reputation. And why not? Glasgow was the Second City of the British Empire, which in turn had a landmass incorporating one-third of the globe. This city had lived up to its motto, 'Let Glasgow Flourish', with trade from the Americas and the rest of that far-flung Empire. It built the finest ships in the world, both for the merchant marine and the Royal Navy, at yards from Govan to Partick and in the heart of the Red Clyde: Clydebank, Harland & Wolff, and John Brown's. Known as *No Mean City*, Glasgow had a police force second to none. The Glasgow Police Pipe Band had been world champions many times over. Having been accepted as a recruit, Constable Angus MacDonald returned to the city of Glasgow and the Clyde.

Glasgow Police HQ was at St Andrew's Square, not far from the Central Court and High Court off the Haymarket. Across the river in the salubrious suburbs of the Gorbals at 22 Oxford Street was the Training School, a solid grey sandstone building. The Force came into being in 1886 and gradually absorbed the smaller forces in neighbouring boroughs. By the end of the nineteenth century many of its recruits were coming from the Highlands of Scotland, where they breed 'big men' in every sense. Around the turn of the century, when the Inspector General of Constabulary for the United Kingdom carried out his annual inspection, he remarked in his notes that he found it difficult on occasion to communicate, as a large proportion of the Glasgow Police were Gaelic speakers and conversed mainly in their mother tongue.

Most of these men were over 6' 2" (188 cms) and built in proportion: their forearms were equivalent to the average man's thighs. Putting it kindly, they were not over-endowed academically, but they were ideally suited for the duties they had to perform.

The thirty-five recruits, of whom MacDonald was one, formed a cross-section of young Scots, mainly ex-servicemen: 'Scots Guards' provided almost automatic entry. There was Peter MacNab Downie, a shepherd from Glencoe turned dairy farm manager who became MacDonald's lifetime pal; Donald MacLean from Islay, a former third-year electrical student; Jim Harvey, the miner and Coal Board heavyweight boxing champion; Donald MacCulloch from Stornoway, an all-in wrestler; Bill Piper, Commonwealth high jump, long jump and pole vault champion; and cross-country runner Alex Slessor. A couple of attractive policewomen made up the class.

The Training School had the usual lecture halls, a first-class gym, accommodation in a dormitory kept in spotless condition; catering was up to three-star hotel standard, and the cleaning and cooking staff took pride in looking after their 'boys'. Like a normal school, the day was divided into one-hour lectures or periods from 8 a.m. to 5 p.m. with an hour for lunch break. Lectures were very basic: all on police duty, all taken from the Glasgow Police Instruction Book, which covered every subject: Criminal Offences, Minor Offences, Court Procedures and their Jurisdiction. As Scotland had its own legal and educational system, the Road Traffic Act of 1950 was then the only English or 'imported' legislation. Unlike other police training establishments, however, there was one hour's lecture followed by one hour's physical, which produced extremely fit young police officers. There was one hour of swimming and life-saving daily, one hour's ju-jitsu and one hour in the gym. Wednesday afternoon finished with freestyle swimming – only on completion of the six-mile cross-country, run within time. In the evenings was badminton in the gym or 'pumping iron'; most did both.

Friday mornings brought two hours' foot drill as per the Guards Brigade, conducted by Inspector Willie Burns at

Govanhill Drill Hall, one of the Cameronians' establishments of the Scottish Rifles (a Lanarkshire regiment nicknamed the 'Glasgow Sweeps'). During these drill sessions the art of directing traffic was taught: a multi-road crossing including tramlines was marked out and those on parade took the place of vehicular traffic. Like everything taught to the young police, it was simple but most effective. They also learned where to punch and what to punch with, including the use of the boot, and were taught the invaluable 'Come Along' holds — where to get hold of a prisoner and stop him from getting himself down on the floor, wrist locks, hammer lock and bar, the half nelson and some others invented by the cops themselves with generations of experience. All movements had to be carried out with military precision, including use of the baton — the 'hickory', more commonly known in the force as The Stick.

Chief Inspector Ratcliffe was a sadistic Commandant, Inspector Willie Burns of Olympic fame the Drill Instructor/Swimming Coach, doubling up in First Aid and Civil Defence and occasionally allowed to lecture. They also had Sergeants Blackie, MA, LLB, and Giggles, MA, Sergeant Joe Riley, Scots Guards, boxer and judo expert; a number of the instructors had double degrees and were former schoolteachers who had become cops during the aftermath of the Depression. Most had war service as well. Sgt Blackie's occasional lectures were half from the Instruction Book, the other half relating an experience which had actually happened to him or one of his 'neighbours'. A policeman's lot may not have always been a happy one, but the police always made an effort to add their personal touches, usually humorous or downright 'cheeky' to some degree.

Inspector Willie Burns was known to be a brilliant swimmer, a magnificent specimen of manhood — six foot, with a 56-inch chest and built like a stud bull — but in some respects Willie was not over-endowed. He lectured in First Aid and Civil Defence, Life Saving, Drill, and Judo, all without par, but on the odd occasion if another instructor was sick he would chance his arm at the Criminal Code, reading from the Instruction Book after studiously having placed his wristwatch on the lectern. Having wasted some time with various pleasantries, he would commence

121

reading, the rest of the class being enjoined to follow in their own copies. On occasion a few pages of the lecture would be jumped, but the favourite Inspector continued reading without hesitation right up to the end of the lecture period, which always finished with his well-known summing-up: 'That is all, sorry we do not have time for questions.'

Who said the 'Polis' (Glasgow for police) were stupid? Inspector Willie Burns was au fait with the Criminal Code, all right, as it pertained to the street. Mind you, he did put you in mind of the famous Glasgow Police stereotype that revolves around the man with the horse and cart selling briquettes in Sauchiehall Street, near Bath Street. The horse drops dead in the shafts of the cart; a huge Highland cop comes on the scene, starts to write up the Occurrence Report in his notebook but has difficulty with the spelling of Sauchiehall Street, so he scratches his arse and immediately drags both the dead horse and cart round the corner, where he slowly spells out 'Bath Street' and completes his report...

Chief Inspector Ratcliffe, silver hair plastered well down and immaculate in his barathea uniform with pearly white Van Heusen shirt, would sometimes take the 'Come Along' holds class with Inspector Burns and Sergeant Riley. Joe had been a Lance Sergeant in the Scots Guards and came from the Silver City of Aberdeen. As his semi-flattened nose betokened, Joe was a boxer of some experience. He was possibly a fraction punchy as he shuffled his feet, but a real decent laddie, greatly respected for his disciplinary standards and impeccable manners to all who came in contact with him. He also had a dry sense of humour, suggested by that twinkle in his eye. 'The Rat', as the CI was known, would use Joe as a guinea pig to show off his considerable prowess in judo, to the extent that he caused Sgt Riley considerable pain. Joe would look him in the eye and address him very quietly as 'Sir'. Luckily for The Rat he never met Joe on a dark night, and his performance was greeted by a stony silence from the young cops. Not that it bothered The Rat: he was on a different plane. And he did have his uses: his favourite lecture was how to get on in the police without a 'wire' – a benefactor: sit tight for the first few years and when you come into plain clothes duty for the one year, you resurrect all your informers and friends who have been lying doggo so your star bursts into the ascendant for all the bosses to see. Young cops take note.

Swimming was treated seriously with Inspector Willie Burns at the helm: Willie could come out of the water without touching the bottom and land on the side of the pool. Some even qualified as Life-saving Instructors. This high degree of fitness was pressed home in the hope that the cop would retain it in the fight against the Ned on the street, who was very fit and a light-weight, fast mover. Cross-country running, up to six miles, was conducted at Pollok Park's Haggs Castle Golf Course every Wednesday afternoon. Those who completed the course in a set time could splash about in the Pollokshaw indoor pool to their hearts' content; those who had not made the requisite time were given fifty lengths to swim before being allowed off the training hook. In one of the runs, MacDonald missed out part of the course and sprinted home in great time; he was then detailed to report Saturday afternoons, if not playing rugby, to take part in runs with the cross-country team, then second best in Britain only to the Metropolitan Police. At least it got him fit for rugby. Coming almost last at the National Meet at Hamilton Race Course about six months later got him thrown out as team reserve, for which, though not too bad a runner on occasion, he was duly thankful. His swimming was not too bad either, so he was drafted into the life-saving team as a reserve. The same fate followed: he was not strong or proficient enough, so finally he was allowed to train with his former teammates — every afternoon off when on duty — and of course his fitness for his first love, rugby, was enhanced.

The last period of each week saw a delightful elderly lady come into a class of some seventy budding cops, an old-fashioned tuning fork giving the required note for the hymn and psalm singing. The Glasgow Police hymn was 'We have an anchor that keeps the soul, Grounded firm and deep in the Saviour's love'. Of course some of the hymns reverted to versions outwith the Psalms and Church hymnary, such as 'We will follow Rangers' instead of 'Jesus' — the Catholics substituted 'Celtic'. Luckily the lady who dearly loved all her 'boys' was quite deaf. A rousing good time was had by all, a real evangelical feat.

As a Probationary Constable, MacDonald gathered he had entered an elite force run on time-honoured systems. Probation lasted two years: at the end of the first, the probationer returned from his Division for a six-week Refresher Course, where he was expected to perform as a qualified Police Officer. By this time he had done his bookings, made arrests, covered a dozen or so accidents, directed traffic, looked after school crossings and had a few sudden deaths and all the normal domestic accidents. He had also learned various methods, additional to training, of dealing with obstreperous individuals: knuckles took six weeks to heal with the usual cracked scabs. At the end of two years on the beat he was back for his Confirmation Course of four weeks, during which he was assessed. Most managed over the two-year period to arrive without 'Failing to become efficient' or 'Ceasing to be efficient', both of which resulted in discharge from the Force. All tests and exams had to be passed: the academically weak were catered for provided they could perform in the real world of rough and tumble and showed pride in their uniform. At every level, practicality was stressed above all else.

Friendships were made in training which would last a life-time. Some would be 'neighbours', which meant working beats next to each other and doing everything together. Some even had the same 'digs' and social life, so one had entered a kind of brotherhood. The Glasgow Police motto, *Semper Vigilo* (Always Vigilant), was instilled into the probationer: there was a war on out there with Robert the Bobby versus Edward the Ned. Robert had to be the winner and the Ned put down and kept down. Saturdays and Sundays were days off, so the local lads did the usual and the ones from beyond *No Mean City* went to the 'fitba' or played sport and in the evening, after a few bevvies (a half and a half − small whisky and small beer) went on to the 'jigging', some to the Highlanders' Institute for Old and Modern, others to the Albert Ballroom, a reasonably sedate affair, to see if they could get a 'lumber' − Glasgow parlance for a date. Sunday was usually given over to reading the papers, trying to get rid of a hangover and wondering if one had behaved oneself − and if not, was it worth the candle?

After three months (fourteen weeks) of this routine, MacDonald passed out. The question was, where would he be passed out to? Glasgow was divided up into Divisions. 'A' was Central Division, taking in the City Centre, and the boys had to be 6' 2" to impress the public and passing tourists. 'B' was Marine Division to the North of the Clyde River on the West side, residential plus docks. 'C' was Eastern Division, heavy industrial and working class, with the odd slum; its policemen were known as 'The Wise Men of the East'. 'D', Southern Division, was famous for the Gorbals; 'E was Northern Division, the City Centre out to the north, mixed industrial and residential, as was 'F', Maryhill to the north-west; 'G' to the south-west was Govan, shipbuilding and engineering mixed with residential; PHQ, which the odd queer had penetrated, amazingly enough. It included Training School and Signals/Radio. 'T' took in Traffic — Jaguars and Norton motorbikes — and 'M' the Mounted Police. Last but not least was CID, the Criminal Investigation Department, popularly known as The Defectives. The Establishment was in the region of 3,500. Chief Superintendents headed the various Divisions and Departments with a Chief Constable, a Protestant, and his Deputy Chief, a Catholic, and two Assistant Chief Constables. The top brass was mainly appointed by the magistrates, who were themselves mainly Catholic.

MacDonald and his mate, Peter Downie, were posted to the Eastern Division, 'C', known as the Breach Division or the Working Division. At twenty-one, MacDonald was the second youngest in his class and had come third without too much effort; he had enjoyed the indoctrination. Now to join the Wise Men from the East! Since he was going out to wage war of a different kind, another uniform was called for. Until April 1952 the Glasgow Police uniform incorporated a helmet made of cane and linen, which was light and protective, adding height to the wearer; a Police Force badge, large, to the front and a crest to the dome in bright electro-plate for day use; at night both badge and crest were a non-reflective black. A button-up tunic with two breast pockets was worn, and guard-cut trousers — high at the front, low at the heels — in a black serge; black boots, without toecaps, of the wearer's choice, two pairs (one working, one parade) from a generous annual boot allowance; a heavy serge greatcoat plus a similar raincoat, large enough to go over the greatcoat; four pairs slacks, four tunics, a referee-type whistle and chain, handcuffs (Victorian era) and a truncheon. The latter fitted into special pockets. Also carried: regulation notebook, two pairs black woollen gloves worn under leather, provided by the wearer. The young cops were encouraged to wear lightweight boots so they did the running. QM Store, Police HQ, had tailors who were usually ex-Guards Regiments and were meticulous in their tailoring and fitting: one had also to look the part.

Mac D and Downie reported for duty and were allocated the same shift and rest days: work seven and have the eighth off. Mac went to '1' Section, a bit like the Army, comprising ten cops and a Sergeant. 'C' Division was divided up mainly by its principal thoroughfares: Dalmarnock Road was '1' Section, London Road '2' Section, the Gallowgate '3' Section, Duke Street '4' Section, Alexandra Parade '5' Section, and the subdivision of Shettleston made up '6' and '7' Sections. Each Section was divided into eight beats with four shifts, early from 7 a.m. to 2 p.m., late 2 p.m. to 11 p.m., night 11 p.m. to 7 a.m., and patrol, 5 p.m. to 1 a.m. Every beat had at least one Police Box built of reinforced concrete with a red light on top and a direct phone line to Div HQ Switchboard, also a pull-open phone for public use in calling Police or Ambulance. Inside was a desk for report writing and a tall stool, plus a first-aid cabinet. The beat book described the boundaries and topography, and with it was a key-holders' book of all premises which was checked every six months by the early shift cop so that all businesses knew the man on the beat and his 'neighbour'.

Most of the time it took at least two cops to make an arrest, besides which the Scottish Laws of Evidence favoured two liars instead of one. Evidence had to be corroborated, preferably by an eyewitness giving Direct Evidence, so your 'neighbour' was all important to your survival or advancement. The Yanks call it the buddy system, the Jocks 'your mucker' (i.e. the man who mucks in with you). The highly functional Police Box also contained a photograph album with descriptions and past records of all criminals on the beat and their associates. Cops were well advised to study it and memorise the opposition.

Early shift called for the relief of pointsmen directing traffic and the covering of school crossings, delivering of messages and the execution of warrants. A 45-minute break was taken for your 'piece' – Glaswegian for sandwiches and tea – in the tea room at Divisional Headquarters, while the beat was covered by your 'neighbour'. Late shift was the arrest shift; Friday and Saturday nights produced four to eight arrests per night, usually after the boozers had 'scaled' (come out at closing time). The East was known as the Breach Division, a nickname stemming from the offence of 'committing a breach of the peace to the alarm of the lieges', which in turn was defined as putting the public in fear. Cops did not count as they at least theoretically could not be put in fear, only trepidation. A charge for a BOP would go like a good jingle at the Bar (Charge Office), given to the Duty Officer, an Inspector: 'About 10 p.m. Saturday on 13th of December 1952 in the London Road at Fordneuk Street he did bawl, shout, curse and swear and challenge the Police to fight, to the alarm of the lieges.' The breach had many variations and could be applied to just about any instance of disorderly or drunken behaviour; at times it was stretched to the limit.

Night shift, normally 11 p.m. to 7 a.m., lasted six weeks, so the body became accustomed to the unnatural timing. New cops did at least twelve weeks so that the senior man could break them in to the various routines and areas. The new boy was mainly kept out of sight of the public and did not get involved in situations he could not handle with confidence. The beat, especially during a night shift, has to be 'tried' (examined) at least twice during the tour of duty. Trying the beat meant the men on the beat had to shake hands with all padlocks (testing their security) and check all business premises' doors and windows, or any other possible entrance including roof and subterranean access. Should the premises be insecure, the keyholder was called out and the beatman stood guard. Hair or matchsticks were placed on doors: should the door have been opened, the second inspection would pick up the fault. A Subject Sheet was issued to the beatman to explain any failure to discover break-ins, a lapse which could result in disciplinary action. The public certainly got value for their money. A 'good' cop was expected to make a capture of at least one housebreaker per night shift and on the odd occasion he would receive a commendation, a stepping stone to better things.

Patrol shift, 5 p.m. to 1 a.m., was in the Divisional Patrol car, which was considered a sinecure – a regular driver, a beat Sergeant and usually two young cops who were fleet of foot. All 'Hurry Up' (Emergency) calls were dealt with and property checked, as per the Aberdeen City Police system, which is now international but does not produce the results of the Beat Cop.

Each shift paraded half an hour before the appointed time to hear the Read-out involving all reported crimes in his Divisional Area and elsewhere if of some import. Stolen cars and wanted persons were dished out to the various beatmen, and action later followed up by their Sergeant, who visited his troops twice a shift and gave them a 'Time' in their notebooks. The Inspector did likewise over a shift, so there was a constant check of the bodies on the ground and exactly what they were up to. All reports, whatever the occurrence, were made in writing in a set style using the prescribed phraseology: dog bites, chimney fires, dangerous pavements, fire hydrants – action had to be taken and the result obtained. For example, a broken window would produce a report that read 'Day/Date/Time/Place… a stone was impinged with dynamic force whereby a plate glass window was shattered from a point of contact in the lower right corner which shattered the window in question.' Laughable, yes, but exact and to the point, down to the last detail.

The cops were constantly trained in many ways. Every Monday, which was a quiet night, the men on night shift would have to parade an extra half-hour early for the readings and inspection and march off to take part in questions from the all important Instruction Book of some 1,000 pages. This effort was called 'The Guesses', although the subject was given out for preparation in depth; each cop had to answer, or at least guess an answer, and on occasion the 2i/c Division or the Division Superintendent would be there to take the salute as the cops were let loose on the unsuspecting public. The 'back' or late shift was the 'huckle', meaning it was when you apprehended the Friday and Saturday night drunks. Of course the keen young cop was expected to 'fill his book' with bookings, mainly lower-level summary offences such as loitering or causing an obstruction to the footway, more clearly defined as 'hanging about' the street corner.

Juveniles and young adult males would collect on street corners: they included the unemployed, unemployable, the petty criminal, the professional criminal – the flotsam and jetsam of the industrial community. Some had not worked for years and had no intention of doing so. If the cop on the beat had control of his 'patch', he had only to look up and down the street to get the 'mob' on the corner to move forward, place their heels on the kerb-line and their feet in the gutter. Should the mob fail to pay due respect to their 'Polis', they would be 'booked'. Ned, the opposing force in this daily battle, would sometimes be accompanied by Neddess, the female of the species, also referred to as a 'wee hairy'. The object of the exercise was that the man on the beat got to know his 'public' at this end of the spectrum – and they him. Assaults on a policeman were always by persons the cop did not know and when on his own and outnumbered at least five to one. Most police received a 'kicking' at some time in their careers: get the cop down and put the boot in. A joyous time was had by Edward, of course, but Robert the Bobby had already responded accordingly: most arrests resulted in the suspect being 'tobered up', 'hammered' or just plain thumped. This was only administered when asked for, when Ned refused to shut his 'curry-hole'; if sober, he was schooled in coming to attention when addressed.

10: The Terrible Twins and the Three Musketeers

One of Glasgow's favourite football phrases is 'We are the people' –
condensed in Glaswegian to 'We arra peepul'. After passing out,
MacDonald was to come across two people with whom he formed
a happy band of three during those years on the beat; he would also
discover that the 'Polis', like the City of Glasgow itself, was full of
personalities, some of whom were bent on moulding him and his
fellow constables to the tasks ahead. MacDonald had joined young
to be a 30-year man; this the Sergeants and Inspectors knew, and
groomed their young fellows accordingly. The senior cop was the
one who made the decisions and did the talking when working
with his 'neighbour'. In the presence of other cops you soon
learned to speak only when spoken to. One night shift, about
3 a.m., MacDonald had come in for his break. At the table were
Constable Roddy Craig, with 30 years on the beat in the
Gallowgate, and his 'neighbour', Constable Donald MacLean, 29
years on the beat in the Gallowgate. Both had wives who ran shops
on each other's beats. MacDonald noticed the foursome were
playing cards and began to speak out of turn. Roddy Craig looked
up and said, 'How many years have you been in the job, son?'
MacDonald replied, 'Nine months.' He was told to keep his mouth
shut until his probation – two years – was up. Those two old cops
were real characters, avoiding promotion like the plague – if it
came, they would automatically be transferred to another Division,
to say nothing of those two shops raking in the loot...

Constable Geordie Bennie, ex-Eastern Division and a former
Fife miner, had taken riding lessons and was at last accepted as a
fully-fledged member of the Mounted Branch. Their mounts, a
cross between Clydesdales and racehorses, produced a huge
animal who could cross-leg step and push the football queues into
line but would stop when near a cop. They too were in the
Brotherhood. On the first day on his mounted beat, Geordie
asked his boss who was to show him around the area. He was

simply told to mount up and move off. The horse took off, stopped at the traffic lights, took him down a back wynd and stopped outside one of the better-known restaurants. Within seconds a waiter appeared in his white jacket, gave the police horse a pie and handed up a glass of whisky to the mountie. This carried on for the rest of his four-hour shift.

Another time-server who worked the area around Police HQ was Willie MacFadyen, who had organised a raffle without bothering to acquire the usual licence. Visiting his outlets once a week to sell tickets, Willie was making a small fortune. His original 'neighbour' was by now Chief Constable, who received an anonymous letter of complaint. Called before the Chief, expecting no more than a warning from his old mate, Willie owned up, but before agreeing to give up the lucrative lottery he politely informed the Chief that the winner of this week's raffle was none other than the Chief himself. Accepting the luck of the draw with a good grace, the Chief promptly put into practice the old adage about 'live and let live' and no more was heard on the subject.

Cons Willie McEwen, known as 'The Daddler' from his famous football dribble in his younger days, was the regular Pointsman at The Toll (Bridgeton Cross) who worked one of the five point crossings. During the festive season The Daddler would not move off his crossing as the managing directors in their Rollers and Bentleys got complimentary passage to their factory offices, their chauffeurs slowing down to drop off a bottle or the sealed envelope of Christmas cheer. Taking the bus as he came off duty, The Daddler was also seen by fellow passenger MacDonald fishing in his tunic pocket for a clear glass bottle, removing the cork and gulping some of the contents. Without a blink of his eyes The Daddler said to all the old dears on the bus, 'Good afternoon, ladies! That's the stuff to put hair on your chest – nothing like cold tea.' Corporation trams also provided their moments of enjoyment. When the 'caurs' that had been repaired were tested during the night, the repairman would allow the cops to drive them at alarming speeds up and down the London Road, their bells clanging as they did so and bets being laid as to who could clock the fastest time.

MacDonald's Sergeant was Big Bob Henderson, also known as Toffee Legs due to his ability to duck and weave while performing as a heavyweight boxer. He was the Force champ and one of the old school. Bob, at 6' 6" and all in proportion, was famous for his appearance and had performed at the Empire Games in 1938 while a probationer. If you were in favour with Big Bob he would address you as 'Angus Son', 'Ian Son' and so on, so his favourite young cops were known as 'The Sons'. The Sons were the ones who made more arrests and bookings than the rest, a reflection on Bob's prowess where his senior Officers were concerned. Should you get no 'Son' you knew you were out of favour: no time off, overtime or sports training. Bob ruled with an iron fist and expected his 'sons' to perform. His sidekick was Sergeant Archie Hay, nicknamed 'Handsome', ex-Life Guards; Archie had been a Physical Training Instructor both in the Army and the Scottish Police College at Whitburn for Sergeants and Inspectors. Handsome Arch had married into money, which he advised young cops to do in their turn. He used to regale them with the story of how he had once courted twins without ever finding out which was which, but it made no difference as he did not marry either of them, instead following his own advice and choosing a girl whose parents had money. Archie too was a magnificent physical specimen of 6' 6": the pair of them made an awesome sight striding down the road together, sometimes with a Wee Ned in each hand as they carried on their intimate conversation, banging the unfortunates' heads together now and then to emphasise a point. Other cops had nicknames of their own – the White Knight, the Black Prince; a cop called Eric Whale was known as 'The Fish'; an ex-RAF Wing Commander was known as 'Soldier' because of his exceptionally upright bearing; another, 'The Bosun' because he was ex-Merchant Navy.

Out on the battleground, three flashes of a torch or a whistle meant a cop needed assistance. This could raise all cops to the gallop; broadcast on the radio, it would produce police cars out of the blue. Taxi drivers would also bring assistance at a rate of knots. You never let your 'neighbour' down. Should there be a complaint from the public, closing ranks was the norm, both outside and inside: a boss (Sergeants and above) could not pump the cop for information about his 'neighbour'. The Mafia would have been proud of the 'omertà' within the Glasgow Polis. Usually a cop took anything up to five years to get his own beat. You had to go through the system: sixteen weeks' night shift then 'fly' the whole Division, first of all being shown round by a senior cop then going from Section to Section until all fifty beats were done. This took about a year, then the young cop would be posted to a Section, ten men and eight beats, which was worked for about six months, then to half a Section, four beats, mainly relieving people on their days off. MacDonald, lucky, keen as mustard and having kept the voice box out of action, was awarded his own beat after nine months to work with his new 'neighbour', who had only a few years' service.

This was Ian Murdock Nicholls, an ex-RAF Flight Sergeant. An Air Force rigger by trade, he had done three years in the 'Brylcreem Boys'. To MacDonald this was a form of life lower than either Military Police or even Regimental. Nicholls was tall, dark and handsome − a real Glasgow boy, about 6' 4", with black wavy hair and a flashing smile to match, obviously very popular with the ladies. But despite MacDonald's initial reservations 'Big Ian' was an outstanding cop with several commendations up his sleeve. He was a local boy from Stepps in Lanarkshire, just outside Glasgow, so he knew the score and could speak the language. He too was desperate to get on in the world and was prepared to skate on thin ice and go where angels feared to tread. MacDonald was more conservative in his approach and preferred to be on solid ground before committing. Both were reasonably well educated and realised if they played their cards right they were going up the way. They were to make a deadly combination and were nicknamed, even by the more seasoned cops, as the Terrible Twins, 'Big Ian' and the 'Man from Aberdeen'. They were to have a lifelong friendship and share many a scrape and laugh together.

For the uninitiated, Glasgow was divided between Catholic Irish and Protestant Irish; schooling was originally sectarian, the rivalry fuelled by loyalty to the Rangers Football Club in Govan, who in those days recruited only Protestants, and Glasgow Celtic, who were mainly Catholic but superficially at least not quite as biased, based out east in Parkhead. The supporters used different transport routes to the games and at the venues they were segregated. The section of the Parkhead stadium opposite the main grandstand – 'The Jungle', where the radical Celtic fans held sway – was half-full of priests. Pubs in parts of Glasgow were mainly either Protestant or Catholic: if you were of the wrong faith when you entered it was not long before you were made aware that the 'hundred thousand welcomes' of the Irish was non-existent, and the Protestant pubs were on the same footing. Most cops were Protestant and were expected to be of the Masonic Lodge, whereas the Catholic minority were Knights of St Columba. Despite the divisions, on the whole cops carried out their duties without religious bias. MacDonald, being from the north-east, was not biased, as in his neck of the woods all sides went to the same school. Religion was not an issue.

On the Glorious Twelfth of July each year, an organised breach of the peace called the Orange Walk took place, marchers led by bands doing their best to provoke the Catholics by marching past the various chapels and parading down mainly Catholic streets to stirring renditions of 'We'll fight and no surrender' and other echoes of the Battle of the Boyne. Deputy Chief Constable McCulloch, a good Catholic, would lead in the City Centre by standing on the front seat of his vehicle with the roof open. Waving to the Protestant crowd, he wondered why they were cheering and waving back to him – his driver, a 'Blue-nose' or Rangers supporter and Protestant, had wired a huge orange lily to his radiator.

MacDonald shared 'digs' with his mate Peter MacNab Downie, and now he had another mate, his 'neighbour', Ian Nicholls. The three had the same days off and holidays, so soon they became known as 'The Three Musketeers'. On occasion, at football matches and the like, they formed a team, MacDonald in the middle at 6' 1", the other two at 6' 4" and 6' 2" – quite impressive. They went to various dances at places like the Highlander, Overnewton, Govan Town Hall, the Locarno, the Playhouse or Denniston Palais. They also had their favourite 'howfs' or watering holes, like Morrison's a businessmen's pub, the Ingram, a swish cocktail bar, and the State, opposite the Albert Ballroom. Definitely not racists at this stage of their development, they would sometimes go to the Palais at Eglinton Toll on the south side to see if they could score a Jewess, provided they were good-looking. MacDonald's social graces had been somewhat neglected during his sojourn in HM Forces, which he remedied by going to the Locarno Ballroom on Tuesday afternoons, when the mill girls from Paisley Linoleum Factories would come to town.

The Glasgow Polis were issued with a Warrant Card which was a means of identification only, but the enterprising Polis used it as an 'Open Sesame' to enter places of public entertainment and to obtain their expected 50% discount on all items. This was considered tribute. In fact most vendors who came in contact did not require the production of the Warrant Card but politely intoned, 'You're a Police Officer. Well, we must offer you a discount.' Free travel on Corporation Transport was the norm and taxis would stop and pick up free gratis off duty cops on their weekly rest days. Of course they too would come to a cop's aid and were well looked after by the Polis on occasion. Mac had just come on duty at Bridgeton Cross about 11.15 p.m. one night when a taxi pulled up. The driver motioned for the cop to get in; he sat in the back seat next to a well and truly inebriated lady of the night. She was giving the taxi driver the run-around and had intimated she was not going to pay the fare. Young MacDonald, the knight in shining armour, would come to the rescue. She got out of the taxi and dived into a single-end, ground floor, right rear and slammed the door. MacDonald went round to the rear and prised open the window to be given a view of the lady in bed with her man, no drawers on but still wearing her high heels and smoking a fag. C89 was greeted by the customary mouthful about being a fornicating illegitimate and told to go elsewhere, quick.

Our young do-gooder went round to the door in the close (alleyway), took a look and applied the boot key to the lock. This method had stood the test of time, but on this occasion the whole architrave and door fell in with a loud bang and the Officer was left standing on the door in a cloud of dust. The lady of the night was told to pay up. The taxi driver had said a couple of quid would do, but MacDonald considered otherwise and demanded ten pounds, which was produced from one of the high-heeled shoes. Boyfriend had dragged himself from his 'pit' and demanded the police Officer's number; he was told if he was big enough he could see it, or words to that effect. Fortunately Ned was about 5' 3" and could not. A hasty retreat was now required. The taxi driver expressed his gratitude and gave MacDonald a lift back.

When 1953 came, the Coronation of Queen Elizabeth II of England and I of Scotland saw MacDonald get a medal. A contingent of about 300 with Pipe Band went off to London; their train was drunk dry before Carlisle and so they progressed to a fine show in the capital. All or nearly all were awarded a Coronation Medal. All the senior bosses got one, and some of the Sergeants as well as the old cops. Sergeant Big Bob had been given a few to award to chosen Sergeants. On that particular night he and 'Angus Son' managed to get a housebreaker: Bob, elated at the young cop's observation, provided a commendation and added, 'You had better have one of these things, or maybe a shaving mug with one of these things.' Medals in the Polis did not count for a great deal: the cop's reputation was more highly prized.

When a soldier, MacDonald had discovered that there is nothing more dangerous than a fool. When he became a Glasgow Polis, that principle still applied: the meek may inherit the earth, but that is all they are going to get. Sections of all Police Forces are corrupt to some extent, in fact a degree of efficiency goes with it. You don't send a Boy Scout to investigate a serious crime or catch a professional criminal. From a 4/- a day National Serviceman to a £6 8s 3d a week cop was a step in the right direction: digs cost £2 15/- a week, leaving £3 15 s 9d. It was not exactly a princely sum for smokes, drinks and clothes, and a few of the other necessities of life, and it made the cop hungry in a hungry world. When called to a break-in, the cop attending invariably had the help of the complainant to fill in his Crime Report, in which a list of stolen property was reported to the insurer for recompense. The amount of the claim would be enhanced to the benefit of all parties, including on occasion the insurance company. MacDonald did not approve, but he was soon corrupted: standing on guard outside a pub that was 'away', being the junior cop present with the Inspector and Sergeant and the CID, plus the odd traffic men who had immediately responded, MacDonald felt something being eased into his large raincoat pocket, with the soothing voice of his Sergeant saying, 'I hope your father likes brandy?' Despite his lofty ideals, MacDonald was compromised!

Publicans on the whole expressed their appreciation by donating a bottle of whisky to the man on the beat. Reciprocation took the form of priority attendance when any disorderly behaviour took place on licensed premises. While having a woman on the beat was taboo, alcohol was merely frowned upon. During his first year MacDonald did not imbibe whilst on duty and received zero information in return. The second year, when on back shift after the pubs had closed, Monday to Wednesday before going off duty was considered fair game. Having let the beatmen slide into the pub, the publican would ask the traditional question, 'Would the boys care for a refreshment?' Funnily enough, lemonade and the like did not feature. A number of 'refreshment places' would be visited: the publican and bar staff would let slip that so-and-so was just 'out' and seemed to be flush with the folding stuff, and follow-up action would duly be taken.

One evening, while inspecting licensed premises after hours, there was a discreet knock at the pub door. MacDonald decided to answer by opening and peering out through the letter box and lo and behold, he was looking straight into the eyes of his Inspector, who was with the Sergeant. 'You can't get into the pubs these days for young cops,' he was heard to comment. 'We'll go to Morrisons.' His meaning was, of course, 'You buggers get out of the pub and stand up for your visit by your Inspector and Sergeant up the road near Morrison's pub.' The Inspector later would say, 'Have you anything to report?', at the same time passing around a bag of Pan Drops at arm's length.

The street bookie was another source of revenue if you were so inclined. The man on the beat and his 'neighbour' would be handed envelopes containing a pound or two on a weekly basis. This was for the cops not to disturb the illegal punting. MacDonald did not accept his envelope but made it clear that information was to be his return for lack of harassment, an arrangement the bookie appreciated.

After a year or so on the street, MacDonald, an ambitious individual, realised that promotion was mainly by seniority once you had passed the Sergeants' and Inspectors' exams, educational and professional. You did four to six years on the beat, then a year in plain clothes, relieving in the office (Police Station), a year in the Inquiry Department (minor complaints), then in the Bar (Charge office), followed by a stint as Turnkey (cells guard). By now ten years had elapsed, so you could transfer to Criminal Investigation or Traffic, or remain in uniform on the beat. The youngest Sergeant had fifteen years' service, Inspector twenty. MacDonald thought he would be better off in the Forces. At fourteen service months, he was told by both his Sergeant and Inspector that he was going places. But not fast enough.

Britain in the mid-Fifties was preparing to hand over her colonies as local aspirations to independence or self-rule gathered pace. India had gained independence in 1947 at the cost of millions dead in internecine strife on the subcontinent; African colonies were at least restless; in Malaya a full-blown emergency was in full swing. Colonial Police Officers were in demand. This meant a warrant or commission, more authority and responsibility with the rank, a doubling of pay, promotion prospects, a higher standard of living and a widening of vista. Mac had itchy feet: the other side of the hill was always greener. But for the time being he decided to soldier on through Refresher Course at the end of the first year and Confirmation Course at the end of two. During this period former National Servicemen did a 14-day stint in the Forces Reserves. Much to Mac's disgust, he was transferred to The Corps of Royal Military Police, the hated Redcaps. At Aldershot, Headquarters of the British Army, he was asked if he could drive. 'Eh, sort of,' he replied. 'Oh well, if you could we were going to make you a sergeant.' Next question: 'Can you ride a motorbike?' 'Yes, Sir!' 'Then you are a corporal.'

Mac drew a motorcycle – a 500cc BSA – from the Motor Transport Pool, pushed it round the side of the building and gave himself a crash course in motorcycle riding. He was later to come off at 70 mph and collect extensive gravel rash. Aldershot with Operational Coy 284 RMP was a holiday. The fortnight reserve was spent running in bikes, one-ton trucks and Land Rovers for the Regular Army, map reading for convoy work, signposting and the various priorities – 'Wounded', 'Ammo', 'Food', 'Reinforcements' and so on. The Company Commander was a solicitor; the RSM owned a transport company. All the military policemen were regular civil cops, so they all had a little in common, and the various forces were discussed in detail. Glasgow, in Mac's opinion, still came out tops.

On return to Glasgow, Mac had a visit from ex-Captain Jack MacDonald, a former Seaforth Highlander, who was a quarry master at Perth and also the Major commanding the Scottish Special Investigation Branch (SIB) of the RCM Police (Reserve). Would Mac like to join? Both were Banchory Loons, so Mac was promoted Sergeant, the lowest rank in the SIB – a detective at last. MacDonald and his musketeer mates, 'Big Ian' and Peter, would take themselves off to the Silver City of Aberdeen on their weekends off, where they visited a variety of hotels and places of entertainment. Jackie Robertson, the local bookie and car dealer of Kirkpatrick Street opposite the Police Box, was always pleased to give the trio a car for their weekend: one taken up to Aberdeen, another brought back – obviously some shady deal was in progress. Speaking of which, Cons Wullie Wylie was an ex-RSM with the Royal Corps (i.e. the Military Police) who, after service in WWII, had got himself a sinecure as Divisional Patrol Driver, the vehicle being manned by a Sergeant and two young constables. Wullie had a friend in Luigi, the proprietor of a real 'flash' café, whom Wullie would visit every evening when on patrol. The greetings over, he would be offered the customary four fish and chip suppers, two bottles of Barr's Irn Bru, a popular soft drink, and four chocolate 'sliders' (ice cream wafers). Wullie would start to take a 10/- note from his trouser watch pocket, but MacDonald said to Wullie, 'If you took that out completely it would disintegrate!'

Still, one evening at the change of shift Wullie the Wylie was on his own when he received a 'hurry-up' call that Tollcross Post Office was being held up by a Big Ned with a revolver. Wullie decided to answer the call and picked up a young beat cop on the way. Arriving at the scene a few minutes later, he saw a Big Ned running down Tollcross Road on the footway. Wullie bumped his vehicle up on to the footway and pinned the gunman up against a brick wall, still waving his revolver. 'Drop the fucking gun or I'll take your bloody legs off!' yelled Wylie. Ned dropped the firearm and that was how Wullie Wylie became the recipient of a British Empire Medal for Bravery.

But now MacDonald really did feel it was time to move on. He had repeatedly applied for Hong Kong, Malaya, Southern Rhodesia, Northern Rhodesia, Nyasaland, Kenya or the Forces, but his old man had talked him out of it, usually on the grounds that the remuneration was insufficient. Police Lieutenants in the Malaya Police were having a 50% casualty rate in their counter-insurgency against the communist terrorists – the same casualty rate as expected for infantry in a Line Regiment. Not an encouraging prospect.

This state of suspension lasted for over a year, but MacDonald decided he still had itchy feet in spite of his father's wishes. So, in July 1955, he had his interview in London for the Kenya Police, a force in the middle of the Mau Mau emergency. Inspectors of Police were being called for on a contract basis. MacDonald was more than impressed by those attending the interview: they appeared to be mainly commissioned Officers, all of whom seemed to have gone through the public school system, if their plummy English accents were anything to go by. Sir Ivo Struton, HM Inspector General of Colonial Police, and a psychiatrist were the two interviewing Officers.

The trick cyclist sat behind an impressive desk, MacDonald seated in front. Sir Ivo sat on a stool-like contraption doodling on a scribble pad, sporting a well-worn sports jacket and corduroy trousers and matching shoes, with beard and straggly moustache. The doctor of the head went through the application, making ticks along the way. The scruffy individual on MacDonald's left came to life and started firing questions:

Q 1:   Why do you wish to leave the Glasgow Police: Sergeant or Inspector trouble?
Ans: Hope to better myself.
Q 2:   Why do you wish to go to Kenya?
Ans: I feel I can make a contribution.
Q 3:   What standard of golf and rugby do you play?
Ans: Twelve handicap and second-grade rugby.
Q 4:   Would you book me for no lights on my vehicle?

Ans: Have arrests to make, we do not book trivia.

The conversation then lapsed into a few well-chosen semi-insults, one of them being that golf was an old women's game, to which the answer was that it depends on how you play it. Keeping one's temper was obviously the correct response.

Sir Ivo then switched tack: 'Go and get a medical, laddie, you'll be all right, and I think you will do fine in Kenya.'

Off to Harley Street − nothing but the best! A week later he was informed he would be flying BOAC to Kenya. Mac resigned from the Polis, went back up to Banchory and, to the surprise of his parents, said he was off to darkest Africa to join the Kenya Cowboys. Last time he took off, he was six weeks in the Army before his old man was informed; this latest move at least heralded a slight improvement in family relations.

Part Three
The Wild Colonial Boy, 1955–64

11: Kenya, Land of Endeavour and the 'Mickey Mice'

'Umtumishi kwa watu wote — Serve the people'

The background to Kenya and the Mau Mau, a secret society that originated in that country's Kikuyu tribe, was that in October 1952 a State of Emergency was declared in three provinces: the Rift Valley, Central and Nairobi Area, where the KEM (Kikuyu, Embu and Meru) lived, three tribes with a common language and customs numbering about one and a half million strong out of the six million in Kenya. Many of the 'Mickey Mice', as the Mau Mau became known, were labourers on European farms where they had been given their own plots to hold and subdivide. In the 1920s there were stirrings of political revolt, including the founding of the Kikuyu Central Association by the man who would eventually become known as Jomo Kenyatta. The indigenous Kenyans sought greater rights and the expulsion of European settlers from the 'White Highlands', a very fertile part of the central mass of Kenya. Mixed farming had been going on since WWI, when ex-servicemen were granted lands bought from the African at a low price. It was underdeveloped, and the claim that the land had been illegally taken was untrue: the Rift Valley, for example, had names given by the Masai, the highland pastoralists of the nineteenth century, not Kikuyu names. Nairobi in Masai means 'running water'. Ol Kalou, Oleolondo, Gilgil, Nakuru, Naivasha all were originally Masai territory. The labour force on some farms would number up to a thousand, some claiming their ground had been alienated due to the greedy white man.

Other sources of unrest included the Burma-boys, who had been given the same uniforms and equipment as their white bwanas (masters) and had fought the same battles, as many of their proud soldier songs signified. From time immemorial the serious criminal class had disappeared into the forest, the domain of wild animals, where police seldom followed: the criminal himself had learned and adapted to live like a wild animal. This pot-pourri held all the ingredients for a terrorist rebellion. Kenya's farming community marched on Government House in October 1952 and demanded the Governor-General declare an emergency. It was also in 1952 that the Mau Mau, calling themselves the Land and Freedom Army, emerged. This was the highly dangerous situation into which Inspector Grade I Angus John MacDonald (24), single, formerly of the Glasgow Police, now of the Kenya Police, was heading. Armed with gifts from the aunts — a pigskin writing case and washing kit which lasted him for many years — the Wild Colonial Boy was ready to go and play his part in a situation that would make Glasgow seem like *No Mean City* indeed…

On first sight it was quite an experience: a trip to Darkest Africa and a new career. MacDonald boarded his Viscount aircraft BOAC at Heathrow, eager for a new adventure. Looking round him, he noticed it was an all-male plane complement of passengers whose ages ranged from the early twenties to the mid-thirties. Quite a few wore regimental ties. As MacDonald exchanged a few non-committal pleasantries with his fellow passengers, a frightfully Oxford accent suddenly proclaimed, 'Oh, I say, chaps, look, that's Mont Blanc on our port wing!'

The immediate rush to view Europe's highest peak produced a sudden lurch to port: passengers were promptly requested by the Captain to resume their seats and replace their seat belts. The chap with the Oxford accent lent over MacDonald's seat and, with a wide grin, added, 'Well, we can't be right all the time, what?'

MacDonald was unimpressed by the accent, which belonged to ex-Captain Arthur Gordon Brelsford of the Hampshire Regiment, who had on MA in English and BSc in Forestry and had just packed in being a schoolteacher. But Brelsford was a future pal, a very funny — and hard — man.

By the time they reached Rome, the aircraft's alcohol ration had run out and it had become clear that all passengers were for the Kenya Police Force or Prison Service. Around 90% were ex-services. One hour on the ground refuelling and on to Alexandria in Egypt, then to Khartoum in the Sudan. Next was Entebbe, Uganda, and they were in East Africa as dawn broke. Some hours later the seventy-five passengers disembarked in Nairobi. The trip had taken twenty-seven hours. As MacDonald clambered down the steps from the plane he saw Inspector Ian 'China' Ross, formerly of the Glasgow Police and one-time rugby teammate, a very useful stand-off. Ian called everybody 'mate' – as in 'china plate' – hence the nickname.

'Welcome, gentlemen,' Ross intoned. 'Former UK coppers on the left and the rest on the right. Left goes to South Hill Mess and Right goes to Hospital Hill Mess. Good, no questions.'

Later, arriving by safari vehicle with open canvas sides, 'China' Ross appeared in ceremonial/walking out blues, a blue barathea uniform with silver buttons, wearing a highly polished Sam Browne and cross strap, unfastened, signifying he was off duty, and his Colorado Beetle Ribbon (Africa Service Medal). He appeared to be wearing a clerical collar, which in fact was a dress white Van Heusen shirt collar turned back to front. 'China' sidled up to the Mess bar, where some of the new arrivals were having a quiet evening beer. His opening gambit was that he was one of the Assistant Padres to the Kenya Police, and on behalf of all ranks he wished the new members welcome, pointing out that while he was a Presbyterian of the Church of Scotland he was willing to help out any denomination with any welfare problem, and he knew what a wrench it was coming to a new country. He was aware of the demon drink but would accept a whisky just to be sociable. Quite a number were taken in by the ex-Glasgow Polis palaver and bought the joker a drink: 'China' was always a funny man who could get away with murder, to coin a phrase.

For a new battleground, a new uniform: the following day the new boys were issued with equipment and accoutrements, including 22 yards of khaki drill for tailored uniforms – four shorts, four bush jackets, two pairs slacks, two long-sleeved tunics with two SD caps; two pairs boots, two pairs short puttees, two pairs long puttees, four Van Heusen shirts, Sam Browne and cross strap, baton, handcuffs, two lanyards and whistle, .38 or .45 revolver, black leather holster and ammo pouch; on top of all that:

blankets, small pack, water bottle, greatcoat, raincoat plus a score or so rounds for the revolver, which was to be carried at all times as this was an Emergency Area.

The next two days being the weekend, the bars of the Nairobi hotels got a check-out, as did the other Mess. Some of the chair-borne commandos, base wallahs who had not taken any active part in the Emergency, showed gruesome photos of Mau Mau atrocities and spun yarns about what they had done at the 'sharp end'. The Mayor of Banchory had, as an act of kindness, given MacDonald the address of friends of his family who lived in Nairobi. Gus phoned them up and was invited for lunch on Sunday: most acceptable, large gins and tonics served by a liveried African houseboy, who was rather 'lovely' with a delightful lisp to his halting Swahili. Gus found he had landed in a den of practising queers and took off at a rate of knots, wondering just how close this mob was to his highly respected Mayor.

Come Monday, most of the latest intake were posted to various provinces in the Emergency Area: Rift Valley, Central and Nairobi. Gus was shunted off to Nakuru, the Provincial HQ for the Rift Valley, along with a few others, Brelsford of the Hampshires being one. After a few hours' drive up the Rift Valley floor, Nakuru appeared. Here the group was further divided up and re-posted to various Divisions. After another overnight at the Inspectors' Mess, Nakuru, the Police Land Rover climbed up a 2,000-foot escarpment and after a 50-mile trip covered in *murrum* dust arrived at Divisional Headquarters for the Laikipia Division at Thomson Falls, made famous by some Hollywood film star stubbing his big toe on a rock while filming at the base of the 300-foot waterfall.

The youngest Superintendent in the Kenya Police, Sherrard-Smith (27), ex-Hong Kong Police, gave a welcome on board. MacDonald was posted as 2i/c Ol Kalou Police Station, Arthur Brelsford as 2i/c to Gilgil West Police Station. They were twenty to thirty miles down the road running parallel to the Aberdares, a forest region that climbed to some 12,000 feet. Thomson Falls was about 6,000 feet above sea level, with dry warm days, but fires were lit at night.

On another overnight stop at the Thomson Falls Hotel, the

two new Inspectors, fast becoming friends, got quite uproariously drunk after having to disarm some drunken, loud-mouthed farming types of Belgian extraction who did not require the Kenya Police, The Kings African Rifles or the British Army's assistance to sort out a few beastly 'munts' (a derogatory term derived from the Zulu *umuntu*, a man). The other settlers at the bar were suitably impressed, most being commissioned ex-servicemen of sound British stock, so the party broke up after a few rousing choruses in the wee small hours of an African night, right in the heart of Mau Mau country.

Next day the merry men arrived at their respective stations. MacDonald was greeted by Jim Burns, a fellow-Scot, ex-Scots Guards and BSAP (British South African Police – Southern Rhodesia), and his wife, who acted as the station Girl Friday. They had not had a day off in nine months and admitted the obvious, that they were both beginning to be a wee bit rough around the edges, as virtually about every night he would be out for at least two hours between 11 p.m. and 4 a.m. when Very lights fired by farmers indicated they required police assistance against surprise terrorist attack.

By this time, the mid-Fifties, the Emergency had been festering for a number of years. The first overt acts were the slashing of farm animals, the killing of domestic animals, then the odd attack on isolated farms, slashing the Europeans themselves with bush knives (*pangas*) and African swords (*simis*). The latter started off narrow at the grip and gradually got broader, then tapered to a semi-rounded point – a beautifully balanced weapon for delivering hacking wounds, the wielder relying on centrifugal force. A backhander could easily lop a head off. Fighting spears and steel- and feather-tipped bows and arrows were less common. Many used home-made firearms consisting of a rubber band arrangement with nail-like firing pins discharging .303 ball or shotgun ammo, almost as lethal for the user as the intended recipient.

The Kikuyu had a traditional practice in which they would be called to take an oath, originally in the legal sense, to guarantee the performance of an act. It had been bastardised into all forms of depravity and bestiality. There were now a dozen or more oaths on an ascending scale: 'If called I will destroy my employer's crops and beasts.' 'If called I will maim as directed.' 'If called I will kill as directed' – and so on, even to the extent of killing the oath-taker's own family. The hard core volunteered to take the various oaths. Soon recruits were enlisted by force; in some cases the innocent who refused were slaughtered. Taking the oath was accompanied by drinking animal and human blood, urine and milk, unnatural sexual acts and grotesque acts of physical violence against both men and women. Farm labourers who had been looked after turned against their masters and trusted, long-time servants would assist in the slaughter of families. It was hard to convince the settler that he had to surrender his servants and workers for interrogation. Loyal Kikuyu chiefs and headmen in the Reserves were also intimidated and murdered. The really bad years were 1952–53; by 1953–54 the Security Forces had taken control; come 1954–55 the tide had turned. From 1955–57 the 'Micks' were almost completely wiped out, and the Emergency was lifted.

Like so many others, MacDonald was dumped in at the deep end. His instructions were to answer all night call-outs, and as there was a General Service Unit attached to the 50-man station, he would also check out the two platoon Officers, expatriates without any previous weapon or bush experience – a fine kettle of fish. GSU (General Service Unit) was the paramilitary wing, wearing maroon berets and the normal jungle gear, better equipped than the Army equivalent: six LMG Bren guns, six Sterling or Patchett sub-machine guns, the remainder Mark V short-barrelled jungle rifles, plus the odd shotgun. Officers also had the choice of side arms. The squad were mainly from the warrior tribes and raring to go. MacDonald had the pleasure of being tutored in the use of the fighting spear by a 19-year-old Reservist Samburu. When correctly thrown it could nail a telegraph pole at 35 yards. The Samburu told the new boy his Chief had told the young men of his *menyatta* (protected village) that the Government required a few Kikuyu killed off, and he was to go and do that before returning after his two years' service.

MacDonald taught and demonstrated the use of the various weapons and had the 'mob' firing at specified targets. After a few days, in spite of the language barrier, the troops could handle, strip and maintain their weapons and had an acceptable degree of accuracy. On one of the nightly call-outs, a red rocket signalled that a settler needed help down the Valley. MacDonald roared off in a long-wheelbase Land Rover to answer the call. The farmer and his three sons had laid out a number of bodies, stating the trouble had been taken care of and police assistance was not required; they were a tough Afrikaner family all the way from the Union of South Africa. As thanks, MacDonald was offered his first biltong (jerk-dried salted meat), not bad to be going on with. As this would suggest, the settlers were in some cases a law unto themselves.

The farms were of an excellent standard; some employed managers with specialist degrees in agriculture and animal husbandry. Herds of matching cattle were the norm. The settler worked hard and played the same way, especially in places like the Wanjohi Valley, which had earned the alternative name of 'Happy Valley'; but for all the wild antics they made great people, generous to a fault. Usually the farm economy was subsidised by the *duka-wallah*, of Indian extraction, usually a BP Patel 'from Bombay-side, Sahib'. The *duka* supplied all manner of things: foodstuffs, alcohol, petrol, clothing and in some cases ran the local post office and bank. Good harvests were not a frequent occurrence, so the arrangement was that when the farmer was flush he paid off his debts to the *duka* owner, sometimes considerable sums of money. Of course the Indian was a wily gentleman, but the settler clan could almost come up to the Indian benefactors' standard by never paying off the complete debt. This form of blackmail was considered acceptable by all parties as it ensured continuing interdependence.

A big percentage of the settlers' sons and daughters were Kenya-born, having grown up in this unusually independent circumstance with servants doing the menial tasks. The youth went to school together, the boys to the Duke of York or Prince of Wales, the girls to the Kenya High and Limuru Loretto Convent Girls' Schools. Some were sent to the UK or South Africa, some came to the Kenya Police and others to the Kenya Regiment (TA), a militia which had won a VC at Karen in the

Abyssinian campaign. The Kenya Regiment was the most feared in the Mau Mau campaign as they knew the African, spoke fluent Swahili and Kikuyu, were naturals in the bush and could handle firearms with deadly accuracy. The Police were the only other unit of the Security Forces accepted in their camps on operations due to the non-bleeding heart procedures adopted. Information was vital: both Police and Kenya Regiment had a close interest in the hunt as this was their country too.

The British Army was not in the same class. If the County Regiments, such as the Gordons and Devons, were popular and efficient, some of the City-orientated ones were not quite up to the same standard. The King's African Rifles, mainly expatriate Officers, made their own significant contribution to success. Even a private soldier in the Kenya Regiment had his batman, usually an African servant; surprisingly, this did not hinder their operational performance. Discipline was more of a consensus of opinion, as all ranks had gone to school together. It never created a problem. Strategy and tactics came from the pool of experience available from past and recent wars and emergencies. The Colonial Police moved from one Force to another on transfer once men were gazetted to assistant superintendent rank. In the commissioned ranks there were groupings of former Palestine Police, Malaya and Hong Kong Police, plus the other African forces.

They adopted General Templar's move from Malaya, where he grouped hamlets into villages in the form of defended areas after the inhabitants had been screened. Loyalist guards were armed first with a spear, then a shotgun and finally the prized firearm, a rifle. Next was the *Kipande*, an ID card giving the individual's particulars, his district, location, chief, headman and photograph as well as his fingerprint classification and a 'print' of the right thumb; it even told the reader if he was literate, his employment and employer, pay and ration scale. It was illegal to pay anyone without his *Kipande*; in other words, without the *Kipande* the person was reduced to a displaced vagrant and vulnerable to arrest. Authoritarian, but a brilliant concept. All juveniles and adults had to have this ID, which was a boost to police work. Civil libertarians would have had their knickers in a knot, bless 'em! Spot checks and raids were carried out in the urban areas, in the farming region sweeps like grouse drives into stop-lines, also successful in bringing up the kill rate.

The Forest was either Army- or Police-patrolled by map co-ordinates. Ambushes were set on various tracks and points of sighting. The elite pseudo-gangs who had been designated terrorists at their time of capture had an immediate choice: change allegiance or be shot. Surprisingly, those who did switch camps never betrayed the trust placed in them. The others were summarily executed, dying a hero's death with defiance and dignity, even to the point of sarcastic remarks. Braver men I have not known, on either side. The pseudo-recruits stank, were verminous and some had wounds healing. They were led by Officers from the Kenya Police Special Branch. A large proportion of the boys from the Kenya Regiment were local lads who had been brought up on the ground and had no illusions about what was required. They would go bush immediately for three weeks, and when these elite men came out it usually took as long to get their scratched, infested and emaciated bodies back to some semblance of health.

Ian Henderson, a superintendent, Special Branch, was repeatedly decorated for his work in the bush. The idea was to contact a gang of Micks in the forest, win their confidence and at nightfall wipe them out. Various methods were used: the use of cheese wire produced decapitation without too much mess. Some nearly had their top-pieces removed by a *simi* stroke; for the less skilful, a rock to the cranium did the trick. The greatest force against the insurrection was the Home Guard of Loyalist Kikuyu, who in some cases saw an allegedly legal opportunity to kill rivals even within their own family circle, thereby gaining power through land and stock. They had the greatest kill rate of all the Security Forces. As MacDonald soon realised, there was no love lost between the opposing teams and 'no quarter' was not asked or given without an ulterior motive. This was no Church Social.

After MacDonald had spent all of ten days in this new 'Land of Endeavour' called Kenya, a Kikuyu woman in her twenties came to the police station. When her babble had been translated it transpired that she had been engaged to be married to a Mick, who was in a hide with a gang of about 250 others on the slopes of Kipipiri, a feature in the Kinangop area of the Aberdares. She had gone with another friend to visit her fiancé, taking in drugs, food and arms. The boys had used her as the village bicycle, which she was not pleased about, and her dearest wish now was to lead the Security Forces to the hide.

A team led by 0i/c Police Station, Jim Burns, 2i/c Gus MacDonald and District Officer from the Labour Department, Sergeant Major Dicky Daniels, with a hand-picked team of fifteen to twenty askaris, were loaded into three LWB Land Rovers bristling with automatic weapons and the odd sniper's rifle, and set off to Pencil Slats, BHQ of the Royal Irish Fusiliers, who were ensconced a half-mile below the hide. Unbeknown to them all, their moves were watched by the Micks. The Kenya Police contingent paid their respects to the Commanding Officer, Royal Irish Fusiliers, hoping he did not mind the 'Cowboys' doing a wee op in their area. Jim Burns had good operational sense and drove about half a mile beyond the entrance to the bamboo forest so the Micks could get the roar of vehicle engines as they passed up the mountain road.

The police disembarked and quickly wandered down the road. At the entrance to the bamboo all weapons were cocked and safety catches off, preparing for immediate action. It was decided to enter the forest by crawling so as not to disturb the heavy dew on the bamboo; despite the slow movement there would be no target on the skyline and little, if any, noise of movement. All talking ceased, including orders: only hand signals done slowly and with care so as not to disturb the vegetation. After 1½ hours' crawling, soaked to the skin by the wet undergrowth, plus the constant dripping off the bamboo clumps, knees and elbows were pretty red raw. Blinded by sweat, the team had covered possibly a quarter of a mile. The signal to open fire was on the first shot being let loose, but where possible a visual recce of the Micks' position would be made. The fifteen police had divided into three subsections of five in line, about three to five yards apart. When they came upon the Mickey Mouse camp there was no 'cockatoo' or sentry, when usually there were two, a hundred metres out, on circular patrol. The 'goodies' were in luck.

A creek ran down the mountain side, its rushing sound providing covering noise. There were a number of small campfires – not the hoped-for 250, only about thirty to fifty bodies in and around the camp, a few rough tent-like structures. In the creek was a huge greasy log covered in lichen and other green stuff like moss. The KP patrol had now managed to crawl into a semi-circular formation and taken up firing positions, picking targets who were at five to twenty-five yards, point-blank range.

All of a sudden the crash of automatic weapons broke the forest silence. Bodies were dropping all over the shop. MacDonald had chosen a Bren gun as his personal weapon and had one mag in the gun and four others in the top and bottom pockets of his bush jacket. His loader, whom he had instructed back at the station, was the young Kikuyu female who had betrayed the gang. She had a metal box of some ten mags strapped to her back. A group of Micks tried to run the gauntlet by racing up the stream, dodging in and out of the rocks, but their luck had run out when they attempted to climb over the slippery log blocking the creek. MacDonald had a field day, firing in controlled bursts of two to three rounds. Then the leader of the gang, Mwangi ('Big Foot' – he too a size 16 boot), attempted to skirt round the log and succeeded. He was hit with a burst to the right rear shoulder; bone and blood flew, so he was at least very badly wounded. Out of the twenty-five, there were only three prisoners, all wounded to some degree, plus the Kikuyu girlfriend who had come out unscathed. 'Big Foot' was tracked for a few hundred paces through the heavy forest. The tracks were clear to start with, plus the drops of blood on leaves. He hit a rocky patch, his tracks petered out and so did the blood spoor: he had got away, perhaps to fight another day.

The prisoners helped carry out what was left: three .303 rifles, numerous home-made bush knives and *simis*, plus the usual oathing paraphernalia, cooking pots and animal skins. They proved quite talkative, needing no persuasion to tell who they were and confirm all that the Security Forces already knew. Back at Ol Kalou Police Station, Supt John Sherrard-Smith had arrived and offered his congratulations on a successful 'bump', bringing the Divisional scoreboard well up for his nightly SITREP to Colony HQ. He informed MacDonald that Officers did not carry light machine guns as personal arms, but nevertheless he would buy them a beer in the mess that evening.

Next day MacDonald got the dirty job of going back and fingerprinting the dead for identification. This was done if rigor mortis had not set in. If it had, hands were cut off at the wrist and taken back so that some of the more skilful could peel off the skin and take the prints: hence the expression 'Coming down a hill with a bag of hands'. Land of Endeavour? MacDonald was being rapidly broken into the Land of Grim Reality that was Kenya.

12: Training for the Kenya Police

After a few months, word came that Brelesford, MacDonald and all the other new boys were to attend a 14-week Training Course at the Police Training School at Kiganjo, just outside Nyeri in Upper Central Province, on the other side of the Aberdares. Mac duly said 'Cheerio' to his adopted Mess dog, a friendly German shepherd named 'Gipp', and to Jim's horses and the rest of the mob hoping to return to Laikipia Division of Rift Valley Province after their induction. He had been accepted by his contemporaries and African Other Ranks, who liked his practical training, especially the live firing side, as they now sported fresh colobus monkey skins for their tribal dances.

Just before they left, a Senior Superintendent paid a visit to a Forest Post in the Wanjohi Valley in the Ol Kalou Subdivision. It was typical of its kind: on the verge of the forest and the farming area, built on a self-help basis, mainly of cement blocks with the usual all-round trench with bamboo spikes and barbed wire double fence, with a main gate and sentry box; up the tower was a searchlight and a Bren light machine gun, manned at all times. The Inspector in charge of this post was a former Lieutenant Commander, RN, the visiting Senior Superintendent was a former Chief Petty Officer Stoker, RN. The Inspector piped his Snr Supt aboard from his perch on top of the guard tower. Pleasantries were exchanged and it was pointed out in no uncertain terms that as their status was now reversed, it would be appreciated if the Inspector only passed the normal compliments. This was 'The Bastard's Way'.

Another visitor to this police post on the slopes of the Aberdares was one Barbara Castle, a Labour MP from the Midlands. Usually political visits were engineered in such a manner that the visitors saw what the Kenya Police wished them to see and no more. The Guard of Honour was drawn up and Mrs Castle was invited to inspect. She immediately picked on the youngest-looking askari constable and asked if his Officer was treating him well. The Sergeant Major, a Kipsiki, snarled *Nyamasa*! (Shut up!), *Si-mama* (Attention), *Tu-lea* (Stand still), then gave Mrs Castle a smart salute and in perfect English, which until now he did not speak, 'Memsahib, the constable says he is very happy with his Officer.' As the tour of inspection progressed, it came to their attention that on top of both gateposts were two fresh skulls and crossbones nailed up for show. Aghast, Mrs Castle pointed and asked, 'What is that?'

The Inspector in Charge replied, 'Ma'am, trophies of the hunt.'

She looked him up and down and said it was her intention to report what she had seen to the Commissioner of Police. Labour MPs on fact-finding missions were always worth a few laughs: their socialism did not fit into the Kenya picture, especially in the middle of an Emergency.

MacDonald was sorry to leave Ol Kalou. He felt he was beginning to fit in and make a contribution. He farewelled the troops, some of whom he was beginning to know, and by now he had the odd word of Swahili, the lingua franca of East Africa – Uganda (The Pearl of Africa), Tanganyika (Tanzania), Zanzibar, the Island of Cloves, the Kenya Colony and Protectorate. The Tame Colonial Boy was on his way.

After some hours of dusty travel in a safari truck, the Kiganjo Police Training School hove into view, with the Tavern Inn just outside the main gate, alongside the Instructors' Quarters. ACP Jim Sweeney, a heavily beribboned Irish gentleman with service in both World Wars, plus thirty-odd years in the Kenya Police, welcomed his new Inspectors of Police and gave them the rundown on the Training School. There were 1,200 African recruit constables (askaris), and 200 European Cadet Inspectors. Jim Sweeney was exceptionally proud of his 'Boys', explaining how the Africans came in from their reserves as pastoralists and herdsmen – some not even that – and in six months they would become constables, who could read and write in Swahili and had a smattering of English, could handle the basic infantry weapons, arms drill, foot drill, first aid, riot drill, and make arrests with a knowledge of the law. Hygiene was targeted and their medical and dental needs taken care of.

Some appeared only in a *shoka* (blanket), carrying a *simi* and fighting or hunting spear, cut earlobes dangling down, chewing betel nut — fine specimens of manhood, most around six foot and athletically built. They came from warrior tribes like the Turkana from north-west Upper Kenya, the Samburu from upper Rift Valley Province (Mac's favourites), the Somalis from the Northern Frontier, the Masai from the Southern Province on the Tanganyika border and the Kalenjin tribes from the mid-Rift Valley, the Kisiis, the Tugens, Nandis and Kipsigis. From the coast, Giriamas, Mdigos and the Jaluos, Maragoli and Kakamega from Nyanza near the shores of Lake Victoria, and the Suk from the north-west border with Uganda. These tribes were divided into racial groups such as Nilotic (Nile basin), Hamitic (Abyssinia), Bantu, all the way down to Kwazulu in the Union of South Africa, some 3,000 miles away, the Kikuyu, Embu, and Meru from Central, also the Wakamba from Southern Province. Throughout the Kenya Police there was an attempt at tribal balance. Only the Northern Frontier had Turkanas, Somalis and Wakamba.

Europeans expressed many opinions about the various African tribes: some were warriors of distinction, others less warlike, some made good servants — the Kikuyu in particular, bearing in mind that they had the most contact with the white man and appeared most intelligent. They were the largest tribe, 1½ million out of six million. The Europeans numbered about 60,000; they could be divided into various categories, but were mainly of British extraction: the settler, who invariably was the farmer; next in pecking order the official, the lifetime serving Government servant who usually retired in Kenya or carried on a close association; and finally the commercial element, or businessman, usually just passing through unless he owned his own business. Settlers versus officials was carried on at all levels, including sport. The commercial type was not in this league, nor did he speak fluent Swahili or any other African language, therefore his understanding of the African was limited. To be considered part of the system, one had to serve at least five years and was expected to read and write good Swahili and another local language. The

Asian from India was the artisan (*mistry*), also the trader (*duka-wallah*); they were from Bombay-side, the Punjab, a few from the North-West Frontier, some from the Central Provinces of India.

Like everyone who comes to a new land, MacDonald had a lot to learn. Outsiders usually ask if there was a colour bar, like the apartheid system of South Africa: the answer could be yes or no. There was a social bar, as in any other society. The colour bar, if any, was best demonstrated in public toilets — European, Asian and African — which eventually became Management, Staff and Workers, a social segregation. Places of public entertainment such as cinemas reserved downstairs for the African, but if he could afford the price no one objected to his presence upstairs. The transport system had first, second and third class, and there again anyone could buy a ticket for any class — though it has to be borne in mind that the European was paid at least five times more than the African, which produced discrimination on an economic level. Sadly, the country could not support its local population any other way.

The newcomers had to learn some of the history of '*Inchi ya Kenya Mwafrika Mashariki*' — East Africa. Missionaries like Livingstone and Mungo Park had come to East Africa to find what they thought was savage, wild land where the poor blacks were in need of being converted to Christianity so that their souls could be saved; some, for their zealousness, were promptly put in the cooking pot for their trouble. The British Government could not allow this to happen to their chosen few, so the Army was sent out to protect the Bible-thumpers. Spears were not much chop against Lee Metford rifles: the tribes were subdued and forts established, such as Fort Hall, Fort Portal. Wives and families followed and so did the supply route by horse and cart, mule or donkey. But given that supplies had hundreds of miles to travel, it was decided to build a railroad to facilitate easier movement from Mombasa inland, as the Germans were doing at Dar-es-Salaam in Tanganyika. God had answered the African warriors' prayers: beautiful steel rails to make spears and arrowheads, far better than labouring on the white man's madness. Without labour, the railroad struck an impasse. India with its teeming masses was not too far away, about a week's voyage across the Indian Ocean, so it came to pass that the Indians would provide the labour skills to build the railway all the way from Mombasa up through Kenya to Kampala in Uganda.

The Indian soon realised that here was an opportunity indeed. He became the skilled tradesman as well as the storekeeper. As usual, to escape the poverty of the subcontinent they came in their thousands, were successful and almost lived happily ever after. Rift Valley and Central Provinces showed great potential for pastoral and agricultural farming, so the European farmer came, buying tracts of land from the Masai and Kikuyu – by foul means or fair. At the end of both World Wars, serving Officers were rewarded with land grants and subsidies. Tea, coffee, sisal, and pyrethrum estates were developed as well as livestock, with African labour. Africans were educated to have the three 'R's in mission schools, where the missionary spoke about equality and in many cases created suspicions which eventually engendered rebellion.

All very interesting, thought MacDonald, but he would not delve too deeply into the politics of the matter at hand; like his colleagues, he had been brought up to do his duty and trust that the Government would do its own, fairly and for all.

He had something else to learn, too: concerning the magnificent animals of this mighty land. The King of Beasts, the lion; the multitudinous zebra of the plains along with the wildebeest, eland, various species of antelope; the graceful giraffe of the savannah, eating the *Mwiba* or thorn tree leaves; the hippopotamus, who was far from docile; the Cape buffalo, the badge of the Kenya Regiment, and a most wily animal; the rhino, who in his forest habitat was what the Security Forces feared most; the hyena, scavengers of the plain, the untrustworthy leopard, the domesticated cheetah, with his spectacular speed; warthog and all other relatives, the primates, monkeys of many varieties and the magnificent gorilla, up in the Ruwenzori Range in Uganda, the so-called Mountains of the Moon.

Marching with his squad into the parade ground of the Training School, MacDonald heard a familiar voice ring out: 'What the hell are you doing here?'

The question came from a lifetime friend, none other than

Charles MacLeod, a Highland gentleman who had played rugby with MacDonald in the Glasgow Polis. Also in his squad was Sergeant John Leighton, Mortar Platoon, and Corporal Lionel Mellor, Signals Platoon, formerly of the 1st Battalion Argyll and Sutherland Highlanders. MacDonald was delighted to see 'kin' so far from home.

The Inspectors in Training were housed in tents. MacDonald's syndicate consisted of Captain Arthur Brelesford (34), Hampshire Regiment; and Bill Hopely (34), formerly of the Irish Republican Navy, ex-Palestine Police and commercial traveller by occupation – at 6' 7", few would tackle our Irish friend. Other members were Colin Robey (23), ex-RASC Lieutenant; Noel Black (26), Ulsterman ex-Lieutenant RA; Jim Halliday (35), ex-Captain, RM Bandmaster; and Jack Fyffe (36), MC, Major, ex-Scottish Horse. There was some nondescript individual who claimed to be an ex-Lieutenant, Grenadier Guards... more like Fire Guards; he went home within the week, homesick.

It took all kinds to make the Kenya Police. Squad 22 Instructor was Inspector Mike Webley (29), former Flight Lieutenant, RAF, who flew Meteors and was also an ex-cop from one of the Midlands Forces. He was the first to admit that most of his class had more experience than he. But Mike was treated with the respect he deserved, and on parade it was not difficult to give him 'Sir!' The lad had done his fair share in the Emergency and had already shown great love for Kenya, its people and its animals.

The training subjects were Penal Code (Crimes), Criminal Procedure Code (Courts), the Indian Evidence Act, Pay & Accounts (the most difficult), Allowances & Travel, plus the usual Traffic Act, Firearms, Children, Cruelty to Animals and so on. Infantry weapons were taught and fired on the various ranges. Ki-Swahili was invoked. There was did ju-jitsu and of course Rifle and Foot Drill; also Sword Drill, First Aid, Civil Defence, Public Speaking. If one studied hard (which was problematic) one would pass the 'A' Exam (Inspectors) and Preliminary Swahili (oral), also qualifying in First Aid. However, as the Course was going to culminate in the biggest Passing Out Parade in the history of the British Colonial Police and all the 'bigwigs' were to be invited, most time would be spent on the parade ground sharpening up drill and deportment.

The 'bullshit' factor was also going to be of a higher standard, intoned the Chief Instructor, Chief Supt Eric Lindsay, who was of the old school, with a lifetime in the Kenya Police, to which he always referred in reverent tones. While on parade, the PTS Band Fife & Drum (Bugle) would play the Kenya Police March: *'Tufunga safari, tufunga safari, Amri anani, Amri anani? Amri ya Polisi, Amri ya Polis'* ('We are going on a journey, What are the orders? Police Orders Police Orders'), co-opted from the King's African Rifles.

Nobody in the world has better rhythm than the African, who enjoyed drill and marching and being smartly turned out on parade. Some orders, like those given to the constable questioned by Mrs Castle, were given in Swahili: *Si-mama* (Atten-*shun*), *Tu-lea* (Stand still). The European Inspectors were hard-pressed to maintain the standards of the African recruit. Chief Superintendent Lindsay, who took the parade from the Senior Sgt Maj (RSM), was seen arriving in his 600cc Fiat with open roof, Lindsay like Rommel with his head sticking out over the top; he got out of his vehicle, placed a large mirror on the side of an outhouse off the parade ground and proceeded to do up his collar and tie, then tunic with Sam Browne cross strap and sword frog, produced his sword from the boot of the vehicle – only to discover he had forgotten the scabbard – arranged his head-dress in the mirror to the approved jaunty angle, not forgetting yellowish gloves, then proceeded to march on parade, stabbing at the odd empty cigarette packet on the ground. One could hear his mutterings of disgust. The parade was standing rigidly at attention. He addressed the parade with *'Hamjambo ninyi, noyte'*, ('Hello, everybody'), and then added to the European Inspectors' Squads, 'And that includes you, you long-haired duffel-coated atheist products of the Welfare State.'

Next up, the inspection. He called over a Cadet Assistant Superintendent, who had recently been demobbed as a Pilot Officer RAF Regiment and had luckily got in at the cadetship back door. 'Mr Whittaker,' he said, 'you will pretend to be the Governor General inspecting the parade. I expect you to speak to the odd Inspector, ask him what his background is.'

'Yes, Sir,' the reply.

A few paces down the rank he asked a fellow with a General Service Medal from Malaya, 'Did you enjoy being in the Regular Army?'

The Inspector answered, 'No, Sir, National Service!'

Lindsay was heard to mutter to his Asst Supt Colleague, 'For the love of God, wake up, man!'

A few paces further on in the middle stood Inspector Jack Fyffe, with a couple of rows of gongs. 'Now, young man,' came the next question, 'did you enjoy your National Service?'

Fyffe went brick-red, spluttered, then exploded 'No, Sir! Scottish Horse, Major Fyffe, Military Cross, eighteen years Regular Army.'

The Cadet Assistant Superintendent was told to fall out. Chief Superintendent Lindsay then had the parade stand at ease. 'Some of you may think I'm mad,' he said. 'That is not so, and I have a certificate to prove it, which is more than most of you lot.' Eric then produced a piece of paper from his right-hand top tunic pocket and held it up, letting those close enough read it: 'This is to certify that one Eric Lindsay is of sound mind' – a signature and the stamp of Mathari Mental Hospital. The 1,400 bodies then performed 'Advancing In Review Order' for the next two hours. Obviously a high standard of drill was to be reached and to hell with trivia like law procedures and enforcement.

The new Inspectors were encouraged to take an interest in the African recruits, amazed by how quickly they adapted to their new circumstances and the pride they took in themselves. Not only were their African Reservists doing a two-year stint of National Service, this also applied to the European and Asian population, which had the choice of Kenya Regiment, Prisons Service, Immigration, Customs or King's African Rifles. Should the KR be chosen, the potential Officer went to the UK and was usually commissioned into a County Regiment before being seconded to the KAR. The Kenya Police always considered themselves the best, as with the exception of the Kenya Regiment, they topped all other rivals at all activities while in the bush. This intake of expertise from the civilian ranks produced higher standards than was the norm: garage proprietors took over Police Transport Workshops; there was even a vet to the dog section with its 100-odd dogs, and to the mule and camel sections of the Northern Frontier Province. All were police-trained in abbreviated courses at the Police Training School, the only difference being that reservists wore a brass cap badge as opposed to the Regulars' chrome badge.

Training on the practical side involved taking part in sweeps and ambushes for real, as this was in an Emergency Area. It was quite tame to those with some Mickey Mouse experience already under their belts. The Force was divided up into Provinces with an Assistant Commissioner of Police commanding 1,500, Divisions (Snr Supt) 500, Subdivisions (Asst Supt) 250, Stations (Chief Insp) 150, Substation (Insp) 75, Post (Insp) 35. Ancillary Provinces of varying size were Training School, Criminal Investigation and Prosecutions, Traffic and Transport, Special Branch, General Service Unit (paramilitary – riot police), Signals, Police HQ, Admin, Pay & Accounts, Quartermaster, Air Wing, Dogs, Railways & Harbours. The General Duties Provinces were Northern Frontier Headquarters, Isiolo; Central, Nyeri; Nairobi Area, Nairobi; Rift Valley, Nakuru; Southern, Ngong; Nyanza, Kisumu; Coast, Mombasa. This chain of command is directly related to the British Army model of three Sections to a Platoon, three Companies, three or four Rifle Companies to a Battalion, three Battalions to a Brigade, three Brigades to a Division and so on, the idea being that a Commander should never control more than three to five units.

As the end of training approached, judo classes came to a sudden end, and for a good reason. Senior Sergeant James, the Instructor, had made a habit of using MacDonald and John Leighton, a stocky Yorkshireman, to demonstrate the superiority of judo over boxing as a form of defence. While Leighton boxed, MacDonald was to make the arrest by using judo. The ex-Argyll mates invariably ended up off the tarpaulin and needing to visit the MO room for treatment to gravel rash and cuts from their spiked buckles. Then one day Leighton voiced the opinion that he could beat anyone by using fisticuffs rather than judo. Sgt James walked into it in more ways than one. Accepting the challenge, a few seconds later he was carted off to the MO room himself after being knocked cold by a right cross from Johnny Boy.

Towards the end of the course one could choose one out of three Provinces, one out of three Duties. MacDonald chose all three Emergency Provinces and stated 'General Duties' in each case, hoping this was the road to quick promotion. Little did he know, to quote his national bard, how 'the best-laid schemes o' mice and men gang aft agley'. He was asked if he was a drill pig (Instructor) in the Army, as there was a vacancy for a Chief Inspector, Mbaraki Lines (Barracks), Mombasa: he was frank and said no, he had been an ordinary infantryman and had no formal experience of 'They stand on the Square, And they bawl and they shout...' It was explained that a former Sergeant Major Ken Dawson, Royal Northumberland Fusiliers, ex-NW Europe and Korea, who had been in the British Transport Commission Police (Railways and Docks), had been posted to Railways & Harbours Province but had claimed the necessary qualification, and MacDonald would take his place. Charming, bloody charming, MacDonald thought. He had no wish to be involved with Railways & Harbours.

As usual a minimal amount of study was done before Officers and Gentlemen paid their nightly visit to the Tavern, the No.1 watering hole and unofficial Mess, where battles dating back to the Boer War and some later conflicts were re-fought in sessions of 'Swinging the Lamp', usually followed by individual ribald songs from HM Services, including those from Australia, New Zealand, South Africa and Canada. Even the Republic of Eire had its representatives, the odd rebel song being joined in without malice aforethought. Pop, the owner of the Tavern, was making a mint as he dearly loved his 'Gentlemen', as he had often to refer to them in an attempt to restore order when things got a little more exuberant than usual. All 'Barrack Room Damages' were doubly paid for; in fact the standard of furnishings was permanently being improved. Here was the scene of the compulsory debating society, heard and seen through an alcoholic haze, where subjects of global consequence were hotly debated such as 'Should Mt. Kenya be towed out into the Indian Ocean and sunk by naval gunfire?'

Like all worthy innkeepers, Pop had a good-looking daughter who helped out from time to time in the bar. Despite her looks, she felt she was not over-endowed in the chest and obtained a blow-up job. One evening a Scottish piper leant across the bar and gave her a kiss; but when the piper asked for 'a wee look', she hesitated – and said piper lent over the bar once more and deflated the magnificent bosoms, earning a spontaneous round of applause from the gentlemen present and having his parentage volubly called into question by the lady herself.

The more naughty boys who had enlisted under false colours and who did not appreciate what was required of them were discharged with expediency. One such imbecile awakened his sidekick by firing off several rounds from his personal firearm, a German Luger, close to the earhole. Unfortunately for him, several shots landed in and around the verandahs of the Instructional Staff. Jim Sweeney, Commandant, gave his immediate blessing and the culprit was on the 2 p.m. plane back to The Land They Adore, fully paid up and the necessary fine deducted, with an escort to the plane's closing door.

As the Passing Out was to be the largest and, they hoped, the best in the history of HM Colonial Police, week-long festivities were planned, with cocktail parties, skits, cinema shows, dinners, suppers, lectures, demonstrations and any other jollifications you could dream up. This was to climax in the Passing Out Parade on the Saturday morning and a formal ball in the evening. The Police Band was brought up from Nairobi; units of the General Service Unit, plus camels from the Northern Frontier Province and also the Police Dog Section were represented. The original parade of 1,400 had expanded to the 2,000 mark plus a fly-past by the Police Air Wing. All that was required were a few comedians from among the residents of the Training School! The inspection, 'Advance in Review Order', counter-marching through the ranks in quick and slow time and finally the 'March Off' to the strains of 'Auld Lang Syne' went well, to the delight of thousands of spectators. His Excellency the Governor General, Sir Evelyn Baring, made the expected complimentary noises, backed up by Lt General Lathbury KBE, General Officer Commanding East Africa. Some wag in one of the dress rehearsals had managed to climb to the top of the huge flagpole, leaving a track of dirty footprints all the way up and down, and nailed a beautiful pair of lady's drawers to the top. The lady remained unidentified, although a number of punting persons laid large bets.

Speaking of ladies, two hundred or so fair maidens had been invited from Nairobi to partner the Officers and Gentlemen at the ball; they came, to the delight of the Inspectorate, and were suitably chaperoned to the quarters of the resident instructors. But MacDonald's syndicate had decided there were insufficient ladies to go round and so the merry men had simply concentrated on imbibing, all turned out in their Number Ones and on their apparent best behaviour, bowing and scraping in the most gentlemanly fashion when they thought it was required. Colin Roby spotted a beautifully turned-out female sitting immediately below the band's platform. She was a honey, but obviously something was amiss – no male escort. Colin was in like Flynn and after a few rounds of the floor was forced to introduce his brother Officers, who were applauding their efforts. Brelesford in the background leant forward and fondled the lady's posterior, whereupon the Colin boy got a smack in the ear. The lady told him to cut it out and everyone returned to watch the other dancers. Again, Brelesford in his exuberance gave her bum a 'wee touch-up'. Colin was awarded another thick ear, but this time managed to notice Brelesford's wolf-like grin and merriment. Roby immediately pointed out the culprit, who stepped forward and with a most gallant bow said, 'I beg your pardon, Madam, some c— pushed me.'

She appreciated the crudity but refused him the pleasure of the next dance, saying she would have to go back to her husband – the band-leader, who had almost fallen off the stage trying to keep an eye on his wife while waving his baton. The ball was also enlivened by a skit by Chief Superintendent Lindsay and a new Inspector, a Welsh wag. Both were dressed up as Senior Superintendents with the same uniform and decorations, and rode onto the stage on horseback. No telling who was who: the pair did a slapstick act on the training methods and idiosyncrasies of the Chief Instructor, each aiding and abetting the other. A huge cheer of appreciation went up.

The Commissioner, Sir Richard Catling, was not amused and did his best to hide in the midst of the distinguished guests. Anyway, the boys managed to get themselves a few dances with the odd farmer's daughter. All was not lost, in fact some almost became farmers by default.

When the exam results came out, to the surprise of most of Squad 22, credits had been gained in the 'A' Exam for Inspectors. As Mike Webley, the class instructor, put it: 'Some of you buggers had to get something,' – from which it might be construed that he was not really instructor material. But 'Auld Lang Syne' was duly sung and the Inspectors (Grade 1), now fully qualified, caught the train at Nyeri Station or took a safari vehicle to their various Provincial Headquarters.

Turkana Tribal Police, 1958

Turkana Matron, 1958

13: Port Police Station, Kilindini Division, Mombasa

The Port Police are happy,
The Port Police are free,
The Port Police are happy,
When they're on the spree,
For the motto of the Port Police is:
'Come and have a drink with me!'

Wally Belcher IP, KP

MacDonald had been posted to Kenya (Railways & Harbours) Police at Nairobi. On arrival he was greeted by 2i/c Province Superintendent Pat Refroy, who lent a sympathetic ear to MacDonald's statement that had he wished to be a Railway Police Officer then he would have been one in the UK. MacDonald was handed over to a fellow Inspector and former Colonel in the Indian Army who had been briefed to talk him out of a transfer request. Colonel Blimp did not impress the young Lochinvar, but he pricked up his ears when he was told that the following evening he was being posted to Crime Branch, Kilindini Division, in the Port of Mombasa, where he would undergo three months' training covering railways and harbours documentation and practice before taking up duties in Crime Branch. The idea of meeting daily passenger ships, with all those gorgeous girls from the Union of South Africa and the Federation of Rhodesia, on holiday and requiring escorts, swung the pendulum in favour of Port Police instead of bundu-bashing (forest patrol).

The overnight train journey from Nairobi to Mombasa, some 333 miles, was up to any world train journey: Second or First Class, the 'One Up and Two Down' had no Third Class, but it did have a luxurious dining car with three sittings, the last being the best, with excellent food, coffee, cheese and liqueurs being part of the treatment, and all on a Travel Warrant. He was accompanied down by an ex-mate from the Glasgow Polis, Inspector Charlie MacLeod, who had been posted to General Duties, Coastal Province. Many a tale was swapped en route, and MacDonald was still shaking his head at MacLeod's antics: from Nyeri to Nairobi he had walked the length of the train and decided to stretch his legs by climbing onto the roof and trotting the length of the 'rake' before descending to join his fellow-passengers. A Sikh conductor had heard the thunder of hooves on the roof and kept pace, but not quite exactly enough. He did challenge MacDonald on his whereabouts; the altercation ceased when Charlie lifted the six-foot Sikh off his feet by his collar and intoned that he was a Scottish Highland gentleman who did not tell lies. Agreement was reached.

MacDonald was welcomed to Mombasa by Divisional Assistant Superintendent Broadhead, ex-Palestine and Nigeria, then handed over to Chief Inspector Max Cable, also ex-Palestine and Royal Artillery. Max, a cockney who had been the light-heavyweight boxing champion of the Palestine Police, had twenty-odd years in. He was a decent stick, respected by all ranks, but his dreams of advancement had long been shattered. The Port operated on a three-shift basis, 8–4, 4–12, 12–8. Max as 0i/c Station had his own routine: lunchtime was 12–2, so Max and his buddy, Chief Inspector Edgar Wallace, Irish Guards and Palestine Police, could sleep off any indiscretion or flatulence. Edgar could tell a joke at any social occasion but his Police commitment was non-existent. The time from 12–2 would see the old comrades ensconced behind pint jugs in the British Legion Club. The 0i/c's Office was closed in the afternoons due to pressure of work – Max asleep in his chair, likewise Edgar. They would return to the strenuous exercise of raising the pint at 4 p.m. until wives gave the dinner call.

Bwana Saini, an Indian of Punjabi extraction, was MacDonald's new boss as Chief Inspector, Crime. He addressed MacDonald as *Burrah Sahib*, both flattering and embarrassing. Anyway, MacDonald did his three-month course, visiting all 26 sheds parallel to the 26 deep-water berths, learning and gleaning from the sheds' superiors how the various fiddles in a big pond were perpetrated. Some of them showed a certain nervousness as the young Detective Inspector learned the ropes from some of his future customers: D & DO (Declaration & Disposal Orders), Removal Orders, Tally Sheets in the hold at the point of hook, into the shed, from the shed into the CGB (Covered Goods Boogie), the different types of seals — Acme, light, with numbers, heavy wire and padlock bolts — Customs Forms, Immigration, all to throw the investigator off the scent, Specie (money), Red (ammo), Firearms Bond, Liquor Bond: a whole new world of complications. A world-wide phenomenon, too: the more complicated and less well understood the system, the greater opportunity for the *mivi* (thief). Another stalwart of the Crime Branch was Inspector John Hawley, ex-Palestine, who had a leg in callipers after a bout of cerebral malaria. Better a job than a pension: he eventually had both. There was also Assistant Inspector 'Baba' (father) Kundalal, another Indian gentleman from Bombay-side, an expert at copperplate writing in his investigation file, but things always resulted in an 'NFPA' — No Further Police Action — due to a stock of excuses he mounted. Clearly he was kept on to satisfy some theory of Full Employment. A back-up of thirty-odd African ORs (Other Ranks) dealt successfully with petty crime, captained by Senior Sergeant Nelson, a Luo gentleman from Nyanza Province, Lake Victoria.

Inspector Roy Chalkley, ex-Chief Petty Officer, Gunnery, from the battleship HMS *Nelson*, headed up the Marine Section. A triple-screw Admiral's Launch of doubtful reliability provided the visiting brass and the junior, single, expatriate Officers' girlfriends off the ships with moonlight fishing cruises around the harbour and to estuaries up the channel at Port Reitz. Chalkley was also the Shipping Officer, Firearms and Traffic; at the time he was deciding whether to become a Lieutenant Commander REAN, or take up a vicarage in the Missions to Seamen.

He lived with his brother-padre, David Seamen, who was at least bisexual. Our laddie was not, but knew a good thing when he saw one. The ladies loved him for his sermons written while under the affluence of incohol and mira (a benzedrine drug); he loved them back. Roy had a charming disposition and cancelled many a Traffic Ticket. His PR on the gangway of ships, especially with passengers, was outstanding. He had a good rapport with the Chief Purser, who advised as to which female tourists were worthy of a guided tour around the bars and nightclubs of the Old Port of Mombasa for an exquisite repast of curry and samosas. Speaking of female tourists, one day John Hawley, then Shipping Officer, was meeting a ship and on coming alongside heard a delightful popsie remark, 'Look, there's one of those *Salus Copuli* fellows!' The Kenya Police motto was *Salus Populi*, meaning 'Serve the People'; near enough is good enough...

The Port Police was used as an R & R Centre for Officers who had done their time playing with the Mickey Mice and those who were being given a final chance to soldier up. MacDonald had his work cut out doing all manner of investigations; as it was a semi-specialist arena, there was also the prosecution side as well, so that justice was done. Despite the cushy holiday atmosphere of the Coast there were plenty of crimes committed, both on paper and more brutal. MacDonald decided he would go on a 'Jews' Course' (save money), which put the kibosh on any amorous and alcoholic adventures, but he usually had a couple of days' binge every six weeks to show he remained human.

Inspectors were posted in from the Emergency areas, most of them having spent two or three years at the sharp end and all having played their part in the downfall of the Mau Mau. Jomo Kenyatta had been tried for subversion and incarcerated at Loikitaung in the Turkana part of the Northern Frontier Province; surrenderees were coming in at long last, and the prisons were bursting at the seams. Crime had gone up throughout the colony, taking advantage of the fact that the Police were hard-pressed. The new Inspectors were Contract Officers, mercenaries of the new fraternity, originally on an 18-month, 2-year or now 3-year contract with a higher salary and gratuity than the regular 'Permanent and Pensionable'. This did not create any division, as most Officers were more concerned with the job at hand.

Inspector Edwin Walter Belcher duly arrived in Mombasa after three years commanding at Naro Moru Police Station on the north-western slopes of Mount Kenya, that magnificent snow-capped mountain of almost 20,000 feet where the wild animals roamed at will. Wally had many a tale to tell: he was ex-Life Guards, having been educated at Liverpool's Merchant Taylors' College, and like so many others from the Metropolitan Police of Greater London he had come out in 1952 at the beginning of the Mau Mau period. Another lifetime friendship was to develop between two kindred spirits. Inspector Mike Wade from the Rift Valley had seen a fair bit of action upcountry too; Inspector Alex Myburgh, likewise Uganda-born, had lost a brother KIA.

Kilindini Division embraced the Railway Police Station Mombasa and the Railway Police Post at Voi, a hundred or so miles up the line – around 360 Rank and File plus some fifteen Officers, ten married. The Port of Kilindini (meaning 'Deep Place' in Swahili) had 26 deep-water berths, each a shed for Imports/Exports, run by a stevedoring company of Landing and Shipping ('Lazing & Sleeping') and assisted by the African Marine Co. Each had its own security service. Also in the Port Area were Customs and Immigration, Health, and the Port Manager, who was an East African Railways & Harbours employee and controlled all operations including the extensive railway marshalling yards. There were sixteen gates to allow people and goods in and out.

Kilindini Harbour also provided an anchorage for the Royal Navy's Far East Armament Depot on the south side of Mombasa Island – *Mvita* (Place of War) – commanded by a Lieutenant Commander, Royal Navy. East African Railways & Harbours was British East Africa's lifeline, and very much a pseudo-Government Department covering Tanganyika (Tanzania), Uganda, Kenya, Zanzibar, all ports, railways, bus routes, hotels, guest houses, including 500- to 800-ton steamships on Lake Victoria and paddle boats right up the Blue Nile to Nimule on the Sudan border, which had come through the Uganda lakes around Nyamasagali into Lake Albert.

Kenya (Railways & Harbours) Police was a cushy posting. Police Stations controlled sectors of the Kenya–Uganda Railway also in Tanganyika, with Dar-es-Salaam (Haven of Peace) as both capital and main port. Housing, vehicles and furniture were in addition to the Kenya Police allocation, where supplies were free gratis from East African Railways & Harbours. Overtime was paid by EAR & H – unheard of in the other Provinces. An EAR & H Warrant Card was issued to all Officers, entitling the holder to free travel and excellent discount rates on all EAR & H services; most countries throughout the world reciprocated, also most shipping lines likewise.

What a set-up! thought MacDonald, Railways & Harbours may not be so bad after all... He had acquired a car, a Hillman Minx of some vintage, having passed his driving test by driving Inspector the almost Reverend Chalkley to the Mess in his MG sports car. He was issued with every class of Driving Licence 'in case you have to move a vehicle at an accident scene', explained the 0i/c Traffic Section. The 0i/c Vehicle Service Department in the Port Area was a keen supporter of the Mombasa Sports Club Rugby Section and told MacDonald that if he would play for the Club he would have his African apprentices restore the Hillman Minx. Another, George MacLaren, who was 2i/c the Marine Slipway servicing the deep-sea tugs and pilots' cutters, said he would chip in with a set of steel milled weights. MacDonald gratefully accepted both offers, joined the Club and played his usual exceptionally dirty game of rugby. He had bought the car for 3,600 shillings and sold it, in its restored condition, for 16,000 shillings, while the steel weights were his for the next twenty years, much to the delight of his Aberdeen Jew disposition.

MacDonald was now part of the Kilindini set-up and could chortle the Port Police song, when ordered to do so while Chief Inspectors Max Cable and Edgar Wallace were holding court at the British Legion of a night: 'The Port Police are happy because the Port Police are Free/For the motto of the Port Police is "Come and have a drink with me!"'

Most mornings, when the 'Q' (quarantine) flag came down and the 'I' (immigration) flag went up on a newly-berthed ship, especially a passenger liner, the Police contingent would troop on board for breakfast at the Officers' Table, sometimes lunch, and of course in the evening wives and sweethearts would be invited down for dinner. Drinks were at uncustomed prices, likewise tobacco goods. The Purser would feel sorry for the bachelor Inspectors and would insist that the young fellows take ashore at least an odd ham or so for their Mess.

Life could be rough in the Port. A story did the rounds about the Inspector assisting with landing formalities at the bottom of a gangplank, when a Retired Brigadier made his way down the gangway; stopping to have a word with the Police Shipping Officer, he enquired, 'What is this I hear, that the longer you are in Africa the black women seem to get lighter in colour?'

The Police Officer was taken aback and asked him to repeat his question, which he did. Back came the reply: 'What black women?'

Major Flood, who had possibly been a Sergeant Major, was proprietor of Flood's Tours. He would dash on board and advertise his exciting safaris accompanied by a couple of real good-lookers in most attractive safari gear. His brochure showed Major Flood in full White Hunter regalia, standing on a dead lion which he had shot: bush slouch hat with a leopard's tail hanging there, a safari jacket covered in pouches for cartridge cases, a pair of jodhpurs and a pair of highly polished lace-up boots from the Victorian era, with paisley-pattern cravat around the neck. His shining boots were on the (stuffed) lion's neck, on which rested his Purdy double-barrelled shotgun, giving day, date, time and place of his first kill in East Africa, back in the pre-war years.

The Yank tourists loved it and were thrilled to learn that all safaris were in big American 'Spam cans' from Chevrolet and Dodge. Most of them had little suspension left, which added to the thrill of their safari in Darkest Africa. The off-duty Police Officers were the drivers, who became for the day *Bwanas mkubwa sana* (very big masters). They too were suitably attired to fill the role of the White Hunter. The gentlemen-drivers were paid 400/- a day, about a week's pay, plus meals and drinks. They would belt up to Voi, about 100 miles up the dusty, potholed road, have lunch at the Voi Dak Station Bungalow, take the unsuspecting tourists to Mzima Springs in the Tsavo Game Park to view hippos frolicking in the pools, and return their charges to their ship, ensuring that sufficient dust had blown through the car windows to show they really had been to the bush. If there were any good-looking females they would be offered equally exciting free tours of the Mombasa nightspots. Great value for money was enjoyed by all.

Inspector Ian K Connell (22), ex-Corporal 2nd Battalion Black Watch, from Arbroath, arrived. He and MacDonald had plenty in common: they played golf and rugby, a bit of soccer and swimming, and the occasional game of badminton. Being also of the Highland Brigade, Ian and Gus saw the world through the same eyes. They also shared the same social pleasures. Next to join the area was Insp Archie Archibald (35), married with two offspring. Ex-Parachute Regiment, Archie had been commissioned in the Somaliland gendarmerie after the war, where a dissipated life had corrupted his way of thinking while in East Africa. He was a qualified naval architect who had also worked as a shot-firer in a pit in Fife, his native kingdom. He had been a taxi driver, had given a Conservative political address at a communist-inspired pit, and as usual in his misspent life had moved on and on. Archie was gifted with an exceptional IQ, which to date had succeeded only in getting him into trouble. He had been given a Police Station in Nyanza Province, and when the troops' pay arrived early he had taken an advance to go on the turps in Kisumu, the local town, returning after a few days. He did the pay for the troops, augmenting it to the best of his financial ability, but fell short and was disciplined for his effort.

Posted to Eldoret Police Station as a Duty Officer, one night the whisky ran out at an Officers' Mess party, so Archie borrowed some from the local *duka*, opening the locked door by means of the Police Land Rover. Again he was disciplined and transferred to Special Branch where, with his IQ and talent, he should have found his niche! But next thing was that informers' money, a prerequisite for SB operation, was being spent entirely on entertainment − his. Again, and finally, he was transferred, this time to Port Police EAR & H. Archie the Arch must have realised that his days were indeed numbered. He continued to visit ships on duty and imbibe the brown amber. On one such trip, Connell and MacDonald found him on board the MV *Europa*, of the Lloyd Triestino Line, an Italian job, at the Captain's table in the First Class dining room, drunk as a skunk. His pearly-white bush jacket had been unbuttoned, his singlet and front of uniform were covered in the remains of his spaghetti Bolognaise – a bright, sickly red mess. His cap and Sam Browne were on the deck.

MacDonald found a nerve pressure point in his neck, applied pressure and whispered in his lughole, 'You are disembarking, sir' – to which he received a mouthful.

Luckily, no diners were present. Archie seemed to have got the message, and weaved his merry way in the direction of the gangway. The other two gentlemen proceeded to have a quiet refreshment in the Saloon Bar; on leaving they noticed 'hero' in the cocktail bar, cap on back of head, dragging his Sam Browne as if it were a dog on a lead. This time he did leave. When his mates returned to their buggy they discovered that 'Wonder Boy' had managed to pull out the leads of the car and the usual three 'Hail Mary's' were offered up.

For his swansong, Archie had partied into the wee hours on the SS *Kenya* of the British India Steam Navigation Co (BI). The Port Police normally invited the Matron of the European Hospital and her sisters to the party; she always accepted, provided she was invited. The ship's Officers invited the purserettes and nursing staff of the ship's company; the *Kenya*'s orchestra provided the dance music. Archie, Officer and gentleman, had fallen asleep and was not fit to negotiate the rise and fall of the pilot's cutter at the turning buoy. Despite his mates' covering for the idiot, the pussy cat was out of the bag. So it came to pass that a week later, on his return from Aden, this particular Wild Colonial Boy, crestfallen at last, paid a quick visit to the Div Supt and found himself on the boat. He ended up some years later as the rector of a commercial college in Edinburgh, his Errol Flynn-like adventures – 'My wicked, wicked ways' – at an end.

Two years had come and gone, and MacDonald had served in every section of the Police Station and returned to Crime Branch. He was awarded a 'Highly Commended' for a complicated investigation into the theft of thousands of tons of ferrous metals from the Railway, and the Asian concerned received a seven-year term of hard labour. The Assistant Superintendent for Regional Crime, based at Nairobi, was impressed; MacDonald was transferred to the Regional Crime Squad on promotion to Chief Inspector, but this elevation never eventuated as an Asian Inspector, Mohammed Sitar Khan, a time-server, had beaten him to the punch. No hard feelings. The Crime Boss, Harry Lawrence (35), ex-Met Police, had been overruled by Senior Supt Ian Dundas, the Railways & Harbours Province Commandant.

Regional Crime Squad dealt with all sophisticated frauds and paper fiddles within the orbit of East African Railways & Harbours. MacDonald would miss the Coast, with its permanent holiday atmosphere, its 500 miles of silver coral beaches, the swimming and fishing within the five-mile reef, to say nothing of fabulous hotels like Nyali Beach, Whitesands, Diani and Malindi, a world-famous holiday resort, and the quieter but equally marvellous fishing of Kilifi. Diani, a beach hotel on the south coast, was the watering hole for Inspector Charlie MacLeod, 0i/c Diani Police Station. Charlie in the first instance had the sweet posting of Nyali Police Station, next door to Nyali Beach Hotel, another famous tourist destination just outside the environs of Mombasa Island. He was supposed to be residing at the hotel until accommodation was built; instead he had installed himself in a store and was pocketing his Accommodation and Travel Allowance. For this breach of etiquette he was given Diani, plus a personal motorbike, so as to attend the weekly conference of Station Commanders. The bike became a snake-killing machine on the road in and out of town. Charles was determined to save money. Though again supposed to live in the Diani Hotel, he reverted to being a store-dweller with his pet monkey. The Indian *duka* supplied the Police Station with petrol and oil for the three Police vehicles, paid for by Local Purchase Order; the Indian thought he could throw in the odd bit of food and alcohol to meet his favourite Police Officer's needs. Charlie had two askaris out hunting to provide meat, and two more out fishing to provide fish. In other words, he had achieved the impossible: he was living free.

On a Divisional Superintendent's Inspection, Cookie the SP was almost shat upon by the pet monkey; the sign swinging in the breeze outside with the Kenya Police badge on it read 'Mac's Inn' and 'Mac's Out'. The locals' appreciation of Charlie's humour and discretion was not shared by his Superintendent. MacLeod's style was now being cramped, so he consulted the oracle and managed to have his contract determined after two years. Full pay-out was made, all entitlements and gratuity. Charlie's adventures continued elsewhere, eventually making him the No. 1 insurance assessor for oil rigs in the Gulf of Mexico – a most mercenary fellow!

As for Gus, his new posting would at times require him to travel into Uganda and Tanganyika to work with his respective equivalents, who were all Assistant Superintendents. These two Protectorates had the full Colonial Officer rank gazetted as Officer in the *London Gazette*, which gave them the opportunity of transferring on promotion from one Colonial Force to another when vacancies were advertised in the Gazette. His opposite number in Tanganyika was an ex-Glasgow Polis, MacFadyen – also ex-Scots Guards. They had played rugby together, so a few snorts of the 'water of life' were always called for at each meeting. Small world.

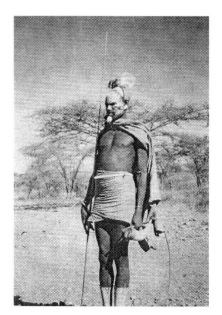

Turkana warrior, 1958

Turkana maidens, 1958

14: Not all Beer and Skittles

Nairobi was over 5,000 feet up on the Rift Valley plateau, which made for a European summer climate but called for the occasional log fire at night. It was back to lounge suits for MacDonald, as he was now a fully-fledged 'Defective' with the rank of Detective Inspector. They made an interesting team: MacDonald as the Investigation Officer, Alex Henry, the EAR & H Chief Auditor, and Chief Inspector Peter Greathead, the Prosecutor. Alex, the accountant, could pick up a fiddle of regular or 'regular irregular' figures; MacDonald collated the evidence and made up the file; Peter the Prosecutor was put in the picture with the usual morass of documentation. Quite a few enterprising Asian gentlemen were given accommodation in HM Prison, despite the usual offer of a case of dirty 5/- notes. MacDonald played rugby for the Police 2nd XV – the 1st XV were the EA Champions and had been for a number of years.

Years later, MacDonald learned that this was the stage of the game where he was deemed socially unacceptable. In one of his many undiplomatic moments he had taken the boss's secretary out – a Nairobi beauty, right down to her high heels and nylons with all the bits and pieces in the right places and a really seductive walk, pet cheetah in one hand and parasol in the other. She was engaged to one of the more unpopular Senior Superintendents, for some years known as 'The Bastard', whose party piece was to carry out inspections in the wee small hours. It was pointed out to our bold laddie that dating Senior Superintendents' fiancées was not the done thing, but MacDonald remained noncommittal and adopted his most innocent air. They visited the better nightspots in the city: Green Door, Sans Chez Ché Magambo and the Swiss Grill. Even in darkest Africa, Glasgow Polis traditions were observed: no entrance fee, welcoming drinks and meals prepared by the chef in person. Big grins all round from the African staff when Inspector MacDonald gave them his blessing in almost faultless Swahili. Happy days were here again, and the lady was most appreciative of the royal treatment.

A couple of his brother Officers in the detecting business were Dalgit Singh Kehar and Inderjeet Singh Raniga, both fine investigators. Dalgit, the traditional Sikh with immaculate turban with silver thread flap and magnificent beard, was an Olympic hockey player. His father was the best upholsterer in British East Africa. Inderjeet was a non-traditional Sikh with a European haircut who sported an ivory cigarette holder. He was popular with the Assistant Superintendent, Crime, as both had interests in the gee-gees. Dalgit had a pal in the Post Office telephone section who received all the odds as they changed around the UK and Africa. Armed with this information, many a successful bet was laid. In addition, Dalgit was his brother Officers' money-lender, as he was always flush with the folding stuff. On Saturdays, 11.30 a.m. saw MacDonald and his two Sikh friends in the Railway Bar, a mainly European watering hole. The Sikh twosome were soon accepted for their hilarious humour about having to go back to India and marry their future wives, whom they had never seen. They also opined how corruption-free Kenya was compared to the baksheesh system of their homeland. They informed MacDonald that he was 'too bloody British honest' and that there was gold in them thar hills. From the gin and tonics of the Railway Bar the trio would adjourn to the Sikh Union, where MacDonald had been made an Honorary Member and would greet the rag-heads with the Punjabi greeting of '*Sashragaleh, Burra Sahibs*' in his best Urdu. It was against the Sikh religion to drink alcohol – so everyone had a good Scotch whisky, and to hell with religion...

By 1957 Emergency Regulations had been relaxed and revolvers were no longer carried by the European and Asian population, but the cowboy atmosphere was still there. Nairobi was the hub of Kenya: everybody passed through at least once a year. The tourist industry brought in the Americans and Europeans to hunt the big game and eventually to photograph the magnificent animals of the East African plains with the green-tracked water-courses of the *mwiba* (thorn trees) and acacia over the sunlit swaying grasses, where at certain times of the year tens of thousands of animals migrated in search of water and pasture. After a night of party and dance the could toast their existence with a spot of champagne as they watched the huge African sun come up and saw the animals go down to the various waterholes – a glorious spectacle of nature at peace with itself and the world in balance. Nairobi had world-famous hotels, the New Stanley and the New Norfolk, where the settlers and tourists rubbed shoulders, and the chair-borne commandos of the Security Forces 'shot the breeze'. Many a hair-raising tale of adventure in the bush was told over a frothing pint of East African Breweries' 'Tusker' beer. The Stanley Grill on the footpath had a display of the best-looking 'popsies' of all nationalities.

MacDonald lived in the Hospital Mess, his room directly above the Mess Bar, where every night there was the boisterous sing-song of male voices giving the ruder and cruder renditions of songs of the British Armed Forces, together with representations from Canada, Australia, New Zealand, South Africa and even the odd Kenya Police reservist from the US or some ex-French Foreign *Légionnaires*. Here were the future mercenaries of the African conflicts. 'Saris Marais' from the Union of South Africa and the ever popular 'We're a shower of bastards, bastards are we', even 'Show me the way to go home' in Swahili hit the air waves. Every night, because of the noise, MacDonald was forced to go downstairs and contribute his share. Paul Westcott would strum his guitar, Doug Hill would drink his ration of whisky and report for duty – to all appearances as sober as a judge. Vernon Roberts, a crack marksman, would do his party trick by firing between the fingers of some fellow-inebriate until he nicked the tip of some idiot's finger, bent down, picked up the tip and expressed his concern with, 'I'm helluva sorry, but is this yours?'

The episode was carried off by the wounded party stating that his idiot driver had started his Land Rover and the fan belt had done the damage. On some evenings, ladies were allowed to attend. Eric Hastie, to express his disapproval, would get his box of needles out and pull them through the lobes of his ears, his eyebrows, his nose and lips, then finish off this party piece by chewing on a brandy glass, to the effusion of a considerable quantity of bright red blood, accompanied by the screams of hysterical women who could not believe their eyes. Saturday, once a month, brought the Mess Dance, the most popular night spot in Nairobi — good food and cheap drink, the best bands striking up foxtrots, rumbas, tangos into the wee sma' hours.

But as the saying goes, it was not all beer and skittles. Johnny Waugh, 0i/c Kilimani Police Station, had received information that an armed gang were going to rob a certain Indian *duka* and house, so he and a group of his police hid out in ambush on the premises. Sure enough, the gang appeared, about a dozen in number to the half-dozen police. Waugh drew his revolver, which was immediately hacked out of his hand by a blow from a panga (bush knife) to his upper right arm. Several of his askaris received gaping slashes. A corporal who had come to the aid of his Inspector had his skull fractured. Despite being badly wounded, Waugh recovered his revolver and shot dead five of his assailants. The African police set about the remainder and made arrests, despite only having handcuffs and regulation truncheons. The gang were later rounded up and given various terms of imprisonment with hard labour. Waugh and his Corporal were each awarded the Colonial Police Medal for Gallantry – deservedly so, despite some criticism that he should have armed his party. Many members of the Force received this award and in all circumstances it was well earned. During the Mau Mau operations, normal police duty was still carried out, despite a huge increase in crime, particularly in the Nairobi area. For a more romantic picture of police work you had to go to the Northern Frontier Police.

Along the frontier which borders Uganda, Ethiopia and the Somali Republic, the Force operated by mule or camel, backed up where possible by Land Rovers and Police Air Wing, and sometimes reinforced by a General Service Company. The frontier was desert scrub country of vast dimensions inhabited by various Ethiopian and Somali clans armed with Italian weapons. Their hobby was to raid into Kenya, driving off stock such as cattle, goats and camels, and on occasion committing murders, rapes and other crime. Foreign Legion-style forts were established in the border regions with romantic names such as Mandera,

Wajir, Moyale, Marsabit; they were also Divisional Headquarters. The Police uniform was also similar to the Legion's: kepi-type caps, brown leather ammo bandoliers, rifles, bayonets, sub-machine and light machine guns. Patrols would go out for three to four weeks, return for a week and go back out on patrol again, possibly in a different sector. The Police were mainly occupied disarming the nomadic bands. Sometimes patrols were attacked or ambushed, or a gentlemen's agreement would be reached that the hunt was on during daylight but when night came hostilities were called off. Many an affray resulted in Police being killed or wounded, while great feats of courage and endurance were displayed by all ranks.

MacDonald had pals in the frontier who encouraged him to put in for a transfer, as life up there was rewarding: after eighteen months, six months' overseas leave, and fourteen days' local leave every six months. Salary could be banked, as there was a Safari Allowance, plus the fact that the troops were well rationed and their Officers could help themselves. Beer was a luxury as it took up space on the supply trucks, so walls of empty gin bottles appeared. Game was abundant, shooting for the pot encouraged. Frontier hands returning to the more civilised areas would sit and stare into space for hours without speaking, deep in thought of the never-never land. Waterholes were often fought over by tribesmen referred to as the 'Shifta' (bandits). When in for a rest up at Divisional Headquarters you could hear the musical clank of camel bells first thing in the morning light as the camel train brought up water from the wells: Beau Geste all over again, and who got the ugly camel?

MacDonald, chafing at the lack of recognition, put in for a transfer to the frontier and was knocked back. Next option was Cyprus, which had an Emergency between Greeks and Turks, but again he was refused; likewise for Uganda and the Seychelles, also Zanzibar. The lust to gain promotion somehow was upon him, but before applying yet again for a transfer, MacDonald and Jack Sullivan decided to take some leave and suss out the frontier for themselves. Sullivan (35), ex-Royal Artillery, India, a Welshman who did not play rugby but was soon indoctrinated, had missed the Burma Campaign and had bomb blast to his eyes, forcing him to wear glasses and keeping him out of his desired Parachute Regiment. On completion of War Service as Staff Sergeant, Sullivan joined the British Transport Commission Police and was on the beat in Tiger Bay (Cardiff Docks), then finally joined the TA Parachute Regiment (Reserve Volunteers) and had done 189 jumps, breaking his ankles on occasion. Jack had seen action at Thika versus the Micks but due to his linguistic ability was now in Special Branch. He eventually spoke fifteen languages and was also a realist painter of famous actions and battles, including Stalingrad. Jack knew that Jomo Kenyatta was being held in detention at Loikitaung, well up in the Turkana Division, almost on the Sudan border. All they had to do was catch a Police supply truck from the QM Stores at Nairobi, journey up the great Rift Valley through Naivasha, of flamingo fame, Nakuru, the Rift Valley provincial centre, Eldoret, mainly settled by Voortrekkers all the way from South Africa, Afrikaners who had come up early in the century in search of their 'Eldorado'.

Next was the Usan Gishu Basin with Kitale, mainly peopled by British settlers who had the luck of fertile African basin pasture and beautiful cattle – verdant green to be seen, most unusual in the brown cloudy dust of Africa. Then Mt. Elgon formed the backdrop over the Ugandan border, the land of the Karamajong – tall, stately warriors. All the way up the Rift they climbed hundreds of feet until the metal road petered out and they began their descent to a couple of thousand feet below sea level, where there was a climate change and they entered a new world: 120° F (just under 50°C) in the shade was not uncommon, but not uncomfortable as humidity was zero. All the Europeans had great tans at the frontier location.

The Police truck was a five-tonner Austin, which had to be coaxed along the track serving as the border with Uganda. Here there was a border check in the middle of nowhere. They eventually reached Lodwar some twenty-four hours after leaving Kitale, having crossed dried-up river beds a mile wide and flat red ochre thorny scrub country. The occasional rain fell, causing flash floods which could be heard roaring down the stony, sandy river beds miles away; a wall of water several feet high could wash vehicles and animals away. Lodwar was the Turkana Headquarters, with a Police fort and the residence of the local District Commissioner, who extended his hospitality to the two Police Inspectors that night. Next day they arrived at Loikitaung. The Asst Supt in charge welcomed the 'civilised' pair, but he had received a signal from the Dist Comm Lodwar that they had entered a Restricted Area without permission, and it would be in the best interests of all concerned if they returned from whence they came asap. Jack Sullivan, who spoke fluent Kikuyu, went down to the detention compound where Kenyatta was being held and had a long conversation with the detainee, referred to by the Kenya Governor, Sir Evelyn Baring, as 'the Leader of Evil and Darkness'. A few years later Kenyatta was released to lead his KANU party to victory and became Mzee Kenyatta, President of Kenya. 'Restricted Area' applied to the whole of the Frontier Province, mainly to keep out unwanted persons – especially the media, who as usual would beat up stories of Police engagement and offer their unsolicited condemnation where possible without considering both sides of the picture.

Apart from the cross-border raids by the Shifta, at times fierce tribal fights would take place in other remote areas between warriors carrying bows and arrows, cowhide shields, *simis* and throwing spears. The arrows, steel-tipped and feather-flighted, were effective up to ranges of a couple of hundred yards. The fighting spear, about three foot with a bladed spearhead, was made of soft iron and razor-sharp at one end; in the middle there was a wooden part, then another three-foot steel probe at the other end. A competent spearman would easily split a target at 30 to 40 paces, and on occasion could pass through the body of the first protagonist and nail the warrior behind him. The *simi*, tapering to a broad end, was the hacking sword, inflicting grievous wounds – in fact all weapons were extremely lethal. A good fight was usually arranged so that Police and KAR were not within interfering distance. Casualties on both sides could reach 50 dead and 100 wounded. An Inspector Simpson had inadvertently got caught up in the middle of one of these miniature wars and by means of threats, pleas and gutsy bravado had talked them out of the clash. Lucky to have escaped the chop, he was awarded an immediate Colonial Police Medal for gallantry, but said he had no wish to add a bar to the decoration.

The KAR broke up these fights by mortar and machine-gun fire; hence the Restricted Area, as the bleeding hearts of the Press Gallery would not appreciate Government action. Sullivan and MacDonald retraced their steps by Police truck, leaving off the beer and mistakenly their food rations, so a couple of days' slimming was in order. Neither was any the worse for the naughty visit to Turkana, but no sooner were they back than Jack met his future wife, and the pair ventured into the very different world of Scottish country dancing at the Church of Scotland's Church Hall. MacDonald withdrew before any further entrapment could take place.

People in the Colonial Service of Great Britain her Dominions and Colonies were never well paid for their labours, but there were compensations, depending on your posting. Leave of six months paid came round every three years; advancement at a steady rate was there for those who did their duty, but the pension of two-thirds pay after twenty-five years in the sun was worthwhile. Widows and orphans got double pension when required, and education of a high standard was given. In this scheme of things, MacDonald was due overseas leave after 3½ years' service; he was also ordered to take fourteen days' local leave, as he had not taken any to date. Heading off to Mombasa was on the cards, to do a liaison job with the Crime Man at Kilindini — none other than the Irishman Edgar Wallace, who had a novel filing system: anything that was beyond his ken was hurled into the waste paper bin. Our Colonial Boy, tamer by now, visited the Port Police and uptown Messes looking up weel-kent faces. Various sorties to hotels and beaches ensured a No. 1 tan for his overseas leave. A couple of weeks later, the MacDonald bird was being poured aboard a BOAC Bristol Britannia jet to the sound of the pipes playing one of his Tunes of Glory; this time not twenty-seven hours, but a mere twelve to London Town.

On arrival, MacDonald phoned his oldest pal, Jack Cook, who was well up in the Shell Oil Company. He was informed that Mr John MacPherson Cook was in a Board Meeting, whereupon the secretary was told to put him on, as 'Cookie' was coming out to play. King's Cross Station Hotel was the venue for a few hours, then a leap along the platform to catch the *Flying Scotsman* and the laddie was home, having enjoyed First Class travel, meal and complimentary drink due to the courtesy of British Rail and his magic wand, the EAR & H Warrant Card. The prodigal son was greeted by his parents and aunts, his father, Old Bill, introducing him as Superintendent MacDonald of the Kenya Police — despite the police being, as Old Bill put it, a necessary evil. The colonial network soon came into play: his school friend, Sandy Fraser, was on leave from the tea estates of Assam in India; Dougie Simpson, ex-Captain King's African Rifles was there too at the George Hotel in Bon-Accord Terrace, Aberdeen, plus a few others from around the traps. MacDonald had scraped together £3,000 and was financially independent for the first time in his twenty-eight years. A trip to the tailor, a Standard Ten loaned by Aunts Tib and Mary, and the laddie was ready to trip the light fantastic as the festive season of 1958 got into full swing. Reunion Balls, Balls for the Tennis, Hunt, Golf — MacDonald was in great demand, though the flash of a fiver over the bar helped his cause. He was home. Everyone knew him and complimented him on his new-found happiness in Darkest Africa. Ted Warren, ex-Royal Marine Commando, now also with the Kenya Cowboys, came up to the north-east of Scotland and further helped with the scenarios. Young MacDonald was becoming a connoisseur of the better life… The local halls still had some great Scottish dance bands playing; Jimmy Shand and Bobby MacLeod would rattle out rousing Gay Gordons to regimental pipe tunes and Gaelic waltzes and the wild eightsome reels of Northern Scotland. MacDonald even attended the Auld Kirk and listened to that most articulate divine ask the better-off in the gallery to chuck in more to the collection as the proverbial hole in the roof was getting bigger.

Having visited relations of the clan in MacDuff and Banff, the fishing side of the family, he went back to see his two old 'neighbours' in the Glasgow Polis. Peter was now a hard old cop, having had his skull fractured when attempting to arrest a safe-breaker. He passed out due to loss of blood. He was now 'stick-happy', and any wrong move by Edward resulted in the hickory being introduced to the skull. Big Ian was doing well: he was out of the Polis and had his own driving school and garage. Most of his former colleagues from the old haunts of *No Mean City* were edging into seniority at last. The Polis had not basically changed, and MacDonald was repeatedly asked to return. Considered a good cop, among the very best, he was chuffed to the bollocks with the reception from his former mates and Senior Officers.

Next stop: the ancestral stamping-ground of the Isle of Skye. Portree was full of MacDonalds, so he was again at home among his ain folk. He knew some of the island girls from his Glasgow days, some real beauties with their gentle Highland lilting voices, so he was invited to the odd ceilidh, where everyone participates as the water of life is passed around to the accompaniment of fiddle and accordion, played and sung to by experts in the Gaelic tongue, a language steeped in historical mystery and full of romance.

One Saturday night early in the piece, at the Douglas Hotel Ballroom, our boy met a charming lass called Lorna Sutherland who had complimented Mac on his tan, unusual in Scotland in midwinter – or any time. Horrified by the number of drinking hours in a day, Good Samaritan Lorna said she would take Gus ski-ing the next day in the Cairngorm Mountains at Glenshee on Devil's Elbow Road. Ted Warren and his antique-dealing girlfriend joined the party. The instructions were a bit vague, and MacDonald ended up on one ski, colliding with a dry stane dike (stone wall) and breaking a couple of small bones in the right foot. After the next day's X-ray our skier went out and bought a pair of skis with bindings and a pair of ski boots; old climbing boots obviously were not the answer. But ski-ing became a passion: MacDonald went to Dinnet Hotel to meet the Swiss ski instructor Michel Bouchatay, (30), from Champéry in the Valais. There were other Swiss instructors like Jean Maurice and Fergie, all skiers of some distinction. Most were Alpine Guides. Friendships were struck up all round which lasted many years. The ski instructors were all decked out in Gordon Highlander kilts and accoutrements, and a Scottish contingent of skiers held Scotsmen's Day in February each year in the beautiful Alpine resort of Champéry.

If MacDonald was keen, so were the other skiers of Aberdeen Ski Club. There were no lifts: you had to hoof it up the hill outside Ballater, then on to the Cranwell at the Devil's Elbow or sometimes up the Letch and drop into that real country pub at Cockbridge. The weather was inclement, a mixture of sleet and rain and occasional snow. The laddie went for his daily dozen and picked up the rudiments. Eventually an old Bren gun carrier was roped in to provide a crude rope tow for a few hundred metres. Michel decided to stay on in Scotland to improve his English (Inverness speaks the best in the UK) and explore the Cairngorm Mountains. They did a few scramble climbs together, not that MacDonald had anything like the same expertise, but they climbed Cairngorm, Cairntoul and Ben Macdui – the latter even had a 600-metre ski-run in late May after they had humped their skis fifteen miles in and out. Many a yarn was swapped between climbers and skiers in the cosy Dinnet Hotel.

On Wednesday afternoons, MacDonald played rugby for Aberdeenshire in their fun games. On Saturdays he played more serious rugby for Aberdeen Wanderers. As their name suggests, they came from the Services – Merchant Navy, the Colonials on leave and from the Dominions – a grand bunch of 'wasters'. His favourite howf was the George Hotel with its three bars. Each corner and table had a different club: Etchen Climbing Club, Aberdeen Ski Club, Aberdeenshire Rugby Club, Wanderers RFC, Gordonians FPRFC, Grammarian FPRFC, Aberdeen Accies RFC; there was the East African table, the West African, Malaya/Singapore/Hong Kong, and of course the locals who had come to see the animals water. The lassies came in and out and enjoyed the company. What a pity that one had to moderate one's behaviour – no singing! When Dougal Simpson, ex-KAR, who had also trained to soldier in the Union of South Africa and Rhodesia, decided to give a rendition of 'Saris Marais', the unofficial South African national anthem, Roy the Head Barman was most diplomatic, pointing out that he would not have the pleasure of being of any further service.

A couple of years earlier it had been MacDonald's sad duty to represent his Division when Inspector Denis Bowden (27), a fine upstanding Officer who had spent years in the Frontier before joining Mac's mob at Port Police Kilindini, Mombasa, dropped dead due to a cerebral haemorrhage. Mac had also acted on behalf of the Public Trustee winding up his affairs, so he asked his mother to accompany him to visit Mrs Bowden, Denis's mother, at Newlyn, Penzance, in Cornwall.

On a visit to Edinburgh in March to see Scotland play Wales at Murrayfield, a Kenya contingent came up from the south and the Royal Café Restaurant and Gloucester Hotel were glad to see the last of the boisterous colonials, kept in some sort of order by the Chair, Mac's girlfriend of the time. By mid-June, his long leave was up; he was looking forward to returning to his Land of Endeavour.

Kenya Police Uniforms, 1960

Mosque, Nairobi, 1957

Major Jack Sullivan (Mercenary), Oman, 1972

15: From Mombasa to Marriage and Back, 1959–60

Back in Kenya, independence was in the air. Jomo Kenyatta was released in August 1961, and political rallies of the main parties, KANU and KADU, were in full swing. The word '*Uhuru*', meaning 'freedom', had made its appearance and as in West Africa it became contagious. Rallies were held even in the Mombasa Port area with its 11,000 labour, where heaven and earth were promised. The political part is easy to give but more often than not the economic side was left in abeyance. Kenyatta, the wily passive, would give his speech, tapping the floor with his leader's carved stick to signify the opposite of what was being said. The man had charisma: MacDonald was to do the odd escort and guard of honour at a later date, so he was at least on speaking terms with the future President. Despite the Emergency, the major killing time was over. Official figures tended to play down the casualty rate on both sides, but a multiple of at least three would be nearer the mark. The figures were about 10,000 Mau Mau, 200 Security Forces and about 100 settlers, as well as at least 1,000 innocent loyalist Africans.

The bitterness that was expected after the state of unrest and murder was almost non-existent and both combatants, at least the passive and moderate sides, began to work together. Britain has always educated up the rebels who eventually take over. Kenyatta had spent fifteen years overseas in England and Moscow and had married an English schoolteacher, Edna, and there was a son from this liaison. Fifty to sixty, maybe even hundreds of years after events, it has been shown that the black man does not rule well – which is a great pity, as so much effort was invested by the colonial administrators. Despite world opinion, they should have stayed longer and given more.

On his return to Africa, MacDonald was given the acting rank of Chief Inspector and sometimes Asst Supt Crime, but after a few months he was posted back to Kilindini Division to run Railway Police Station Mombasa with Voi Police Detachment, one hundred miles up the road to Nairobi. He had now passed the Inspectors' and Superintendents' Exams plus Basic, Standard Oral and Standard Written Swahili, and could at least swear in both Hindi and Urdu. Swahili, meaning 'coasts' in Arabic, was the lingua franca of East Africa. It was, like others, developed as a trading language made up from the Swahili of the Coast plus the odd words of Arabic, German and Hindi, as well as the odd touch from the Coastal tribes. Like English, it had a large vocabulary and when spoken grammatically conveyed exact meanings, attitudes and passions. Government bodies like the Police had to be at least proficient up to Standard Swahili or the Officer did not receive his annual increment.

His next move took him back to Port Police as 0i/c Traffic, Marine Section, Shipping Officer, Firearms, so he became reasonably skilled with the triple screw on the Admiral's barge, the MV *Makonde*: great for taking the bigwigs around the harbour and island, but more show than go. 'Shipping Officer' encompassed helping out the Medical Officer, Immigration Bodies and Customs, also the security of all passenger and cargo vessels. Firearms were mainly imports; the Emergency was on its last legs but a firearm was always good insurance. MacDonald rejoined the Mombasa Sports Club, where almost every sport was played, each with its own section; there was a sports bar and saloon bar in the main hall, all the various pitches, swimming, croquet, squash and running track for a membership of some three thousand Europeans. Down the Kilindini road was the residential Chini Club (Below Club), which was more for the senior department heads and the older set. There was a Golf Club on the seafront and a Yacht Club which catered for the aquatic side, but rugby was the main interest. Mombasa Sports Club had a good team of various European nationalities plus Australian, New Zealand, South African and the usual British mix; Welsh and Kiwi coaches saw that training was of a serious nature.

The team travelled extensively, to Dar-es-Salaam, the port for Tanzania, with its own magnificent sports club plus a racecourse, motor racing track, a large restaurant and four different lounges for the various sporting sections, and to play the rugby teams of Arusha and Moshi, towns on the lower slopes of snow-capped Kilimanjaro, where game abounded. On two occasions the Sports Club team travelled up to Nairobi to play at various venues, usually departing Mombasa Thursday night and returning Sunday having played Friday, Saturday and Sunday, which produced a prodigious injury rate. The club was runner-up in the EA Championship, and MacDonald was picked to play for Coast Province (Dar-es-Salaam, Moshi, Arusha and Mombasa), much to his surprise and delight. He was fit, thanks to two games a week plus weights, despite being a light thirteen and a half stone for the second row, making up for his lack of weight by various foul tactics, most of which he got away with.

As the Old Port Police Mess had become married quarters, MacDonald moved into the uptown district Mess, originally the African Mercantile Company's, a beautiful, typical old coastal colonial building of blocks three feet long and two feet thick hewn out of coral by axe. The heat of the sun could not penetrate, and there was a twelve-foot verandah: all round the building were open-and-shut, up-and-down hardwood slats. The floors were cement, painted the customary red; the houseboys polished them with their sheepskin slippers until they shone like glass. With accommodation for 35 to 40 Officers in huge quadruple bedrooms and some doubles, a dining room which could seat twenty, a large lounge with a bar adjacent, bathrooms galore with showers and baths, all beautifully tiled, and a good kitchen in the rear quadrangle, this was luxury indeed. 'Tojo', an ex-Indian Army Colonel nicknamed for his similarity to the Japanese leader, was the honorary Mess Caterer. Jim Smythe, Queen's Police Medal for Gallantry, was the Barman: he had won his medal in a celebrated murder case in London known as the Craig and Bentley Affair in which a cop was shot and killed. The underage robber was instructed to shoot and did so; the Old Bailey decreed that he swing for it, and he did. There was still justice.

'Tojo' was deposed as Mess Caterer and the unsuspecting MacDonald installed. With his Scottish frugality he managed to charge ten shillings a day messing fee, with a three-course meal three times a day, but only brunch served on Sundays. This also included a servant to do the Officer's dobhi, clean his kit and car, plus the provision of toiletries, shoe polish and so on. It was all achieved by slight of hand – the Mess was only half-full of bodies, so sporting teams and other Government servants down for the weekend were accommodated at thirty shillings per skull. Of course, the only meal the visitors had was Friday evening dinner, as the rest of the time they were out on the town. The bar run by hero Jim did a roaring trade, as drinks were half-price thanks to various donations. Senior Officers with wives would attend both bar and dinner sessions. On Friday nights musicians from various bars around town would be welcome to come and play for free drinks and food of a high quality.

Alibhai Essa and his Forty Thieves was the Mess Purveyor; and Munshi, his bookkeeper, got MacDonald out of many a spot. Jindibhai Abdul, the tailor who made the Police uniforms, could make a good profit on the generous supply of Khaki Drill; his cousin was the excellent *fundi* (craftsman), a shoemaker who could turn out excellent 'brothel-creepers', desert boots with leather three-quarter top and a sponge-like sole. Veggies came down from the Teita Hills near Voi, one-hundred miles inland; one of the Police Officers was engaged to the daughter of the Agricultural Project Manager, supplying the Mombasa market with fruit and vegetables, so he was kindly required to contribute at reasonable cost to the Mess.

At this time Ron Moyes, a Government doctor who was a Mess resident, got himself into big trouble. A detention camp at Hohola, north-west of Lamu, contained about 900 Mau Mau, all of whom had taken the third oath, which meant they all had committed murders but had surrendered. Prison authorities in charge of the camp under Superintendent Jock Simpson were unaware that oathing was still a feature of their existence. This time the oath was that they would refuse to do any form of work. When the Prison Officers realised what had gone before, they decided they would place each detainee's hands on the tool he was supposed to use, place their hands on top of his and then go through the motions so as to break the oath. It succeeded to some extent, but also produced a prison riot in which a European

Officer and two of his unarmed askaris were killed, and other parties injured.

A Company of Kenya Police GSU was sent in; they in turn came under attack, in retaliation for which eleven detainees received serious injuries, including fractured skulls and broken ribs, with lungs pierced. The injured detainees took a further oath to die – and nine of the eleven did – they lay down and died. The Prison Superintendent did not inform HQ but decided to try a whitewash. He requested medical assistance in the form of Ron Moyes, who was just out of Medical School and inexperienced in the ways of Happy Africa. The injured were treated, and Moyes issued death certificates to the effect that nine prisoners had drowned – mainly true, because of excessive blood haemorrhaging into the lungs. Dr Moyes was told this would cover up the deaths satisfactorily. Unfortunately, news of the riot had leaked out on the 'jungle telegraph' and the London tabloids were in possession of at least part of the story, according to which innocents had been beaten to death by prison and police officers in far-off Kenya. The resultant panic prompted an inquest into the affray. Doc Moyes was put on the spot and advised by his Police friends to tell the truth; his inexperience was also subject to evidence before the inquiry. He was given a 'rocket' and a few heads rolled. Hohola was immediately renamed Gallole: whether this was perfidious Albion at work it will never be known…

For bar flies, including many expat Port employees, there was no shortage of choice. At the foot of Kilindini Road, near the Main Port Gate, was d'Souza's; just up the road was the beautiful Sundowner, a restaurant/bar run by an Italian family. Splendidly done up in marble and granite, it had an upstairs gallery where you could watch the gyrations of Chief Inspector Jerry 'Brer' Fox, former Commando and ballroom dance instructor, on the floor, doing the tango and other Latin-American dances with a comedy routine thrown in. Its latest proprietors were Hong Kong Chinese whose three daughters, nicknamed May-Ling, Fan-Ling and Tremb-Ling, delighted in flirting with off-duty Officers while their parents served warm rice wine. Next came the Anchor Bar run by Aussie Paul, the oysters and Guinness, brown bread and butter a great accompaniment to a *chupa mkubwa* (big bottle) of

Tusker lager. They offered classical music during the week, but come Sunday night the gays from the various shipping lines put on a Folies Bergères performance that packed the place. Next to that the Carlton Hotel, with its '5-Alls Bar', was positively sedate, and MacDonald never found out what the '5-Alls' were. Ignorance is bliss...

Now in his 29th year, MacDonald had covered a pretty large spectrum of Army and Police experience. Rumour had it that when independence came in the next few years the expatriate government servants would receive golden handshakes before relinquishing their positions to the local population, now fast coming into more senior positions. Then, out of the blue, Cupid struck, which was not part of the game plan at all. The lady was a charming English girl who had been brought up in Kenya, the family having migrated after the Second World War. Her father, an ex-Major, Artillery, who had seen action in the Abyssinia Campaign, was with the EAR & H Industrial & Welfare Department. The two of them fell in love and, after a short engagement, were married in Nairobi. As MacDonald was then playing his best rugby for Mombasa Sports Club, the wedding was attended by his brother Officers and rugby teammates and other reprobates from all corners of the colony.

Their first night was spent at the Breckenridge Hotel, up in the Limuru Hills outside Nairobi. Next morning MacDonald suggested a large signboard was required for such an excellent hotel; management concurred, but upon departure he realised the signboard was about three foot broad and twenty-one foot long, so perhaps there had been an alcoholic haze the previous evening... On they went to the Brown Trout Hotel in the Kinangop, then down to Nakuru to board the train, the Two-Up all the way to Uganda in a First Class double compartment; their Ford Anglia also given a lift. Then, stops at Eldoret and Kitale, over the border into the Kabaka's Kingdom of Uganda, paddle steamer across Lake Kyoga to Namasagali, bus to Masinde Hotel for an overnight halt, and then Butiaba on Lake Albert, source of the Blue Nile. Joining a lake steamer of some 500–1,000 tons they journeyed on to Para on the Victoria Nile, then by launch up the river. The last few miles was a bit of bundu bashing before sighting the Murchison Falls in all their splendour.

MacDonald almost became a missionary on this side trip. Aboard the steamer was a group of nuns; the captain asked MacDonald to kindly chaperone these intrepid ladies once they were ashore. There were herds of *tembo* (elephant) about, and the *kiboko* (hippos) in the deep pools of the river, where they broke crocodile backs with one to three bites in vengeance for the crocodiles eating their young. The Game Ranger on the river was a sight to behold, flashing in and out of shallows and up waterfalls in his Hamilton jet-engined, aluminium-hulled boat. The Ranger accompanying the party urged MacDonald to *chunga* (move) his ladies along as the jumbos were coming down for their midday drink: not advisable to get between those magnificent beasts and their watering hole. Elephant annoyed would pick up the annoyance with its trunk, smash it into the ground, stamp on it or gore it — not the best way to go to heaven! Back to the Blue Nile, and another paddle boat, viewing all kinds of game on both banks, then finally over the border into the Sudan at Nimule, where members of the Sudanese Army boarded the boat and bought out almost all the booze and smokes. Independence had reduced them to an unkempt rabble. Then the newly-weds did an about-turn and returned to Mombasa after the honeymoon of a lifetime, which cost the two EAR & H employees all of £20 in tips for services rendered. MacDonald and his bride knew all the skippers on the boats, likewise the train staff, who expressed their African happiness with big broad grins and flashing teeth. The Asian staff gave a '*Tighai, Burra Sahib, Memsahib*' with a polite bow.

Back to Mombasa, 'auld claes and parritch', as the saying goes: both had jobs to go back to. Mrs being secretary to the Dockyard Superintendent, the Dockyard made the couple a complete set of furniture including packing cases. Alibhai and his Forty Thieves were generous as always and stocked their bar in spirits and liqueurs. The Indian tailor had curtains of their choice run up, also seat covers for the Government-issue chairs. The wedding list had been more than successful — colonials and the like were always a generous bunch.

The Chief Electrician at the Port of Kilindini was a Kiwi with a penchant for handgun shooting. MacDonald had licensed a firearm for him, and in exchange he took MacDonald out in his Mercedes Benz 190D and advised him to get one, as the diesel version ran on the smell of an oily rag and would last a lifetime. MacDonald was tempted, but could he afford such a beautiful piece of machinery? Narrowly avoiding the costly mistake of a new Rover, MacDonald turned to the Arab car dealer Saleh and was shown a 180D Mercedes formerly owned by a groundnut (peanut) plantation manager in Tanganyika. It still smelt new, with the original plastic covers still intact. It had been hammered over the *murrum* (stone and mud) roads, but once the shock absorbers were replaced and then steam-cleaned, *voilà* – a new Merc appeared.

On the other side of the island was the Old Port in the original Portuguese town where stood Fort Jesus, guarding the Old Port and the entrance to Kilindini Harbour. The Old Port was used by the Arab dhows which came down on the south wind and returned on the north wind to the Persian Gulf. To go out to the deep sea in a dhow – a low prow and a high poop with a triangular sail, picturesque in the sunset, built of wood and some with a diesel engine – was an adventure in itself. Some came all the way from Bombay carrying spices of the Orient and giving the Old Port a distinctive aroma; they also brought Persian carpets, offloaded by the muscle men of the Old Port. There were no unions here and the stevedores carried the cargo on their bare shoulders, a gunny bag draped over to protect them. They were all developed like professional weightlifters and would wave, chant and dance as they performed their prodigious feats of lifting and carrying, all movement being done at a graceful jog-trot. They took a great pride in their performance jogging up and down rickety gangplanks.

As time marched on, a daughter was born unto the MacDonalds. This coincided with their Long Leave, four months after a two-year tour of duty. Lloyd Triestino was the shipping line and the MV *Europa* sailed out of its registered port of Trieste. The MacDonalds boarded her at Mombasa, having downgraded from First Class to Tourist, and managed to squeeze their car on board at no extra cost. First port of call was Aden ('Where the girls wouldn't but we made 'em'); a few days sailing up the east coast taught MacDonald that he was not the good sailor he thought himself to be. The Italian ship's doctor suggested a suppository; Typical of the Wops, thought MacDonald, but surprise, surprise, it worked like a charm. Aden was still a British Base on the way to the Far East. Its Principal Officer (Mayor) was a friend of his wife's family, so a duty call was in order.

Bill Gunn had served HM the King for many years, but had an unusual hobby: he collected wild animals from Africa, mainly the East, and he had a gift of making friends with the creatures before they were shipped off to European zoos at a handsome profit. After a few perfunctory beers, Angus MacDonald thought he was seeing things: what appeared to be a bloody huge dog wandered through the lounge area. Bill scratched its ears and spoke soothingly to it. In answer to his question, 'What the hell is that?', MacDonald was told it was a young, full-sized lion and would he like to come and see the others? The invitation was politely declined and MacDonald gulped down a few rapid ones without moving from his lounge chair. His wife explained that sometimes the leopard could play up: when visiting Hamburg Zoo a new suit had been torn and ruined by an over-affectionate beast. 'Possibly not 100% trustworthy' was her closing remark: back onto the ship and a few more suppositories!

After about ten days they landed in Venice and did the usual tourist things, with trips on gondolas on the Grand Canal. It was an educational experience for MacDonald, who was most impressed with the fine cuisine, wines and other alcoholic drinks, clothes and the general standard of well-being, which appeared to be well ahead of anything Britain had to offer. Having had their precious 180 diesel offloaded, they set off north for Switzerland. The autostradas of Northern Italy were another new experience: Italian ingenuity had built roads where, at certain speeds in a bend, the camber brought the car round without steering thanks to the centrifugal force. This was civilisation. They decided to spend the night on the shores of Lake Como in a reasonable *albergo* in the heart of town. MacDonald was immediately identified by Mine Host as a Colonial District Officer (DO) from East Africa, partly due to his tan and dress, and possibly his attitude as well. The pair did have something in common: the

Italian had been a POW both at MacKinnon Road, which the POWs had built, and again at Kiganjo, the Police Training School. He reminisced as if he had been on a holiday rather than a prisoner. He served them an excellent three-course meal, followed by drinking each other's and families' health through several bottles of wine and a rendition of 'All over Italy, the girls sing so prettily' to the tune of 'Santa Lucia', camouflaging the more vulgar bits with a drunken mime. An almost good night's rest was had, despite the wire mattress sagging significantly in the middle. The night's lodging cost 35/-, suggesting that this Italian gentleman must have been exceptionally well treated as a POW.

Up the picturesque shores of Lake Maggiore and through the Simplon Tunnel to Switzerland they went. It was February and the ski season was in full swing. MacDonald had warned Michel, his Swiss friend and ski instructor, that one day he would visit and ski those great slopes. Down the Rhône Valley, admiring the towering snow-capped Alps, then up the mountain road to Champéry, in Valais. Champéry was about 3,500 feet up, with a lift up to Planachaux, another 1,000 feet higher, a plateau divided up into different ski runs – La Croix de Culet, Les Crosets, Champoussin.

Bouchatay had become Director of the Ski School along with the other instructors Gus had already met back in 1959 in Scotland, a great bunch of personalities with their flamboyant lifestyles. He was popular with the group and was invited to sit at the Instructors' Table, an honour in itself. They settled into the Pension de la Paix, run by M Monier-Stettler and family, where the cuisine was excellent. Gus's schoolboy French had never amounted to much, but at least his attempt to resurrect it would show he was trying to be polite. As a result, the locals in the downstairs bar took an interest in the Colonial Boy. Mine Host introduced him to the various spirits and liqueurs of Alpine Europe, also dishes of fondue and raclette with their cheese bases, much more sophisticated than the solid British roast beef and Yorkshire pudding. MacDonald and wife took to the slopes with varying degrees of success: a poor snowfall meant icy conditions prevailed, and Mrs Mac ended up with a black and blue posterior, much to her disgust.

MacDonald was now at the Silver (Intermediate) level but could ski most runs and enjoy the mountain scenery carpeted in silvery snow, the pinnacles of the Dents du Midi probing the southern skyline to the south across the Champéry Valley. MacDonald had a trunk full of carvings of African animals, some of which he gave to M Monier-Stettler as a token of respect — just as well, as he had run broke after five weeks on the hog's back, and his dear mother back in Scotland refused to forward money from his bank account, which she controlled on the assumption that she would never see her brand new granddaughter as long as the snow held in Switzerland. So, cap in hand, he was given a loan by M Monier-Stettler of £100 to take them over to the UK.

After a farewell party the Colonials took off for England, sobering up as they wound their way down the mountain. Snow was beginning to fall but chains were not required as yet.

They had decided to make for the Channel port of Calais, travelling through the night to avoid heavy traffic with daughter of four months asleep in the back seat. After Montreux and Lusanne, they wound over the Vosges at Vallorbe. A blinding snowstorm swirled around the French city of Dijon, and in hilly country around Auxerre they were directed to park off the road as there had been an accident up ahead. Next moment a lorry careered down the right side of the car, out of control thanks to black ice. MacDonald shot out of the car, grabbing the baby, and Mrs Mac scrambled out of the driver's door because of the damage on the passenger's side. Having asked the driver of the lorry for his particulars, he was handed a shovel and told to spread grit on the road. There was a heated exchange, both in English and French, with a bit of Swahili thrown in for good measure. Luckily, despite being lifted a few feet off the ground, the Mercedes did not roll over and down the 300-foot embankment to the right. Eventually, the journey was resumed. Much later, shaken by the rudeness of the Parisians after going through a 'No Entry' and by a rough crossing from Calais, the exhausted family arrived at the Oxfordshire hamlet of North Leigh, a couple of miles outside Witney, famous for its blankets. Jack and Betty welcomed daughter, granddaughter and son-in-law. Gus enjoyed his week's stay in the Cotswolds with their quaint stone and thatch cottages, and pubs with some decent lager to quaff. Jack had retired, and his mate, an ex-master mariner and the younger MacDonald swapped yarns of better days and harder times.

Before heading for Bonnie Scotland the Macs looked up a couple of old pals: Cookie, still going well with Shell in London; and Ken Craig, a schoolmate with whom Mac had also served in Korea. Ken had done well after being severely wounded and was now in the paper-manufacturing game. Although a brilliant mathematician, Jack's driving did not impress the insurance companies: he jumped into his car and reversed it into the Merc's front, but not to worry — it would all be part of the original bump in France. By now MacDonald could hear the pipes a-calling, and it was time to head for the north-east of Scotland and Bonnie Banchory, his home. The usual routine: relatives and old friends, a bit of Scottish ski-ing up on the Lecht near Tomintoul, MacDonald's family delighted that he was married with family.

The leave passed all too quickly and they retraced their steps for another week's great ski-ing in Champéry, where M Monnier-Stettler put out the welcome mat, his loan having been repaid. They then travelled back to Italy and boarded the *Europa's* sister ship, the *Africa*, at Trieste. A few weeks later they were back in the land they loved.

16: The Leaving of Africa

By now our laddie had completed every aspect of Railways & Harbours policing. On his return from leave he asked his Senior Superintendent about his prospects and as usual was told everything was just around the corner. But he was posted as Officer-in-Charge No. 3 Sector Kenya (Rlys & Hbrs) Police, Nakuru. He got on well with all ranks, so what was the hold-up? Nakuru was the main provincial town for the Rift Valley Province, about 100 miles or a couple of hours' drive north-north-west of Nairobi. An agricultural centre, it had had its fair share of Emergency problems. The climate at 6,000 feet was temperate, with warm days and cool nights. No. 3 Sector covered various stretches of railway track, going west to Kisumu on Lake Victoria and north-west to Uganda, plus the odd branch-line. Place names come to mind: Lumbwa, Londiani, Solai, Eldama Ravine, Gilgil, Naivasha – this was very much in the 'White Highlands', as the European farming area was called, bordering areas of Kalenjin-speaking tribes. The farming area was formerly Masai but required clearing; labour on the farms, was mainly Kikuyu. The white community were nearly all ex-Service on farms or government servants of the various departments, and all got on well.

The Inspector's residence for the Railway Police consisted of a duplex knocked into one house with a surrounding verandah. It was vast. When the telephone rang in the lounge it couldn't be heard in the bedrooms, a situation that had to be remedied. The residence stood on about an acre; there were servants' quarters for three families and a triple garage. His houseboy, Mwajalo, a Teita from the Teita Hills near Voi, and wife, had followed on from the coast, and they had a Shamba boy and wife to look after the garden in which European vegetables thrived – a half-acre of cabbage, sprouts, beans, cucumber, mealies (sweetcorn), lettuce, tomatoes, you name it. MacDonald's driver used to come round and load up the long-wheelbase Land Rover with cabbages and take them back to the Police Lines for the troops. The average African lived mainly on *posho* (ground mealies), which could be produced in many forms: porridge, pudding, roasted, boiled, and supplemented occasionally with meat, fish and vegetables, nuts and fruit, tea, coffee, milk and sugar.

The Rift Valley Club and Nakuru Golf Club housed various expatriate sporting bodies. The golf course, a par 75 rated at 73 over 18 holes, staged the Coronation Open (the East African Open Championship). MacDonald was now down to a seven handicap and was sleeping, breathing, reading and practising golf at least one hour per day. He had the disease bad! His golfing mates were Irishman John Edwards (35), the local Magistrate, and his Scottish wife, Sheila, née Cameron, from Perth. Besides playing off a 2 handicap, John was the Dublin University High Dive and Springboard Champion. The pair would startle their fellow members with their duets and solos of 'The Wearing of the Green' by Presbyterian MacDonald and 'The Sash My Father Wore' by Edwards, a staunch Catholic. They would finish off with some rebel rendition of 'The Irish Soldier Boy' – who said they could not unite the Papes and Proddies? With the help of Tusker lager many impossibilities were achieved.

Another of his golfing friends was Frank Smyth, the local vet, a down-to-earth Yorkshireman. A novel fellow, was Frank: he subdued vicious dogs by rattling their noses up and down the hot radiator. When entertaining guests he would produce his hunting horn, a thing about nine feet long, open all the windows and play quite a musical hunting call, to which his pack of pet dogs would respond and come flying through and out of windows in all directions, over, under and on top of guests, with drinks and eats also going in many directions. Just another Colonial nut, but a highly respected vet among the farming set.

Assiduous practice brought MacDonald down to a 7 handicap. He won the Toby Gibson Cup at Njoro, twenty miles outside Nakuru, both he and Edwards in great form, much to the settlers' disgust. Njoro, in plains country, and Molo, boasted the highest golf hole in the Empire at 10,000 feet. Ian Connell, MacDonald's best pal, was Officer-in-Charge CID Molo, having topped both the CID and Prosecution Courses for middle-rank Officers. Edwards played immaculate golf with his 2 wood, saying he did not require a driver thanks to his great skill. This was almost true, but he invariably three-putted the 17th and 18th due to 2 wood strain through his game. Bob Shoyer from the Coast came up for the Coronation and Bendor Trophies, the East African Open Championships; in fact there were professionals from South Africa, while Southern and Northern Rhodesia, Nyasaland, Tanganyika, Uganda and Zanzibar sent up their low-marker amateurs of 9 handicap and under. Africans were beginning to blossom – mainly ex-caddies, who were truly remarkable for the way they hit the ball prodigious distances and had a complete disdain for the rough. Some Europeans expressed the sentiment they had no nerves, even with critical putts. This was not the case: like all other golfers of note they had practised long and hard and had a burning desire to be winners. MacDonald's caddie, Mweiga, off 8, was also taking part. He was in his teens and was looking forward to *Uhuru*. Asked what it would mean to him, he told MacDonald that he would go to the biggest Indian *duka* in town and demand that the shopkeeper hand over some of his goodies gratis, otherwise he would bash in the Asian's head with his *rungu* (club with a ball end). MacDonald asked him what he would do if he, MacDonald, were the *duka-wallah* (storekeeper) and was told this would be different, as Mweiga could expect to be shot in his tracks. Not a bad summation!

MacDonald too practised hard for the Long Drive competition over 350 yards, with a fairway only 40 yards wide. He did well: out of three shots his best was 285 yards, putting him second. One of the African caddies pipped him at 287 yards. Some were creaming the ball up to 340 yards, but all over the shop. MacDonald did not do well in the main event, as his short game became a nightmare of shanking – dangerous, but only good golfers have this disease within a disease. Later on, in 1962, another Inspector, Tom Heron, 4 handicap and MacDonald, 7 handicap, took out the 4BBB Civil Service Golf Championship at Karen Country Club, outside Nairobi. The pair were delighted. ASP Hugh Mainprice congratulated them, informing Gus that he was lucky to have Heron as a partner. He was slightly deflated (hard to do) when told that Gus had finished with birdies on the last four holes. Golf was decidedly looking up.

On the more serious side of life, MacDonald's askaris had picked up a number of KKM (Kiama Kia Muingi) supporters. The latest offshoot of the Mau Mau, these were potential murderers. The Resident Magistrate, His Honour Mr John Edwards, was presiding and dishing out three-month sentences. When instructed − highly illegally − over a bottle of lager that this was ridiculous, he invited the Inspector to attend court the following day. Half a dozen men accused of being members of the proscribed KKM were brought in, and through the interpreter asked to plead 'Guilty' or 'Not Guilty'. They pled 'Not Guilty'. His Honour, who was seen to be suffering a hangover and relieving same by aspirin and gulps of water, replied, 'That's what I thought, you can have three years' hard labour.'

Later, at the Golf Club, he asked his favourite Inspector if he wished him to increase the sentencing side of things. Justice had been seen to be done.

A few months later MacDonald picked up a coded railway telegram − all were sent in code in an abbreviated form. There had been a derailment at Gilgil Station. This usually meant that a bogie or coach had jumped points and come off the rails; that was not serious, but when a locomotive came off it was a different matter. The former required a few jacks and manpower, the latter a heavy-lift rail crane. Next up was a phone call from his boss in Provincial HQ, Nairobi, requesting a SITREP (situation report by radio) on a derailment and capsizement of a mixed passenger and goods train on the line between Gilgil and Nakuru. This was a bird of a different colour. MacDonald dashed off towards Gilgil, found the derailment/capsizement and faced the sarcastic comments of his railway friends as to what had happened to their usually efficient Police Inspector.

On a curve on the line with a bit of camber, New Zealand bolts and a couple of fishplates had been taken out on both sides of the line: when the locomotive came to the join in the line, the flange of the loco would spring outwards to the rails causing a derailment, then the camber would cause a capsizement down the 30-foot embankment. The couplings between the coaches and wagons would spring apart and the individual bits and pieces with people and goods would roll down the hillside. In spite of the derailment and capsizement, the couplings had held and the whole train had rolled over onto its left side and slid down the embankment in slow motion: thanks to God, the only casualties were two African children with bruising. No other injury was reported. Obviously a prudent driver observing the speed limit had contributed to the good luck.

This piece of sabotage obviously required railway gang knowledge and the use of heavy-duty railway spanners. There were track gangs housed in *liandis* at five-mile intervals. At least here was a starting point for any investigation. The next clue was that the Mixed Passenger train was behind schedule and was followed by a Passenger train of Second and First Class coaches bringing home several hundred European schoolchildren on holiday. The distinct smell of Mau Mau or KKM had appeared. Teams of Police scoured the landies and screened railway workers at both Gilgil and Nakuru and further afield. A dozen or so suspects had their alibis and movements checked out. At this stage, particular interest was being shown in any disgruntled sacked employees, and as usual there were a number of them. One, a huge, 6' 7" Mteso tribesman from the Tororo area of Uganda, was not popular. He had worked with that particular maintenance gang in the area before being sacked for incompetence. He was a bushie, with a pair of tattered shorts and car-tyre sandals, unkempt dreadlocks and a few animal skins in place of shirt and jacket. He also carried a *simi* and a Somali-type knife. People including his workmates were scared of him. He did not communicate and drank copious amounts of *pombe* (native beer) to no apparent effect. He had allegedly been seen in the area at the time before the sabotage, carrying a railway spanner and other tools.

Our bushie was personally checked out by MacDonald. Oh yes, he was in the area and was carrying a bag – but no tools. As he trudged through his movements for hours before and after the sabotage, with his hands secured behind his back (ordinary handcuffs were too small), it became apparent that 'Bushie' was just that: a simple, honest, quiet, reticent, lonesome person who preferred his own company. His hands were unbound and he in turn expressed his thanks by bounding into a culvert followed by the Police party, who were soon to discover that he was after a wild bee honeycomb. Despite bees, wax and stings, our wild man stuffed his face – literally – with the contents, bees and all. There he was, covered in bees and honey, with the gallant Kenya Police taking flight in all directions up and down the line.

He immediately ceased being prime suspect and told the Police that a few years before he had worked with an evil man who had threatened he would wreck the line one day and kill a lot of Europeans; he had also taken the Mau Mau oaths on a number of occasions. After more enquiries the Kikuyu they were looking for was identified, living down the road in the Naivasha area. Naivasha Police confirmed his whereabouts. Over that period he had failed to appear on a Reporting Order (criminals having served over five years had to report for five years on a weekly basis to the local Police Station and give an account of their movements). Some came out as good informers. He had two sidekicks of similar disposition who had recently been released from the 'Queen's Hotel'.

Detained for questioning, they were a surly bunch. They did not speak any English and claimed that their Swahili was also non-existent and that they only understood Kikuyu. Nonetheless their alibis, which were numerous, did not check out. A mate of MacDonald's who had an electrical business and did various radio and tape recorder repairs set up a microphone in their cell, which gave encouragement for further questioning. Having been cautioned and the statutory warnings given, they were given the opportunity to make a voluntary statement. A microphone was again hidden on MacDonald's desk and his personal tape recorder in the tea room next door. This palaver started at 7 p.m. and went on for hours, because a Police Kikuyu interpreter was used, then everything had to be transposed into Swahili and then put into English by a Higher Swahili African Inspector. Although laborious and slow, typing with two fingers, it did the trick.

MacDonald had adopted the role of the new *Mzungu* (European-foreigner) in Africa who was unaware of the score where Mau Mau or anything else was concerned. The 'White

Man Fool' paid off: the main suspect, Ngoroge s/o Kamau, a common Kikuyu name, broke his silence in a violent rage, first in Kikuyu, then Swahili and finally in reasonably fluent English. 'You are looking for the man who destroyed the railway,' he raved. 'Well, I am he and you cannot prove it because I am not going to give a statement or sign any paper. Also you wait and see, I will do it again and my brothers again will be there!'

Thanks to recent legislation, the tape recording was accepted. The three men broke into uncontrollable rage on hearing their voices, stating that they were sorry that they had failed in their object. To secure a conviction, the EAR & H's Act was used under a Section dealing precisely with sabotage. The trio got nine years' IHL, MacDonald received a 'Highly Commended' and there were commendations and rewards for his troops.

One day as MacDonald was belting down the highway between Gilgil and Nakuru a 'Johnny' British soldier was thumbing a lift. MacDonald came to a halt and in climbed Aussie Potter, who had been a reinforcement from the Gordon Highlanders in Berlin to the Argylls in Korea after Hill 282. The Potter had a cheeky, upturned nose and had both arms and a considerable part of his body tattooed in commemoration of campaigns in the Western Desert, Italy, North-West Europe and Korea, which Infantryman Potter had survived despite the 50% casualty rate in each and every one. MacDonald recognised the old soldier but let Potter carry on with his 'Three bags full, Sir' for the lift, until he eventually said, 'Aussie, for Christ's sake cut the crap, I'm MacDonald, "B" Company, remember?'

Aussie, in his inimitable way, declared, 'Jesus fucking Christ, they've made you a fucking Officer, you bastard! My fucking congratulations! Oh, MacDonald of "B" Coy the Argylls a bloody Officer – and a copper at fucking that! It's good to see ya, you bastard!'

Along with his enlightening turn of phrase, Aussie was a most genuine chap – a real old sweat, difficult to fit into humdrum civvy street. He had once shown compassion to a North Korean prisoner who had his hands tied behind his back and was being booted down the road by some Yank truck drivers. Aussie stopped this and the Gook had a chance to wash his face in the nearby river and regain some soldierly dignity. Aussie was not all bad, just a wild man and a bloody good soldier, not lacking in fortitude after five campaigns. On his way to Korea, Aussie had been interviewed by one of the newshounds who wished to ascertain how an Australian had joined the British Army. He was told that one day Aussie's Pa had taken his 17-year-old son down to the docks in Sydney, where he blessed him with the following advice: 'You have the whole of the Australian Police Forces behind you and the whole of the British Army in front of you.' Could the average person ever imagine what our Scottish-Australian friend had been through in his life?

MacDonald dropped Potter off in the centre of Nakuru and, after several double rums and *chupas* of Tusker at the Stag's Head Hotel, Aussie finally arrived at the Rift Valley Club. He proceeded to expand on his various campaigns, failing to note that a considerable number of his audience at the bar were former servicemen themselves and had mostly held commissions and senior posts. Some hours later MacDonald got a phone call to come and pick his mate up, as he was now a bloody nuisance. He was greeted by Potter giving a vivid description of how the pair of them had won the Korean War on their own after repeated bayonet charges. MacDonald took Aussie to his residence, where he promptly fell asleep in his steak and kidney pie, with expressions of apology such as, 'I can't help my fucking self from fucking swearing and I'm fucking sorry.'

MacDonald drove him back to the Gordon Highlanders at Gilgil, and as luck would have it bumped into his old classmate, Colour Sergeant Bob Strachan – small world. Several weeks later they ended up at the Mafeking Ball for NCOs and the Ladysmith Ball for Officers, saying 'Hello' to several of the Jocks from the north-east of Scotland in that very clannish regiment. When next heard of on his discharge after twenty-four years' service, Aussie had bought a ramshackle house adjacent to the Gordons' camp and turned it into a brothel with African talent to service his former comrades. He never short of initiative, our old soldier!

MacDonald was then transferred back to District Police from Railways & Harbours Province. He had been up and down like a yo-yo for seven years in acting ranks: his superior considered him socially unacceptable because of his after-rugby antics, so he was informed by his father-in-law, a drinking mate of his boss, who considered him to be too much of a disciplinarian – the first and last adverse report in thirty-two years' disciplined service. Of course the letter came a day early and, keeping his temper at his presentation in Nairobi, he accepted a tankard from his chief critic, a thorough gentleman to all appearances but as a Police Officer lacking in intestinal fortitude. MacDonald gave a hilarious speech of thanks, to the amazement of his brother Officers, and had to be hustled off the stage before he went too far.

It was good to be back on the Coast, with its tropical climate of a steady 30°C and the golden sunsets over Port Reitz, travelling through the coconut groves and the sparkling waters of Kilindini Harbour. They were housed in the Mbaraki Police Lines, cramped but central to town. MacDonald was posted to 999, a Patrol Car System with an Officer, driver and two fleet-footed constables. Their job was to be first on the scene of all calls from Control: it was back to pure city police work – accidents, riots, murders, rapes, assaults, drunks, affrays, anything went. Survey the scene, take immediate initial action and call in the back-up boys of CID, Traffic, Riot Police, GSU, Scenes of Crime, even Special Branch; nothing new, all old hat, covered in ten years of service. Next up, he was the Controller in the Operations Room with half a dozen radios and telephones to play with. He was allowed to control all operations, thanks to his Superintendent's faith in him. Disappointed not to have been promoted despite all the promises, he agreed with the saying, 'Put not your faith in Princes'. In some respects he was still a naive country boy at heart and believed in a code of honour which could not be broken. A man's word was just that. Unequivocal was his way, with no reservations. He thought he should perhaps have stayed in the Army after all.

Taking refuge in his golf, he was soon down to a 2 handicap; he became Secretary of the Mombasa Golf Club, joined the invitation-only Nyali Golf Club and won the Lord Lorne Monsoon Bowl for match play. John Wylie, a fellow Scot, was the Assistant Superintendent, Kilifi, which had a prison and a golf course – nine holes with browns instead of greens. The surface was a sand and oil mix and the levelling was done by a sack pulled in a slide… not bad. The main feature was that two hundred prisoners were released from the prison where the 0i/c had trained them up as caddies and fore caddies, grass-cutters, levellers of the browns and so on. It was quite a performance to see the mob of 200 prisoners trotting down the road to the Golf Club in unison – scary but laughable. There were never any escapes: it was a day out for everybody.

Jomo Kenyatta had been released from his detention and was back in politics before the granting of independence on December 12th, 1963. He and his entourage made several visits to Mombasa, and MacDonald did escorts and helped out with traffic arrangements, plus the usual street lining by police for crowd control. In fact MacDonald got to know the African leader to some extent and found him to have considerable charisma and a great sense of humour. At times a wicked twinkle in the eye became obvious – a man who did not tolerate fools. On the opening of a new oil refinery the usual dignitaries were there for what is politely termed 'the Cocktail Party'. After the speeches by all interested parties the bun fight got into full swing. The bar staff were not dispensing beers but doubles, triple spirits of all kinds. Within an hour Hopley, the 6' 7" Irishman who was 0i/c Traffic, and MacDonald, assisted by the Police present, were dragging out the inebriates into a large shed with a concrete floor.

Tom Mboya, a Luo politician, came over to Hopley and MacDonald and expressed the hope that they were staying on after 'Uhuru'. Hopley said he was; MacDonald said he was moving on, to which Mboya rightly said, 'Yes, you tell us about a better economic future but you do not stay to see it put in place.'

At this stage one of the upcountry church types with his missionary zeal thought he too could contribute his bit to the conversation, adding, 'You must realise that all men in the eyes of God are born equal.'

MacDonald could see the look of disdain both from Mboya and Hopley, so he replied, 'Yes, I agree with you in the eyes of God, but not when he is looking down my rifle barrel.' The missionary's face expressed alarm and disappointment, especially when Tom Mboya cracked up laughing.

Chief Inspector Roy MacGregor, ex-Scot Guards, had become a Company Commander of a general service unit stationed at Likoni, south of Mombasa by a ferry ride. Roy had been jilted on the parents' instructions by a lovely Jewess. He had soon fallen in love again with a beautiful Indian dentist, Sacha Rashid, a koja from Hyderabad, one of Ali Khan's mob. In fact, the Cons/Askari directing traffic in Salim Road at Kilindini Road did not fulfil his function as Sacha literally wriggled her way across each morning on the way to her surgery. The traffic came to a halt. Ribald and suggestive remarks filled the air from viewing motorists. Sacha Rashid's uncle was a fellow member of the Mombasa Golf Club and contacted Mac requesting a meeting with MacGregor as Sacha was already betrothed. Roy MacGregor was offered and accepted 1,500 pounds sterling, a year's salary. This was to cease the romance. However, the pair flew off for a week of 'fireside wrestling' in Aden. Soni Rashid protested to MacDonald, saying that MacGregor was not an English gentleman; he was informed that Roy MacGregor was a Scottish gentleman.

The European police officers were being asked to stay on: all who did would be given two promotions, but no more. MacDonald thought he should have already had three on his track record, so as far as he was concerned it was all too little too late. What to do next? A number of his expat brother Officers had already left on the golden handshake and limited compensation scheme whereby depending on seniority, age and position you could choose a pension, gratuity or a mixture of both. MacDonald chose the latter. The ideal age was 42, with ten years' service and the rank of Superintendent. Doubling the compensation involved would have been the ideal position. Like servicemen, especially infantry, you don't join a service just for the filthy lucre, but an adventure and a sense of belonging to an organisation to be proud of. There was, too, a strong element of wishing to do good for the people in general. The African at all levels knew that he would be justly dealt with, which was illustrated in the lack of bitterness shown by both protagonists on cessation of the Emergency. Zanzibar at this time had the Africans hacking up the Arabs, who proved pretty useless in their own defence. A couple of companies of GSU were dispatched, plus the Gordon Highlanders, and law and order was restored to the Isle of Cloves off Dar-es-Salaam. Tanganyika too was in the grip of independence fever, as were many of the African colonies, protectorates and mandates.

The words 'freedom' and 'independence' are powerful catalysts for creating new political bosses, but the average person does not really benefit, as can be seen in most – if not all – of the territories formerly under British sway. At least the British gave an ideal to strive for, as opposed to our American cousins who merely throw dollars in the mistaken belief that you can buy people. The sun that never set on the British Empire was at last going down: one-third of the world had that British red over it at one time. What an achievement for such a small island nation!

The MacDonalds were blessed with the arrival of a son in February 1964. Mwajalo, the houseboy/cook, had got himself a position at the Oceanic Hotel, Mombasa, as a sous-chef, and was as proud as punch to order up a meal on the house for the MacDonalds. Mrs MacDonald had taken him under her wing and his standard of cuisine was a great achievement. The decision to leave had been made, all arrangements in hand. The pipes were playing one of MacDonald's favourite 'Retreat' marches as he and his family flew out of Africa for the last time. His education, like his understanding, had been enhanced by the sojourn in *Mwafraika Mashariki inchi ya Kenya* – East Africa, the country of Kenya. '*Salamu zote kwa ninyi note, Kwa herinikwa Watu Wote. Royo yangu leo si frai sana. Kwa heri ya kuonana.*' ('Greetings to you all. Goodbye everybody. My heart is heavy. See you later.')

Interlude

Glasgow and Australia, 1964–66

17: Paradise Postponed

What followed were two brief interludes on the MacDonalds' way to paradise. After nine years with what he thought was his lifetime career in the colonies, Mac returned to the Glasgow Polis and was welcomed back with open arms. 'The Rat' had become Deputy Chief Constable, and the Inspector who escorted Mac to his interview warned him to be on his best behaviour. 'You may have been an Acting Assistant Super,' was part of the advice, 'but you're back to the beat as a Constable, and if you don't forget that you should be all right.'

Offered a posting to 'A' (Central) Division, MacDonald asked to go back to the Working Division, 'C' (Eastern), where more arrests were made than in any other; posted to the Subdivision of Shettleston, he was given the pick of the pops, the 'gusset' beat. His 'neighbour' was Eddie Blair, known as 'Yogi Bear', the senior cop on the beat in the East with fifteen years in on the street. MacDonald now had almost fourteen years, so the old sweats were a team: Eddie was easy-going, MacDonald still ambitious, so between them they gave the public a fair balance.

The Training School Commandant, a former Provost Marshal of the Military Police, had been a Major at the war's end and was sympathetic to MacDonald: it was hard to start at the bottom all over again. After a couple of quick refresher courses, MacDonald drove to duty in his Mercedes 190D and discovered that the promotion stakes had changed in the Polis. There were Sergeants with six years' service and Inspectors with ten; all of his former sidekicks were bosses, some even up to Superintendent level, so MacDonald hoped for support for his own ambitions. But that support came from a different source. His Chief Superintendent noticed he had been a Corporal in the Argylls; he, the Chief Super, had been a Sergeant, and he wished MacDonald to apply for a CID vacancy. The Board was to sit at Police Headquarters and there were only two other applicants who he knew stood a chance. But he wished MacDonald to refuse the offer at the interview, as his quicker line to the top was through the uniformed branch. MacDonald had six Commendations for Criminal Arrests and two Highly Commended from Kenya; the other two applicants had around thirty-six, so he bent the knee to the better men and opted out.

'Grasses' were what the Police called informers, and like all informers they too had good criminal connections. Even the local Catholic Priest helped out in the fight for Law and Order!

The second-hand dealer, Harold Wilson, was a Russian Jew well up in the Masonic Lodge. He would give the cops a refreshment on the beat (a glass of whisky) which was welcome on cold days and the chance to sit at a blazing fire. Electricians would bring in scrap wire cuts, obviously new and in great lengths, which had the outer covering burnt immediately to destroy recognition. MacDonald sensed that Harold wished to speak which he did by giving him the lion's share of whisky. Beaney, the young 6' 5" cop, was keen and would have 'had' Harold on any pretext, so he was ushered out to answer the light on the Police Box across the street. Harold said if the CID was to visit such-and-such an address they would find a number of stolen TVs in the loft. Almost on a weekly basis, MacDonald was getting the good griff. Harold and MacDonald respected each other's positions. Harold said that MacDonald had the bearing of a boss and should go places and he was willing to see this happen.

Harold's brother, a former villain, and a good break and enter and steal merchant, had, after doing time, decided to further his career by setting up jobs for the boys. He would coordinate all persons and things involved, including cars and timings, also fences (resetters) to buy and dispose of the ill-gotten gains – *but* his charge in advance was 10%. What Brother was doing was a payback to any rival syndicates who were in the game. Brother ran a pub in St Enoch's Square with an Operations Room behind the bar. The information kept coming, and eventually MacDonald was put to the Regional Crime Squad where, found answering the phone, was Alex Simpson – now Detective Inspector – who had been in MacDonald's class at the Training School. He demanded to know the source, and MacDonald told Simpson where to go and what to do!!

Next up, he was summonsed to appear before the CID boss, Det Chief Supt Neil MacDonald, who offered the chance of a job with CID MacDonald suggested it would be a good idea if he spoke with his Chief Superintendent – an amicable arrangement was reached all round.

As always, Glasgow threw up more than its fair share of characters. MacDonald's patron, the personal bookie, told him that next time he was at the Carntyne dog track he must put a bet on the winner of the first race and it would become a cross roll-up right through the programme. At the end of the meet he was £600 the richer but declined to come up to the Bookies' Bar to celebrate. Jim Frame, known in Ned circles as 'Frame the Grass', had operated a kindling business down the London Road before Mac went to Kenya, and now had expanded his business. He had a number of lock-ups which he rented out, thereby creating a large yard where long-distance transport could park securely overnight. Payment was varied: 'things that drop off trucks', depending on the load, or diesel fuel, was procured for resale. James was a member of the Masonic Brethren and an Elder in the local Church of Scotland. He had over forty commendations from the Chief Constable for assistance given to the Polis – little wonder he had his own protection squad. Father O'Flaherty, the Catholic Priest for Parkhead, rewarded the boys on the beat for their attendance at Christmas Mass with communion cake and a few glasses of good malt whisky. He and Yogi Bear used to lord it in the back seat of the Holy Friar's Rover 90 with Gus at the wheel; on each corner he would point out the Neds that should get the gaol for a variety of good reasons, both domestic and criminal. Gus wondered if the odd breach from the confessional was added for good measure.

The Boys had a one-legged man on their beat, a real big, awkward, dirty Ned who wore a ragged evening suit. His modus operandi was to enter the bar of a public house and demand a 'hauf and a hauf' – whisky with a beer chaser. If prompt service was not forthcoming he would take his crutch and smash any glasses within striking distance, and go on his merry way. He was about 6' 2", weighed a good 15 stone and could hop on his left leg like a two-year-old. If you were silly enough to attempt an arrest, he would sit with his back to the wall feigning unconsciousness, then suddenly strike out with the crutch across the unsuspecting shins. After the arrest he would jettison his crutches and bring all his weight to bear on the arresting Officer. A charming fellow. MacDonald had arrested this clown about six times in his return year when he began to think once more of warmer, sunnier climes. The day they moved in to their £4,000 house in Old Cathcart, Mrs MacDonald said she had a gut feeling that they would be on the move again, and eighteen months later this was to come to pass.

MacDonald had met both an Aussie and a Kiwi at the Crow Wood Golf Club, where he was a member. Mac had already applied to emigrate to New Zealand but would have to pay his way, which meant an outlay of £3,000 to get all his goods and chattels to the Land of the Long White Cloud. Although he was said to have great prospects in the Polis, and still believed they were second to none, after the sun of Africa he could not stomach the climate. Besides which, the Brits were too slow to adopt or adapt to any new ideas. The NZ Government had a job for him as a screw (Prison Warder), but his reaction was it was bad enough being a cop and arresting the villains without having to cohabit with them. His dream was more golf and ski-ing, even if that meant no advancement. His Aussie mate said there was plenty of both in Oz, which surprised him as he had not realised there was snow in the Great South Land. He tried the Victoria and New South Wales Police. They regretted he was six months over the age limit, but said try Tasmania, which he did; and after an extended parley, was accepted. The Australian Government paid the airfares with only a £20 contribution required: God was still smiling down on MacDonald. He bade farewell to old Glasgow Toon with regrets at leaving the Polis, such a fine body of men.

After 27 hours' flying, via Singapore and Darwin, the immigrants arrived at Tullamarine Airport, Melbourne, Australia. It was early January: midsummer, bloody marvellous − the sun shone again and there was a beautiful blue cloudless sky. Next day, off to Tassie, their new home. They were greeted at Hobart Airport by an Inspector of the Tasmania Police, George Dowling, who proved to be more British than the British. Like the taxi driver, he asked Mac again what he thought of Oz and was told, 'Good, Sir, but ask again in a few weeks for a more elaborate answer.'

They spent the next week in a guest house in North Hobart where Mine Host was an ex-Infantry Lieutenant, so the pair got on well. Gus was warned to look out for Aussies — they were not all honest. At the local, the beer was good and the locals showed genuine interest in the latest immigrants. So far, so good.

MacDonald reported to Police Headquarters and was told that the Training would begin in a week or so, as they were putting together a class half made up of local recruits and half of migrant personnel, and that he should, like the rest, report to the Inspector i/c Traffic. Their duty was washing, cleaning and polishing police vehicles. The recruits had been given grey overcoats as overalls. On the second day MacDonald was called into the 0i/c's office and told to put on a white overcoat as he appeared to be an experienced man; also the Inspector had a problem in that the readings in the underground tank and the records were not balancing. In fact there was a considerable discrepancy, and Mac was told he would have to be very exacting in his new position of Chief Petrol Dispenser at the pump! On dipping the tank and comparing the records there was indeed a considerable loss showing. A vehicle would roll up and the Police Officer would shout out, 'Just fill her up, cobber!' and then jump in and drive off. By the end of the day the dip in the tank and the records matched up, to the delight of the worried Inspector. He was informed that there was nothing to it provided that the vehicle logbooks were not checked for the monthly return. What logbooks? There was a little embarrassment caused when half an hour after being 'filled up' the motor cyclist was seen pushing his cycle back into the yard with an empty tank! 'G'day cobber, you all right?' was replied to by an obscenity. My, my!

When the class came together the following week, who should be there but Willie Foster, alias 'The Bosun', from the same Subdivision of the Eastern Division, Glasgow Police as Mac. The

Bosun had been just that in the Merchant Navy. His method of arrest was to grab the offender by the throat and apply pressure until he was told to desist, as the culprit was indeed choking. Willie never did have too much finesse in his approach but was immensely powerful both in body and head, a most determined individual. He was a cabinetmaker of considerable skill and imagination. He also made some beautiful knick-knacks with rope, having been schooled in the intricacies of splicing, jointing and knots when at sea. The training instruction was given by two schoolteachers, Mr Yaxley and Mr Hooper, and Sgt Thomas, formerly RAAF, so the recruits were given rudimentary Arithmetic and English, plus an introduction to Australiana.

Sergeant Thomas's instruction seemed barely related to any police work that MacDonald had experienced. The course seemed aimed at raw recruits (50% were not, of course), who would remain in their ignorance for years to come. The other Instructor was Constable Peter Collins, ex-Sgt, The Black Watch. His speciality at this stage of his career was Drill and PT. The Swimming/Life-saving Coach also taught some First Aid, a real down-to-earth bloke who could see that most of the Pommie bastards had a fair bit of experience at various levels under their belts and treated them as men, not nitwits.

Arthur Baker, a Londoner from the East End, had been a Detective Sergeant with the Flying Squad. Arthur was around 6' and had done a fair bit of boxing in his youth, a nimble-witted cop who loved to have a flutter on the gee-gees. He had the Londoner's quick sense of humour and the ridiculous, similar to the Glaswegian's. He and Mac teamed up both in the life-saving and the gym, where they made sure they played games on the same side. Ray Knowles, a big Pom from one of the Midland Police Forces, did not take a liking to Mac for a variety of reasons. He liked to obstruct Mac in the various games, so when they jumped for a ball, Mac just happened to bring his elbow down into the big fella's nose. True to character, he immediately started to kick out. Mac and Baker had a good laugh, which did not spread oil on troubled waters.

During the Arithmetic session, a former bookie's runner would shout out the answers before Mr Yaxley had completed his write-up on the blackboard, which was most disconcerting. The poor devil got 49.5% in his exam, as he failed to show any working, although the answers were 100% correct. Baker and MacDonald soon twigged that Sgt Thomas, despite his 20-odd years, had seen little real police work and was a theory man: it was important to define a 'Public Place' in twenty-eight different ways verbatim, but when it came to defining the various crimes, only 'Stealing' was mentioned, as the CIB would deal with crime and it was of little consequence to these ignorant recruits.

By now the Macs had rented a house at Sandy Bay, one of the better suburbs in Hobart. They did up the garden and cleaned up the house, much to neighbours' delight, as the previous lessees had left a mess, both in and out, and were thanked by the owner. In the local park one Sunday morning the Derwent Pipe Band put on a show, much to Mac's delight, as they played some of his favourites with flair. The local pub even served him 20 oz (pint) glasses of Cascade beer. The brewery was situated on the majestic slopes of Mt. Wellington, which gave a great backdrop to Hobart and Constitution Dock, where the world-famous, gruelling Sydney-Hobart yacht race finished. The Commonwealth Bank gave them a 4% loan for a new house on the Eastern Shore, at Howrah, on the other side of the Derwent River from Sandy Bay, a modest three-bedroom place beautifully finished with Tasmanian Oak panels. The lounge had a huge window facing across from Sandy Bay, taking in the Derwent estuary, the new Derwent Bridge, which deep sea ships could pass beneath to collect the zinc upriver, over to Constitution Dock, with Hobart rising up the eastern slopes of Mt. Wellington's 4,500 feet: a magnificent panorama of water, twinkling city lights, forest bush and rocky crags. It was midsummer and the temperature in the low twenties Celsius, but with plenty of sun: not the expected warm climate, but a very temperate one.

They could not have thought more highly of their new neighbours. 'Jenny' Jenkins, a retired master baker, now on the wharf exporting the world-famous Tassie apples, and his wife came over with a case of apples. Jim Carter, the Holden Sales Manager, dropped off a load of firewood with an invitation to the Yacht Club where he was Vice-Commodore. Johnny Chick, a former aerial ping-pong (Australian Rules Football) player from Carlton in Victoria brought in a case of beer and an offer to play at his golf course at Lindisfarne; and Ken Funnell, ex-Uganda and now the engineer on the hydro-electricity dams of Tasmania, came with an invitation to dinner. This was the beginning of a Sunday barbecue rotation of all the neighbours through the winter months, which gave freezing nights with snow on Mt. Wellington and clear blue skies with sunny days. Shelley (5) and Richard (2) really enjoyed themselves, and so did the MacDonalds, but alas the ambition bug was still biting!

The 12-week training period dragged on with little learned, but he did pick up how to frame a charge in detail from the Act or Ordinance, that was something on the plus side. Excellent barathea blue uniforms were issued but were still fifty years behind: brass buttons, belt buckle and cap badge had to be polished daily, and a pair of exceptionally broad beetle-crushers (boots). The cap service dress had a white plastic top just like the Victoria Police: everything, it seemed, had to come from the mainland. Reports had to be written in quintuplicate, with the various addressees getting a different-coloured paper. After the first three weeks Mac realised he had jumped from the frying pan into the fire. In Glasgow he had won his fight to have increments paid for previous service in other Forces, but not seniority. He was told that he would be sitting his Inspector's exams in fifteen years' time and they would be promoted at thirty years' service. Now it was time to hook up and jump! Pay was also less than previous, with few or no prospects. The Tassie Police had only 700 personnel, equivalent to two small Divisions, so advancement was out.

He had come a satisfying third in the class results. At 35, he was the oldest; one of his mates was the youngest at 19, and the brightest − he had just topped the class in all subjects. Mac thought of becoming a lawyer, but not with much enthusiasm, so he went to the Commonwealth Service and took an intelligence test in which he did not badly. His young mate, David Mee, an expert in such matters, said, 'Take another and speed it up,' which he did; he got a much higher rating and was told he could become a doctor, but his age was against him. He did especially well on the mechanical side of things — 90% in this section — by spinning the lucky coin. The good news was that the Commonwealth Government was recruiting Sub-Inspectors for the Territory of Papua and New Guinea, a Colony and Protectorate up in the tropics of the South-West Pacific — Melanesians, black fellows. Contracts were being offered for six, ten, twelve and fifteen years. It was now or never. The other side of the hill had always been greener, so why not?!

Application was duly made, and an interview came six months later. The interview, when it came, was short and sweet: MacDonald was most acceptable for the position as Sub-Inspector due to his background and previous experience, but to use up the time remaining would he like to expand on the reasons why he was leaving the Tasmania Police? MacDonald answered the Force reminded him of visiting Disneyland, and that if the Interview Officer had a couple of hours to spare he could elaborate, but was told that in the present circumstances it might be best to disregard the question.

It would be four months before he heard the 'Tally-ho', so all in all he had ten more months to serve. Back on the beat, MacDonald's Inspector — in fact most of his Sergeants — always addressed him as Mr MacDonald, so at least some presence was acknowledged. There were a number of transfers from other States, mainly due to the fact that the blokes had married Tassie girls who wanted to live in the Apple Isle. Some of these fellows had been Senior Constables, Sergeants and Senior Sergeants, but like everyone else they had to start from scratch, like a qualified electrician having to do his apprenticeship all over again.

One late shift his Inspector told him to go to the Royal Brisbane Hospital and escort a prisoner back to the Royal New Norfolk Hospital. Trooper MacDonald fronted up and the Sister on Duty asked if he wished the patient tranquillised; it was not necessary, as the prisoner was okay. Then the penny dropped: it was a 'nut' from the 'loony bin'. The patient joined the trooper in the rear of the ambulance, the driver up front and the second man a retired Inspector of the Force. Off they went to the Wild West Show. The patient, a powerfully built fellow who would take more than a little subduing, informed MacDonald that to date he had only killed three people. Mac immediately plied the patient with chewing gum, cigarettes and understanding conversation all the way to New Norfolk, where the dangerous ones got the royal treatment inside a compound with a huge cement pit with cornice overhangs so that even a mountaineer if trapped behind these bars would have great difficulty in getting out. On his return to the Police Station, MacDonald expressed to his Inspector as respectfully as his rage would allow him what he exactly thought of the situation.

Late shift on Saturday was a good huckle for Gus. He made eight arrests with the help of his Special Constable driver, who managed to open the door to the rear seat. First arrest was 'Obscene Language', a Greek café proprietor getting his pedigree. Another couple were for an 'Affray' (punch-up), next was a couple of 'DUI' and 'Unlawful Use of Motor Vehicle'. One vomited when the vehicle door was opened, the other fell out of the car in a heap, unconscious. Next came a couple of diggers having an up-and-downer on the footway next to the cop shop. When placed in the watch house it was discovered that both were ex-3 RAR, and like Gus had done a 'Make Korea your Career' bit. A 'Breach of the Peace' was scrubbed and replaced with 'Drunk and Untouchable' with a pound bail to be estreated when they failed to appear before the Resident Magistrate's Court without proceeding to conviction. Gus was now a good Tassie cobber. But on Sunday morning he was called to report to the Superintendent in uniform. What had he done now? After a smart salute and a most cordial 'Good morning, Sir', he was informed that he should take it easy, as eight apprehensions on a single shift was over the top!

Having done nine months, MacDonald was posted to Bellerive on the eastern shore of the Derwent. There he did car patrols with his 'neighbour', a regular trooper, and discovered that the crowd here were a better mob. His new Sergeant was all right and his new District Inspector, George Manning, was an easy-going expert in Australia's history, flora and fauna, a most pro-British, educated gentleman. He even drove an old Armstrong-Siddeley. Manning took a shine to him and had him posted to Sorell Police Station as Acting Sergeant: the Sgt i/c was sick and the rest of the crew were all Senior Constables who did not wish to offend each other — the promotion system was such that one applied on a seniority basis, implying that the applicant had more than the others. This occasioned continual bickering, backbiting and a perpetual filling-in of curriculum vitae which consumed unlimited police work time. So MacDonald was detailed off and given a car to work split shifts, four hours in the morning and four in the late afternoon, and to report at Sorell, about 35 miles outside Hobart.

His job was to do up the Duty Rosters and the Overtime, but he did get to travel around his new area, which was mostly in the 'sticks': Richmond hamlet, with its famous convict-built stone bridge; further up, Carpentaria, another farming hamlet where the publican most generously invited him in for a drink; and on the waterway nearby, Dodges Ferry, where he saw his first Australian wood-chop and the mighty men who competed in the various events.

In one week he had seven serious accidents to attend, one where a wood-chop party had won the event and their celebrations ending up in trying to knock down a gum of 6' girth. The driver was scalped and the passenger had at least six compound fractures. The surfies lent a hand by holding the car above their heads for about half an hour while MacDonald did his damnedest with his limited first aid. He managed at least to say all the right things to the badly smashed-up pair, who responded — in fact their alcohol intake may have delayed the shock.

Powerboat races, open-air barbecues, surfers searching the coasts for the big waves: MacDonald was just settling into rural Tassie society, where the people on the whole were excellent. Then it dawned on him: the average trooper did not join this Force to catch the criminal but to get a country posting where he could shoot, fish, and have a government house where the local farmer presented him with the required farmyard animals and seeds to run his own hobby farm. All very nice, but unfortunately this laddie had another game plan...

To round off his career in the Tasmanian Police, MacDonald did have a high-speed chase over thirty miles one night on the way back from Dodges Ferry to Hobart. The idiot driving was eventually taking corners on the wrong side of the road, although most of his driving had been first-class. MacDonald backed off, switched off his lights and followed overtaking and signalling to him to pull over, which he did. Girlfriend was shaking and white as a ghost; boyfriend was off next day to Pukapunyal to do his Infantry training. He was told to look at the state of his girlfriend and try and think, but good luck with his soldiering, hoping that he too would be lucky in the service of his country.

A few days later the long-awaited letter to report to PHQ Port Moresby arrived and was received with relief. Wives and family were not required but would be notified, the usual Government guff. Surprisingly, MacDonald got a 'Good' Discharge and was gratified, if only to have escaped 'Fletcher's Follies'.

Part Four
The Paradise Years, 1967–82

18: Back Where He Belonged: 'Mosbi' and Rabaul

On January 5, 1967 MacDonald set off from Hobart via Sydney and Brisbane, and as the flight continued out of the Queensland capital he was joined by a smartly turned-out gent in a brown suit who communicated with a pronounced Glasgow accent. By the look of him he could be a cop: quick, intelligent eyes and a sharp sense of humour. This was Tom Mulhern, ex-Glasgow Polis, twelve years on that Force and in the same age group as MacDonald. After a few words they shook hands and had a few laughs on personalities they both knew in the Polis. Tom's Dad had been a long-serving Sergeant in Govan Division; Tom had become a painter to trade, as his Dad could not afford his university education, and had wandered over most of Queensland doing contract painting jobs but had heard they were in need of Contract Officers in the Royal Papua New Guinea Constabulary.

On the trip up Tom was interested to learn MacDonald's background and did a bit of pumping. His main concern was that MacDonald had previous 'colonial experience', but how was he, Tom, going to get on in the job? MacDonald's advice was to get into Police HQ and say a polite 'Good day' to all the Senior Officers, give a respectful salute and do nothing controversial, but keep his nose brown. Was that what MacDonald was going to do, Tom asked? 'Definitely not,' was the reply: Mac would get himself as far from Port Moresby Police Headquarters as possible.

At 6 a.m. on January 6th the pair emerged into the tropical sunlight of Jackson's Strip, Port Moresby: not much of a building, with restricted amenities. Where was the reception committee? Not a dicky bird in sight – an inauspicious start for the Royal Constabulary. A taxi to Police Headquarters, where it was hoped they could freshen up, shave and shower, but it was not to be. They ended up being ushered in to see the Commissioner, Colonel Bob Cole MC, who had been a member of the illustrious band of 'Coastwatchers' who sent messages back from behind

Japanese lines in World War II. Mac was told that the cricket bat methods of the Kenya Police were not acceptable, while Tom was asked what he had done in the Glasgow Police. If he had been in Sydney, he replied, he would have been in the Vice Squad, but in Glasgow he was just a 'whores' man'.

They were quartered next door to the Port Moresby Police Station in Musgrave Street in the heart of town, where they were joined by Bill Southby, another budding Sub-Inspector. A hausboi appeared, introduced himself as Michael, claiming that he was a good 'bush cook', and so it proved: he cooked the bacon and eggs in water, as there was no cooking oil available and made a few other faux pas before being given the Order of the Boot. For the next two weeks they were given an indoctrination/orientation course at the Police College at Bomana, a few miles outside Moresby. As they were experienced Police Officers it was more or less 'Collect your uniforms and equipment, and here are the various Ordinances and Acts you will need, together with the Queensland Penal Code and Procedure Code, and you had better get a book on Neo-Melanesian by the Rev. Francis Michalic, the best Pidgin language instructional.'

Superintendent Robbie Robertson, formerly of the Scots Guards, was the Commandant, and doubtlessly the best Drill Instructor in the Territory – which he demonstrated with relish, giving a show of impressive pace-stick prowess. He had the new boys take command of recruit squads and give them drill, which to MacDonald was nothing new, but others floundered a bit. Other Instructors were mainly expat Brits; a few, like MacDonald, had colonial experience and were known as 'The Africans'. John Revill was the musketry man and had been a Bisley shot when serving as a Sergeant with the Cheshire Regiment in Malaya. The new boys fired off a couple of courses with their .38 Scott Police special revolvers, and a few rounds with the .303, and most seemed reasonably competent. The Instructors at the Police College had it made. Good accommodation, Officers' Mess, gym, swimming pool, squash court, and the Force QM had his store at the College.

The local recruit constables were given a comprehensive six months' course and were well trained, considering most were literate only in Pidgin. They were of good physique and robust. The South-West Pacific has Melanesian people who are dark in colour, ranging from brown to black; in the Territory around Port Moresby there was also a considerable population of Papuans, who were of Polynesian stock and spoke a language similar to Maori and Hawaiian, indicating the places they had most likely come from in the past.

After the orientation, both Mulhern and MacDonald were posted to the Port Moresby Police Station, which had the Divisional Headquarters. The set-up was the same as Kenya. In fact you could go from any of the Colonies, Mandates, Protectorates or Territories and you would find the same procedures and basically the same laws being used. Their role was that of Duty Officer, which means you run the Police Station and direct persons to the various sections such as CIB, Traffic, Prosecutions and so on, but the General Duty stuff – Drunkenness, Offences and all the minor misdemeanours – is all yours. Life is hectic at this level but this is where the trade is learned.

In quieter moments Tom and Gus would go out in the 999 vehicles, which were Toyota Land Cruisers – a great multi-purpose vehicle. They would go round the various pubs and lock up the Drunks and Disorderlies with the assistance of the two constables and the driver. MacDonald's first week back on General Duties resulted in five European arrests, all Dutchmen off various ships. Tom had a revolver stuck in his ribs by a Norwegian ship's Officer at the Main Wharf: he too visited the cells. The various patrols had competitions as to who would make the most arrests, all good stuff. Usually the four Police vehicle crews would lock up around 100 on their shift. They had derived a conveyor belt method where even the most illiterate constable had his little piece of action to deal with. They began to pick up a little Pidgin and Motu, and they would instruct the prisoners how to plead when in court the next day. A score or so would be paraded and in unison shout '*Sori Masta mi mekim*!' – which had the desired effect of a 'Guilty' plea. The holding cell they had devised was more like the Black Hole.

Before 1964 the native population had not been allowed access to intoxicating liquor, except their home brews and palm wine. The years 1965 and 1966 had seen a dramatic rise in crime. The previous verandah-style justice dispensed by the Kiap and Police Officer, such as 'Kick him up the arse, Sergeant Major,' was no longer a deterrent, and the regular Police had found themselves unable to cope with the new 'liquor' situation. Self-government was being thought of, so what to do but get a new breed of Officer – on contract for four, six, eight, ten, twelve or fifteen years? As the British Empire was dwindling, the obvious choice was to use people with previous experience, as a result of which the composition of the Force was maintained at 50% Aussie and 50% Brits. There was little or no rivalry between them. The Regular Officer was better paid and also had an exceptionally good pension/superannuation scheme, much superior to the Contract Officer's gratuity. This was a pity, because it did cause some misgivings. The Regular was delighted to see the Contract Officer, as at least he would be promoted on the 'seniority' way of thinking, and the Contracts would do most of the operational police work.

After three months, MacDonald was posted to Rabaul, the Islands' divisional centre. He was glad to leave 'Mosbi' behind – an unsafe place, as it had been since its inception in 1883. Formerly the administration capital for Papua, which was British, it was handed to Australia to administer in 1902 before the country became the Australian Territory of Papua in 1906. Of course as time progressed it became a squatter city. Moresby was also a dust bowl and could have dry spells of up to nine months, which frayed tempers. The indigenous squatters came from all over the Territory and would fight each other, sustained by the *wantok* system, whereby relatives would descend on the house, room or hut and stay with an individual until he was out of provisions to cater for them. A form of social welfare, the system falls down after a time, so everyone reverts to stealing to provide for themselves.

There were three main companies in the Territory: Burns Philp Ltd, Steamships Trading and New Guinea (Carpenters); they had virtual monopolies on all goods imported and exported, they owned supermarkets, stores, taverns, ships, plantations, docks. Besides the local population, the Chinese element had a variety of stores selling their wares to all.

The two airlines operating the main routes were Ansett-MAL and TAA. The main aircraft was the 35-seater Fokker Friendship, which took around two and a half hours for the 500-mile flight from Moresby to Rabaul. Out of nowhere appeared its surrounding volcanoes, all still active; vegetation was the tropical lush verdant green and the sea in the lagoons a deep crystalline blue. Simpson Harbour was in the shape of a horseshoe, with the cloud-topped hills of New Ireland in the background and the idyllic Duke of York Islands lying off Praed Point to the south-west − a real Pacific Island setting, and a magnificent panorama. The Fokker came down steeply and landed quickly on the airstrip near Matupit Island. Hot tropical air gushed into the plane and a Tolai voice said, 'Welcome to Rabaul.' MacDonald felt the same feeling he had in Kenya: he was back where he belonged, and chuffed to be there.

This time he was met at the airport and whisked off to Divisional Headquarters for the Islands, which include Manus, Bougainville, New Ireland and East and West New Britain. This was the heart of former German New Guinea, on the sea trade routes. At Divisional HQ was '5 foot 17½-inch' Chief Superintendent Brian J Holloway. At 37, Brian had done well and was to go further. He had a twinkle in his eye and welcomed the new arrival, explaining that the Tolai, the local inhabitants, were the most sophisticated in the Territory, and he felt sure MacDonald would enjoy his posting. The single quarter was excellent, right down to new fridge and washing machine. An apparition with the figure of Buddha, middle-aged with bright piggy brown eyes and a cheeky grin, said, 'I'm your *manki-masta* and before I worked for Inspector Max Hayes, he was a good man.'

Sure enough, Butt Solumun, a native of Narmordu near Namatanai, New Ireland, was to prove a faithful servant for the next ten years. He could cook well and do the laundry, spit-polish boots, belts and other leather work. He had been well trained and was about to receive a second dose of 'civilisation'. Later they discovered that he was a 'black' remittance man sent out of his village for attempting to take over the Council business. He owned a copra plantation and was possibly better off than his new 'Masta'.

Next day, having met 0i/c Station, Senior Inspector Noel Cooper, formerly a rugby league champ with the Paramatta Eels, Mac was back as Duty Officer on shift work, with his own shift of about forty men to count. Rabaul had been laid out as a vast arboretum, its two main roads, Malabunga Avenue and Mango Avenue, forming a letter L. There was a Chinatown where the Chinese community did a good tourist and local trade. The Chinese originally had been imported as coolie labour for the plantations in German times, but were not traders then. Burns Philp, Steamships and the New Guinea Company were on Mango Avenue; there were a couple of hotels with boi bars, the Cosmopolitan and BP's Tavern; also the Kaivuna and the Travel Lodge, a wharf area which took large ocean-going vessels and island traders. Namanula Hill was where the Heads of Departments were ensconced, with a view over Simpson Harbour. This was a tropical paradise with 30°–33° Celsius, and 75% humidity and higher. There was a Malay town too, where an Ambonese community resided, and an Indonesian restaurant called 'Marsalaam'.

At the apex of Mango and Malabunga Avenues was the market (*bung*) where you could buy just about any fruit or vegetable for one mark (a shilling), fish, chook, coconuts, galip nuts, plus free-range eggs, *kaukau* (sweet potato), *kindams* (crayfish) and *kukas* (crabs).

The Tolai people were friendly, polite and pleasant and always good for a laugh. Kuanua, the language, was light on the ear. They claimed they were an offshoot of the Fijians, and they certainly were a handsome, well-built group of people. Most of the males displayed European-style tattoos which they had done themselves. They had copra and cocoa and some cattle; they came to market in their half-trucks by the hundreds and stayed behind on Fridays and Saturdays to drink the South Pacific brew, brown and green bottles of beer by the carton, and were quite happy to spend a night in the cells sleeping it off. In fact MacDonald's servant was a great exponent of the amber nectar, he too sleeping off its various effects in the drunk tank.

MacDonald was a member of the Rabaul Golf Club, a nine hole course out towards Matupit and the airport. At this time the President was Mike Wilkinson, a pharmacist, and the Captain was Brian Capp, an accountant. MacDonald was soon back to a 6 handicap and was co-opted as Captain of the club. He also played at Kokopo, Kerevat and Vudal, all good nine hole courses. The climate ensured that the couch grass both on the greens and fairways grew in profusion. Huge, 100-year-old mango trees provided shade, challenge and character, while hibiscus and crotons grew everywhere, making up demarcation lines in the way of fences and boundaries. All you had to do was get a sapling and stick it in the ground in a diagonal pattern and within weeks you had a flowering or shiny-leafed *tanget* (boundary).

When you played you could smell the sulphur from the Southern Daughter, a nearby volcano. The last eruption had been in 1937, when Vulcan Island emerged from the sea as a new volcano. Several thousand people lost their lives, but despite the menace of an eruption Rabaul carried on. *Gurias* (earth tremors) were experienced regularly, right up to seven on the Richter scale. In the Namanula houses, furniture would move round and some decking in the town would spring loose — an eerie experience when the ground moves and shakes under one's feet. *Gurias* could bring down mudslides, blocking roads. Tsunamis — sudden tidal waves varying in height from a few feet to much more — caused flooding in the town. Kokopo, some twenty miles south-east of Rabaul, had a magnificent war cemetery, Bitapaka, where Australian and Allied dead had been buried and remembered. The cemetery, where locals and visitors alike paid their respects, was a mass of beautiful tropical flowers and trees, the grounds trimmed to perfection. The commemoration plates read like a history book, while an abundance of decorations paid tribute to their sacrifice.

Having been in the Territory four months, MacDonald sent for his wife and family. The single quarters was divided up into compartments by the judicious hanging of bed sheets. A week or so later, a quarter was found next door to the Senior Ships' Pilot, a real old salt almost smothered in British tradition — hard to beat! Son went to the local kindergarten and daughter to the international primary school, and wife had a job with a local tourist company.

The family car arrived along with personal effects. One day Mac received a telephone call from his better half and was requested to help out by taking a couple of Yanks and their daughter out and about to see the sights. Why not, as he was on night shift? The Yanks, as usual, had to show off their superiority. He took them to Praed Point to view the Duke of York Islands and Kokopo across the harbour, and the six-inch guns at the entrance to Praed Point, relics of the Pacific War. Next up were the various volcanoes, the town centre, a short trip to a copra plantation, a view of the Blue Lagoon to see the Tolai fishermen with their bamboo fish traps, then a visit to the War Cemetery for lunch and a couple of drinks served on an immaculate white tablecloth and napkins of the best Irish linen.

Then by accident they landed in a Tolai village where they were holding a wake at the *matmat* (burial ground), all done up in their tribal and ancestral finery with the grieving paint on their faces, to the accompaniment of a *garamut* (wooden drum). The Yanks thought the ceremony had been laid on for them. One of the elders was passing round an enamel chamber-pot to gather a collection. Mac dropped in five shillings and made appropriate noises, hoping the foreign presence was not too offensive. Of course Yankee Doodle Dandy had to wave a ten-dollar US note above his head before depositing it in the collection. The Tolai elder had thanked MacDonald but ignored the American donation: pride and dignity were still very much alive. The tourists congratulated MacDonald on his command of Pidgin and said it was obvious he had spent many years with 'his people' – little did they know it had been all of six weeks.

MacDonald tourist tours became a feature. Another time, when escorting a couple of nuns around the Gazelle, he got lost down the Warangoi, a dense area of bush and plantations. He came back the North Road at 70 mph, belting through the coconut plantations on a sandy, bumpy road, giving a commentary as the greenery flashed past. They thought it all part of the tour. He was fifteen minutes late for duty and got chewed out by Senior Inspector Barry Baxter, ex-Grenadier Guards, and quite rightly so!

Next to take the tour was a French architect and writer on the South Pacific, who insisted that the guide be a French speaker.

Mac, who had achieved Lower French at school, volunteered and was delighted when the Frog spoke excellent English. MacDonald mumbled a few words along the lines of the Auld Alliance between Scotland and France. After a few miles they parked under a ficus (fig) tree and shared a bottle of Black Label whisky, with many toasts to old allies, and the Frenchman invited MacDonald to dinner that evening.

MacDonald declined, as he had his duty to perform. In fact that evening he and his crew locked up a number of the locals for various drunken offences, 22 arrests in all. He was called in the following day and made to retype all 22 Informations (Charges) a second time, as they were not up to standard. To his disgust, this chore was not on overtime: that's the worst of being a hypocrite.

There was no Officers' Mess, so the New Guinea Club was the venue when the Boss called his Officers to heel. They were a motley crew, their experience ranging from considerable to negligible. Inspector Stuart Hulbert was an ex-Uganda Assistant Superintendent, and before that a Captain in the Lancashire Fusiliers; Inspector Peter Hewitt an ex-Chief Inspector, Kenya and Cyprus; Sub-Insp Dennis Grove, Scots Guards, Met Police; S/I John Blackwell, Victoria Police; S/I Doug Henham, ex-Lt RACMP & Victoria; S/I D Ilsley, ex-RAF and Northamptonshire Police; S/I Jim Gould, NSW former Secretary NG Gold. One S/I was nicknamed 'Eager Beaver' because of his frequent expression to the boss, 'You're so right!' He had joined the same squash club, he swam on the same beach and to crown it all he even sat in the same pew at the Anglican Church. 'Nearer, my God, to thee' must have been his favourite hymn.

The boss, meanwhile, said he had observed that MacDonald was a bit of a hard case and that he would take him out on the grass. MacDonald asked his boss his weight and height: 17½ stone, 6' 5".

At 13½ stone and 6' 1", Mac said if he was going to trip the light fantastic on the grass he would employ some of his Glasgow experience by use of bottle or folding chair. This seemed to be the psychological answer that was required, as the gentlemanly pair proceeded to down the famous Victoria bitter at a rate of knots ending up at the Sub-Inspector's quarter, having their fortunes read by his charming wife.

The cap badge of the Police was the Bird of Paradise and the Gazelle, like the rest of the Territory, certainly had its share and more of the paradise concept. This was the land of plenty, totally different from the dry dust of Africa: here you could almost hear things growing. The locals even had a dress for this glorious climate; both male and female wore a *laplap*, a piece of cloth wrapped in a fold at the waist down to mid-calf, and the female wore a *meri* (blouse) like a loose T-shirt with baggy sleeves. Their hair was frizzed up to varying degrees and some had bleached the top to a blond colour, using either seawater or peroxide from the pharmacy.

Having completed a year in the Duty Office as a foundation where all things happened, his Chief Super transferred him to Traffic to smarten them up, as he had seen a Traffic cop lying on the tank of his motorcycle when travelling at a slow speed. As 0i/c Traffic, he went up two acting ranks and was paid accordingly, to his gratification. There were about thirty Other Ranks, plus two expatriate ladies who ran the Vehicle Registry and Firearms. Processes (Warrants and Summons) were executed and served. There were also a few local clerks and typists. The whole set-up had great potential, but no one to date had bothered to develop the Section. Some of the rank and file had been neglected: Constable i/c Jack Towatura, a local from Matupit, did broadcasts on the local radio station both in Kuanua and Pidgin explaining the Traffic Law, which had been adopted from NSW; Constable Benny Laukaut and another Constable, Alois Towaragar from Reimber Village, did driving tests and motorcycle patrols. Others were Demeoa, Martin Kuluah, a dog-eater from Manus Island, and Constable i/c Ebenesa, a Papuan, who did Traffic Accidents. MacDonald asked for and got about an extra twenty literate police who spoke English. A course was devised to train them up so they could drive and ride any vehicle or motorcycle, and also do mechanical inspections, right down to stripping down a vehicle and putting it back together. S/I John Marsh, ex-WO, RAE, Victoria Fire Brigade and Police, was a godsend in this technical area.

Next up to join the Section was S/I Dave Ilsley, who devised an Accident Report Sheet and how to investigate and prosecute a traffic offence, then S/I Doug Henham, a whiz on motorcycles who taught how to drive and test. MacDonald himself introduced the Traffic Infringement Notice, and a year later it was expanded again right up to a Warrant of Commitment – when the offender, having Failed to Pay, was imprisoned, the whole procedure being on one piece of paper. By now the Traffic numbered more literates than any other section, to the Divisional Commander's delight, so they were posted out in pairs to other stations within the Division and more came through the abbreviated but first-class Traffic Course. Eventually the Commissioner heard and expanded the idea for the whole Force. In a year a Traffic and Transport Department was up and running.

When the ex-Army hut at the rear of Traffic became the Officers' Mess, with a small servery at the rear for the marrieds' use as a takeaway, the Traffic boys soon managed to bribe the barman to allow them a little bit of the action. New motorcycles had arrived, Honda 250 and 500cc machines, as well a couple of Mini Coopers: when topped up with aviation gas, 135 mph was clearly achievable. One Friday, as a shift was going off duty, they collected their beer at the rear and decided it was time to give extra instruction to a new boi. The uncomfortable four-seater was jam-packed with seven bodies. The heroes had all had a few beers so they went on down Nonga Hill towards the *haus sik* (hospital), which in the circumstances was fortunate. They were helping out the new boy by using his controls when disaster struck and they contrived to make the vehicle somersault forward a number of times. In the process they bailed out through the two front windows. The vehicle was a write-off but they were not: all received gravel rashes, contusions and bruising, some to the soles of their feet as they had discarded their police boots for comfort. Monday saw the sorry sight front up for Orderly Room proceedings, where the merry band were docked one month's pay and no promotion for one year. The insurance company, luckily for all, was understanding and the matter died. Bandages were still being worn a month later.

Mac was then shunted off to help out in Prosecutions, where the 0i/c was a hypochondriac and a pill-popper of some standing – a nice fellow, but he had no wish to appear before Court.

There were two Courts, with Resident Magistrates Paul Quinlivan and Keith Walters. One was to be a Supreme Court Judge in Australia and the other was a former 'Kiap' (Patrol Officer). Both were good at their jobs, the former highly qualified and the latter extremely capable; they had a friendly rivalry which suited MacD down to the ground. Paul Q had a pooch that needed to be put down so Mac obliged. Both Keith W and Mac were off a six handicap so they crossed swords on the golf course from time to time. Keith also had seen a good twenty years' service in some tough areas such as Menyamya Sub-District and had been wounded by the wild Kukakuka, 4' 8" savages with 6' bows and arrows and weighty stone 'head-crushers'.

Mac managed to achieve 100% Committals to the Supreme Court by enlisting the aid of each magistrate in looking up case law and seeking legal advice as to how to achieve his goal. They were both apprehensive at the year's end as they would have to explain how there was a 100% success rate by the Prosecution. As they say in Pidgin, *Mi grease em gutpela tru.*' Mac had done his Prosecution side of things in Kenya and was not struck with the idea of spending his days in court, even as Prosecutor.

The Tolais had founded an illegal society which they termed 'Mataunganism', meaning to look forward or expect advancement. This resulted in the takeover of alienated land which the government claimed. In 1969 a civil disobedience campaign began, including refusal to pay poll tax, failure to support Local Government Councils and protest marches. As usual the ins and outs of the trouble were never fully explained to the Police. Oscar Tammur from Malavunan village in the Kokopo Sub-District was one of the ringleaders. He occupied some ground at Raviola Plantation near Kokopo and was driven off by two mobile squads (riot police). MacDonald, in charge of one because the normal commander was on the sick list, was asked to bring his previous experience to the fore. The Tolais, he found, could be bloody awkward but did not expect any viciousness. 1,500 extra reinforcements were flown in on C30 Hercules RAAF Transports that could carry a payload of 90 bodies and more, which came from all over the Territory. The Rabaul Barracks had quarters for 350 Police, and all of a sudden there were 1,500 more. The Barracks Officer's job had been considered a sinecure, and the older Inspector i/c could not cope. The new Chief Superintendent thought MacDonald had some experience in sanitation, so he was sent to the Barracks, where the carpenter nailed up the toilet blocks; trench latrines were the order of the day and chloride of lime was the aroma of the month. The PNG Volunteer Rifles lent 100-man tents so each airlift was divided into three Platoons of 30 R&F and a 90-man plane load made a company as per an Infantry battalion. The Divisional Clerks had sent pay sheets which made ideal muster rolls. After a couple of days and nights things were semi-organised. The Chief Superintendent came to inspect the Old and the Bold on a scale-A Parade.

Mac handed over to his boss who immediately started rearranging the troops: he certainly made the parade look neater but forgot the admin tail that has to wag the dog. All the companies were successfully mixed up and had to be untangled. Next up was a Flag March, with the Band playing some rousing music to celebrate before the operation. Civil disobedience continued, but scaled down towards the end of 1969. In any case, MacDonald was on his merry way once more.

Port Moresby 1967, including Hanubada (left), Konedobu (centre left),
Sir Hubert Murray Stadium (centre right), Toguba Hill (right)

Tolai kids, Rabaul 1967

Tolai fishermen, Rabaul, 1967

Rabaul, 1967, before the eruption in 1995.
Malaguna Village (foreground), Watom Island (top left),
New Ireland visible on horizon (in clouds).

19: Eden: New Ireland

A truly tropical paradise, New Ireland is five degrees south of the equator; by sea 24 hours, by air an hour or approximately 300 kilometres from Rabaul, it is some 500 kilometres long and fifty wide at its broadest, with an indigenous population of some 60,000 and 1,000 expatriates. The people in the northern half speak Tigak, those in the south Kuanua; they are well educated and self-sufficient. When it became clear, for many reasons, that District Inspector Dave Nixon's days were numbered, Mac volunteered. Another Chief Superintendent, Bill Burns, had taken over the Islands Division. He asked two other Senior Inspectors, who refused the posting as they had done a bit on what they termed 'outstations', so MacDonald was given the opportunity. It was to be a 'temporary/permanent' posting, which MacDonald did not understand as he had asked that a time-frame be given. 'Could be weeks or months,' he was told. Even when he tried to explain that he was married and had family at primary school, there was still no decision, so he set sail in the Government trawler, eventually with family, including his trusty servant, Butt Solumun, cat and dog.

Before the move he was told to fly over, do an inspection and report back: rather difficult, as he was the junior Officer. MacDonald flew over, was not met at the airport but hitched a lift to the 0i/c's house where he was wrongly identified as another Officer. He was asked if would like to have a look at the Station and town or just have a few beers. At the Station the 0i/c's cap and epaulettes were displayed on top of the safe, covered in cobwebs of some antiquity. Next was a visit to the Kavieng Hotel, where he was introduced to the local expatriates at the bar. Mick Gallen, a former Chief Superintendent and a golfing acquaintance, gave MacDonald the nod and the wink, which was appreciated. Next was the Kavieng Club, where he was introduced to Fred and Dawn Grosser, who ran the establishment with a high degree of efficiency. After a few more 'jugs' they boarded a Clan Line boat loading copra for the UK, whose Captain and Chief Engineer were roped in to provide the Constabulary with their beer ration. This merry-go-round lasted into the wee hours of the morning, after which MacDonald flew out at 6 a.m., having reached some definite opinions as to the Police presence − or lack of it − in New Ireland. His report was non-committal but expressed the opinion that the District needed a good shake-up.

The District Commissioner was Les Williams, MC, a former 'Coast Watcher' who welcomed the MacDonalds. He too was a golfer. Mrs MacDonald later became his secretary, an auspicious start. DDC Mert Brightwell enquired whether or not Mac was interested in Asian cooking: it seemed the former District Inspector's forte in life was instructing the Chinese ladies in the art of preparing Indian curry. He also took an active interest in the Transport Department auctions of used vehicles: he would bid an undisclosed amount and become the owner of all vehicles for sale, then conduct his own private auction. There was a Police Detachment at Taskul on New Hanover (Lavongai) Island, some 40 kilometres through a maze of island plantations of copra and logging. About 100 kilometres down the road was Konos Police Station and a further 100 kilometres on was Namatanai, both with 30–40 police, which with the 50 at Kavieng meant there were more than enough to do the job. One Police vehicle at Kavieng, however, was a joke. Within a month there were an additional nine vehicles and various sections had been set up. A 12-year-old Land Rover represented the local Fire Brigade, which was another Police function. There was a *kalabus* (prison) and an expatriate Corrective Institutions Officer, John Hynds. Another expat, Mrs Sue Baartz, ran the office side of things as typist and registry clerk for Firearms, Motor Vehicles and all documentation. MacDonald had enough experience under his belt not to do the 'new broom' act, but delved through files, showing that there had been a system but it had fallen into disuse. Some previous Officers, such as BJ Holloway and Peter Hewitt, had run an efficient set-up, but it soon became clear that another Officer was required to do the Crime and Prosecution side of things.

Mataunganism had resurfaced again on the Gazelle Peninsula

at Rabaul, and MacDonald was called away to help out with the organisation, returning after a few weeks to run his District of New Ireland. While having a few drinks in the Mess he was approached by Senior Superintendent Frank Hoeter, 2i/c Division, one of his favourite senior Officers. Frank had been a soldier with the NSW Cameron Highlanders in the New Guinea campaign, returned to the Reserves and had become a lieutenant-colonel with the United Nations in the Kashmir dispute in India and Pakistan. He had picked up a couple of gongs plus an MBE, much to the disgust of his brother senior Officers, who said he should decide whether he was a soldier or a policeman. Frank was both, and a straight shooter who liked a pint and did his best to please the ladies. He had been Commandant at the Police College. He thought highly of MacDonald and felt Mac would not let the side down in a 'stoush'. Hoeter explained that there was a new breed of Officer, the Assistant Inspectors, middle-aged and experienced in their various fields. MacDonald was not keen on the experimental breed, but on learning that the one selected for Kavieng was ex-British Army and an Inspector Manchester City Police, that was different. Chris Hanlon seemed pleased with his posting, as he had heard that Gus was a good man. He was briefed on the spot and told after a few jugs that he was flying at 6 a.m. the following morning by kind permission of TAA.

The pair arrived at Kavieng at seven in the morning and by 10 a.m. the new Assistant Inspector, a one-pipper, was ensconced in a four-bedroom fully furnished house, which meant he could now send for wife and family from Adelaide, South Australia. Further briefings and showing around happened over the weekend. Chris had thought it was all beer and skittles, but he was brought back to reality when at 9 p.m. that Sunday a serious assault by an expatriate manager on a plantation on the West Coast in the Namatanai Sub-District was reported. At 6 a.m. Monday he would pick up a Land Cruiser, driver and Senior Constable Sam Bung Sapa, plus another constable, and they would go and do the necessary. Chris was going in at the deep end — the quick way to learn! Snr Constable Sam Bung was a highly capable, literate man who had already been awarded a Bravery Certificate after saving a coastal vessel on fire with fuel drums on the deck in Rabaul. A Manus Islander, he was a deep-sea fisherman and was nicknamed 'Elephant' due to his powerful legs. He was a dog-eater − a delicacy in Manus, while the dog teeth made carved necklaces and other decorations.

Twenty-four hours later, Asst Inspector CJ Hanlon came on the 'blower' to say he had done it hard. A 20-mile four-wheel low-ratio drive, a 20-mile hike by track and about the same by canoe and he had arrived at the plantation, where he ascertained that one of the Labour Line had been beaten up by the expat manager, and when the complainant had responded had been stabbed in the guts for his trouble. The question was, what to do? Poor old Chris got the sharp end of MacDonald's tongue: 'Do you want me to come down and show you?' Another expat appeared in court and got a term in the 'pokey' for his trouble. Chris was well and truly baptised as a Colonial Police Officer and continued his good service for the New Ireland population.

The Magistrate was Mike Cockburn, a former Kiap Assistant District Commissioner at Maprik in the East Sepik, who had married into the Stanfield family, members of the local plantation fraternity. Old man Stanfield had been a brigadier in the Indian Army and retired to New Ireland, where he owned a number of the 154 plantations. His daughters were married to three other plantation owners. John, the only son, had taken over. Mike Cockburn was a stickler for protocol at all times – or to use the vernacular, he was rather up himself. He did appreciate, though, that he now had a Crime and Prosecutions Inspector, pointing out to MacDonald that he was also the Fire Chief of the District and that he had a couple of fire extinguishers which were overdue their yearly maintenance. This check was done by a constable struck off for the task.

Every Wednesday morning, MacDonald, with the shift on duty, did Fire Drill which consisted of sounding the alarm, *pitim belo*, by belting a strung-up oxy-welding cylinder with another chunk of metal: primitive but effective, and traditional throughout PNG. The 'team' would pile into a dilapidated fire engine and try to arrive at the Airport office, about a couple of kilometres away, in the scheduled time, play out the hoses, link up and pump water from a well − with varying results.

Sometimes the pipe basket would clog up with frogs, or the hoses would burst, as they were rotten in places. Water pressure usually produced a sort of dribble, but all concerned were full of misplaced enthusiasm, which did not augur well for the firefighting capability. Things did improve: Ken Bonnett, the Regional Firemaster at Rabaul, sent over replacements and was most helpful.

About two one morning, MacDonald received a phone call at his residence to say that one of the doctor's houses at the hospital had nearly burned down following an electrical fault to stereo equipment, but by expeditious use of extinguishers the fire had been put out. MacDonald sympathised with Resident Magistrate, Cockburn, who for some unknown reason was at the scene and demanded that the 0i/c Police be present immediately. He was informed that Asst Insp Hanlon would attend, as he would do the Fire Report and attend the Inquest. The former expressed his dissatisfaction, and when the Coronial Inquiry got underway, MacDonald as Fire Chief had to attend by order of the Court, where the following exchange took place:

RM: 'What formal training have you as Fire Chief?'
FC: 'None.'
RM: 'What experience have you in firefighting?'
FC: 'None.'
RM: 'Do you practise?'
FC: 'Yes.'
RM: 'What are the two fire extinguishers used for?'
FC: 'Putting out fires.'
RM: 'One is red, the other blue: what do you use them for?'
FC: 'I would read the label.'
RM: 'This is not satisfactory.'
FC: 'Agreed.'

Luckily for Gus, Ken Bonnett had given evidence before him, and as MacDonald had just returned from an outstation inspection, they could not have concocted the same story. Much to the frustration of the Resident Magistrate, they said pretty well the same thing. One reason for the Coronial Inquiry may have been that the RM's brother-in-law, John Stanfield, had been locked up the previous week for inciting a riot and being in possession of unlicensed firearms.

John Stanfield was a character in his own right. He hated having to oversee plantation life as he believed he was cut out for better things, and to some extent this may have been true. Stanfield had been a Lieutenant commander in the RANVR, and from what could be gleaned from his naval friends, he was a bloody good seaman. Anyway, JS vented his frustration in a number of ways. He would sit in the hotel bar and lecture all within earshot on multiracialism or simply the colour bar; luckily for all concerned, his remarks were treated by all as more to be laughed at than pitied. He had been told to get his firearms licensed, some being years out of date. Seemingly he had a protest from his Labour Line over rations, so he heaved a couple of large tuna into the mob, who took exception; there was a scuffle, so he phoned Mac and demanded that he attend in person. Instead, Cadet Officer Leo Dion and party attended, resulting in JS being 'placed' in the cells. Since there was only one it was multifunctional. Would Mac go to the Club and have him bailed out, as he had been arrested on warrant for firearms offences? He had a weekend lie-in to appear on the Monday before his brother-in-law, the RM, who managed to convict on all counts but fined his relative a few dollars on each. Chris Hanlon was informed in the Club Bar that there was a 'Law for Them' and a 'Law for Us', but explained that as far as MacDonald was concerned it was the same law for all.

Once again MacDonald was called over to the Gazelle and Rabaul, as more civil unrest was on the way. He had reported that even in Kavieng there were anti-Government mutterings among some of the Tolais in the Public Service. On arrival at Rabaul he managed to get another Officer transferred on a temporary basis to take over his District, as someone was needed to do the admin side at least. Chris Hanlon was now in the saddle as far as Crime went. Chief Supt Bill Burns said Supt Clem Henney had asked for Mac to be his 2i/c at the Vunapaladig area, where the Tolais of the Mataungan group had allegedly taken over alienated ground formerly owned by the Bainings people, who had been driven further back into the hills. MacDonald reported to Supt Henney, an excellent Officer with a straightforward manner and a great sense of humour. Clem did not beat about the bush: MacDonald had Army and African experience and he had heard that he could get things done operationally. Clem as CO would do the admin and PR side, MacDonald the Ops. There were 1,000 Police, mostly the Old and Bold but 200% reliable, tested in dicey situations all over the Territory: they did not know how to 'run'. Many had fought the Japs and wore both medals and service stars with pride. Could MacDonald turn them into Mobile Squads overnight? 'Oh yes, miracles later.'

Snr Supt Frank Hoeter lent a regular squad of the Mobile Force to assist. They were put into 20 squads of 40 bodies each, given an Officer, and then off to the North Coast Golf Course at Kerevat, where a bugler sounded a 'G', the Regular Squad did a movement on the second note, and the remainder copied. At the end of a week the Old and Bold were acceptable.

The following week bush patrols were sent out to keep the Mataungans out of the copra and cocoa blocks they had created, possibly illegally over the years. Lexy Brown, one of the Comworks construction managers, was roped in with his Caterpillar D10 and scrapers and graders and levelled off a Defensive Area. To gladden his medieval heart, MacDonald had a moat built from the run-off of nearby creeks; a cement bridge was the entrance overlooked by about 40 riflemen as the final resort. All work and no play makes Jack a dull boy, so every *apinun* (afternoon), there were sports on the adjacent beach. This was prior to the rumoured Matangan attack. As days rolled into weeks, a tent town with duck-boards, beds, mattresses and 'mossie' nets was bunged into place. Sub-Inspector Jim Ramm was co-opted as Quartermaster. Clem and MacDonald noticed that the 'Down South' (Australian Government) were in panic mode, and that in turn American-style money was no object. The Government Stores Officer i/c was an old golf crony of MacDonald's, and offered anything he could to help the boys in blue: generators appeared, as did fridges, deep freezes, diesel cookers and the most generous of rations, right down to Coca-Cola machines. The rank and file dined on peaches and cream. Fresh meat had also been supplied, but QM Ramm had forgotten to take the other ranks' meat from the rear of his hired car, and in the tropical heat it had turned a lovely greenish colour with a good whiff of putrefaction about it.

MacDonald volunteered to help out the QM by going downtown and speaking to the various parties involved in supplying the troops. The Divisional Clerk who controlled the funds let slip that he had a signal from Police HQ that the Australian Government had approved almost unlimited funding on the Gazelle operation. MacDonald went to Anderson's butchery, who had supplied the meat, and explained the position. They said they too were aware of it and would help out. Anderson's was also a licensed grocery with heaps of goodies. The meat was replaced; various spirits, liqueurs, imported beers, wines, cigarettes and some cigars were ordered for the Officers' Mess, and the troops had coke, ice cream and peaches; so morale was maintained at a very high standard – as was gluttony.

New Britain Motors came to the party by supplying a vehicle for every four Officers so they could have R&R at the Kaivuna Hotel or Travel Lodge one night per week from the rigorous campaign that was going on in the bush, some 30 miles out of Rabaul. The Air Hosties from TAA & Ansett Airlines were most impressed by the lavish wine-and-fine spreads that the boys in blue could put on, and they came to the party too. When the Administrator for the Territory of Papua New Guinea, Mr Johnson, decided to pay a visit to the troops at Vunapaladig it almost caused a panic: fridges and deep freezers had to be concealed in the bush, which was an unattended copra and cocoa plantation, while all grog and accessories were put aside. Mr Johnson was most impressed with the ham and tomato sandwiches and cups of tea and coffee for his entourage and the 'brass' from HQ. Even the cups and plates had received a bit of chipping to provide the 'roughing it' effect, right down to mossie coils throughout the tent camp. After Mr Johnson's departure it was 'Carry on up the Khyber' in the best colonial tradition.

The civil disobedience by the Mataungan Association proceeded with a march of some 5,000–6,000 male Tolais on the

Vunapaladig encampment. ACP Operations Brian Holloway attended and was suitably impressed at the brilliant white plastic tape being rolled out in the middle of the cement bridge entrance to the camp with the forty-odd riflemen waiting on the order to volley fire. The Riot Act was proclaimed in English, Pidgin and Kuanua: 'Her Majesty Queen Elizabeth II, our Sovereign Lady, commands that persons assembled disperse and go about your lawful business or sufficient force will be used to disperse this riotous gathering. God save the Queen.'

As MacDonald would no doubt use this many times in the future, he had the Proclamation typed up in five or so different languages which he kept in his service dress hat behind a piece of clear plastic – most impressive, but it usually ended up being disregarded in favour of those two international words which can be loosely translated as 'Go away quickly'…

With the uprising quelled, MacDonald returned to his beloved New Ireland and took up the reins as sheriff, his Officers Jim Napkai and Chris Hanlon having held the fort in his absence. Mert Brightwell, Acting DC New Ireland, complained that he had a problem on the remote West Coast at Lambu, where a number of tax evaders were holding out against the Administration and the Kiaps were at a loss in their tax-gathering endeavours. Warrants for the tax evaders' arrests were issued. A Police party consisting of Insp Jim Napkai, S/I Ben Hamboken and Snr Sgt John Korau, plus twenty other ranks, was placed aboard the Government trawler skippered by Hans Schmidt, along with a Patrol Officer who was nicknamed 'Mandrake' because of his appearance and manner, and later his attitude. Three 17-foot aluminium-hulled speedboats were loaded on with outboard engines and extra fuel tanks, plus six boat boys to handle the craft. The main village to be raided was about 160 kilometres down the West Coast, the area where the New Ireland shark fishermen had a unique approach: they attracted the sharks by beating together hollowed-out coconut halves and used a halter affair to lasso the shark and then have their outrigger canoes towed in by shark propulsion.

The 'commandos' landed at dawn the following day. Three sections of the Police party stormed up the beach, showed their warrants and made ten or so arrests. At this stage it was realised that some 300 villagers were not amused, and the odd shotgun had begun to appear as the menfolk gathered. The Police had the odd shotgun too. MacDonald decided discretion was the better part of valour and ordered a hasty retreat to the beach where the trawler and speedboats were to have been waiting, but hallelujah – the marine side had deserted their station and there was no sign of them!

The prisoners were handcuffed and the Police party took off quick-time north along the pebbly beach. 'Mandrake' was blessed in a variety of tongues. After a few miles a large party was seen approaching along the beach from the north. They were not reinforcements but 100 or so angry villagers who had out-marched the Police along a track parallel to the beach. Shotguns, bush knives and the odd bamboo or spear were being brandished. A stoush was in the offing. Simultaneously the Government trawler appeared round a headland and saw or heard the Police party: Cpl Sam Bung Sapa, as instructed, fired three warning shots in the air. By a matter of yards the boys in blue were taken by speedboat back to the trawler, where 'Mandrake' was informed his balls were to be garters when back in tranquil Kavieng. Some more speedboat raids were carried out along the coast and about fifty tax defaulters apprehended. Sr Sgt John Korau was left on the trawler with specific orders that 'Mandrake' could walk the plank if any further breach of cooperation was spotted. The Police party sailed for home with a good catch of red emperor and coral trout on board!

Chief Superintendent 'Snow' Feeney, the new Islands Division boss, visited New Ireland some time later. MacDonald accompanied him around the traps and did the normal introductions. Belting down the Bulaminski Highway, made up of crushed coral and created by a former German Governor of New Ireland, MacDonald noted his boss was not over-impressed. All of a sudden they were flagged down by a plantation owner and invited in for a drink or coffee, the latter the order of the day. The copra planter went on to tell Supt Sweeney how he had a riot of his labour some weeks back, the Kavieng Riot Squad had attended and what a great bunch of boys they were. On resuming their safari to Namatanai township, another 100 miles down the road, MacDonald was asked about the non-existent Riot Squad and had to explain that in the armoury he had discovered some shotguns, gas guns and gas masks, helmets and shields, so with a few pick helves he had created his own Riot Squad and all his Police had received 'live' riot training. Despite the ranks being made up of the young and inexperienced as well as the Old and Bold, and not much to look at, when dressed up as a Riot Squad they were quite impressive. The troops also enjoyed their newly found expertise.

On arrival at Namatanai, a small township with a few Chinese stores, pub and a club, ADC for the Sub-District Harry Redmond complained that there were more tax defaulters at a village called Uluputur on the West Coast, some 30 miles distant, and several hundred villagers who also supported the Mataungan Association in Rabaul, another 50 miles over the sea to East New Britain, and the Namatanai Police were not strong enough to effect the necessary arrests. Chief Supt Feeney said he would allow a mobile squad from Rabaul, but it was to be denuded of its shotguns and tear gas, which rendered it almost ineffectual. Nevertheless a week later MacDonald flew over to Rabaul and picked up the Mobile Squad under the command of Inspector Geoff Brazier, an old acquaintance, a big solid lad with a cool head to match. A Government trawler was procured and the merry men set sail for a dawn landing in the best tradition. Orders were overlooked and thankfully the squad brought its full complement of equipment. The overnight trip was most pleasant on a flat tropical sea with shoals of flying fish, and the odd dolphin and shark also sighted. The troops had a party in the evening and the two expat Officers shared a bottle of 'bundi' in the best naval style. Skipper Doug Schmidt had taken part in similar efforts. At dawn the trawler had tied up and the squad was sent ashore to be joined by the Namatani contingent of some 30 police under S/I Joshua Nelson, a Tolai who spoke the local language and knew the exact whereabouts of the wanted bodies. Apprehensions were swiftly made and the two units returned to their original bases of Rabaul and Namatanai. No Police brutality was required: a successful operation.

When MacDonald did his monthly visit to his outstations,

especially Namatani, he would usually take down from Kavieng his esteemed friend Mick Gallen, who had eight of a family (8 pints to the gallon) – to his and his wife's credit. Mick was a former Chief Supt of the Islands Division, now the licensee of the Kavieng Hotel and the owner of the Namatanai Hotel. Among his many attributes Mick, a solid North Queenslander of good Irish stock who had considerable respect for former British Colonial Police Officers, was also a six handicap golfer. At sundown, the expatriate males of the Sub-District would gather for a few 'wets' and chew the fat. Along came the local planters, and Tom McKellar, the local Catholic Priest who had been in Namatanai for fourteen long years. He and MacDonald struck up a close friendship and sank a bottle of malt between them after the club had closed and the group had dispersed. Between toasts to all sorts of worthy and not so worthy causes, the pair would set the world to right and insult each other in the extreme, as only good mates can. Tom was a character and, like MacDonald, not all good. MacDonald always overnighted at the guest house-cum-store of the Chinese gentleman called Luk Poi Wai, whom he had re-christened 'Lukewarm Pie'. The Government Accommodation Warrant was the proverbial 'open sesame'. About 5.30 p.m. MacDonald would count the number at the club and then send a chit over to his Chinese host ordering dinner for the gang, about 15–20 hungry persons.

The Reserve Constabulary came into being about 1970, partly in response to those who had served in the British Colonies in Africa. While MacDonald was in the Kenya Police, both Regular and Reserve had excellent Officers from the dominions such as Canada, Australia, New Zealand and South Africa. These expatriates were of commission calibre and came into the Force as Officers; the Africans were mainly the other ranks. The concept worked. In PNG everybody would start at the bottom as Constables, an egalitarian idea but a sure-fire way to slow up indigenous recruitment; MacDonald's, New Ireland, had the largest proportion of all the Districts/Provinces. He had about thirty Recruits, mostly expatriate planters, some mixed race and a few of the local elite. The reservists were mustard-keen, their intention being to lock up their brothers at the drop of a hat.

Training consisted of two hours every Thursday, 7–9 p.m., with lectures by S/I Napkai and A/I Hanlon. Inspector MacDonald personally took some lectures and drills. After the weekly exercise thirty bodies would descend upon the Kavieng Club, which was used as a Mess, an area set aside for the jollification. Some travelled over 100 miles by motor vehicle or speedboat for their weekly training. Some gained NCO's chevrons, one being Peter Ross Kennedy-Murray, who had a booming Oxford accent and had served in the RAN. MacDonald asked him if he had been a Lt-Cdr due to his commanding presence. He was around 6' tall and about as broad. No, he had been the Quartermaster on one of HM ships; for Quartermaster read Helmsman. His accent, he claimed, had been acquired at King's, the number one school in Sydney. Another plantation manager with a pronounced mid-England accent claimed he had been a lieutenant in the Scots Guards. His idea of arms drill would have made a nun kick a hole in a stained glass window in any chapel. Another claimed a commission in the Australian Army, but on the rifle range he could not hit a cow in the arse with a banjo.

After a year's training they were allowed out on the beat with strict instructions that they were in a supportive role to the regular Police and that the indigenous NCOs were the boss. Surprisingly, the merry band of would-be desperadoes acquitted themselves well. All had hilarious memories of some aspect of their spell as Reserve Police Officers.

One Saturday when MacDonald was on the golf course, he could hear a fracas coming from the Public Bar – a good going punch-up. Some time later the DC, who was also on the golf course, asked MacDonald what he was going to do about the situation. MacDonald said S/I Napkai was the Duty Officer and would handle the matter. Some minutes later it was discovered that S/I Napkai had stripped off into gym shorts, and so far had knocked out three persons in the bar and was threatening to continue. MacDonald called in at the Police Station, picked up a couple of his merry men and went to the hotel, still in his golf gear with golf shoes and spikes to boot. A good time was being had by all: at least six fights were in progress in and around the hotel and in the main street. MacDonald entered the saloon bar to go through to the public bar, was prodded in the chest by a Tolai gentleman and when he grabbed the offending digit was pounced upon from behind. A melee erupted, with about six Tolais from Rabaul throwing punches at their favourite Inspector of Police, who responded in kind. The floor was tiled, and with the spikes in his golf shoes, attempting to throw a punch or take one was difficult, as he slipped all over the shop. One Tolai attempted to pinion MacDonald's arms, another on his back; one went over the top, the other let out a roar as MacDonald got hold of his 'goolies' and squeezed.

S/I Napkai appeared and gave a good impression of a light-heavyweight. Eric Lauder, a big Kiwi, was hesitant about coming out on the Police side. Jim Copland, his Scottish sidekick, was attempting his peacemaker act, entirely out of character. By now the mob had managed to drag their District Inspector and themselves out into the main road. At this stage MacDonald had lost his shirt, shorts and socks, a most undignified sight. More drunken off-duty Police arrived and joined in. Eventually six Tolais were bundled into the Police vehicle. Bob Murray, the manager, was told to close the Hotel and shut windows, as MacDonald was going to get some tear gas and shotguns – and if need be have a Tolai's balls.

MacDonald phoned his residence and asked his Missus to bring a change of clothing and the keys to the armoury as (l) it had been raining and (2) there had been a disturbance at the hotel. S/I Napkai was ordered and escorted to his quarter next to the cop shop, which he did with reluctance. Seemingly he had received a letter from his father telling him to leave the Police and return home to help out in their gardens. Jim did not want to and had become morose, to the extent that he had taken on a group in the saloon bar and had knocked out three bodies so far and possibly more were on the way. The alarm was sounded and a dozen Police and two more vehicles materialised; the rest were at the pub playing their part in what was to be known as 'The Kavieng Riot'! MacDonald returned and with the continued efforts of all, 30-odd bodies were arrested for riotous behaviour.

On Monday afternoon the Magistrate was made aware of the circumstances and Mac was asked to identify his assailants, which he did: they were all there in court with bandages around the holes that Mac had inflicted by stamping on their feet with his golf shoes. As the US Marines would say he had 'Adapted, Improvised and Overcome'. S/I Napkai, usually a good Officer, was in the poo. It looked like a Serious Disciplinary Charge plus transfer, so MacDonald charged him before the Resident Magistrate with Riotous Behaviour and quickly got his Officer out of the way. Later, when ordered to take disciplinary proceedings after reporting the incident, MacDonald managed to avoid this by pointing out that to punish twice would be unjust. The local populace soon forgave with a good sense of humour. At least the cops were almost human. Acting DC Mert Brightwell had a delegation of Tolais stating that MacDonald had threatened to kill them and, knowing him, they were in fear of their lives. Mert said he was disappointed that all the good work of 'his' Police had been undone, to which the rejoinder was 'bullshit'. Chris Hanlon A/I was 'down the road' on an investigation at the time, expressing disappointment at missing out on the fun and games. Just as well: the Bleeding Hearts would have written up racial connotations with Whitey versus Blackie.

Brightwell was a man of large proportions in every sense. He complained that there was a housebreaker on the loose in Kavieng, and that could not be tolerated. MacDonald agreed; on a number of occasions the Police ambushes had almost made an arrest but the gentleman in question was a wily bird. Mert said he would catch the thief – he and the two 'boat boys' secreted in his residence. But the thief got in through a rear open window and was caught in the act of removing money from the Deputy DC's wallet by Mert himself. Discretion overcame valour when threatened at knifepoint, but unbeknown to Mert a couple of Police who had staked out the residence caught the culprit and Police honour was again back in place. To show his appreciation, Mert gave MacDonald the use of his private speedboat − a twin inboard/outboard Volvo Penta plus auxiliary motor and prop, a really nice trim craft, down to galley and toilet, with three of a boat crew − to carry out Police business, as he had dozens of islands offshore where he had to inspect liquor licences and firearms security on the 154 plantations. He also took a trip round

New Hanover, an island of 50 x 30 miles, involving a day in a speedboat of some 168 miles. On New Hanover he had a Police Detachment of some fifteen souls plus their families under an Assistant DC.

Lavongai, a large village called of some 800 cargo cultists who had thrown a Police Mobile Squad back into the sea with a few broken arms and legs a few years previously, had been 'pacified' to some extent, but required a Police presence from time to time. Materan was another small village and a plantation managed by Jim White, an ex-lieutenant who had served with the 9th Australian Division in the Western Desert, one old soldier and a gentleman of sterling character. About 50 miles further on the North Cape at Umbukul was another planter, Jack Gleave, a former Sergeant with the 8th Army who had also been in the desert. When those two got together on their monthly R & R to Kavieng to 'swing the lamp', the Battle of El Alamein was relived within the hallowed ground of the Kavieng Club. MacDonald broke his rule of not drinking on duty when visiting Umbukul and had a few stubbies with Gleave, who was well into the never-never land on the island.

Round the North Cape they went to Noipous, a large village where Corporal Conrad Simeon Tali's wife came from. Tali was the accompanying NCO on the first trip in an open aluminium-hull speedboat. Despite his brown complexion, Tali peeled from sunburn due to the extreme long exposure and the reflection off the Pacific Ocean. Then on to Puas, a leper colony, where in the river dwelt a 22-foot sea crocodile who had taken a number of locals from the hospital. Next was the Tsoi Passage, beautiful flat water, crystal-clear and only a couple of fathoms – you could see all the colourful, abundant marine life. Then through a group of a score of islands where the odd plantation manager would beam in a bright red searchlight to the boat inviting the 'Police Masta' ashore for a neighbourly drink as per the colonial tradition. The day went from 6 a.m. to 7 p.m. and the Inspectorial Party would be back on dry land at Kavieng. Mert's cruiser was a boon indeed in comparison to a bruised backside in the metal 17-foot hull speedboat.

Joe Smythe was the Plant Manager for Public Works

Department who saw that the roads were maintained. He told the tale about one of his grader drivers, the driver had decided to see how fast his grader could go so he gave it a burst going down a slight incline on the Bulaminski Highway. The driver described how the grader's front wheels were 'flopping' from side to side when travelling at a rate of knots. Seemingly the grader hit a bump on the road, took off into the bush at the side of the road, knocked down X number of trees, sheered off palms and came to a rest on top of the stumps, whereby the grader remained firmly wedged. Later that day the driver decided to report what had happened. Joe did not believe the report, so the pair went to the scene and viewed the elevated grader. Joe shook his head in disbelief and added a few customary words. The driver placed his had on Joe's shoulder and began to commiserate in the following terms: 'Masta Joe yu no ken wari long dispela samting, samting bilong God I kamap long hia ples, Masta. Yu nogat wari, yu gat gutpela tinktink long dispella baggarrup, Gavamin I gat plenty pela moni Moa Yet.' Which translated as: 'Mr Joe, don't worry yourself about this; God is responsible. Please don't worry, you must realise that regards this accident the Governement has got plenty of money.' There is attitude on display.

A great two years in the District of New Ireland was up and MacDonald and family were due leave. Accompanied by school-teacher friends, Terry and Judy O'Keeffe, the MacDonalds set off on a Burns Philp Travel charter flight, with stop-overs at Hong Kong and Singapore. Relatives and friends in England, Scotland and Wales were looked up, and the customary drop of the 'craiter' downed. Jack Sullivan, former Chief Inspector Kenya Police, was now a Major in the Sultan of Oman's Forces, and the number one Intelligence man. In Glasgow town, Big Bob Henderson had returned to his original Division as Chief Superintendent and was still personally locking up the Ned at football matches. Producing the malt whisky from his desk drawer to celebrate seeing one of his former 'Sons', Bob ribbed MacDonald that he was only an Inspector and it was time he was a Superintendent. Peter Ross and Bill Hening were both Chief Superintendents: as predicted, both were going to the top and deservedly so.

Mac had been acting Senior Inspector for this time, and of good report, so promotion was due. It was a great temptation to ask to stay in the tropical paradise of New Ireland: he had a good rapport with all members of the community, but he could see himself being sucked into the soft groove. It was time to move on.

Flashing bayonets, 1971

Kavieng, 1970

20: The Other Highlands, 1972–73

MacDonald was transferred to Mobile Force HQ Rabaul, under command of the aforementioned Senior Superintendent Frank Hoeter, MBE. After pointing out that he was a bit long in the tooth to be 2i/c Mobile Force, as suggested, he was told he was to be Adjutant and Training Officer. But it mattered little: after just one week there he was transferred again, this time to the Highlands Division at Mt. Hagen, almost dead centre in the eastern part of the island and some 500 kilometres north-west of 'Mosbi'. The Highlands was the wild and woolly place of PNG — something to look forward to, and decidedly a challenge! Like many of his transfers, this one took effect on Anzac Day, April 25 1972. They flew up to Hagen and their personal effects arrived a few days later, well and truly smashed up: yet another insurance job.

Mt. Hagen got its airstrip in the early fifties. In the sixties the Highlands Highway allowed freight into the Central Highlands. The 350-mile trip took three to five days, up the Markham Valley from Lae, the commercial capital and second city of Papua New Guinea — a rise of over 3,000 feet up the 15-mile Kassam Pass into the pacified Eastern Highlands to Goroka, its capital, 100 miles on and over the Dalo Pass, another 4,000-foot rise into what was to become the Chimbu/Simbu with Kundiawa as its centre, dropping down thousands of feet to a warmer climate, then up the Waghi Valley via Kerowagi and on to Hagen. Here you could carry on bearing south-west in the Nebilyer Valley around the slopes of Mt. Gilluwe, 13,000 feet, to Mendi, the capital of the Southern Highlands where Ron Neville was king, or go west around the hills which abutted Mt. Hagen to Wapenamanda and Wabag and finally, if you so desired, to Laiagam.

The Southern Highlands had come under control around the mid-fifties. Mountain ranges with towering heights, up to 15,000 feet, great alluvial valleys, the foothills densely populated with vigorous people. The climate during the day was around 20 Celsius with extreme UV, at night 10 degrees; in fact the Central Highlands, Chimbu, Western Enga, Southern, all could produce warm days and sometimes frosty nights. A good rainfall could add to discomfort in the field. The Whitlam Government was hell-bent on passing on independence from the colonial yoke, despite the obviously shaky presence of law and order and the fact that economic development was yet in its infancy. Australia was under pressure from the United Nations to give PNG away, which Whitlam did, resulting in the mess it is in today.

The Divisional Superintendent was Jim Dutton QPM and his 2i/c was Ernie Young, two old hands who had spent a couple of score years in the Constabulary. MacDonald was told to report to the 0i/c Police Station, Supt Ian Cluny McPherson. 'Big I' was glad that such an experienced Officer had arrived, and suggested that MacDonald fill in the following: to supervise the Barracks Officer, also there were a couple of Mobile Squads, 7 Platoon and 10 Platoon. They came under Div HQ, but MacDonald would oversee both. MacDonald sarcastically asked if there was anything else he could help out with. Oh yes: the Armoury was a mess and overflowing, and there were about 90 disciplinary offences to be heard. MacDonald now realised that the wool was being well and truly pulled. The nub of his posting was that he was the man in charge of the Mobile Force for the Highlands. Charming: now the Colonial Boy had to soldier up once again…

Mrs MacDonald had a reputation too as a top secretary and was offered the job as the District Commissioner's secretary. Dinger Bell was of the old school, straight down the middle, and of course he was ably supported by his Deputy, Ron Hyatt, and Assistant District Commissioner Ross Allan throughout the Western Highlands and The Enga, which soon was to become an autonomous District. MacDonald now realised that he had been shanghaied as the Group Commander Mobile Force for the Highlands Region. This included Eastern, Chimbu, Western, Enga and Southern Highlands; their main centres were Goroka and Kundiawa to the east, Mt. Hagen itself, Wabag to the north-west and Mendi to the south-west. Each district had one or two Mobile Squads, giving a total of six squads or two companies;

each squad had a strength of some 40 police, giving 240 bodies to work with. The original composition of the squads was twenty baton-men, four gas gunners, four shotgunners and two self-loading rifles, one Officer, one Sergeant, one Bugler, one Orderly/Medic, four Drivers and one Cook/Clerk. The vehicles were four Toyota Land Cruisers and one three-ton Austin truck, insufficient for the Highlands situation: this would change radically in the near future. Again, Police Headquarters in their wisdom were out of touch with the current requirements throughout the various regions. The Police Station itself was an impoverished affair, built by self-help, the bricks having too high a sand content as opposed to cement, so that security was an imagined rather than an actual state.

The natives were restless but not quite revolting. They had always been in a state of warlike flux: the Administration had covered up the real situation because of insufficient funds and a lack of interest down the pipeline. All these inadequacies unfortunately have now come home to roost. The Highlands people always tried to squeeze the opposition up the 'hill' and likewise those up the hill responded in the opposite direction. There was nervousness about independence, planned for 1975; it is always a precious commodity and welcomed by all peoples. Were the Great White Father and Mother Australia going to abandon their offspring? Some welcomed the prospect for a variety of reasons, mainly opposed to the belief that Law and Order = Peace = Prosperity. Naturally there were those who wished to establish 'rights' over land tenure before Oz pulled the plug. The result was simply an increase in clan tribal fighting. The Highlands of PNG has been referred to as the 'human aviary', due to each clan having its own birds of paradise head-dress, passed on from generation to generation. Despite MacDonald's chequered career and background, he realised he had a lot to learn − and quickly − in this new environment. No orientation course was offered: you started at the deep end, with which he was by now familiar.

A couple of days after the MacDonalds' arrival, a clan fight had taken place a few miles outside the municipality of Mt. Hagen. Seemingly, this was quite a common occurrence. The responsibility in the bush lay with the Administrative Officer or 'Kiap' and the town's Police. The Kiaps had attachments of regular Police, mainly the old and bold, whereas the Regular Police kept the pick of the crop. Of course from time to time the Regulars would help out the Field Constabulary, and the relatively new concept of Mobile Force (riot/paramilitary) was now accepted.

The reasons for the clan fight were many, and yet singularly simple: a killing, an insult, a trespass, theft of a pig, a dispute over women or the most important '*Graun bilong mipela*' − 'Our Land!' To simplify, the reasons came down to one from time immemorial: they hated each others' guts and they had to prove that they were real men. Like the Maori, the Aboriginal and the African, the Highlanders were much closer to nature than people of European origin or descent. Animals, fish, trees, the miracles of nature, sunrise, sunset, the rivers, all were part of their very existence. Some experts never tried to understand the Highlander. They attempted to hold him in contempt: just a savage. Little did they realise that this so-called savage could speak up to five languages, plus English in some cases. He was a farmer, hunter, fisherman, builder, navigator, midwife, orator, artefact manufacturer, singer, artist, a warrior and for some a leader. In mourning he would chop off joints of his left hand, small and index fingers; man to man, he would greet you by grabbing hold of your testicles. He was reasonably short in stature, as the mountain men went, but not always: the new generations were adding inches. He was well developed and muscular, and while there were a few runts, they were possibly the most dangerous of them all.

On this first occasion MacDonald was invited out with the Division Superintendent to attend at the *Ples Krai* (mourning area) at a particular village in the *Sing-sing Graun* (open meeting-place like an arena), rectangular in shape and surrounded by bamboo clumps and yarr trees (casuarina). Three dead warriors were about to be 'planted' in the village *mat mat* (cemetery). A thousand or so mourners, covered in the red-brown mud of the Highlands to express their grief, were present, jumping about distraughtly: women and children were present, and the male warriors were all armed with traditional weapons, ceremonial spears of black *limbum* (palm hardwood), carved bamboo bows and colourfully decorated arrows. Most had steel-headed tomahawks with 3-foot shafts in their *lets* (belts made from bark). Some among the Big Men (Leaders) had green stone Hagen axes, which sold for thousands of dollars overseas. Their wailing and gnashing of teeth continued for days, with fresh flowers being heaped daily on the grave mounds, some of which had wooden crosses displaying their Christianity. No mention of the rival clans would be made at this stage; councillors appointed by the Kiaps, who were usually a natural leader or No. 2, would inform the No. 1 Police Master that there was no intention to mount a 'payback' fight at this stage; but compensation in the form of pigs, women, beer, meat, land, money, bird of paradise feathers, traditional axes, goats, chooks, sweet potato or even an apology would at least be discussed and in some cases made.

After ten days in the Highlands MacDonald was informed that the Jigas and Yamugas were now fighting again at Oglebeng, a few miles out of town. The area was hilly, with clumps of yarr and bamboo around the hamlets, and the odd creek meandering its way down into the Waghi Valley. At least 50% of the area was under cultivation in the traditional Highland garden, 200 metres squares, some fenced off to keep out both domestic and feral pigs. Oglebeng was a reasonably flat plateau and had been cleared of trees to make a huge *sing-sing* ground where the fight was to take place. Skirmishing between the two clans had been going on for about a week and a couple more had been killed on both sides, plus a few hundred injured, mainly by arrows. At Mac's disposal were two squads, 7 and 10 Platoons, commanded by S/Is John Pahau and Cosmos Pulai, both with five or so years' service and, like most of the Mobile Force, in their mid-twenties. They had to do four years' service at least before joining Mobile Force, so they were not exactly raw recruits.

MacDonald made his recce: over an area of four square miles the opposing teams were approximately 3,500 Jigas and 1,500 Yamugas. This was not by any means either clan's full potential so a conclusion had to be reached before others became involved. Weapons being used were bows and arrows, tomahawks and spears, plus the odd shield. MacDonald asked Ian McPherson for 20 rifles with 50 rounds .303 ball per rifle; also the odd confiscated shotgun was added, so that baton-men became suddenly obsolete.

Monday was a good day for a fight, as it did not disrupt any weekend festivity, and obviously this was agreed to by all parties. Nonetheless the 'boys' were out there killing each other, so both of Mac's squads spent the rest of the day breaking up company actions all over the shop by the liberal use of tear gas fired from inefficient cup dischargers — the 1.5-inch gas guns proved much more up to the requirement. After a morning of non-stop manoeuvring over broken ground, taking out the wounded and sending them to hospital, the two squads seemed to be getting a bit of control back into the situation. About midday Mac had chosen a knoll for his troops to have a drink of water and a smoke when he noticed a solid bunch of 450 spearmen, some with the traditional head-dress and spears, approaching about 300 yards off. He went out and waved a spokesman forward; the latter informed him that if he did not get the Police out of the way they would come down and kill them so that they could get on with the clan fight.

Mac returned to the two squads and brought 20-odd riflemen to the front; the spearmen continued to approach in a fighting crouch. At about 150 yards the riflemen were given the order: 'Five rounds standing load.' Then came the second order, 'Present!' — and a number of shots went off, cracking past Mac's lugholes. He had been standing some ten paces in front of his troops; he now about-turned and in his best parade ground voice asked, 'Which one of you buggers wishes to shoot your Officer? *As you were*!' During the shooting he had witnessed a body fly through the air and another land in a heap among the warrior spearmen, who withdrew rather smartly: the fighting was over for the day.

Up at Oglebeng the troops filed into the Police tent for a de-briefing. When asked who had fired the shots, a solitary hand went up from a very junior constable. Mr Napkai was told that Mac would return in half an hour and he was to sort out who had opened fire before the command was given. As expected on his return there were no culprits but looks of feigned puzzlement. Next day Mac inspected and found eight out of twenty rifles had been fired. Luckily for the culprits, none could be identified as rifles were not signed out. Mac made further enquiries and it was found that although both squads had been trained to the .303 rifle, they were not interchangeable as should have been the case. There were a few unkind mutterings about the training of a man who was to become known throughout the Force as 'Superintendent Drivel'.

Mac himself was put on the mat and presented his report in writing to ACP Jack Graham from Police HQ, attended by his own Chief Superintendent, Jim Dutton, and 2i/c Ernie Young. Jack Graham was nonplussed by Mac's frankness when he stated that the commands 'Aim' and 'Fire' were not given and that these commands are never given standing in front of one's troops. The result was that he had to hand in his US M1 Carbine, a very personal weapon, and was suspended for 24 hours, then exonerated. Had it been Kenya, a medal and a promotion would at least have been considered. Dinger Bell had a beautiful repeating long-barrelled shotgun sent over to Mac by way of commiseration for a non-event. The following day the carbine was returned and Mac, having explained he did not ask for or wish the job in the first place as he considered himself a bit too long in the tooth to be racing about playing at Mobile Squads, was asked nicely to return to duty. Nobody wanted the job and hardly anyone had the know-how: all part of the pantomime.

The second day of the Jiga/Yamuga fight saw Mac and his two intrepid sub-inspectors, John Pahau and Cosmos Pulai, both dog-eaters from the Manus Islands, head a Police contingent of 7 and 10 Platoons, some 80 bodies equipped with gas guns and shotguns plus some 20-odd .303 rifles. The opposing Big Line of some 3,000–4,000 Jigas were armed with *supsups* (spears), bows and arrows and a 3-foot-handled tomahawk of Swedish steel. They had lined up at about 500 yards, 32 abreast in multiple lines holding their *supsups* horizontally across their front to achieve an immaculate dressing of ranks. They began a disciplined jog-trot in full fighting regalia, pig-greased bodies covered in black soot with bird of paradise head-dresses, a broad belt of bark, a bamboo string *purpur* some two feet to their front and arse-grass of croton stuck in their belt to the rear. As the measured tread began to echo, a SITREP was passed to the Divisional Commander Highlands, Chief Supt Jim Dutton QPM. He and his 2i/c Supt Ernie Young, were on their way. Mac requested the attendance of the Divisional Band with their instruments, emphasising that riot gear was not required. Mac went on to report that he would open fire with everything he had at 100 yards, having theoretically read the Riot Act with the usual two short words. 'Try and hold your fire' was the advice given.

Mac, realising that he was in a facetious frame of mind, decided to gamble on a new tactic. He told his Officers to have the men turn their backs, sit down on their shields and have a smoke. His Presbyterian prayer was answered. The mob ran whooping through the sitting Police and came to a halt some 50 yards on. Precisely at this moment, on the river stone road closely adjacent a 'Mr Whippy' ice cream van arrived. He was instructed to park at the roadside. Police then organised the two opposing lines of Jigas and Yamugas on opposite sides. Mr Whippy did a roaring trade with Police supervision. Next off the rank of surprises was the appearance of the Police Band, who counter-marched up and down playing stirring Sousa marches, to the delight of all present. That concluded another Police Action – or Inaction – in the wild and woolly Highlands.

So in effect the fight had been broken up by accident, but overnight MacDonald acquired a reputation which went by sing-out throughout the Highlands: '*Dri pela man em i kam ap hia olsem long taim bifo hat pela man sootman tru*' – loosely translated as 'A tough nut like those in the past and a real policeman.' Clearly the Mobile Squads for the Highlands Region would have to be retrained according to the local requirements. What they had was a form of clan warfare where there could be hundreds of wounded and a few dead on each side. The powers that be tried to whitewash what was happening; to date no one had put a figure on the economic disruption, or worked out whether this was the beginning of the breakdown in law and order. MacDonald was delighted: the number of clan fights totally prevented him from doing any paperwork in the form of reports and logistics, so he was thankful that Inspector Terry Selva, an ex-Queensland policeman who had spent years in the Highlands, provided them on his behalf. In a matter of days MacDonald retrained and re-equipped his Mobile Group, briefing his Officers and NCOs that previous Town and Gazelle training and equipment were inappropriate for the Highlands, with its volatile and virile people.

The training itself was basic. Everyone fired gas gun, shotgun and SLR repetition rifles at tin cans on bamboo stakes at 100–200 paces. Helmets, water bottles, gas masks, batons and shields, and small packs were discarded, including ration packs. Helmets were steel pots cooking the brain; fresh sparkling water was everywhere in mountain streams; gas masks made the wearer deaf and unable to communicate by voice; shields of steel − too heavy and awkward; batons versus 3-foot axes, no thank you; small packs and rations not required as live off the land, and use village houses for accommodation. Boots, gaiters and socks unnecessary impedimenta: bare feet meant the troops could run faster. Officers like MacDonald wore an old pair of golf shoes with holes cut out to admit sand and water and spikes to cross bridges of felled trees. In brief, personal weapon and ammo and that's your lot. Former retired Police from the lines were recruited as scouts as they could identify the leaders and the main participants. They only identified the opposing side, not their own. They came on strength as labourers and were kitted out with blue Police shorts and shirts, pullover and jungle hat plus liberal rations such as tinned fish, meat and rice, and given a shotgun. Here were the human maps, advisers and intelligence-gatherers.

They and their training were put to the test soon enough. 'Mike Sierra Major to Delta Hotel Quebec. SITREP,' came the report over the SSB Mobile Force radio. 'Report as of 8.15 a.m. today from ADC Kerowagi: Siku/Genu clash this a.m. Reports 3/2 dead so far. Teams are 850/650, usual weapons, bows and arrows also spears. Wounded 300/200; fight expected again a.m. tomorrow. Pn 7 and 10 attending under Sub-Inspectors Pahau and Pulai. Inspector MacDonald flying down this a.m. also by Talair. Cause of fight: ground on their border, also alleged rape of one Siku woman.'

In these clan dust-ups, intelligence was essential to good planning. Plans A to F were conjured up in the middle of the night while MacDonald did his Egyptian PT:

A. All in favour of the Police = A Dream
B. Most favourable for the Law and Order = Seldom
C. Pretty good for all sides, seize the initiative and be a winner.
D. Not in favour, but can be changed to positive.
E. Very dirty situation, probe and hope for opportunity.
F. A no-win situation – 1. Do not go, 2. Go home.

The squads would fly in on Baron Twin and Islander aircraft, one after another doing a shuttle service between Kakamuga airstrip at Mt. Hagen and Kerowagi – quite spectacular. The 0i/c Kerowagi Police Station, S/I Kevin Wilde, a speleologist of some repute among other things, greeted MacDonald and his crew on landing. A trip to the ADC's Office for a briefing and being brought up to speed on current holding arrangements, and MacDonald took off for the fighting area with his two Officers and couple of NCOs. Armed with cheap Instamatic cameras, they took snaps of various groups of warriors along the way, all geared up to perform, right down to the black soot of war plastered over the pig-grease on their faces. Some even posed for their piccie to be taken and when asked what the score was said they would have to defend themselves on the morrow from dawn onwards when they expected to be attacked. Vehicle patrols were sent out between the two opposing factions. The Siku were the larger mob pushing the Gena up the mountain, but as usual higher up the mountain was the more virile and volatile mob. As usual, nobody wanted to fight, only defend themselves, and expressed thanks for the Police presence, but this was as far from the truth as it could be.

Throughout the Highlands the combatants did not fight once darkness had fallen, from 6 p.m. to 6 a.m., whether in deference to the *Masalai* or spirits they never knew. MacDonald spent a pleasant evening with the ADC and his wife and Kevin Wilde and his girlfriend and over a few pots of beer managed to convince the happy pair to get married. Bev Street was the High School maths teacher; their wedding was to be quite an occasion.

Reveille was at 4 a.m., move out at 5 a.m., still in darkness; by 6. a.m. dawn was on the way, with the soaking Highlands mist rolling off the foothills that engulfed Waghi Valley on the Kup side opposite Kerowagi solidly blanked in the heavy white stuff and a chill in the air. The two squads, Nos. 7 and 10, were feeling the cold despite their light Police blue pullovers, and movement was a slow drag. The valleys had gone deadly quiet, which forewarned the initiated that a fight was on the way; even the birds went quiet − bodies in the bush. MacDonald decided to take in both squads in a skirmish line fully extended over a few hundred yards and do a sweep up the hills, hoping to force the Genas to remain in the upper mountain area: if the Sikus decided to attack uphill, an about-turn to deal with them would be an effortless movement.

Various parties of warriors passed parallel to the Police movement using the 'Big Rods', the numerous footpaths between the *kaukau* (sweet potato) patchwork gardens. All were in their *bilas*, black soot and pig-grease base. One group of thirty or so stopped in a gully near where MacDonald was standing and called up to him. Was his carbine any good? The sling went from shoulder to elbow but no further before there were about thirty bows fully stretched with arrows aimed dead on MacDonald. He bowed his head in resignation and said he was only joking. He noticed that the group had their No. 1 arrows with the individual's distinctive colours; usually they came in groups of three to six and were not used in fights as they were for ceremonial occasions. Ordinary bamboo, freshly cut, was the norm. Later the same group were taken prisoners and charged with Riotous Behaviour and Carrying an Offensive Weapon. When asked if he could identify the accused MacDonald picked up three sets of arrows and gave them to the accused. The Magistrate was most impressed, and they showed up on photographs taken earlier. Court procedure was conducted according to the Police Offences Ordinance and Native Law Ordinance; the prosecution, conducted by an Officer or Senior NCO from the Mobile Group, invoked tribal custom as was known from time immemorial. Fortunately for the prosecution the Magistrate, who invariably would be a Highlands Kiap, was sympathetic to the Crown case.

As the Police line advanced up the hill, both sides got a liberal dose of tear gas, depending on the wind direction. The protagonists were kept apart. S/I Kevin Wilde commented that MacDonald was itching to shoot, as he was 'an African'. The response he got was, 'Who has his revolver out and what does that signify?' – and an apology was forthcoming. Gena Leader Siwi Korondo, an acclaimed fight leader, was noticeably absent. Platoon 10 S/I Cosmos Pulai was tasked with keeping post so that the Sikus stayed down in the valley. Platoon 7 S/I John Pahau, with MacDonald, would search for Siwi Korondo in his hamlet area. His son appeared, and said his father wished to surrender to the Police party but he must be protected from the Siku. Siwi appeared, and about 750 warriors. The Councils and Committees (Chiefs and Headmen appointed partially by the Administration) did a headcount by the use of bundles of twigs; as the nominal roll was called a warrior could come forward, join his line and dump his arms as the twig was discarded. Primitive, but almost 100% effective. They called up a magistrate who conducted a bush court on the hillside, and trucks for the surrendering men. Isuzu 10-ton tippers were the favourite. They came from Mt. Hagen, fifty miles away, and parked at a pre-arranged meeting place on the main road some ten miles from the court; the trucks and drivers came from the Government Transport Dept with a Police armed escort up front.

By late afternoon the oracle had been worked and now it was time to take the prisoners out of their mountain hamlets, marching out along back roads and tracks so as not to impinge on Siku territory, which would indicate a challenge to fight. The mob of 750 were marshalled and off they set with their 40-strong Police escort, MacDonald and Wilde out front. The crowd behind began to cram on the pace: from a leisurely 90 paces to the minute they upped the ante to about a 160 jogtrot. What to do? Shoot them with shotgun No. 4? MacDonald took up the singing and jogging with the crowd, as did S/I Wilde, but the rest of the Police guards were soon left behind as they were exhausted from their earlier efforts. After the 10-mile jog they piled into the trucks, singing with the occasional war chant thrown in, making it more of a festive occasion than imprisonment. They decided not to send them to Kundiawa, the local *kalabus*, but another 100 miles to Goroka. Each of the dozen or so trucks had four police shotgunners sitting on each corner or the roof, and off the menagerie went.

For the next two days they went up and down in the trucks to Goroka and Kundiawa. As the Supt Corrective (Prisons) would not accept bodies without a Warrant of Commitment, this had to be done individually by the bush court Informations (Charge Sheets). To stop the rot, MacDonald missed out the chain of command and phoned the Commissioner of Prisons, Bob English, at Port Moresby; he agreed to allow the Police to guard the prisoners in the *kalabus*, circumventing the red tape. It worked. Apart from food and toilet breaks for 48 hours of continued movement, not a 'warrior' was lost. God was again on Mac's side. He was not a great believer in Highlands improvisation, but at times there was little choice. The Sikus gave up about 800, and they, in turn, went to the Kundiawa *kalabus* where none other than Supt John Hynds, Mac's old mate from Kavieng days, awaited. On the 'she'll be right' basis there were no Warrant problems; the Colonial Can-do was still the order of the day. Two police had received arrows in the guts when returning to camp at Kerowagi; a roadblock of trees set up the ambush. As per custom, the arrows were fighting not hunting, therefore no barbs, so the doctor at Kerowagi's *Haus Sik* did the extractions and the boys were okay. A few arses received shotgun pellets in the Police payback. In fact a sorry sight was beheld at Minj Hospital: forty or so gallant warriors with gentian violet-dotted bums in the air having had the pellets removed without anaesthetic.

Mac was fast coming to understand the Highland mentality, very similar to his own from his Scottish upbringing. The Scots were doing the same thing 300 or so years previously, so there was some correlation to be drawn. Father Ross, a worthy figure with forty years in these Highlands, was a revered figure in the Mt. Hagen area, so Mac went and chewed the fat and, lo and behold, they hit it off right down to the nitty-gritty of what was required to maintain a semblance of balance. Next on the list was

Danny Leahy, one of the first expatriates in the Western Highlands. He was getting on and almost blind, but still a pioneer in many ways. He proudly displayed a family photograph of his ten children, all by different indigenous mothers but all educated at different top Australian schools and now holding down plantations of coffee and tea in the Highlands Region. Over a few beers Danny told the story how an employee of his had produced a highly polished skull in the best headhunter tradition. It had a neat bullet hole drilled dead centre between the eyes — Danny had personally put it there in one of his original exploration visits through the area. Danny was well abreast of the current situation and advised Mac he was on the right track, so two of the local oracles had confirmed his Highlands appreciation was correct.

Another two squads were posted to Mt. Hagen, so at times Mac had nine squads available. Eventually the ideal response to a normal clan fight was to use a Mobile Company, one squad up the hill, one squad downhill, one squad as a reserve. Fights usually were around 750 a side, though Wamp Wan MBE, the Moge clan's Leader/Councillor, could muster 6,000 at a few days' notice with another 15,000 in reserve, a real warlike prospect. Luckily they only kept a watching brief. At the height of the fight season, Mac had up to fifteen fights going on simultaneously. The answer: there is no point in going to a fight unless you are going to win. An immediate system of priority was devised where the 'good' ones got a higher rating.

By way of example, one evening about 5 p.m. at Mt. Hagen Golf Club, 2i/c Division S/Supt Ernie Young remarked to MacDonald that it might be a good idea if he took off to Minj, as there was a 'big one' brewing. MacDonald put down his middie and glanced out of the club-house window, shook his head and informed Ernie, 'Sir, rain delays play.'

'What the hell?'

'They might slip and fall and cut themselves on their axes on the slippery, muddy ground. They will not fight if it's raining – bad form; also there are no dead yet. Once we have a few, then it's time for Police Action.'

'Agreed, MacDonald — have a beer!'

'Your astonishingly good health, Sir.'

The conversation continued over a few more middies, then it was Reveille at 6 a.m., cookhouse at 7 a.m., Muster Parade at 8 a.m. and off to see the Wild West Show, arriving 35 miles down the Waghi Valley at Minj about 9.30 a.m. By 10.30 a.m. the ADC for the Sub-District and the local Police Officer would have briefed the troops as to the current dispositions of the sides involved. A five-mile truck to the bottom of the foothills, dismount and pound your way up the hillside; 10.30–12.30 survey the scene, manoeuvre into position – by then a couple on either team would have been killed or if they were still 'at it', cover the mob with tear gas and put a few pellets up the bums of the disturbers of the peace. Make hand signals to come in for a *tok tok* or *kibung* (meeting), ascertain the proportion of blame and number of surrenderees and when and where this *kibung* was to be done, usually at the *ples krai* – the area used as a fighting ground, dance arena or for mourning. Arrange for two separate courts and two separate prisons. Two separate routes in and out and roundabout. Also agree to the terms of imprisonment: District Court was out as there could be an appeal; some of the warriors despite their traditional fight appearance might be Army Officers on leave or half-baked legal eagles, so Local Court was favourite and the maximum sentence was six months. Also Court documentation was not required, only the Warrant of Commitment. It was agreed how many and who would go to gaol and for how long, which depended on a number of factors. An immediate surrender, a plea of 'Guilty' for a smaller number of prisoners and lesser sentence; if there was a delay or hesitation, more to the *kalabus* and a longer sentence. The Government bodies were not dealing from a position of strength, as most supposed, but compromises were reached on every occasion.

To give Kerowagi a less violent face, MacDonald was eventually invited to the wedding of Inspector Kevin Wilde and schoolmistress Bev Street – an occasion to be remembered. One reason for the invitation was that MacDonald's old Mercedes 190D was still presentable enough to be the bridal vehicle. Most of Kundiawa, Kerowagi and Waghi Valley's expatriate population were invited or attended. Bev's parents flew up from Brisbane; her students provided the choir in the Catholic Chapel where they were married by the local priest, even though both bride and groom were Anglican. Who cared? After the church ceremony the 'mob' descended upon the Kerowagi Club, which consisted of a huge native material roundhouse, the roof being of thatch, the shelter of poles cut from casuarina trees and the sides of a bamboo split weave. It had a shiny cement floor, a huge bar, some tables and government-type metal-cum-plastic chairs, ceiling fans, and a central fireplace. A surprisingly good local band was giving it heaps, from modern ballroom to the latest shake, rattle and roll. Alcohol was flowing and the High School girls served finger food in addition to the hot and cold buffet.

Outside was the 'other' facility, consisting solely of a long-drop thunderbox toilet with a pile of newspapers, or toilet rolls for the more discerning patrons. A multiracial queue of both genders was already forming as the reception got into full swing. Protocol was followed with various speeches, not that any particular attention was being paid by most of the guests. Major and Mrs Street (Rtd) had latched on to Mac and spouse and were most interested in all that was happening around them. They were totally new to the PNG customs, including those of their brother and sister expatriates, and felt a little perplexed by it all.

As time wore on, the crowd swelled as a few of the local 'big men' and the Valley expatriates from all walks of life filtered in to send Bev and Kevin on their way. Besides, it sounded like a bloody good party was the go. Harry Field, a 6' 6" diesel mechanic, fitter and turner, appeared in a grease-smeared T-shirt, brief blue work shorts and work boots with a scruffy cardigan to keep off the evening air, also sporting a three-day growth of beard and an inane grin after a few refreshments. Mac knew Harry from his Kavieng days – and his diminutive Chinese wife, who wore the pants and could wield a mean umbrella to her husband. Coffee buyer Jim McCourt and his mate also appeared, none of them averse to a pub punch-up. Robin Lamont, ex Squadron Leader RAF and an old school pal of Mac's, drifted in; he too did a bit of coffee buying and ran the Kerowagi Pub, where the locals in their hundreds regularly descended. Mac introduced his friends and acquaintances to Major and Mrs Street and hoped the motley crew were going to be on their best behaviour for the nuptial celebrations. Even the locals were of a similar frame of mind, as was amply demonstrated in the multiracial toilet queue where the odd Missus was given a chance to jump the queue but graciously refusing the genteel offer.

Then in came the Chimbu 'Princess', a local girl, unusually tall at about 6' 1", with a magnificent figure to match, wearing a shimmering dress of white cotton material and thongs to go with it. She had her hair straightened and was made up to the nines. A cigarette dangled from the corner of her mouth and she was acknowledging the boys of all races with intimate waves until she spotted Harry the mechanic. He obviously took her fancy, as she grabbed him for a dance and the pair put on a show worth paying to see, both with big grins of anticipation. As they gyrated round the dance floor it was obvious she had no time for underwear, and a first-class eyeful was had by all. Major Street could hardly believe his eyes and was advised to try a whisky.

By now the High School girls had finished their duties and were up and at it with the boys. The expats at the bar were giving a rendition of one of their favourites, 'It's a long way to Kerowagi', substituting the local place names for 'Tipperary' and so on. As it was a Sunday, 'Onward, Christian Soldiers' got an airing. At one stage of the proceedings 'Maus Grass', one of the fight leaders from the Kup area of the Waghi Valley, appeared. He immediately latched on to Mac and Missus by sticking his drunken bearded face into Mac's and telling him what a good fellow he was, introducing Mac to all who passed as *'Dispela em i man long brukim pait, em i Numba Wan tru'* − 'This is the man who breaks up our fights, he is very good.' After another half-dozen beers to buy him off, 'Maus Grass' moved on to fresh fields. Cars and trucks parked in the *barrets* (drains) all around the township of Kerowagi next morning confirmed that a good night had been had by all.

One of the clan fights was between the Pipitombas and Linki-san some miles outside Wabag, the principal town of the new Province called The Enga, PNG's main linguistic group of some 70,000 people. The Wild Wabaggers were a more awkward bunch to deal with than the Happy Hagens. There had been a couple each side killed and some one hundred each side wounded. The initial fight had been a few days before the arrival of the Police when the second round erupted. Mac and the boys spent a few nights on 24-hour non-stop roll-ups and arrested only a score or so warriors, some sick and wounded, plus the old and bold. Next ploy was to drive down the Lai Valley towards Wabag, do a sweep from the rear and force the Lenki-san back into their own territory; the step after that was to sit in the village and send the *Kri* out along the ridges that if they didn't come in and surrender their womenfolk would be raped. The *Kri* or 'Sing Out' was done by getting a local to pass the message from *keel* (ridge) to *keel*; they did it by slowly inhaling deeply, raising their arms above their heads and giving out the Enga language '*Eboo eboo eboo*' ('Come in, come in' in the plural). The message could travel forty miles in as many minutes or less, much better than the Police SSB radio. In conjunction with the 'Sing Out', another tactic was also used, old-fashioned but quite effective. A small *haus* (toilet) would be 'cooked' (burned down), then a house, and another at half-hourly intervals until they came in and gave themselves up. The women and children were allowed to remove their ceremonial weapons and artefacts, head-dresses and so on before their *haus* was 'cooked', and a house could be built in a day with fifty pairs of hands from local materials — bamboo, casuarina poles, pine and banana thatch — but the UN had not approved this tactic, so officially it was never used.

The second Jiga/Yamuga fight was now in the offing. As was customary in the Highlands, it took months to plan a big fight as there were certain agreements proposed and met by both sides, such as the time, date and place and their intention to kill a particular number or sometimes particular people. A week before the fight both sides would hold *sing-sings* (meetings involving dancing, singing, and speechifying by numerous leaders; women and children would be moved out of the fight area after having taken part in the *sing-sing* and the feast of meat and beer). Funnily enough, the two expatriate Hagen butchers did a roaring trade in steak. The Kiaps usually allowed the Councillors of the various lines amnesty, even if they were the fight leaders, and arresting them was not on. So Mac decided to cut off the head of the snake, arrest all Councillors on both the Jiga and Yamuga sides, and give them terms of imprisonment on multiple charges to run consecutively in order to disrupt the political structure of the clans involved. When they emerged from prison, new leaders would have replaced them or at least their line of thought would have been disrupted.

Clan fights were breaking out all over the Highlands so the Mobile Force had been expanded by reinforcements from Rabaul, Lae and Port Moresby. Mac had a dozen or so squads or four companies of Mobile Force plus General Duties, mainly ex-Mobile, giving him over 700 bodies, plus a back-up of General Duty Police. Operations would be of several weeks duration. After eighteen months, Mac was finally transferred out when he applied to the Commissioner for 900 self-loading rifles; the powers that be thought he had cracked under the pressure of 150-odd fights, but history shows he was right in his predictions.

This posting was as District Inspector for the Western Highlands and Enga Provinces, once again with the acting rank of Superintendent, to advise some of the Police Station 0i/cs and the Kiaps in charge of detachments in the bush how to respond to various situations and introduce new techniques in the fight against crime and lawlessness. Most of the duties were done by single-engine Cessna aircraft with a group of Highlands pilots, mainly from Talair, some ex-Battle of Britain, both Brits and Jerries, and the odd crop-duster. One such was Scotty Adams, a Scot who had flown with the RNZAF and had been a crop-duster in Australia. Scotty's penchant for strong drink and strong language had got him banned from all clubs and pubs and a number of private residences, but in the air he was a changed man, a most careful and resolute pilot of incredible skill. One Saturday morning he took Mac up to Wabag, where there had been the usual clan fight, the idea being to demonstrate the possibility of bombing the participants with tear gas. Luckily for all concerned, Mac persuaded him to rule it out, even though liberal use of tear gas worked well in other situations. Not to be outdone, Scotty did a few practice dives over a fight, whose protagonists fired arrows at the aircraft. Mac quickly became disorientated as Scotty insisted on tight turns, side-slips and flying upside down in circles. Thanks to a strong constitution and only a slight hangover from Friday night, the inside of the plane was not redecorated.

One evening in early 1973 the Italian Consul and entourage for some obscure reason decided to visit Mt. Hagen. The District Commissioner, Dinger Bell laid on the usual bunfight – a cocktail party with Heads of Departments and business personalities being the invited guests. As the evening progressed the air of conviviality spread in various ways among the invited guests, who included The Venerable the elected member for the Western Highlands. He also was a fight leader to the Link-Jiga Clan. That particular evening he was resplendent in a Filipino shirt and Hawaiian flared slacks with a bright multi-flowered pattern, his shrewd eyes were lit up with good bonhomie and possibly the effect of several stubbies of SP Brown, which he was clutching in each hand. He greeted the MacDonalds with a display of brotherly love, congratulating Gus on his ability to deal with the warring clans and his charming wife as one of the nicest expat ladies in the community. He had a bit of a sway on and having delivered his platitudes, asked in Melanesian pidgin, 'Sma haus i whia?' Mac replied, 'I go i go lik lik long han kais i stap, yu no ken loosim rot bilong yu.' (Translation: 'Where's the toilet?') 'Go a little bit, it is on the left-hand side, it is easy to find.' As this conversation was taking place, a beautific smile creased the MP's shaggy bearded face, obviously denoting relief, as a large dark-coloured stain appeared in the area of his crotch and upper legs! With a grunt of satisfaction, he perched himself on the arm of Mrs Mac's lounge chair and attempted to continue with animated conversation, much to her surprise, horror, then amusement. Who said we could not take them anywhere? The Italian Consulate Party was at least being given the opportunity of further graces of the Western Highlands.

Mac had gained the respect of the various clans, being paid the supreme compliment of being addressed by his surname without title or rank, as was the custom and addressed as '*Bik man i kam up harim tok bilong lapun*' – translated as 'A leader is present, listen to what this venerable has to say'. Although Mac had locked up a few thousand Jigas for clan fighting they never threatened him or his family, who lived in their Police quarter on Jiga ground within 200 metres of a village across a donga. The house had a three-foot *pitpit* fence. Mac's Chief Scout, John Kuli, and Constable i/c

Driver Lexi were both Jigas, which would have ensured some protection. After two years in the Highlands a transfer came out of the blue to Gordon Barracks, Port Moresby. Before leaving, the MacDonalds were farewelled by fellow Scots, tea planters from the Wahgi Valley, from the townships of Minj and Banz, and coffee planters. The Kiaps presented him with a beautiful repeater-action eight-cartridge shotgun worth over $1,500. His fellow Officers, who had done some outstanding deeds, had little or no recognition, as the Highlands was more or less considered a punishment posting.

Fight Chimbu (a sport), 1977

Wabag Base Camp, 1972

Sub-inspector Vincent VM, Mt. Hagen, 1973

Village, Lake Kutubu (Southern Highlands), 1977

21: From Gordon to the Green City

Gordon Barracks was the biggest barracks for the Royal Papua and New Guinea Constabulary. It housed some 1,200 members plus families, all making up a considerable village of some five thousand souls: 100 labourers plus Police, carpenters, plumbers, a first-rate dining hall, a wet canteen, parade ground, guard-room, Officer block, two single/double blocks, a couple of football and cricket pitches and excellent Officer quarters for four families and security fence surrounding the complex. The MacDonald family, the only expat/whites in the barracks, was given a palatial quarter. The barracks housed all types of Police and Mobile Company plus CIB, Traffic and the odd PHQ bod. Snow Feeney was MacDonald's Chief Superintendent; Snow had been MacDonald's boss before and had the opinion that MacDonald was a tough nut and hence was treated as such. MacDonald was a Senior Inspector, equal to an Army Captain. The problem as usual was discipline in the first instance. Secondly, there was a lack of interest in the ORs and families, exacerbated by a lack of back-up at all levels. Morale, that vital ingredient, was lacking. Here was MacDonald's first task.

The wet canteen was enlarged to twice the size and a dry canteen introduced on the same scale. In came Canteen Manager Doug Kirby and an accountant to do a monthly check. A Canteen Police Squad was formed under Cpl Daniel Punsurawa from Sio, Morobe District, a first-class spiv but useful in the circumstances. Prices were reduced, and the money rolled in. Next was the Dining Hall: all Officers and Civilian Staff were expected to partake of the same fare as the ORs, with the exception of a 50c per week fee for additional condiments. A weekly inspection of all quarters and a $20 prize for the best; labourers' quarters were improved by the issue of beds and mattresses, also their own ablution block and toilets; a blind eye to carry-outs from the wet canteen; an operational guardroom and checks on movements in and out of the barracks; a scale-A parade every Friday with the 70-strong Police Band under the familiar direction of Supt Tom Shacklady MBE, BEM: the troops, the band, the watching families all loved it and morale was on the up and up. 'One week Mac' was the 0i/c Barracks' nickname, as discipline – always dear to the heart – was improved by quite a ruthless punishment of one week's pay for all trivial tried breaches of discipline.

As the Barracks were now under control, the powers that be transferred 'One week Mac' to Papua Division as Staff Officer – trouble-shooter – and his new residence was outside the Barracks in Gordon Estate. Before he moved, one day out of the blue an ex-Cadet Officer who had been dismissed from the Constabulary presented himself in Mac's office, ranting and raving that he wished to rejoin the Constabulary and demanding that the 0i/c Barracks reinstate him. As the rave progressed his hands were chopped from him and he lent on the 0i/c's desk in a threatening manner, but it just so happened that his chin came smartly in contact with said desk. He was eventually removed by Senior Sergeant Major Goneni, a man with a reputation: he had strangled one rioter and broken the neck of another during a disturbance in the Gazelle Peninsula at Rabaul. The disgruntled ex-Cadet Officer then went to express his point of view at the guardroom. Mac went over to the guardroom at the Main Gate and told him to take a walk, and he began waving his arms and shouting.

Inspector Martin Haddock, Coy Cmdr of a Mobile Force Company, thought his brother Inspector was being assaulted, came to the rescue with a short sharp right cross to the jaw, and one body spun round and collapsed, unconscious, in the shrubbery nearby. The Guard picked him up and dumped him unceremoniously outside the Main Gate. Martin Haddock was 6' 2" and a good sixteen stone of mid-England county stock, and not to be meddled with. Mac thanked Martin, pointing out that his prompt action had not been really required, but by now the unconscious figure had come alive and was shouting, 'You people will be sorry!' He was the nephew of the then Prime Minister, the Hon Michael Somare.

As this was Friday lunchtime, Mac remarked, they should hear something by Sunday morning as the wheels of justice ground exceeding slow. Sure enough, Sunday morning the new Commissioner of Police, Brian J Holloway, required both Officers to report to him immediately at his residence on Toguba Hill. Holloway had been Mac's Chief Supt in the Islands and they had been known to indulge together in the brown amber refreshment known as VB. Holloway had been personally contacted by the PM and told that an immediate result was required. The Inspectors forewarned were duly forearmed. Mac was senior and would do all the talking. But as the reason for the recall to the Boss's residence was not stated, why not make it a social occasion and take the wives along for the entertainment, plus a 40 oz bottle of Chivas Regal?

On arrival they were welcomed by Mrs H, a charming lady who was well aware of her husband's and Mac's reputations. The jolly company assembled on the main verandah and had large dollops of Chivas with water or soda and plenty of ice. By twelve noon the company was well and truly on the way, but the boss said before he produced any further refreshment that the boys should adjourn to the formal lounge. Mac told the tale of gentle removal: the complainant had merely tripped and fallen as he was obviously under the 'affluence of incohol at the time'. Being a good policeman, Martin made appropriate noises to corroborate the story. After considerable reassurance, the Commissioner was satisfied and would inform the PM that this nephew had been dismissed and unfortunately was a delinquent. BJH gave his Officers a toast and wished them well. Mac could not help saying quietly to his former boss, 'Well, we'll never really know, will we?' – to which the rejoinder was, 'Get out of here, you Pommy bastard!' It could have been a lot stronger. The pair of heroes drew a deep breath and shook hands: they were still 'in'.

MacDonald, Staff Officer Papua Division with the Acting Rank of Superintendent, was mainly responsible for a visiting job to the five Districts. Western had a huge landmass but a small population of 30,000. Daru was the main township, where you could find barramundi fillets and crayfish by the carton; a mangrove swamp area from the mighty Fly River drained the District from the Star Mountains to the sea, some 500 navigable miles with a 30-foot rise and fall, an 11-knot current and sandbanks to navigate. The OK Tedi Copper Mine had yet to come on-stream. Kiwais, the coastal people, had enjoyed a taste of the outside world as seamen with Arabs and Europeans for centuries. Next door, Gulf District's headquarters was Kerema. The coastal areas were swamp land with main rivers such as Kikori, Purari and Lakekamu, the last named navigable for shallower-draft vessels and linking up with the Bulldog Track of WWII importance as a supply route to Wau in Morobe Province. The Kerimas had a migratory streak; they were found in most Government Departments as clerks and tradesmen, while some made good policemen.

Central District had 'Mosbi' as the Administration capital, UNI and Army and Police Barracks and Training. In Northern District, Popondetta was the Headquarters, with Kokoda at the end of the famous wartime trail where, with supreme heroism and heavy casualties, the Diggers halted the Happy Jappy and turned him around in November 1942. Milne Bay at the south-eastern tip of the mainland had Alatau as HQ and Samarai, with its own colourful history as a port in the gold rush days. This was another Pacific battleground, the scene of Japan's first defeat in an attempted amphibious landing during World War II. The Japanese were trying to create a base for their air and naval support operations during the attempt to capture Port Moresby. The action had cost almost 400 Australian lives, but now Milne Bay looked what it was — a place of unsurpassed beauty with its various archipelagos and an island people of considerable charm. The Trobriands to the north, with their bare-breasted, grass-skirted girls, were known as the Islands of Love.

All of the Districts were divided up into five or more Sub-Districts, administered by an Assistant District Commissioner with his District Officers, Patrol Officers, and 'Pikinini' Kiaps (Cadet POs). Inspectorial Duties were one of MacDonald's fortes; most Senior Officers did not relish flying in single-engine or even double-engine planes. As the saying goes, in PNG there are two types of pilots, good ones and dead ones. If one had the time, the Government trawler was the way to visit the islands, with a bit of fishing, including game fish, swimming, snorkelling and collecting tropical shells. One trip to Milne Bay, accompanied by Kim Bineer, an Army Captain on attachment to the Royal Constabulary, included a visit to Samarai Island, where there was a plinth erected to a Patrol Officer who had in fact committed suicide at the age of 32. The plinth was no longer central; it had been moved several inches to one side by a group of locals, no mean feat as the monument was solid granite. The inscription read: 'To the memory of John Smith, a member of the Administration who through his life had endeavoured to make New Guinea a fit place for white men'. The racial quote and the New Guinea reference were both out: this was in the heart of Papua. How to make friends and influence people had clearly not been a consideration.

Six hours in a speedboat was the return trip into a heavy sea with a gale wind as opposed to the downward trip of two hours. The Alatau Club was multiracial, the locals most insistent on shaking the hand. Next was a visit to the local *kalabus*, where there was again much shaking of paws with the inmates, as the majority were from the Highlands and were previous clients of MacDonald's. Next on the Agenda was a flight over the Owen Stanleys – 15,000 feet – to Kokoda and Popondetta and down to Gona, a former mission station on the north coast where there had been bloody fighting in WWII.

Senior Inspector MacDonald's progress having impressed the powers that be, he was taken under the wing of the Deputy Commissioner Operations and given an Inspectorial Role for the whole country including all Police Stations and Detachments. A format of inspection was drawn up, difficulties and requirements, the introduction of literate police to outstations and detachments, and a new transfer/posting system. The Constabulary was divided into Regular, for the cities and towns and settled areas, and Field for the bush or unsettled areas. The Regular was Officered by ex-Police, mainly from the Australian State Forces, with a good percentage of Brits and some from various Colonial Forces, mainly Africa. Until 1964 the Regular Constabulary had an easy life: the locals were not allowed to drink intoxicating liquor, though they did drink both home and commercial brews in their villages. With the advent of liquor came a sudden increase in crime. What to do? Send for the Fire Brigade. So in the late

Sixties came the Contract Officer, who received a gratuity at the end of his service and could almost be described as a mercenary, a dirty word to some who did not understand that certain males love adventure, and fight not merely for money. The Regular was promoted and better paid than the Contract Officer, but little bad feeling existed between the two classes as each realised the other had a function to perform.

There had always been friction between the Field Constabulary and the Regular, for a variety of reasons. The 'Kiap' came from an educated and adventuresome class of young Australian and New Zealanders, with the odd Brit, and were given the accolade by their British counterparts of being the finest in the Colonial Service: they spoke more native languages, did more remote patrols, accepted greater responsibility at lower levels and were much closer to the locals at all levels. They wore an unofficial uniform of battered hat, bush jacket, long khaki slacks or shorts and a sturdy pair of hiking boots; seniority brought a characteristic walking stick or cromach, with a colourful sweat cravat. Sometimes the jurisdictions overlapped, and both parties had differing ideas about how to deal with particular situations. Regular Police were called in to support when the proverbial hit the fan. The Regular Constabulary had all the civilised amenities of suburban life in the main, although they too had the odd outstation where few wished to serve, much to their collective detriment. MacDonald for his part was known as a Kiap lover as he agreed with their philosophy, similar to his own previous training and experiences in British East Africa.

When Police were posted to serve in the Field Detachments, some of the old hands who were also bold and illiterate or semi-literate enjoyed the life and its greater freedom. The younger police with families accepted their lot stoically. Old and young alike were more or less forgotten about and remained to stagnate in the bush for up to ten years, after which they were no longer employable in the Regular Constabulary except in times of emergency when they proved a steadying influence among the less tested. Their promotion prospects were less, so they made up for their isolation by 'going native', planting up gardens and filling in as members of the local population, to the detriment of their function. The Kiap could fill many roles: agricultural Officer (*didiman*), vet, doctor, financial advisor, tax collector (his most disliked role), police Officer, magistrate – in fact some District Commissioners even among the expatriate population had such sweeping powers they were referred to as 'God'. Detachments of Field Constabulary seldom received a visit from a Regular Police Officer, mainly because of the danger of flying.

MacDonald had the ear of his boss, Deputy Commissioner Sari Onamisa Mesa, one of MacDonald's Cadet Officers ten years before, so reforms were put in place. Every two years the Police Other Ranks would go on leave for three months to their Home District. Should they desire a transfer, it would be granted to a different location and environment, and from Field to Regular or vice versa. The longest spell was four years in one posting unless the individual was a specialist in CIB, Traffic or elsewhere. Each detachment would have at least two fully literate members so that regular returns and applications could be made. One should not forget the effect on families in terms of education, medical facilities and courses for members in various aspects of Police Duty. Eventually young Sergeants were running the Police side of the Detachment, which was a great improvement.

One fine April day in 1975, MacDonald was called in by the Deputy Commissioner, Chief of Operations, with the words 'MacDonald, I have a job for you!'

'Sir?'

'How would you like to go over to my home Province, Morobe, and take over the role as 2i/c "C" Division? Chief Superintendent Sam Nuakona requires a back-up; as you may appreciate, he is new and, like the rest of us, new to command. You may be able to help him with some of his decision-making. Also in a few months he is going to Bramshill College in Oxfordshire, UK, on a Senior Officers' Course for four months and you will take over the Division. Any questions?'

'No, Sir.'

'You'll be okay.'

'Sir.'

MacDonald had a confirmed rank of Senior Inspector and had been Acting Superintendent; now he was Acting Senior

Superintendent, so at least it was a step in the right direction. But twenty-four years' service and still comparatively junior... As had so often happened, the transfer took place on Anzac Day, April 25th, so sadly the Remembrance march, two-up and the proverbial PU were all missed yet again. Butt Solomon and Poksur, his servant and wife from New Ireland, plus Mrs Tib the dog accompanied the Macs and Richard, who was at primary school. Shelley, their daughter, was already attending boarding school in Brisbane. A survival kit was taken, and vehicle and household goods came round by sea a week later.

Mac had only passed through Lae before. It was the commercial capital of PNG and considered a plum posting. An airport as busy as Moresby plus the Defence Force Air Wing and a Joint Services College, a Technical University and Posts and Telegraphs Tertiary College; a deep-sea harbour, yacht club, bowls club and of course an international golf course, eighteen holes of hallowed turf, the best in the country. The house provided was first-class, an old Bulolo type with a broad verandah three-quarters of the way round, a double garage and servants' quarters. In Australia the house would pass as a Queenslander, spacious with high ceilings and fans, plus senior Officer's furniture and a decent vegetable and fruit garden. Lae also had a large war cemetery, kept in immaculate condition and providing the Green City with a noted arboretum. Mac paid his respects to all graves and noted the exact places of the VCs and other decoration winners. There was also a separate graveyard for the Indian Army, who had suffered grievous losses as prisoners of war in Japanese hands. There was also a section of British POWs, mainly from Singapore.

Chief Supt Sam Nuakona was in his early thirties and, like most of the indigenous Officers, had been rapidly promoted, as independence was now in the offing. He had been a technician with the Posts and Telegraphs and was extremely bright, but sometimes a trifle indecisive, hence his nickname of 'Slippery Sam'. He and Mac got on well and made a good team.

'C' Division, New Guinea Mainland, embraced Morobe Province, with Lae the main centre. Morobe, the most representative Province of PNG, had a 300,000 population, plus

5,000 expatriates. Dense rainforests, rolling productive valleys, and to the south-west the rugged Menyamya where the unpredictable savage and fearless Kukukuku people, the fiercest in PNG, held terrifying sway. Very few were over five feet but they carried 6' bows and arrows, primitive stone clubs, and most had bones through their noses. When a truck-load of them arrived at one Highlands Show in Goroka, thousands of Highlanders literally took to the hills, such was these fearsome wee men's reputation. In the 1930s, Mick Leahy and his brother were attacked while prospecting and Pat was badly wounded. This type of attack was still reasonably common in the 1970s. Any sign of weakness was always exploited by the 'Kookakookas', as the name was pronounced. They did not like it; seemingly it referred to an insect of some kind.

These charming people smoke their dead in a sitting position, usually up in a cave on the mountainside. Sometimes the skull was placed in the family garden as a way of remembrance. Their dress was a grass kilt, criss-cross straps of red and yellow beads across the chest and shaven head with a topknot. They were fierce in appearance, and quick-tempered. The Kiap in the 1970s was an Englishman from Newcastle, a hard-case Geordie who had brought his 70-year-old mother out to the wilds of PNG as the second expat resident of Menyamya. Police still patrolled with rifle and bayonet, which gave any stranger a clue he was in hostile company.

East of Menyama lay the Wau goldfields, then north of that Bulolo, a company town with the *klinki* pine plywood factory and Forestry Training Schools. The company had the idea that their Police Inspector would conform to their wishes, but not for long. The Police Station at Wau came under the Inspector at Bulolo, and had a complement of about 25 bodies with a Sub-Inspector in charge. Both were medium-pace stations with the normal run of offenders passing through the system. Wau's golf course was hilly, its airstrip likewise − in fact on one of his visits Mac went up with some of the Army boys in a Pilatus Porter STOL aircraft which revved its engines, took off in about 25 metres and was soon flying backwards due to a strong wind!

Down the valley was Mumeng hamlet, one of several with

regular police stations like Finschhafen, a huge mission station of Lutheran denomination. Unlike Africa, the missionaries were a help rather than a hindrance, and did good works without becoming politically embroiled, thanks to the benign Australian Administration, while the natural division of the country helped in its own way. There were a dozen Field Detachments and six Sub-Districts. Crops representing all aspects of PNG were produced. The people on the whole were cooperative with Government policy.

Lae sat at the beginning of the Highlands Highway, which over the past decade had been upgraded to almost highway standard, with some parts sealed. Nadzab Airport, 25 miles out of Lae, was opened to larger aircraft and could accommodate the odd international jet. Up the Markham Valley, 100 miles or so and 2,000-plus feet, you moved from the valley floor into the Eastern Highlands at 4,500–5,000 feet and entered another world. The first town was Kainantu, with its airstrip and coffee plantings, then on to Henganofi and Goroka, the centre, with its various tertiary colleges; Mt. Michael at 12,500 feet, the vast Goroka Valley, a population of 200,000 and a couple of thousand expatriates in the coffee industry and education facilities. The Eastern Highlands was the first Highlands District/Province to be pacified, for want of a better word; it was also the most realistic, practical and co-operative of the five Highland Provinces.

Following the Markham Valley north-west, you arrive in Madang Province, with Madang with its towering Coast Watchers monument, the Venice of PNG, a town built around islands and lagoons and with deep-sea berths – the quietest town and, like Rabaul, possibly the most beautiful and well-laid out, thanks to the German Administration. Here you sent the Officers who deserved a break from a harder environment. There was the Smugglers' Inn, the Madang Hotel and the Coast Watchers Motel, all on the seafront or on a lagoon. This was the conference haven of PNG, where you could leave your car keys in the car, doors were open during the night and possessions were never stolen. Madang had 150,000 locals and some 2,500 expats. Inland you came to Bundi, on the slopes of Mt. Wilhelm at 15,000 feet with occasional snowfalls. Although Madang was mainly a coastal province, along the rear range, the Schrader Mountains, the people were Highlanders. Alexishafen, some miles west of Madang, had a large Catholic mission with a beautiful church. Over the water some forty miles away was Karkar Island with its active volcano. Madang produced copra and tobacco and was a fisherman's paradise, both commercial and game.

Next, heading west, came East Sepik, with Wewak as its centre and its seven-mile beach on a promontory; Moem Barracks, the Depot of 2 Bn PIR, with a good nine hole golf course. The population numbered 200,000 locals and 1,500 expats. Angoram on the Water Sepik had a Police Station, likewise Maprik, and there were six Field Detachments. The mighty Sepik River, navigable for about 500 miles, ran into the Star Mountains in the West Sepik; there was no harbour on the Coast because of the shallows and heavy surf. The Sepiks in the Police Force usually proved themselves to be good steady NCOs, with intense loyalty. The Officers were a mixed bag. The Province had introduced tilapia in the rivers and there was a bit of gold around populous Maprik; on the coast a little copra, cocoa and cattle. The Prime Minister, The Hon Michael Somare, came from the East Sepik around the Muruk Lakes near the Sepik's mouth.

The neighbouring province was the West Sepik, now called the 'Sundaun' Province, being the most westerly in New Guinea. Its population of 100,000 and 400 expats included many Chinese, the traders of PNG. Vanimo, almost on the western Irian Jaya border, was the main township with a club and pub as well as its Catholic Bishop. There were a dozen or so Field Detachments in the never-never land for border patrols. Little productivity: some coffee and rice, experimental rubber and timber. Nearby Sissano had a large, picturesque lagoon next door to Aitape, a Sub-District HQ. There was a track along the coast to Wewak but for the long haul you flew and used four-wheel drive for local hops. In all, the region incorporated about half the New Guinea population. Other ranks 2001, with 156 Officers policed this area, some 700 miles by 100 in breadth. Each District or Province, as they had become, had a Provincial Government elected with a Premier for their local affairs. Moresby housed the National Parliament; at the lower end of the political spectrum came the Local Government

Councils for towns and country areas. It was quite a reasonable system, but the Provincial Governments tended to weaken the national authority in a country with 500-odd languages.

Sam went off on his Bramshill Course in the UK for four months and on his return was shanghaied into PHQ to help with pre-independence problems in Papua, as he was a Papuan from Central Province and knew the political set-up in detail, eventually earning himself an MBE for diplomacy. Mac, still a substantive Senior Inspector, was now acting four ranks senior as Chief Supt and was subsequently paid 100%. He was soon promoted to Superintendent. Back in Lae city, the Divisional HQ and Provincial HQ of the Lae Police Station were one, which was not the ideal set-up: there should have been three substations to a station, three stations to a province and three provinces to a division. This set-up came from the British Army three hundred years before; it had proved useful throughout the British Empire and had stood the test of time.

In the first six months Mac made an inspection of all Police stations and met all his Officers. He had a good bunch; some had served with him before, some had been his Cadets. The same applied to the NCOs and the members. There was sound communication and mutual respect. Monies, weapons, ammunition, prisoners' property, bail monies were checked and exact amounts shown. At this stage the Constabulary was 100% honest and loyal, a disciplined body. Mac insisted this would be unchanging and steadfast. Parades, kit inspections, musketry, courses on all weapons were a weekly event. His two Mobile Squads at Lae and Goroka were regularly involved in all forms of Police work as back-ups and did VIP escorts and Guards of Honour.

The Constabulary had a lot to be proud of, both in war and peace-time roles. The Papuan New Guinean was never found wanting when a little guts was required. Establishments and strengths were looked at and workloads checked. Mac insisted on producing law and order by arrests and summonses, and the disciplined conduct of his Police. The locals knew they would be given a fair hearing, and the expats could expect no favours. A tight ship was being run, so the population said. Officers and

NCOs of competence were promoted and those who showed 'motivation', that modern word, were put on courses to accelerate their way up the tree. The civilian staff throughout the Division were encouraged to give constructive criticisms; the reverse was unacceptable, as some were to learn to their bitter cost.

Mr Ake Lootha, a Morobean himself and a local boy, was Divisional Clerk, and a most efficient, reliable and loyal fellow he proved. Short in inches but large in heart with his distinctive Afro hairdo, he was betting man of some standing. He was nicknamed, but only by the Boss, 'Ake Louvre' − 'Son of Big Window'. Mrs O'Brien was the No. 1 secretary; she harboured minor delusions of running the show and had made a pass at the Boss who, almost to his regret, had scorned her, so she had it in for him.

Mac had made friends with the Lae golf professional, Ted Cates, who was in his mid-seventies − a mighty man who at 58 years had come to Lae as the golf pro but had gone fossicking for gold for a few years, not with much success, then turned his hand to shooting *pukpuk* (crocodile) from a 17-foot aluminium dinghy up and down the Morobe and Rai Coast in Madang Province. Mac took a weekly golf lesson plus numerous hours of free coaching, which served to confirm his self-taught theories: hit 1,000 balls to kill a fault, hit another 1,000 for the new instinct, and a new one from Jack Nicklaus: if over forty, take the hands out of the shot and go for centrifugal force, like swinging a 10 lb axe. It's well worth consideration for the golfing fanatic − and it works. Mac took Ted on his inspections of 'C' Division, usually done in a single-engine Cessna which would take co-pilot plus six passengers and some cargo. At Teptep, up in the Finisterres inland from Saidor on the Rai Coast, they landed uphill and taxied down the strip as on an aircraft carrier, falling off the edge into a ravine before the plane got the required power to fly. There were four policemen and a Kiap and about fifty children gathered round the plane. Possibly because of his white hair and immaculate appearance, white shirt and navy blue slacks with highly polished brown shoes, the kids took a liking to Ted and presented him with a bunch of carrots about 18″ long and of considerable circumference. The largest carrots ever, they were also sweet to the tooth.

In the area of Telefomin in the West Sepik, where locals had killed Police and Kiaps in the past, was a newly opened detachment, Oslobip, in a box canyon about 8,500 feet up. The landing technique involved flying around the box canyon after an approach from an adjacent gorge, then a couple of side-slips to lose altitude and a bumpy landing onto a new strip only 20 metres or so wide, taking downdraught and side winds into account. In 1975 Mac was the second white man seen in the area; the Kiap was a Scottish Spaniard, another new Australian. He had been there six months and was due a break.

After a two-year slog getting his large Division into efficient order, and delighting in being resident in the great city of Lae, Mac received a personal call from the Commissioner of Police, Pius Kerepia OBE. Mac was to relinquish his command and report to PHQ as SO1 (Staff Officer 1), Executive Officer/Personal Assistant to the Commissioner, or as the laddie himself put it, bum boy. Polite protestations that he was now a Senior Superintendent, felt he was an Operational Officer, had no ambition as regards PHQ and anyway his overseas leave was due made no difference: he was told to pack up, go on leave and report for duty in the Ivory Tower.

Officers, Lae Police Station, Morobe Province, 1978

Madang Lagoon, 1978

Chinook, volcano evacuation, Karkar Island, Madang 1977

Madang – 'Venice' of Papua New Guinea

22: Some Never Learn…

Part of the three months' leave now due was spent in Australia, starting with a flight to Cairns and up into Atherton Tableland to see Stuart Hulbert and Mick Gallen, both formerly of Rabaul and Kavieng and ex-RPNGC, then down to Mackay, Brisbane, Sydney, Melbourne and back to Tasmania. Crossing the Tasman to the Land of the Long White Cloud, the MacDonalds arrived at Christchurch and were suitably impressed by that very English country city on the Canterbury Plain. They looked up Denis Holmes, CPM, ex-Kenya Police then headed down to Queenstown, the tourist ski-ing hub of the Shakey Isles, to meet up with the Grossers. Fred was ex-manager of the Kavieng Club, New Ireland, and Dawn had been MacDonald's Girl Friday when he was sheriff of New Ireland. Was this the place to retire to, as everyone said? Impressive mountain scenery, friendly people, a low cost of living, trout fishing, ski-ing, golf… The beer wasn't bad, the Wilson's malt whisky above average, and the rack of lamb excellent. In Wellington, the 'windy city' and capital, they said 'ciao' to Bob and June Thompson of Mombasa and Kenya Police days, headed north to Hastings and Napier and ran across more Kenya and PNG people, one an ex-tea planter from Kericho, another the ex-Matron of Mt. Hagen Hospital. From Auckland and its magnificent yachting bays they went back to Melbourne and met up with more former colleagues at a Kenya Police Association function in the Dandenong Hills. The way back to PNG took them through Adelaide, Perth and Port Hedland, over the Kimberleys to Darwin then Cairns, and back to the Land of Paradise.

Mac wondered why the Commissioner of Police had picked him to be his bum boy. It was thanks to Arthur Baker, who had served with him in Tassie and Rabaul and had been one of Pius Kerepia's Officers while a Cadet. They were famous for their racist greeting – 'How are you, you black bastard?' 'How are you,

you white bastard?' – and were very good mates. When Arthur left PNG he recommended MacDonald as an Officer who could be relied on to perform. Pius Kerepia had been nicknamed 'Treacle': black, sweet and all over the place. Rumour had it that he had been given the position of C of P because he did not drink. He was a burly 5' 11", a handsome lad, very black as he was a Buka from Bougainville. He would have been about 32, with about twelve years' service, coming up the old way: six months at the Police College, and then attached to a section of a large Police Station for six years – which was a waste, as at the end of the day you may have produced an all-round theorist who, like many of the expats could 'talk police', but were shy when it came to the nitty-gritty. The Kerepia bird was an amazing person. Instead of being handicapped with the demon drink, he was addictive to the female population at large, and knew it. Pius was not backward in coming forward when it came to bedding any attractive female. Once in the middle of a function he produced two beautiful Papuan twins, but instead of the planned ménage à trois, he had to be sternly reminded that his SO1 was a happily married man and that introducing anti-social diseases to the family would not be appreciated.

Pius had accepted a rule allowing his senior expat deputy to attend the daily conference supported by the Army Colonels, who had been seconded to the Royal Constabulary in a bid to strengthen the leadership now the Vietnam War was over. Most of the Colonels were a fine calibre of regular soldier. MacDonald would be called in to the inner sanctum to advise on most matters, including the uniform newly designed by Pius for himself and Senior Officers. When asked his opinion, Mac advised it might suit the flamboyant Commissioner, but was a wee bit over the top as working dress. At times the C of P dictated notes to his Staff Officer; usually the first page was to the point, but after that he was 'away with the fairies', as Pius himself generally agreed. MacDonald became a speech writer for the various official and social functions, such as addresses to delegations from the UN.

MacDonald soon realised his main function was to be the meat in the sandwich between the C of P and the Minister, a reasonable expatriate gentleman of the Pangu Party, as they were at loggerheads. Each referred to the other as 'illegitimate' and they refused to speak directly to each other, so the various messages between them had to be toned down and compromises made. MacDonald in his best Staff Officer manner advised his Commissioner to join the Pangu Party; then he would be able to criticise from the inside, which would be more acceptable. Pius agreed but admitted it was too late — he was going to be transferred as Secretary of the PWD Dept in the near future. In the meantime the Senior Deputy Commissioner had dissolved the four Divisions and made the twenty Provincial Commanders report to PHQ. This of course was contrary to any basic system, where over the centuries three to five had been the ratio of the chain of command. This did away with Chief Superintendent and Senior Superintendents, leaving twenty junior Superintendents. Considering each wished to speak to their Asst Comm for Operations for twenty minutes daily, this would cover approximately an eight-hour day. A Commissioner's Personal Directive was issued on paper with a red strip on the right edge, ordering that the daily conference of all Deputies and their advisers was now cancelled; should a Department Head wish to speak with the Commissioner of Police, he would state his business on paper and the subject raised would last 15 minutes only, and the decision given was not for discussion.

The politics of Headquarters, though not Mac's cup of tea, was well within his grasp. Bill Tiden, a Superintendent commanding New Ireland, was co-opted as the next C of P. Bill had about forty years' experience, from band boy to clerk to Jap POW — he had been forced into their military secret service, the Kempeitai, and was not to be issued with any Australian or British war medals. In fact MacDonald on one of his Inspectorial visits had recommended disciplinary action due to a neglect of duty re a 'bookies' raid which was not a howling success, but when Deputy Commissioner Sari Mesa and MacDonald went to meet the new C of P at Jackson's Strip they were immediately informed that Mac was to continue as SO1 as he was a 'good man'. Bill Tiden did not want the job, as he swore he was past doing a young man's work. The politicians as usual had made sure they would have a 'yes-man' to control: it had been explained to the Minister that his function was to direct policy but to allow the C of P to implement it. Bill was reassured that it was a reasonable easy position as the two Deputies each had three ACPs, who they would channel and recommend for signature and despatch all documents and bumph.

Robbie was Admin and most capable – he even knew the Forces Standing Orders almost verbatim. Sari Mesa, who was nobody's fool, had agreed that Divisions should be reintroduced and that they should become Regions with a more Senior Officer Commanding. Some would need an ACP so that PHQ would be relieved of the day-to-day running and free up HQ for policy-making and allow the C of P more time and space to play politics.

A lonely man, Bill Tiden told Mac over a drop of the green devil, Glenfiddich, about being taken prisoner by the Japanese as an 18-year-old Police clerk and given a stark choice: join the Kempeitai or be decapitated. He was now keen to receive war medals, as had most of the old hands and contemporaries. A letter to the Governor General PNG procured an OBE; in exchange Mac received a Jubilee Medal, as he had missed out on the official distributions.

Mac had now almost mastered the art of HQ politics, where back-stabbing was the order of the day and most cared little how their Police Force was going. It was time for a transfer back to his old stamping ground of Lae, with New Guinea Mainland to oversee. Various papers were signed by the Boss, so Mac simply included his transfer amongst the rest of the bumph to be signed. A week later he held a farewell party at Bomana Police College Mess and invited the C of P, who asked what the occasion was. 'Yes, Sir,' came the reply, 'that was the transfer to NG Mainland you signed a week ago.'

After a brief discussion stating that an operational posting would be more beneficial all round it was now verbally approved. Going back to Lae was a pleasure, but the wrong move in the promotion stakes. One should never go back to an old nest, as Mac had already done in Kenya when he returned to Mombasa. Some never learn…

Senior Inspector Paul Van Staveren, a former Kiap and

District Officer, ex-Buin (Bougainville), had been made redundant and posted to the Highlands to open up rural Police Stations around Mt. Hagen and had his fair share of the Highlands fun and games. As Kiaps were not over-popular in the Police, no Divisional Commander wanted the Van Staveren bird, who had the reputation of being a bit of a 'cowboy': seize the initiative, go where angels fear to tread. Mac recognised some of his own traits, and when asked by the Deputy Commissioner if he could fit in a former Kiap, Paul was pounced upon and flown over the same day to Lae to be briefed. He would be Station Commander for six months; if any good, he would be promoted to Provincial Commander Morobe and if he did not perform accordingly the opposite would happen. Paul was 6' 1", strongly built, more than averagely intelligent and a worker. His Pidgin was faultless, and his reception and communication with the indigenous people well above average. He owned two Rottweilers, Hitler and Lisa, the pick of the pack of 26 dogs he had collected in the Highlands when expats left permanently or on leave and dumped their dogs on him. His idea of feeding the pack was to let the two Rotties kill a local pig outside his property, a five-acre plot with a large house in the centre surrounded by an earthworks mound with the usual yarr spikes. This was in Moge country, with a dense population who could put 18,000 warriors in the field. Luckily for the powers that be, they never did. Not that Paul improved the PR with his wolf pack: he paid many hefty fines and compensation on the odd occasion to the local Magistrate. Obviously his Highland ways would have to be curbed, and Paul did a great job with the policing of Lae.

New Provincial Commanders trained up during his previous stay in Lae were posted to the five Provinces, and on the whole were a success. The teleprinter had come to PNG for the Main Stations so there were regular SITREPS giving a statistical printout of all crimes and offences and, where serious, a more detailed report. The Detachment radioed in for 8.30 a.m. to his nearest Police Station, the Police Station at 9 a.m. to Province, Province to Division 9.30 a.m. and Division to Region, so by 10.30 a.m. HQ, namely the Director of Public Relations, had the national picture. He, in turn, further sanitised the report for the press at 11 a.m. and sent them on their way by 11.30 a.m. Provincial, Divisional and Regional Commanders were allowed to give very brief Press Reports. In reverse, the Regional Commander could put pressure down the chain of command for results.

Visits to Detachments now showed that literate Police and NCOs were taking over the running of these posts in the never-never land, making the Kiaps' workload easier. A transfer policy had also taken effect so Police and families were no longer allowed to stagnate in the bush postings. It took fifteen years of training from the illiterate Constable to the one who had a six-year secondary education, although the fact that the educational standard had fallen and a previously good standard six was equivalent to a twelve was disappointing. More than 50%, both indigenous and expatriates, had come up through the ranks the easy way, and did not have the required knowledge and experience of the professional Colonial Police Officer, who held a tertiary education or commissioned rank, or an up-and-coming junior man with top secondary education plus a number of years' military and Police experience.

Obura, in the Eastern Highlands, about twenty miles south of Kainantu, was a thorn in the flesh. Two lines had been fighting off and on for years, but every time a Police response was made the locals disappeared. Mac decided to visit the Eastern Highlands by helicopter, a Bell two-seater type that did about ninety knots. The area was quiet: the fighting season was not in full swing. After a few passes over the area it was suggested that they have a look close in to a few of the cliff faces. Out of the blue, entrances to caves appeared: this called for a careful look-see. On the ground, almost hidden by scrub, were huge caves, 30 foot to 50 foot in height, and some with springs inside; crops could be planted in the entrance where the sunlight shone, and an irrigation system had been constructed. Smoke from cooking fires would curl up the roof and waft gently up the cliff face, unobserved from air or ground. Police attention was given and the pacification of another area achieved.

But there were tougher nuts to crack. The most scary thing a Police Officer may ever have to face is a prison riot, especially if it is a high-security gaol with long-term inmates or, in the old days, condemned prisoners facing the death sentence. One day the Resident Magistrate for Lae, Peter Light, came on the blower and asked if the ACP would be kind enough to call in past his chambers, as he had received some particular information that he wished to discuss. It turned out that the Superintendent of the local prison had been told on the grapevine that there was to be a prison break in the next fortnight, right down to the exact time: 6.30 a.m. on a Tuesday. The same at Goroka and Wewak: the latter long-term inmates would follow a week or so later. Here was a dilemma. A number of ringleaders were named, and about 200 out of 600 had their support. What was the plan of action? Take 200 out and transfer them around the country and spread the disease? Other centres might also be less prepared. Mac asked for a few days to think it over. So that charges could be laid and the Court in its wisdom take action, it was decided to provoke a riot inside the prison, whereby offences would take place.

The conundrum was exacerbated by the fact that although the cell block at Lae Police Station looked secure, with iron bars on all apertures and doorways, plus a mass of iron grillwork in the ceiling, in fact like a number of Police Stations built on the self-help basis, there was more sand than cement in the construction of the walls; a determined escapee could scrape his way through the brick with a spoon, or the mob in the cell would soon realise that a good heave would push the wall down. In theory, the cells could possibly accommodate a few hundred standing up. The alternative was to rig up a barbed-wire holding compound with field accommodation, latrine, ablution block and cooking facilities, which always entailed at least a 40-man mobile squad to do guard duties. Of course, having sentenced the prisoners you return them either to their original prison or a different one. Again, you can expect another break-out at either, plus the spreading of the disease. It was decided that the Court on application from the Police would sentence all to six months' additional imprisonment, but again on the recommending of the Police the Court would not proceed to conviction but place the rioters on a Good Behaviour Bond of one year and up to 18 months for the leaders. Once again a compromise was being mapped from a position of weakness out.

Next was the training of 300 Police, bringing in some reinforcements from other Stations such as Wau, Bulolo, Mumeng and Finschhafen. About 200 warders would be given a role, as would the Fire Brigade and the six-man Dog Section. The 2i/c Senior Superintendent, Leon Dion; the Province Commander, Paul Van Staveren, and the Police Station Commander and Inspector MacGregor, Mobile Squad Commander, were briefed along with His Honour, Peter Light, RM. Police now began a deliberate campaign of intimidation and provocation by getting up on a hill within cooee of the prison and for a week staging a rifle firing practice, along with gas guns, shotguns and the odd sub-machine gun. Firing by volleys gave an impressive crash; they also practised the old-fashioned drumfire, in which one of the 50 riflemen fires followed by the man next to him, resulting in what seems the continuous firing of a machine-gun. All very old-fashioned, but effective. This distraction ceased a few days before the break-out and Police appeared to have resumed normal duties.

On the appointed day, all Police were woken at 2 a.m. and on parade by 4 a.m., with equipment drawn at 5 a.m.; at 5.30 a.m. all Officers were briefed, at 5.45 a.m. all other ranks, and at 6 a.m. they were in position, mainly surrounding the workhouse and dining hall. For the week proceeding, Police observation had been maintained from a camouflage position above the prison. There had been no leak of information. A gap in the rear fence was opened to allow prisoners out on to the road and into awaiting Police vehicles.

The dining hall literally erupted. The construction was of fibro batten walls and corrugated iron roof with glass louvres: it was demolished within a matter of seconds. Prisoners in their frustration punched and kicked holes and tore down the place, many receiving severe lacerations to arms and legs. During this escapade, the Riot Act was allegedly read and tear gas deposited at a very high angle into the hell-bent mob. Within minutes a huge leader appeared and gave his demands. At this stage Mac's 2i/c was attempting to suggest a three-rank manoeuvre, as opposed to the two-rank drill already in position; he was reminded quite pleasantly to keep his eyes and ears open but everything else shut, as he might learn something.

Next came what appeared to be a snowstorm of fibro and glass thrown at the Police. Luckily no one received any injury. Six warders arrested the No. 1 ringleader, a huge mixed-race Morobean Highlander, who was warned by MacDonald that if he did not desist from his act he would receive a .300 between the eyes. He shouted that he would go quietly, without the customary help: he knew Mac's reputation and he would go into the Police truck with his chosen cronies. The warders were encouraged and helped to make the arrests, so they too would remain in charge of the situation and not lose confidence in dealing with their charges.

Some 300 persons were taken to the Police lock-up and charged, appearing in batches of twenty before Court. About 100 were weeded out: they well and truly professed their innocence, usually by being more timid than the angry rioters. The leaders thanked the Magistrate, the Police and the Corrections Staff, saying it had been a huge misunderstanding and they promised to comply with their good behaviour bonds. Everybody breathed a sigh of relief and about 100 of the prisoners were treated for cuts and abrasions at hospital, where liberal doses of stinging antiseptic were used and the barest of anaesthetic.

A new Regional/Divisional/Provincial Headquarters was created away from Lae Police Station for much needed space, although the security of the cells was mentioned in a comprehensive report. Funds were not made available for a new Police complex, although architectural plans with costings were submitted, hence the status quo was maintained. A new Commissioner of Police had also appeared on the scene. A Papuan from the Port Moresby environs, Philip Bouraga had come up through the Kiap ranks to District Commissioner and was a Charterhouse-educated boy. In fact, for a time in the usual bureaucratic foul-up, he had received expatriate salary, as he had resided in Australia. He was a Pangu Party supporter and well quoted by the Government of the day. He was *Mero Lohia*, son of the Chief in his own right, and was capable of making his own decisions. He paid the NG Mainland region a visit with his entourage and was met at the new Nadzab Airport by MacDonald, who had laid on a 'do' in the Mess so he could meet Officers of the Morobe Province, and was invited to dine at MacDonalds' residence if he so desired. In his normal less than tactful manner, Mac had pointed out that the dinner was not an ingratiating event, but his normal hospitality; he was told the new C of P had been well and truly briefed on MacDonald's disposition and found no problem. This was an auspicious start: both appeared to be straight-shooters with a no-nonsense approach.

Around this time two Rottweiler pups appeared on the scene, one called 'Kipsoi Arap Ruto' after an African Sergeant Major, the other 'Nandi Bear' after a rugby team from Kenya days. Kipsoi was a 135 lb, handsome, arrogant gentleman, and Nandi Bear just a likeable bear who thought the sun rose and set on her master. Here begins a love affair between the MacDonald family and the Rottweiler breed. Both were trained by the SI i/c of the local Dog Section, where the Police dogs were terrified of the Rotties – they used the so-called ferocious German shepherds as footballs. The Rottie is a natural guard dog but discerning in all his activities and a deep thinker, 100% loyal and reliable – provided the owner plays his part. Mac began to show them at Dog Shows, and both were due their Championship colours but all good things come to an end. A voice on the phone said, 'Hello, Scotsman.' It was the Commissioner.

Mac was told he was required to relinquish his command and take over National Capital, Port Moresby. He had just dipped out in being confirmed ACP but would continue in this rank in Port Moresby, which according to all reports was fast approaching anarchy, despite Terry Selva's efforts at stemming the tide. Mac protested to no avail and obeyed the order, managing to wring from his boss a condition of being allowed to recruit eight Officers of his choosing to fill critical positions in the National Capital set-up. Sad farewells all round were the order of the day.

Lady and Sir Tore Lokoloko, Governor General, Papua New Guinea, 1980

Commissioner of Police, Pius Kerepia OBE, 1978

Kipsoi Arap Ruto (left, named after S/Sgt, Kenya Police 1962) and
Nandi Bear (right), 1980

23: A Bit of a Bastard: Moresby, 1980

Here was one of the supreme challenges as a Police Officer in the RPNGC, the other of course being the unruly Highlands. While the powers that be tended to accept the state of the Highlands, 'Mosbi' was different: this was the capital and it was out of control – no law and plenty of disorder. Moresby had always been a bit of a bastard. Three-quarters of the locals did not belong but lived with *wantoks* (clansmen) in the various settlements on the shanty town hillsides. The *wantok* system, where you had to provide food and shelter, even drink and clothing, could only last so long, then the merry vagrant would revert to stealing and all the other escalations which followed. The Commissioner, himself a Papuan, would have a special interest, as would any Government, since they had to have some sort of showpiece.

Mac fronted up for the handover and ACP Terry Selva, his old colleague from the Highlands, not only presented him with 800 pages of notes but also spoke for six hours non-stop until hoarse. Mac appeared to be impressed, but those 800 pages would be reduced to 15 and the paper war reduced to manageable proportions. After giving his congratulations and receiving commiserations on the promotional stakes, a shake of hands and it was all his. The following day, Commissioner Bouraga called and asked if Mac had any ideas on how to tackle the law and order problem. He was told regretfully not at the moment but it would be looked at.

Every morning at 8 a.m. onwards, sometimes until 12 midday, there was an Officers' Conference of 56 Officers who should have been out with their men on the street, all 1,200 of them. The Conference Room was most impressive, a collection of tables forming a circle with Mac in the centre flanked by his Chief Supt and two Senior Supts plus the Junior Officers. It was a wonder this lot didn't all hold hands and hold a seance. As the new boy, Mac gave his address along the lines they might have expected, as a large proportion of his Officers had served with him all over the country.

'Some of you are black bastards, some of you are white bastards and I am just a bastard; that should alleviate any racial tensions, gentlemen. Police duty is simple and we are going to keep it that way: during daylight we will lock up the vagrants and during darkness we will lock up the big-mouthed drunks. This will allow the lads and lasses in CIB and Traffic to deal with the criminal and the blatant traffic offender. When support is required we have three Mobile Squads on hand. If you are dealing with a lady or gentleman, treat them as such; if they behave like an animal then get them down and put the boot in. Everybody from the rank of Superintendent down who wishes to be considered for promotion will make a weekly arrest of at least one body. There will be no questions, and from now on there will be each Friday from 8.30 a.m. to 9 a.m. a Section Heads' meeting – that is people usually of the rank of Superintendent only – where they will be instructed on their daily requirements. Now you may dismiss and go about your lawful business.'

Opposite Mac at that address sat Inspector John Holland, a new boy, formerly a Traffic Inspector from the Sussex Constabulary in the UK. His facial expression and his feet in particular made it clear that he disagreed entirely with Mac's outlook on life. Upon returning to the inner sanctum, within minutes Mac was informed by his secretary that Mr Holland wished an interview. She was told to show him in and give him a cup of Goroka coffee. Inspector Holland appeared, gave an attempt at a salute and was told to remove his head-dress, sit down and have a coffee.

Did he know why such a huge desk separated his senior Officer and himself? It was to prevent people like him from assaulting people like Mac. How could Mac be of help? Holland went on to say that he did not like Mac's brutal approach to police work and that in his experience it was counter-productive. He had been six weeks in the fair land of PNG and was obviously already an expert on all Police matters there. It was pointed out that perhaps in time (a very short time) he would realise that with an average of five homicides a night plus fifty break-ins in a small city of only 400,000 he was no longer in Sussex by the Sea. He was blessed and the interview terminated.

Paul Tohian, his No. 2 when Mac arrived, had a desk in the same office. When asked the reason for this, as 2i/c of National Capital he said that this was for personal instruction. He was given time to find a decent office as far away as possible, and then to go down to Transport, pick out the best two Mazda station wagons, one for himself and one for the new Commander, National Capital, as the latter's Merc was not going to be used for Police business, despite the travel allowance.

Mac got a chopper and took with him his two operations fellows, his No. 2, Chief Supt Paul Tohian, and Supt Paul Van Staveren, transferred over from Lae, to check on the topography of the city. It showed three hill ridges and valleys, then they flew over the Bomana *kalabus* where 700 prisoners doing various stretches at Her Majesty's pleasure gave the Police party the Royal Salute in reverse. Without extra Police there was a problem, as the Constabulary had lost confidence in its ability to make arrests. In fact they were on the run from the so-called 'Raskol' gangs. Mac brought in the three Mobile Squad Commanders and the Company Commander of the Mobile Force and proposed that each squad would be beefed up by ex-NCOs and Officers of the Mobile Force, or specially selected 'hard nuts', so that the Squads could operate SAS-style in subsections of four to five storm troopers.

The 40-man squad would have two Traffic, two CIB, two dogs, two Policewomen, two Scenes of Crime (Photographic) and additional transport, such as a 10-ton Isuzu tipper six-wheel drive that could take up to 50 prisoners. There would be an additional squad of ex-Mobile Force, plus the young and bold and fleet of foot, each man to carry a personal weapon plus an axe helve – lighter than the traditional pick helve – and ten plastic handcuffs. These squads were to operate on overtime on a hurry-up basis: no head-dress worn, black baseball boots, no gaiters, no service numbers or badges of rank. A target would be selected, such as an unruly pub – and there were many. A briefing of 15 minutes, travel to target 15 minutes, on target and make arrests 15 minutes, return 15 minutes; 60 minutes to prepare Information (Charge

Sheets), to 24-hour sitting court, 15 minutes; Court 30 minutes, and back to the 'slammer' 15 minutes. Two persons to make initial arrest, plus two as back-up. Another two to reinforce; all prisoners to be handcuffed with hands to rear.

The first night op began at 6 p.m. and went through to 10 a.m. the following day. It was discovered that the cell block could take 350 persons standing up or 150 lying down. Additional cell guards (watch house keepers) were required, plus typewriters and typists. All subsections had their own walkie-talkie radios on an ops frequency. The Ops Room too required additional staff. All extra work was done as overtime, to the delight of the well-paid troops. Thursday, Friday and Saturday were the ops nights. On the first night, six persons wanted on warrant for serious crimes were arrested. Within three weeks the University Chancellor phoned Mac with his congratulations, as the campus was now quiet and serious assaults, rapes and break-ins were almost non-existent. He wanted to write to the Commissioner, but Mac expressed the view that it was too early in the piece to accept accolades. The C of P was impressed, and called Mac accordingly.

Less impressed was a Goilala leader from one of the shanty settlements, who came in to threaten the new 'shoot-maun' for Port Moresby. His gambit was that if the Police expected cooperation they should discuss all raids with their Goilala representative. When this Goilala leader said that Police could be killed if they were foolish enough not to cooperate, Chief Supt Tohian, a big boy of about 6' 1" and broad to match, was asked to show him the door. Thrown down the concrete stairs and booted into the cells, he soon wished to apologise for his rudeness and said he could guarantee cooperation. His settlement was raided that evening with 50-odd arrests and a certain amount of stolen property 'recovered'.

Another day dawned with Col Brian Cooper RAA being ushered in. When he and Mac shook hands, the vibes were good: Brian had been the No. 1 chopper man for the Aussie Army and, like other attached Officers, had been shunted up to help the modernisation of the Constabulary. His role was Personal Adviser to the Commissioner, who appeared not to require his help or advice. Mac responded in his best Horstralian that 'that would be rait, mate'. Could Mac find something for him to while away his time? 'Certainly,' Mac replied.

With Supt Rex Wardle, formerly a Chief Inspector with the Lincolnshire Constabulary, as the Operations Room man with his communications set-up of radios, phones, teleprinter, maps and statistical data, the pair made a formidable team, and overnight the Ops Room became something to behold. The Policewomen were good on the radio with their clearer enunciation than males. When an op was on, the various sectional channels switched to a single, and Supt Wardle took over. Brian had recently returned from a tour in the Vietnam War so he was well up to date with the latest technology. Mounted patrols for the hills and scrublands around Moresby were dreamt up and discarded, so instead, bush motor-bike patrols with night scope field glasses and telescopes were a hit. All the trouble areas could be observed and the Mobile patrols directed to the various trouble scenes. As was customary, the *big rot* or tracks on top of the *keels* were the route for stolen property and Wanted Persons, so many a 'baddy' was snatched by Police ambush. Choppers were looked at and a 'night sun' − a searchlight from a chopper − considered, but the budget did not extend to such luxurious items.

Being the disciplinarian he was, Mac decided a good way to raise morale in and out of the Police was to put on a parade at the Hubert Murray Stadium. He invited all the 'Big Boys', so every Friday at 7 a.m. a Scale-A parade was held. Even the CIB and Traffic were on parade and a skeleton force left to look after the fair city. The Police Band of 70 musicians and the Pipes and Drums of the Corrective Institutions Service were enlisted, as was the former Deputy Commissioner, Robbie Robertson, now the Governor General's Official Secretary. As a former Drill Instructor with the Scots Guards, he knew his kit. Brigadier Ted Diro could not understand how the immaculate dressing and covering off had been achieved at the parade. It was done by hanging red towels over blue from various buildings around the Stadium at right angles so that the Markers and Guides could march on the Police colours. Tin cans with various numbers painted in white on their base were driven into the stadium grass to act as markers for Officers and guides for the NCOs.

It took about three months of hard practice and rehearsal in full ceremonial — even coins were placed in the old .303 rifle magazines and the 18-inch bayonets sparkled in the sunlight. The Parade movements were to the accompaniment of the massed bands and of course the Tunes of Glory were to the fore: March On: 'Highland Laddie'; Advance in Review Order: 'Gary Owen'; Royal Salute: 'The Cross of St Andrew'; March Past in Quick Time: 'Blue Bonnets'; March Past in Slow Time: 'Old Gaul'; Inspection: selection of Scottish Gaelic waltzes; March Off: *Rani La* (Papuan March); and finally 'The Black Bear'. Congratulations all round: the Royal Papua New Guinea Constabulary could still do it with a bit of swank! On one of the practices Mac had handed over to his 2i/c Paul Tohian with the instruction, 'Once more and fall them out and have the Officers under Superintendent Brant [ex-RSM Armoured Cavalry] do a bit of sword drill.'

After two hours in the office Mac wondered where the hell they had got to. Paul had given them those extra two hours in 33° Celsius and 75% humidity: when he returned, like the others' his blue uniform was black with sweat. The troops took it without a snarl. Morale had been restored, as had initiative, through pride.

At the same time Moresby was set up as three Divisions, Port Moresby, Boroko and Gerehu, each station having its own General Duties (Beats and Mobile Patrols), CIB and Traffic Sections, Process (Warrants and Summons), Firearms Section, Prosecutions, Transport and a Mobile Squad posted to each. There could be no illusions of complete success, but homicides were down to less than one per day and break-ins to a handful. Serious assaults and rapes were now containable and could be thoroughly followed up. A curfew was proposed but the Government said 'no'. ID cards were proposed again, the reply also negative. Civil rights were raising their piggy little heads, but what about civil responsibilities? Identity cards showing a person's particulars in detail can control a footloose itinerant population of the kind the *wantok* system encouraged. This had been Moresby's problem since the early 1900s.

Meanwhile Mac had taken a shine to some of his new Officers. Garry Garvie, a Kiwi, was 2i/c Homicide and an excellent detective of the old school. Garry had founded the Armed Offenders Squad in NZ and was a Senior Inspector with a warped sense of humour like Mac's. He made sure never to be on parade and always had a fresh homicide to deal with. However, to show his agreement with Mac's policies he presented him with a plaque from the Royal Yacht *Britannia*; as Garry put it, he thought a birthday present in appreciation was appropriate. A Crime Report was never raised. Another was George Howell, 0i/c Homicide, an ex-BSAP Sergeant who had been blown up three times in the war in Southern Rhodesia, now the mess known as Zimbabwe. George was obviously bomb-happy and nervous: he had to be told that compliments to senior Officers were fine, but not all the time. A most conscientious Officer and painstaking investigator, he had a really sickening case on at this time. A Papuan girl of 17 had gone to a dance in town when a gang of nine 'raskols' raped her and then killed her, mutilating her in the process. All nine were apprehended and received anything from five to fifteen years: totally inadequate. The American Consul, a woman, also suffered a gang rape by 'young pups', fortunately without being mutilated or murdered. The press showed their usual tact by demanding the gruesome details at the daily 15-minute Press Conference, where they were given amended copies of the SITREP book sheets. One idiot from Australia informed Mac that he had to give details of the alleged rape, as the hospital had no comment, or he would personally see that Mac and his command received bad press. After two hours in the cells, which were not salubrious, he saw the light and was born again, but instructed not to venture back for one month. He must have realised that he was not back home in the Bowling Club.

One Sunday about 7 p.m. Garry Garvie phoned the boss at his residence and said he had some bad news. There had been a prison break. Contingency plans for this type of emergency were already in place. The Corrective Institution would immediately let the Duty Officer know of any untoward action by prisoners. On receipt of a code word, roadblocks were set up in a circle at various distances. The roadblocks were based on the theory that an escapee would run six miles in thirty minutes and then the speed would decrease. It sounds good in theory, but as Scotland's national bard so rightly said, 'The best laid schemes o' mice an' men gang aft a-gley.'

The Superintendent i/c of the Bomana *kalabus* decided in his wisdom not to report the break-out, which happened at 3 p.m. when 700 prisoners rushed the wire fence set in concrete and it gave way. The Duty Officer finally got the report two hours later and mentioned the circus act to Garry, who went out and got nominal rolls of the escapees, which took until 6.30 p.m. Mac held a brief meeting of all Officers at 7.30 p.m. and set the hunt for the escapees in progress. Of course details required would take 24 hours. Docks, airports, tracks were ambushed and sweeps made of the various settlements, an exercise that lasted a week, during which photographs and details of the escapees were given to all Regions, right down to Detachment/Post level. Despite the SNAFU, within six months all had been recaptured or had surrendered, demonstrating that the Constabulary when it ex-digitated could still be efficient. The odd body had died or been killed on return to his environment.

Deputy Commissioner (Chief of Operations) Michael Vee contacted Gwen, Mac's secretary, and informed her that an OBE (Other Buggers' Efforts) was in the offing for her boss in the New Year's Honours List. Mac was unimpressed and phoned Michael Vee to say that many years ago on the field of battle he had had the opportunity of earning medals for bravery, but being a professional coward he had passed them up. To date these political baubles did not impress him, and the chain of command should have been observed.

This was a big booboo, as recently C of P Bouraga had been awarded the CBE. Mac's uncalled-for remarks were taken as a personal insult and he was required to attend at the Ivory Tower. The C of P informed Mac that he would hand over RAT One to ACP David Tasion; as from now it would come directly under PHQ and the Squad would operate outside the constitution, pick up and beat up prisoners and dump them off the Police trucks. Mac did not mention that there were four RAT teams, but with considerable respect attempted to advise that as a professional Police Officer and as an Asst C of P he might be allowed to advise against this idea, as this would amount to thug versus thug. Not that this fact bothered Mac too much, but if the Troops were allowed this illegal freedom in the exercise of their duties, then

(1) it would result in a break-down in discipline and morale, and (2) the public would not appreciate a totally illegal operation.

The C of P said he knew that Mac on occasion had operated outwith the strict rules, to which he agreed, but Officers and Men were not informed of this particular illegality. The outcome was that Mac was transferred sideways into the Ivory Tower as Commander, General Ops Division, which meant he ran the Police Force in the field, as 2i/c to the Deputy Commissioner Chief of Operations, so he could plan strategy. Hindsight is a great asset. Usually the C of P would only spend ten minutes with expat Officers; Mac still got his two hours' worth, so he was not completely out of favour for his transgression.

CDR Ops was the proverbial 'doddle'. One of his sidelines was to be seconded to the Bechtel Organisation, who were opening up the Ok Tedi Mine in the Star Mountains, Western Province, some 600 miles up the mighty Fly River. It was a pleasant surprise that one of the company bosses was a John Newell, who recognised Mac's 'Colorado Beetle' (African Service Medal) and asked if he had been in Kenya at the time of the Mau Mau Emergency. A reply in the affirmative led to Laikapia Division, Ol Kalou: John's father had been a farmer at Pencil Slats on the North Kinangop, where Mac had seen some action in days gone by. This was the same company who had involved him in the Panguna Mine in Bougainville Province, where there had been problems, mainly with the expatriate miners.

Mac was to advise the company on security arrangements and report back to the Chief of Ops, then draw up the Police Establishment/Strength required. Mac had no experience in this area, so he phoned ex-Inspector Jan Jansen, now in Australia, who had been through the 'troubles'. At the mine both had a long look and took in the various issues involved. What transpired was that each group of tradesmen, skilled, semi-skilled labour and the various levels of management would have their own Messes, wet and dry, run by themselves or on an elected committee basis, as opposed to one big Mess which produced exactly that: riotous behaviour and a lack of control at all levels. There would be a compulsory day off per week, a long weekend at Cairns every six weeks and a maximum of 12 hours' work per shift. These areas had been the cause of work stoppages and riots. Accommodation at the site would be segregated. A blind eye might be turned to illegal gambling, the various schools would have their own committees, and a proper floodlit area with facilities would be provided. The 'ladies' who would frequent the campsites were to be registered and have a weekly medical check.

Although not essentially to do with security, these measures would alleviate security problems. In addition, a Police Station and Compound was to be erected in a fort design; the Security Personnel would be immediately adjacent, with a similar set-up. In all 350 Security and 350 Police would be required, creating a sub-division; Security at all levels would be recruited from the Disciplined Service and Police and were to work together to provide mutual back-up. MacDonald was fortunate that Col Brian Cooper came into the picture again, and with the help of Transport Dept (Water) a Sharkcat, twin-hull, twin-prop with inboard outboard engines was developed in a tube shield. It had special tempered-steel propellers, so that in the Fly River with its 11-knot current, sandbanks and semi-submerged logs the launch could skid over the obstacles and churn its way through sand and mud. Various light aircraft and choppers were proposed, as was their incorporation into the Police as an Air Wing. As usual, funding was a problem and it is doubtful they ever got off the ground.

At this stage MacDonald had been informed that his contract might not be renewed. John Newell had suggested that Mac was the man to head up the Mine Security and that the conditions offered were even better than his Police Contract. After about a year of being 'God' a new challenge came his way. Many of his colleagues would have liked to see our hero come off the tightrope: his operational success, some said, was just a matter of luck. Few paused to reflect that planning and experience might have contributed. Unfortunately he had developed a cocky disposition, due mainly to his unspoken disgust that so many of the expatriate Officers made conditions to their tenure of service. Most wanted to be chair-borne commanders playing with bits of paper, submitting theoretical treatises on how the Constabulary should be run. Few had any commitment as to the welfare requirements of their members and Juniors, but toed the self-aggrandisement line. Most of them never had the necessary exposure to become leaders.

ACP Terry Selva, now A/Deputy Com Admin, had been the Director of Training and Personnel. He and Mac were old colleagues and had a healthy respect for each other's capabilities, although at times they agreed to disagree. Rumour had it that MacDonald, despite his operational flair, would come off his perch in the role of Dir T & P. He almost did when he saw the huge office, desk and chair to match, and the floor piled high with various files from the Directorate's various Sections. Terry said he had been flat out from 8 a.m. to 12 midnight most days. There were about 15 Sections, each with its own clerical staff headed by Officers of exceptional calibre, some with double degrees. There were Majors, Captains on secondment from the Defence Force of Australia, their own legal eagle plus a Defence Force psychologist, an RNZAF Squadron Leader, and Barbara, the Confidential Records lady. Even the Commissioner could not see his confidential file, as she had been sworn to secrecy by the Chief of the Civil Service Commission. Shortly Mac had to add an admin cap when Pay and Accounts were dumped on him. Oh, what a familiar feeling — up shit creek again, and still without a paddle!

Heads of Sections got their humble boss's address along these lines: 'You are better qualified than I, but I do have the say in the hire and fire stakes, and if given a chance we will live together happily ever after and do our duty. Not really inspiring stuff. But to start with, you people can identify your files on the floor here and take them back to your Section where you will deal with them to their conclusion. Your new Director will not have tea or coffee breaks and you will not come into this office for discussions or seances; all are barred without appointment with the exception of the Commissioner and his two Deputies. You may discuss your findings and intended results direct with those persons involved. I will not rewrite your reports, but merely agree or disagree to your comments, which will be based on researched facts.'

There were the usual mutterings to the effect he might be a 'cop' but he was no HQ's Wallah. The NZ Sqn Leader made an appointment to say he did not know whether he would salute the new Director or not. It was jokingly explained to him the basis of a salute was only a hallmark of friendship and not all that important, and that Mac would not be broken-hearted not to receive the normal compliment between friends. He said he would consider this and let Mac know. When he appeared the following day he was surprised to discover that the new Director had removed the seat of his chair and was sitting on a spike-like end: could the Sqn Leader help him? Both broke into laughter, the Sqn Leader came to attention and gave a smart salute and advised that they were both nuts. MacDonald got his own back by advising the Sqn Leader that the painful hair transplant he was going through for his missionary girlfriend was not really necessary as there were more fish in the sea than ever came out of it.

Now that he was the boss of the relevant Department, MacDonald asked Lady Barbara to let him see his Personal Confidential File and got a flat 'no'. But when he issued the order, 'Send up ACP MacDonald's file, I wish to see it,' he got the desired result. It was full of compliments, with the exception of one report going back to his Rabaul days. As Sub-Inspectors, he and Dennis Grove had mimicked a senior who had written to the C of P, Bob Cole MC, to complain that the two Subbies were disloyal and should be discharged. Det Supt Don Potgeiter of the CIB was sent over from Mosbi to Rabaul to investigate and report. In fact he gave the pair a glowing write-up: they were loyal, most experienced and even, socially, a pleasure to meet. Both were promoted on the next list. The Senior Inspector in question had a short neck with bulging eyes, sweated profusely and was always 'pulling wind', breathing heavily like a frog that has just surfaced. So naturally the poor bugger got the nickname of *Torokrok*, Kuanua for frog.

To add weight to Det Supt Potgeiter's comments, one day Sharon Reinhardt, 0i/c of the Officers Overseas Section, was asking advice from Mac. 'Just take it from this old colonial racist bastard,' was the reply, 'that is the way to do it and no other.'

Sharon responded that the last thing Mac could be called was a racist.

'Who said so?' Mac rejoined.

'Your National Officers and men think you are okay.'

Mac was delighted to hear it: Whitey was convinced he was a racist but Blackie had come to the opposite and appropriate conclusion.

Sharon's current boyfriend was Supt Simon Kawi, a Highlander from Minj, and she got a surprise when the pair were ordered overseas on an Officers' Recruitment Drive which included Hong Kong, Singapore, the UK and Canada. Both enjoyed the experience; Simon was aware of the type of Officer Mac wished to recruit and in addition both had enjoyed a glorious holiday. Reports were streamlined to the Chief of Admin through to the C of P, and only a few comments of Mac's were added, to the delight of his Sectional Heads, who were receiving accolades for their efforts. Even the Police Force Band came under the Training & Personnel & Administration umbrella. The familiar figure of Tom Shacklady would stick his head round the door and be given Mac's blessing: 'Do what you think, Tom, send us a copy of your schedule, I'm not a bloody musician.'

The Commandant, Chief Supt Pat Barry of the Police College, got similar blessings, so paperwork was reduced and people could get down to the job in hand.

To give an added interest Nandi Bear, the MacDonald's Rottweiler bitch delivered her second litter with the expected minimum of fuss. All thirteen pups were well formed and in good health. In a matter of months the pups were ready to sell to the expectant market. Various buyers came round to view the litter and pick their pup. Mrs Mac had an odd experience when a prospective buyer was being shown the pups for inspection. Kipsoi, the proud male sire, appeared on the scene, gave the fellow a precautionary sniff, cocked his leg and piddled down the gentleman's leg. To some extent fortunately, the fellow was only wearing sandals. Mrs Mac did her best to handle the situation by informing the potential buyer that Kipsoi only favoured certain people, and that was his way of showing his affection. It has not been recorded whether a pup was sold.

One fine day, a voice over the telephone intoned, 'Hello, Scottish gentleman, do you know who this is?'

'Yes, Sir.'

'Good, come out and see me now.'

'In uniform?'

'Yes.'

'Have you cleared this with [C of P] Philip?'

'Yes, he knows.'

The voice belonged to Israel Edoni, Chairman of the Civil Service Commission. Some months earlier at the Golf Club, the Nationals had gathered in one wing of the bar, and the Expats round the corner. It was noisy and boisterous: the Moresby Golf Club had about a 50/50 local and expat membership and was one of 'the' clubs in the city. By now the most popular 'dram' was Glenfiddich malt whisky, translated into the Motu language as 'Kone dekenai mogani' or 'The Valley of the Deer'. The crowd Mac was associated with were a real mixed bunch. 'Bettsy' (Betts), a construction manager, would burst into opera when the spirit moved; 'Noise' (Noyes), an electrical businessman, could be heard any time, anywhere; 'Kraut', a Lithuanian design draftsman, was a brilliant bridge player with his mate, Lindsay Knight, Deputy of the Reserve Bank for PNG, a sophisticated Kiwi; Jack, a senior Customs Officer who was drinking his stubbies unto death, was a true gentleman; Ken Armstrong was a quiet architect who always had a joke to tell, Dr Jim Jacobi OBE, President of the Rugby League PNG, was alleged to have cures for the pox and malaria only; and then there was Mac, the lightweight walloper. These fellows had 15–30 years dedicated service to PNG and had been told that in a year's time they would be redundant, so there was an air of bolshiness, bitterness, defiance and possibly even sorrow – not just for themselves but the country. For some, therefore, life tended to be a continual piss-up, though to be fair that was only in the afternoon, as all had responsible positions.

Anyway, 'Noise' could be heard above the din and Bettsy had just completed a stanza of Figaro. A diminutive Papuan lady appeared, looking a little nonplussed. Mac got up and offered her his stool and put it round the corner where she indicated. A minute later a large glass of Glenfiddich appeared with the insistent word of '*Taubada* [Sir], Mr Edoni's compliments.' The bar steward was instructed to repay the compliment, Mac guessing that the lady was Mr Edoni's wife.

Israel appeared and said, 'Thank you: do you know who I am?'

'Yes,' Mac replied, 'therefore I cannot accept a drink without repayment and you are the man who will eventually hire or fire me.' They agreed that a game of golf together was on the cards.

On arrival at Waigani, a conglomeration of Parliamentary Offices and Departments, Mac was ushered in straight off and offered a Glenfiddich, which he declined. Did he know that C of P Bouraga was being co-opted into the Somare Ministry as Treasurer? Mac had heard the rumour. What was required of him was to recommend the next C of P, as he would provide the files and sit on the Board as the C of P's representative. He recommended Henry Tokam, the present Senior Deputy Commissioner and Operations Chief, a Highlander from the Chimbu Province. Henry had served with Mac as a Cadet and as one of his Company Commanders in the Highlands. He was teetotal and religious and not bigoted in any way – a brave, powerful Officer, both physically and morally.

Mr Edoni expressed the Cabinet's opinion that they did not wish a Highlander but would prefer a Papuan Colonel from the Defence Force. Mac said they had past experience with Colonels and Brigadiers, recruited both locally and overseas, and at no time did any of them appreciate the intricacies of PNG or its Constabulary. He was told that a former Deputy might be considered, one who had outstanding administrative ability but little or no charisma with the rank and file, and who was also out of touch after two years on the Governor General's staff.

Told to go away and think about it and come back in a week, Mac duly answered the second summons and was informed that there was a fourth candidate.

'Who?'

'Yourself.'

As the expression goes, you could have knocked him down with a feather. After a few seconds he enquired who had backed this extreme outsider. Advised that it was the Cabinet, he asked who in particular and on what criteria. The answer: Mac was apolitical and Sir John Kaputin had spoken most forcibly on his behalf. Fifteen years previously, during the Matangaun affair, Sir John had received a boot to the posterior, but obviously had not held it against this candidate, as his cousin Zakius Mangut had served with Mac at Gordon Barracks and knew the score. Mac once again insisted that Tokam was the man: it would be a retrograde step for an expatriate to hold the position even for one year instead of a minimum of three. Tokam went on to hold down that unenviable position on two occasions.

Mac was then offered the Commandant's position at the Police College but would have had to revert to his substantive rank as Chief Superintendent and declined. Next up, Senior Deputy Henry Tokam himself told him that with the C of P's imminent departure he could be seconded to the Corrective Institutions Service for six months to do the Admin portfolio, as they were in dire straits where training, discipline and performance were concerned. Mac agreed – provided he was offered a new contract and a guarantee of three years' service. When, despite assurances, this was not forthcoming, Mac declined. Air Niugini said they would like him for their Security Branch, but the sentiments expressed did not bode well. They were looking for a saviour and, as Mac pointed out, walking across water with holes in his feet was not one of his accomplishments. It was a sad time at 51 years of age and after thirty years' service in five Police Forces. Mac was starting to hear the sound of the pipes playing some of the great slow airs: 'The Skye Boat Song', 'The Dark Island' and some of those stirring Retreat Marches – 'The Highland Division at El Wadi Akarit', 'Cock o' the North'…

Had he done his duty, he wondered, and what would he change if he had to do it all again? The answer: probably not a thing. Perhaps he should have taken his father's advice that one should be diplomatic (even if it meant telling lies, except in court, of course), or about being honest – but not too honest. But it was not in his nature.

There were more than he leaving the Royal Constabulary as time-expired men, so there was a great round of parties and presentations of beer mugs with those kind inscriptions on their sides, some true. One of his haunts in town had been the Police College Mess, where a particular decorative coach light had taken his fancy. The stem underneath had a concave hole which went unobserved, unless critically inspected. Mac used to shove his beer mug under and up, so that his beer glass appeared to be replenished, a trick often watched by various inebriates who shook their heads at the magical powers of the white witch doctor. The coach light too was presented and still has a place of honour in the MacDonald establishment. Eventually Paul Van Staveren told Mac he had a job interview arranged for him with Mr Heddle, the General Manager of Burns Philp, as they too required someone to head up their Security. Mac went and secured the job with all the usual promises. A couple of weeks' compulsory leave to the Great South Land, and then, having been issued with an employment card, Mac returned to take up his new position in Lae.

Interlude

Burns Philp Security, 1982

24: Bastards of the Pacific

Back to the Green City... Burns Philp Ltd, sometimes referred to as 'Bastards of the Pacific', was a large Australian company, founded in Townsville. It had its own ship, the Bulolo, which travelled around the islands of PNG and down to Sydney, calling in at the major ports. Burns Philps also had plantations all over PNG, the Toyota franchise, Coca-Cola, a nylon rope factory, its own wharves, numerous supermarkets in all centres, butcher shops, hardware – every kind of consumer goods you could lay a finger on. MacDonald thought a company of this size would be super-efficient and on the ball: not so. His boss was the company auditor Alex Richardson, an ex-Master Mariner and a well-qualified chartered accountant. An honest man who dearly loved playing detective, he had a weakness for a 40 oz bottle of Black Label per day, but like most with the habit was never under the influence in public, just topped up.

Strangely, Mac was not given an office from which to operate, but had a free hand in forming a Security Branch for the company. What they had at present was a handful of bodies with no Police training or any other kind. Crime detection was kept within the company and punishments meted out accordingly if at all, depending on the popularity of the individual. Mac had only assurances from Mr Heddle that the company would abide by Mac's decisions in all security arrangements. After a week's sniff around (orientation period) it was blatantly obvious that security in any form did not exist. The next week Mac visited all the various centres around the country at Rabaul, Kavieng, Madang, Mt. Hagen and back to Moresby. One word summed up the situation: unbelievable.

A climate existed in which no one had any responsibility for security. As an example, a large godown in Lae had eight gates in and eight gates out. Lorries came and went at all hours; drivers had an invoice for their respective loads. Mac and two other

Security men had a truck unload at one exit and discovered that half the load of mixed goods — TVs, washing machines, stereo equipment, refrigerators — did not appear on the invoice and the driver had no explanation for how they got there. When the manager of the godown was informed he showed little interest in the fact that goods were being stolen under his nose. The same operation was repeated on a number of occasions with the same result. Simple solution: one entrance, one exit, with two security men to check cargo in and out. All movements of goods would be tallied in and out and all goods checked against invoices and signatures of persons receiving on all documents. Security men were moved on a monthly basis so that familiarity could not breed contempt or bribes.

When word got out that Mac was back, there were queues of ex-Police and Disciplined Forces such as Army, Navy, Air Force, Customs and Prison Services. He decided on three levels of Security: investigators who could investigate at any level and prosecute the offender, patrolmen for the stores, godowns, wharves and factories who could arrest and prosecute thieves, and then guards for the various yards, such as the Toyota one, with its hundreds of vehicles. The new personnel came from the boxers, wrestlers, weightlifters or simply the thump merchants inside the various compounds. Sports equipment was supplied for the musclemen. Pay would be generous, promotion automatic and liberal based on results, i.e. arrests. Recruits for the three sections of Security were mainly former senior Officers, junior Officers and NCOs, who could all get off their tails and move and appreciated the opportunities offered. One of Mac's favourites appeared: former Sub-Inspector Simeon Conrad Tali, who had married a Kung Islander off the coast of New Hanover (Lavongai) in the New Ireland Province. Tali had just been released after a year or so in the *kalabus*; he had been a great cop with a brilliant arrest record but had repeatedly gone to water when in possession of a chequebook. He may have believed that the white man just wrote cheques to get money, in which he was not alone. Tali came from Morobe, and was a Siassi Islander known to the locals of Lae; in other words he heard the *Tok* at all levels of society.

Once an office had been established, there was a constant

stream of informers, mainly reporting the managers of various departments who had their perks lined up, but with the inception of the Security Department had them curtailed. Hence the new Security Manager was not the flavour of the year. The nylon rope and string factory was of particular interest, so two security men were installed as a clerk and a labourer. They were eager beavers, as undercover jobs meant double pay. This particular manager gave away a set of sheepskin car covers to the value of $800 a day. He was popular with the management as his profit showed 28%, but when shown it could be 35% nobody was particularly interested: he was one of the boys and the use of undercover security did not go down well. Elsewhere, to be a cash register operator was a plum job throughout BP. One attractive Morobean lass who was married to a betting man, always broke and unemployed, had a beautiful diamond engagement ring worth about 8,000 Kina (A$12,000). She just happened to be one of the cash register girls in BP's supermarket. Mac invited her up for a cup of coffee and a fatherly chat, offering his word that there would be no prosecution provided she explained in detail how she came to be wearing this most expensive engagement ring. All cashiers, if junior, would dip the till for $50 per day; the more experienced managed $100, and if they had been one year in BP's employ, $150. There was no check, or only a vague one, when cashing up at the beginning of the day, and at handover no monies were signed for, it was all done on a 'friendly' basis.

The Macs were invited to a social drink at the Lae Lodge by the Manager and Staff of BP's Lae outfit. The Macs arrived to discover that they and one other couple were the only heterosexuals; the remainder of the company were of the other persuasion. Not that the Macs were bothered, provided they were not imposed upon. In fact a large percentage of the management were queer, and some – in the words of the prophet – were AC/DC; in fact Mac's neighbour was in the last category. One Personnel Manager who had played second row rugby for PNG had spent six weeks at Ambunti on the Sepik River had been confirmed in his gay habit by celebrating the fact with having a crocodile scarified into his back and buttocks. Also down the upper rear part of his arms – quite a mighty feat, involving six weeks of cutting and healing by placing charcoal in the cuts to raiser the welt rough like as a crocodile skin. This was dedication to his sexual performance. As Mac was not anti-queer, they gave him a lot of information as to who was stealing what.

The Senior Physicians at the hospital and the Airline Manager, both friends of the Macs, invited Mac to their party, and what a night it was! The company was excellent, the servants danced on every whim right down to Mac's whisky, Glenfiddich, being served in double dollops into fine crystal with ice and filtered water from a silver tray with fine Irish linen napkins. The meal of Wiener schnitzel cooked in white wine was way ahead of most chefs. One of the guests, in full Highland dress and resplendent in a MacLean kilt, played the pipes and piano; also, their local beautiful Dr Ross Terry gave a duet on the piano, and the rest present gave a fine rousing chorus of some of the old favourites. But what a gay time in the old sense was had by all.

One fellow, the head of the Butchery Department for New Guinea Mainland, seemed to be doing exceedingly well. He entertained daily at the Melanesian Hotel, buying his guests their lunches and dinners, even down to their individual bottles of wine and other drinks. His arrangement with the suppliers of vegetables, fish and meat was the age-old practice: if you don't have the particular product or the desired quantity or quality, who cares, just supply what you have – convenient all round. But in appreciation for this understanding you are required to provide a cash donation to my personal welfare fund. This would come under the various headings of 'dropsy' (Met Police), the 'bung' or 'iron lung' (Glasgow Police), a 'present' (Kenya Police) or simply a reward for services rendered or promised in the past, present or future. Corruption was here to stay.

Another fellow came to grief after spending $25,000 in a six-week spree in the US. Documentation showed the importation of two Toyota Crowns, but their whereabouts for physical inspection were never discovered: another popular and influential figure in the upper echelons. On a visit to Mt. Hagen hardware store, for a 'wee giggle' it was decided to chalk-mark the level of nails in a barrel. In ten minutes the level had lowered several inches but there were no sales. One old Jiga tribesman complained that he had been short-delivered, which he had. On checking the invoice the amount showed 124 but the carbon duplicate showed only 24. The ploy was simply brilliant: the original showed as 124 but a plastic board was placed under the original so there was no tracing made. Later a piece of paper plus carbon recorded a different amount and price, and the culprit pocketed the difference in the cash payment. Not bad for a semi-literate thief or Security man. The Highlanders were never slow on the uptake.

Life back in Lae was good, especially once the Macs, Kipsoi and Nandi Bear moved into a spacious Bulolo/Queenslander house opposite the Lae Lodge Hotel and its pool and tennis courts.

But one day Deputy Commissioner Michael Vee gave Mac a call to say that his uncle, the illustrious former Prime Minister Michael Somare, would be back in the saddle in a few months and that he, as his nephew, was to take over the Pangu Party business wing. BP's General Manager, Mr Heddle, had agreed to give the Security job to him, as he did not really wish to be C of P after all. Michael Vee was invited to come over to Lae and inspect his future accommodation and the BP set-up in general; he declined, stating that if Mac had anything to do with it, it would be well organised. The usual reference – 'Due to pressures of localisation and economic restraint in this developing country, Mr MacDonald's services regrettably had to be terminated' – was followed by the usual drivel. It was good while it lasted, but clearly the Bastards of the Pacific did not require an efficient Security service under any circumstances.

Lae, 1975–82

Part Five
Out of Uniform: 1982 and After

25: The Shaky Isles, 1982–84

Mac was 52, his wife 47. Their first decision: where to go? New Zealand had always made a favourable impression, so why not start with the Land of the Long White Cloud? They came down from PNG via Brisbane then made the 3¼-hour flight to Christchurch on the South Island, where they were met by Denis Holmes CPM, ex-Kenya Police, who was now a Kiwi resident. The Merc, loaded to the gunwales with survival gear, was waiting at the Lyttelton docks. The two dogs were in quarantine in Oz for nine months, so off they set down through the Canterbury Plains with the snow-tipped Southern Alps as backcloth, into the High Country at Rangitata, through Geraldine and Cromwell to Queenstown, the tourist capital of Kiwiland. A place for all seasons enjoying an international reputation, Queenstown has a population of about 3,500 with only 1,000 ratepayers. Many folk have holiday homes there and come from all over the country. In the 1860s, when gold was discovered in Otago Province, there was an influx of Australian and American miners, as well as Chinese, who went over the tailings. Most of the settlements died with the departure of the miners, but Queenstown survived as some brave souls in the form of sheep farmers arrived. One by the name of Rees had two peaks named after his eldest sons, Cecil and Walter. The local War Memorial pays tribute to the highly-decorated Kiwis who gave their lives in the service of King and Country, the cemetery an unspoken reminder of the hardships the pioneers suffered.

After PNG, Mac found it hard to adapt from a tropical to a temperate climate, though the warmth of the Macs' reception by the locals helped. The Kiwi dollar was 30% lower than the Aussie but the cost of living was cheap and the produce excellent – Steinlager was good beer, and the Wilson's malt whisky almost up to Scottish standards. Enjoying the scenery – Coronet Peak and The Remarkables, Cardrona, Lake Wakatipu and its twin-screw steamer SS *Earnslaw*, the Skyline Gondola in the town centre – was all very well, but it was time for the MacDonalds to seek gainful employment. They declined the chance to run a town-centre motel; Mrs Mac did a short spell at another nearby, then at the local kindergarten which she enjoyed, but out of the blue a secretarial job with the Lake County Council came up. Mac flirted with the premature but worthwhile notion of using his 280E Mercedes for whirlwind tours around the South Island, but instead he accepted a job as manager of a local tourist tours/taxi firm. Depressed by relatively menial duties and the drop in earning, his spirits rose at the end of the first week on discovering that Saturday and Sunday were also included, and his day off was Monday: this suited him very well, as weekends gave time and a half and double time and special overtime rates, so it ended up not too bad after all. At least so it seemed, but despite having been employed by the Labour Department, his weekend allowances were not paid. Here was a pretty kettle of fish. When the proprietor, Graeme Scarlet, claimed he couldn't afford the payments, the Labour Department was asked to inform Scarlet's solicitor that the matter would be pursued. What had angered Mac was that Scarlet had taken on as a daytime despatcher a young fellow who had a conviction for being in possession of drugs, which he held over him. Mr Scarlet would learn that Mac was an animal of a different colour.

The cars left a lot to be desired, but the drivers were a good bunch. Fraser Campbell, 35, had been in the NZ Army but had smashed himself up in a bad accident and got himself medically discharged. He then qualified as a Forestry Commission Officer and became a crack shot with his .22 rifle, taking out feral goats in the local ranges at 50 cents a tail. An adventurous sort, he had toured the USA and Canada, skied and worked as a roustabout, kitchen hand and waiter for a couple of years. It was Fraser who enlightened Mac on the wondrous snowscapes of North America. Also hang-glider of some renown, he suggested that Mac take up this exhilarating sport; however, despite the relative cheapness of entering the hallowed realm of hang-gliders, Mac was put off when he discovered that lately Fraser's mate, who had trimmed the wingspan to execute more intricate manoeuvres, had plummeted to his death on Walter Peak, compacting his more than 6' frame to slightly over five foot on impact. A horrified Fraser glided down some minutes later to discover the remains. Ski-ing would do this 53-year-old, thank you.

Neil Campbell, another of the drivers, seemed to have lived a charmed existence. He had no previous visible means of support, but owned his own residence up Fern Hill with a grandstand view of the lake. A competent fisherman and shot (poacher), Neil's piano playing had earned him a reputation, not for his accomplishment but because the better hotels were only too willing to pay up in jugs of beer to see him leave. American tourists thought he was quite a guy, with his battered orange squeezer (NZ Army hat), his red bandana, tartan shirt, well-worn frilled buckskin jacket and hand-tooled cowboy boots making up the picture of the Kiwi Frontiersman. Neil doubled up as one of the stokers on the 'Lady of the Lake', the SS *Earnslaw*, on which he was known to leave the stokehole and appear in all his sweaty, coal dust glory in the saloon bar to thump the piano and lead the sing-song. He would also ski with the best of the locals.

The third character was the owner of a swish seafood and local cuisine restaurant around the first bluff who had been an Alpine guide and ski instructor in Austria. This trio, with Mac tagging along, decided to ski Cardrona one bleak day. Going up the mountain in the back of an ute, the four demolished a bottle of vodka, as there was a snowstorm brewing. The three experts took off over the top and rattled down a steep slope, dodging electrical pylons and ending up well down the terrain. Mac followed, but not with the same grace; a dozen falls and several fits of swearing later he too arrived, to be congratulated on joining this brotherhood of idiots.

On the quieter slopes of the golf course, a friendship had developed between 'Bob the Greek' and 'that Scottish bastard', otherwise known as Messrs Triviates and MacDonald. Bob had enjoyed a varied career and, like Mac, had been a rebel at heart. A student protestor in his native Greece, he had fought on the side of Elias in the late 1940s as a beardless youth of communist persuasion. Over the years he had been ground down slightly and now had a strong right-wing outlook on life. Bob had met a charming Kiwi girl, Kathy, who was on holiday in Greece. She was a sheep-farmer's daughter, so Bob married in New Zealand and settled in Queenstown, where he took up a job as kitchen hand in the Frankton Motel, a tourist overnight destination. Soon he could cook a hearty breakfast; that earned him promotion to the role of cook proper, in which he quickly picked up the traditional lamb crown roast with trimmings and could open an ice cream container and place a quantity over tinned peaches. After a number of years the motel came under new management. Bob was now Chef. The new proprietor required an à la carte menu, which Bob obviously disputed; he was sacked, claimed unfair dismissal and won $20,000 compensation. He had a Greek friend who owned a fish and chip shop and a market garden. Bob bought him out and worked the shop for five years, seven days a week with no holidays, making about $1,500.00 a day plus his pinball machines for the unsuspecting local youth, and accumulating some $3 million or thereabouts from potatoes with the black eye still in them, and all cooking done on a pre-heat basis. 'What do these bloody Aussie tourists know anyway? They're usually half pissed,' was the reasoning behind this successful operation. Mac would only partake of the Bluff oysters, as Bob had nothing to do with their preparation! Bob, being astute, bought the family a new house on acreage on the path of a new highway; he had become a chef on a half-day basis at one of the better restaurants in town, where he ruled the roost and was popular all round with his outgoing personality. Somehow he had learnt the art of cooking from another chef and excelled. With the build of an Olympic athlete, Bob the Greek was also the best golfer in many a country mile, playing off a 1 handicap. He asked Mac for a few tips, as Mac had an educated swing. Mac refused as his lowest handicap had been two, but after several rounds with Bob he realised the Greek golfer did need a little polish in chipping and working his fairways in match play. Bob eventually played to a +1 handicap, and in his later years a comfortable 3 handicap. He was known all over Otago and Southland and in the Canterbury Plains and had a number of championships under his belt.

The Macs had leased a property from a Dunedin doctor,

brand-new from top to bottom, with cathedral ceilings, an open wood fire and four double bedrooms. The Doc obtained permission to use the establishment as a ski-ing guest house. The first guests were a Yankee couple: who bounced up and down on the beds, declared them too soft and moved on to a downtown hotel at five times the expense. Bless 'em! Next came the Happy Jappies, a few Poms and the odd Aussie. Mac would entertain them with his stories of former colonial days and get a laugh. They enjoyed the Memsahib's excellent cuisine, from Kashmiri curries to rare old English roast beef and fine Kiwi seafood, washed down by Aussie reds and Kiwi whites, the occasional hand-picked Highland malt and the above-average Steinlager. After six months the MacDonalds took on a bigger property owned by a professor at Dunedin University. Perched on a promontory about 2,000 feet up looking over the lake, it had downstairs bedrooms with bunk beds to accommodate the budget skier.

There was the odd Colonial like Mac around. Roy Heath, ex-Hong Kong, had been a Pilot Officer RAF Regiment in his National Service days, joined the Royal Hong Kong Police some thirty years before and married a Kiwi. As was customary, the wives made sure their husbands returned to the Shaky Isles on retirement. Roy played golf and enjoyed the regular hand of cards with a flutter on the side. He had two fishing launches on the Lake where he took tourists on fishing trips to catch the various classes of large trout. John Perkins, an Englishman of Yorkshire stock, had flown with the Royal Fleet Air Arm and gravitated to PNG as a pilot of light aircraft, flying out of and around the out-stations of Madang Province. John enjoyed flying and the life in PNG, but had the initiative to add to his repertoire a few small stores run by the locals on his milk run round the traps. He made a success of his venture, especially when he flew in his cargo and took out his earnings on a daily basis, landing for thirty minutes while being loaded with passengers and some cargo. His boss at Talair got a whisper of what was afoot and instructed his pilot either to quit his store operations or buy the plane from Talair for $20,000. While the tirade was being delivered John produced his chequebook. His operation expanded, but when John had had enough of the 'hairy' flying around the central cordillera of PNG he moved to the Land of the Long White Cloud, opened up a leather goods store in the mall in Queenstown, and became a competent skier.

Dawn White, who had been Girl Friday in Kavieng, New Ireland, came up from Dunedin where she was ensconced with her new legal eagle husband. They were to visit her mother in Christchurch, so the Macs were invited down for a couple of weeks to look after their house in Dunedin, about 150 miles south-east of Queenstown. Dunedin in the Gaelic is 'Edinburgh'. It was like an old lady who had seen better days, but it had a quaint charm and resilience and St Clair was a great golf course to score on with wide open, interesting holes. The other course was Ballymacewan, a championship layout where you had three options into each hole and drive placement was imperative for good scoring. A real traditional clubhouse matched the course. A voice in the pro shop boomed, 'What the hell are you doing here, Angus MacDonald?' It was the former pro from Port Moresby, who introduced Mac to the esteemed members who were having a Veterans' Day, so they enjoyed several cracks about Moresby over a few pots.

The golf had improved and a comfortable 7 handicap was the best Mac could do, due to arthritis, which had now plagued him for a number of years. By now the attacks were severe because of the cold and changeable climate and sudden changes in barometric pressure. But he won the Skyline Classic by the skin of his teeth, an 18 hole competition for the best nett score. The prize donated by Mt. Cook Airlines was a trip for two up north to the Bay of Islands, with a four-day hotel stay at Kerikeri, where Queen Victoria had made the Treaty of Waitangi with the Maori people – something that has been debated ever since. $400 spending money was also provided, the total value in the region of $1,500. Mac had to think about it: this was a professional purse. After some consideration, and having won two raffles on the same day, he accepted – if he had not, the donor might have been disinclined the following year. To placate his conscience he gave the air tickets to a local rugby captain and his girlfriend on the condition they would be 'Mr and Mrs Mac': this was their honeymoon in advance.

Mainly because of Mac's arthritis, the family decided to return to Australia. The convoy of two vehicles loaded to the gunwales with personal and household effects, including visiting mother-in-law and the two dogs, set off for Christchurch, where Mac sold his Mercedes in a take-it-or-leave-it deal with the Mercedes people. On arrival in Oz the arthritic condition improved immensely.

26: Tamer now — but still a Colonial Boy

A rolling stone gathers no moss, but receives a fine polish. All very well, but back in Brisbane some of life's realities had to be faced. As the MacDonalds soon found, rolling stones do not gather enough for the retirement they deserve, either. Determined not to be caught out as his parents had been in the Wall Street Crash, over the years Mac had bought housing in the UK and OZ, which he leased, though the nett income amounted to more or less what the banks were showing as interest. His own property was not in too bad shape: his old mate, Tom Mulhern, had done the painting, but the gardens were run-down. The estimated time to get the properties shipshape – six two-week stints – in practice became six times six weeks; in fact a whole year came and went in which all members of the family played their laborious part. The real problem was that at the age of 54 nobody wanted to employ this has-been. It was a new experience, being unemployed and unemployable: both the Macs had worked all their lives, but the money they had thought so good overseas never really was.

An advert in the *Courier Mail* for an 'Investigation Manager with International Detection Services' set the ball rolling at last. There were two partners in the IDS, Keith Schafferius and Keith Gillespie. The former had held a commission in the RAAF, the latter had been a Senior Superintendent with the Federal Police, and both were on the ball. Their business was divided into sections, with a manager in charge of each. Keith S did the more secret and confidential work, which culminated in him being a retriever in child abduction, with cases inter- and intra-state as well as overseas. The business had 'sources' in most departments who provided information. There was a Mercantile Section, which acted as debt collectors; a Missing Persons Section (or Skips), persons who had disappeared for a variety of reasons; and a Repossession Section (Repo) for individuals who had fallen behind on their payments. Keith G headed up the Investigations, but was keen to go out and drum up trade with the various legal, government and business people who might further expand the business.

Despite his varied career in Police work, this was a new game to Mac, who had to piece the puzzle together bit by bit. The Investigators were the men and women out on the street, exerting profound patience in their observations and surveillance. A considerable amount of work came through Workers' Compensation Claims, those professional cheats of the system. An injury – actual, self-inflicted or imagined – would result in a visit to a physician, who would certify the patient's inability to continue in that form of employment. 'Compo' led to millions of dollars of taxpayers' money being fraudulently paid out. Even some of the would-be old soldiers who had served in a recent conflict would suddenly develop the inability to sleep or to communicate with their peers. A sympathetic psychologist would recommend a TPI pension, although in fact the individual's lifestyle had not been impaired in the slightest. A few drinks at a bar and a tape recording would help establish the truth, as did the prudent use of long-range cameras. The Court would enjoy a few hours of entertainment from both stills and movie of the 'Compo' case limping into the surgery on crutches for his medical check, then hurtling out, crutches under his arms, for a game of tennis.

Mac was of special interest to his new employers: he had professional investigation contacts throughout the world, as his ex-Kenya Police colleagues were scattered to the four winds and held managerial positions in insurance, commerce, even in other Police Forces. Here was genuine networking. It was a most professional set-up; the secretarial and clerical back-up was of exceptional standard and all 'hands' were happy with their remuneration. Everything down to industrial espionage was dealt with; successful enquiries were made throughout Europe, North, South and Central America, the Far East and even multicultural India and the Far East. Even the legal eagles, both Defence and Prosecution, would come and have evidence redefined. These were the days when you get a 'contract' job done in dear old Brissie for a miserable $250; but like all good things they came to an end. The Victoria and NSW Governments' Compensation representatives decided that in most cases it would be better and cheaper to pay out than to hire people to investigate and put the matter to rights. This was a blow: Mac was moved sideways again to help out in Mercantile, which was managed by Dick Barton, who eventually went out on his own and netted $350,000 the first year — not bad for a Bachelor of Business.

'Mercantile' was a nice way of saying 'debt-collecting'. Given the 'Too Hard' basket, Mac asked for a briefing on what to do. 'Phone up the debtor, put your cards face up on the table and Allah in his wisdom will smile down and the poor debtor will agree to pay up, mostly.'

It was quite a surprise for the uninitiated Mercantile Assistant. As the weeks rolled on it became clear that here was an avenue the world's Police Forces had neglected. Debtors could be categorised in the following ways:

1. The person who is naive and borrows when unable to afford to pay the debt off, but has every intention of honouring the commitment.

2. The average person who finds it easy to raise a loan, can back up the play and intends to pay the debt off but creeps further into debt by being careless.

3. A person who starts off as a category 2 but gives up and no longer cares but continues to borrow, cannot honour the debt and is satisfied with that situation.

4. These people realise that money can be borrowed under false pretences and have no intention of paying but are now making a practice of borrowing with intent to defraud. They usually move from place to place and lending agency to lending agency. They change their identity when close to the crunch.

5. As 4, but now moving interstate, adopting a new identity with each move.

6. The same as 4/5, but they even change their background and appearance and move from country to country, NZ usually,

then Fiji and the Islands. This process can take up to five to ten years, then they are back at the beginning. Most aliases used are similar to their original names. A good operator can net around $100,000 to $200,000 a year; sometimes crime does pay.

After a week or so Keith G said to Mac that it showed on Mac's face he was not enjoying the Mercantile side of things. Too right! Another reference was collected and an advance to the rear was made.

Justice delayed is justice denied. In 1987, Mac returned to NZ to submit his claim of $10,000 back pay owed by Mr Scarlet's tour company. The Tribunal was impressed with his presentation, and despite one dissenting assessor for the employer, the judge awarded 100% of the claim, to be paid over the next few years. Crime, it seemed, wasn't the only thing that paid.

The return to Kiwiland whetted his appetite for more and better ski-ing, so in 1988 he took off to visit his daughter, who was a biologist/environmentalist working temporarily in the UK. They met in London and took off by British Air to Geneva, where they boarded a train for Lausanne, transferred to mountain railway at Aigle, on up the mountain to Champéry of early sixties fame. The Pension de la Paix had become a 3-star hotel right beside the cable car, which could take about 100 skiers at 30 kph up from the village to Planachaux, a plateau a couple of thousand feet above, to ski down to Les Crosets and up and over the range to Avoriaz, a modern resort dominated by the British. Michel Bouchatay, his old ski instructor, former Ski School Director and Mayor of Champéry, accompanied them. They did the World Cup run, not in the style of the racers but nonetheless a great run down to Les Prodains for a bite of lunch, washed down with many toasts to such wonderful people. The area was now one of the largest in the world, with 300 km of runs in Switzerland and France *called 'Les Portes du Soleil'* (The Gates to the Sun). The Monier-Stettler Juniors had now taken over the hotel from their parents; Mac's African carvings were still proudly displayed. A couple of years later, when Mac was back in Switzerland with a golfing mate, Jon Currell, ex-3 RAR and SAS, a Canadian instructor rekindled the wanderlust for North America. In Europe, he said, the snow began at 4,000 feet and finished at 6,000, but in the States it went from 8,000 to 12,000, so there never was a problem, only a predictable abundance. While Jon made his own way to Chamonix and then Vail, Mac and son did a whirlwind tour of former Glasgow Police and Kenya Police mates, plus the outlaws, before heading for Aspen, Colorado, via Denver.

Aspen to Mac will always be something special. Son had got himself engaged to a former girlfriend, a braw Scottish lass from Falkirk, an air hostess whom he had met in Australia. They flew into Aspen to discover that the airport had lines of private jets on both sides owned by the billionaires, who could push the millionaires out of the way. The Little Red Ski House was run by Kiwis and Aussies for an elderly lady, an original Aspenite. John arrived from Vail and could now ski. Richard was a natural and took to it like a duck to water. Aspen is an exciting Old West silver mining town with numerous pubs, restaurants, art galleries and a comprehensive collection of shops whose prices range from reasonable to most unreasonable. The Colonial contingent had an excellent budget room with cooked breakfast. Aspen has five mountains: Ajax, in town, for the more advanced skier, with Bell Mountain adjacent; next is Buttermilk, the beginners' mountain, then Highlands, which has the lot, and finally Snowmass, twelve miles out of town, with its four peaks and seven-mile runs, its own village and infrastructure, and possibly the best ski school in the USA – a great mountain with wide open cruising runs to steep moguls and triple black slopes in the hanging glades. Thanks to Bob Georgie, a man of Mac's vintage with a droopy moustache, cowboy hat and a very laid-back attitude, who had been a Detective Sergeant in the LA Police Dept, a Park Ranger, a Minister of Religion, a physicologist and now a Ski Instructor, Richard progressed to 9.5 and Mac to 9.25, 10 being 'expert'. They always managed to have an extra hour's ski-ing at the end of the day, as Bob liked their 'give it a go' attitude. If you can walk, you can ski, irrespective of your ability; even learning is fun and there is a rejuvenating process that goes with ski-ing, both mentally and physically. It is an adventure involving skill, speed, feel, sound, and the chance to appreciate a glorious white winter wonderland. Obviously Mac was becoming addicted.

Thus 1992 saw Mac back in the States, this time to try out resorts like Breckenridge, a couple of hours out of Denver, 10,000 feet above sea level and with ski-ing up to 14,000 feet; then over to Aspen for another couple of weeks. Prices were going up, but it still took a lot of beating. Our dear old proprietrix was there on holiday at the Little Red Ski House with her Hawaiian companion, who was her bodyguard, an interesting hunk of a man – well over 6' and built to proportion – who was also a Methodist Minister. Mac and he discovered that the Motu language in PNG was close to Hawaiian, so the South Pacific Islands, their traditions, attitudes and cultures were on the agenda. It was refreshing for Mac to realise that he had grasped a fair picture of the South Pacific during his time in PNG.

They took in Salt Lake City, home of the Mormons with their world-famous Tabernacle and shrine, Park City, another Old West silver town, now home of the US ski team, and Deer Park, a luxurious resort with all mod cons and immaculately groomed runs. Mac met up with a Swede and the pair skied Snowbird, down the valley and up Cotton Wood Canyon an hour distant. He got paired off with two charming old ducks, both in their seventies, who in their day had been champion skiers and still performed at comfortable advanced level. Led by their instructor they were ski-ing the Peruvian Gulch run when suddenly there was a 'white-out' and a snowstorm. On their right were cliffs of several hundred feet. Mac was instructed to ski as close to their instructor as possible in the same tracks. After a hair-raising twenty minutes there was a burst of sunlight through the timber: all were heartily relieved, as they had come down the mountain at a fair lick to beat the weather. Next day a further couple of miles up the canyon they tried out Alta, which is laid out for the better skier and is famed for its champagne powder.

The Swede and Mac took off for Wyoming, cattle country in the summer, freezing cold in winter. The Tetons separate Wyoming and Idaho; in the valley nestles Jackson Town with its own ski run and twenty minutes away in the Tetons is Jackson Hole, a resort mainly for advanced skiers and some of the world's best extreme skiers. Mac met up with a Canuck who had just competed in the Veterans' Downhill Race, which he had watched, impressed at the Veterans' performance. Most were ex-champions; the Canadian had taken up ski-ing at 49 and now, at 64, was an instructor and racer. He was kind enough to compliment Mac and gave him a few tips as they did a few runs together. After ski-ing at least five out of seven days per week for seven weeks the man was satiated at last. He flew back to Denver and spent a couple of days in San Francisco on the way back to the Great South Land.

After a few sallies over to NZ, in September 1997 it was time to try South America, and Chile in particular. They had decided to try a ski resort 300 miles south of Santiago called Termas de Chillan. A couple of days in Santiago, a fascinating city in centuries-old Spanish architecture and an exciting throbbing city, then their travel rep took them to the Central Station which, like the rest of Santiago, had seen better days. The rails were rusty and there was a profusion of weeds, with the odd stray mongrel prowling and the local children peeing onto the rails. Half an hour later the passengers were invited to embark on a couple of unwashed coaches; an equally grubby diesel locomotive linked up and they were off. After a few hundred metres it was apparent that the suspension matched the outward appearances. It seemed to Mac that the coaches would leave the track as the whole set bounced and swayed alarmingly. In their heyday these had been very plush, sophisticated passenger coaches. Theirs had double glazing and a venetian blind in between; the seating was in double leather chairs with fold-down footrest in front. Mac was in the act of putting his feet up when the American couple seated in front literally took off in a neat slide forward; part of their seating had become detached from the side of the coach. Numerous rail crossings were taken at no reduction of speed. To go to the toilet was like negotiating a fishing boat in a heavy swell.

The rail system was North British, which meant there was a precise camber to allow a train to negotiate bends at 100 kph, so the train did not depart the rails after all. Next was the wee man who got up, put on a red waistcoat, disappeared and reappeared with an annoying cry of '*Bebidos, bebidos!*' which one took to be refreshments, a pantomime repeated immediately after each station — and there were many, one about every ten minutes. After seven hours the towering, snow-capped Andes emerged on the left, the sea on the right through miles of vineyards and poplar trees with the attractive haciendas of Chilean farms and wineries and their tiled roofs, all flying their national flag on this national holiday.

Mac realised he was a month late, as the spring thaw had set in. It was late September and the season was June to August. At the ski base he picked up a Spanish instructor from Barcelona and spoke to a couple of female instructors, one from Scotland and the other a dinky-di Aussie, who were leaving the next day. The run from mountain top to bottom was mainly intermediate; despite being unfit, Mac managed to almost keep up with his Spaniard instructor, but when they ended up on the beginners' slopes with their melting snow Mac caught an edge and went down with a muffled scream and a few four-letter words. He had done the tendon in his right ankle: his most expensive ski run ever, all $13,000 worth — not a Happy Little Vegemite.

Back at the Lodge, a charming lady doctor, doing her spell as locum, told Mac all would be well in a few days. It was not. So the receptionist, with a little English, an accommodating female who had been nicknamed Toyota Corolla because her name sounded like that (it was actually Carola Espinoza) said her uncle owned the taxi company at Chillan and that before they left they should take a trip to Concepcion and Talcahuana, the former an old city on the coast and the latter the Chilean naval base. They agreed, and Carola came along as it was her day off. Some shady-looking males followed the party when they went to change money, and the naval base had a definite flavour to it — drying fish. The taxi driver crossed himself at every road shrine, and there were many, while Mac was doing likewise at his suicidal driving. The tendon was still useless, so it was time for a withdrawal, back to the Great South Land.

In 1992, shopping in Brisbane, Mac bumped into Colonel Harry Green MBE, of the PNGVR, whom he had known back in 1967 in Rabaul when Harry was a successful importer/exporter and one of the local personalities. Harry was now a resident in

Vanuatu and strongly recommended the place, which he said was like Rabaul forty years ago and an ideal place to retire to. Mac did a bit of research and with the help of daughter-in-law Mairi was put in contact with another former PNG resident, John Smith, who also gave Vanuatu a great write-up. The indigenous people were Melanesian and similar to the Tolai of East New Britain. A score or so islands north-east of New Caledonia around the 18° latitude mark, it was tropical with occasional cyclones, had an abundance of fish and produced copra and very special beef cattle. Like most of the South-West Pacific Islands it had won its independence in the early 1980s. Mac, who now suffered wearily from chronic arthritis, knew this could be the answer to his ailment.

In March 1998 they boarded Air Vanuatu and landed 2¼ hours later at Vila Airport. The locals were friendly and the climate tropical, a steady 30° and 75% humidity. The arthritis disappeared immediately. Next day they hired a small Toyota and did the rounds. All fences were of hibiscus and the town had the usual stores, with the Chinese well to the fore. Port Vila was built on a hillside overlooking the island resort of Iririki. It had three distinct lagoons named 1, 2 and 3. Housing was an interesting proposition: you could lease a house for fifty years with a possible 25-year extension. The average four-bedroom top of the range residence with the inevitable sky dish antenna would be around $750,000, then you would require a boat of around $50,000 and a vehicle to tow, about the same. The Old Colonials had left, some to be replaced by what would be termed as carpet-baggers, out for a quick buck, none of whom could speak basic Melanesian-Pidgin, which was a very anglified form. Most locals spoke English and French. They were nice people, well-built and fed, but both their previous Colonial mentors, French and British, had spoiled them. It was another South Sea paradise wilting on the vine. Arthritis would have to be tolerated after all; a tropical island life was fast becoming a dream.

In 1999 the Macs took off to Canada via Honolulu. Vancouver is quite a city: it too has its fair share of Vietnamese and Indians, brown as opposed to red, in a population of some three million. North-north-west was Whistler, one of the great ski resorts on the American continent — two big mountains with plenty of lifts and many runs from 'beginner' to 'expert'. Mac was a bit shaky on his pins after radium therapy for a touch of cancer, but quite determined to give things a go, and after a week he had a bit of strength in his legs and began to really enjoy the thrills and spills of those first-class slopes. The accommodation was reasonable and the food comparatively cheap — the Aussie dollar was on a par with the Canadian, so his Scottish heart did not haemorrhage after all. They spent a few days at Sun Peaks, where Olympic gold medallist Nancy Greene and her husband have developed Todd Mountain near Kamloops, a logging town, then went on to Red Mountain in the Kootenay Mountains near the US border and an area called Paradise before heading to Fernie, over the border in Alberta.

Banff, with its famous hotel, was full of Japanese, both tourists and shop owners, and loads of Poms. The secret of a reasonably priced visit was to live in a satellite town like Canmore, 20 km out, the land of the lumberjack and coal miner and almost 100% Canadian. There were a number of Pipe Bands in this territory, which was also the country of Princess Patricia's Canadian Light Infantry. Their 2nd Battalion had served with 27 Brigade in Korea, so Mac was a welcome guest in the Royal Canadian Legion, where a few of the Old Korea sweats were still about. Norquay's ski school left much to be desired, but Mac got the Chief Instructor, Edouard, self-named 'Speedie Eddie', a French-Canadian and chef at the Railway Restaurant in Calgary. A new form of instruction was given, racing crouch and less movement from one ski to the other to minimise the effort. As commented on by Edouard, Mac now had three techniques at his disposal: jump the end – old-fashioned; unweight or roll – very modern. Mac had reached 69 years, thinking 65 years would see the end of his ski-ing, but had now decided to go on until 75, God willing. His ski guide at Panorama in the Purcell Mountains was a local gentleman from Invermere, a sprightly 82-year-old who could ski blacks with the best, but hoped Mac did not mind if they missed out double blacks and the humps and mumps of a mogul field. The other two couples had trouble keeping up with the Silly Old Bastards, who sank a few rapid beers over lunch. Thank you, O Canada…

Things might have been going downhill in more ways than one had Mac not found a way of financing these travels. Years earlier, he had returned from that two-month holiday spent ski-ing in Champéry to be greeted by the hard word from his better half: 'Your self-made pension precludes you from these expensive ski holidays. If you intend to continue ski-ing sojourns you had better get yourself a wee job. In fact, they are advertising for driving instructors…'

Thinking this was a sedentary job where he could bring in the booty to maintain his lifestyle on the snowfields, Mac was offered employment with the Olympic Driving School. He was trained to a limited extent — he failed his test four times, the first deservedly and the other three because of his forthright criticism when called for by the Department of Transport Examiner. Little did he realise that his autocratic, authoritarian, Army and Police background would be a drawback, but in the event the leopard managed to change a few of his more obvious spots. He was supposed to have been allocated the south-west as his home area but instead he was shunted off to the SSE, but he was desperate to keep up his lifestyle as he had become accustomed. On some of those long days he would return vibrating to the rhythm of the engine. This was overdoing the role of Driving Instructor, but his normal determination carried the day at the tender age of 58. Soon he got to know his new area and became a happy Vegemite, especially when he made over $200 a day. There was considerably more to being a good driving instructor than met the eye, but he never became so involved that he became one-eyed about the occupation or let it become the overriding aspect of his existence. As the years rolled on, Mac developed new techniques for teaching strictly accordingly to the book as required by the Transport Department.

Mac's daughter suggested that she would like to have a business, so after having been associated with various driving schools over a six-year period, it was time to open his own School. The first year was a struggle, the next three years a learning process, then after another three years a profit at last was being made. Then the Government in its wisdom introduced the GST. For those under $50,000 gross a year the single operator did not pay the tax. The 10% increase in price effectively reduced the number of students by 35%, hence there was no profit margin. At 70, Mac resolved to train his own instructors, again creating a considerable loss. On the whole the young people Mac came into contact with as a driving instructor were a pleasure to teach. Driving Instructors unfortunately are not rated particularly highly in the community, although about 50% are well-qualified people. The rate charged leaves very little room for error and the unenterprising find it hard to earn a substantial living, so the lesser 50% resort to dishonest dealings with their company.

In politically correct terms, some nationalities are quicker learners than others. One group of Indians would always ask for a student rate, then a discount. They usually got the standard answer about the profit margin. One student in her late forties saw that Mac was a kind gentleman and after eight hours' instruction said she loved the automatic car, although it was in fact a manual. Another 82-year-old gent who had been picked up by the Police after failing to obey three 'Stop' signs and six Give Ways asked Mac what gear he wanted, trying to slam it into 1st at 80 kph; his pebble glasses had not been cleaned in months and his hearing aid had a flat battery. After ten minutes of free instruction he thought it a good idea that the pair have a few snorts of Johnny Walker Red Label – not a bad suggestion in the circumstances. Driving Instruction was not the Golden Gateway to a Golden Existence, though it did help Mac indulge his passion for the snow. But in 2003 the school was closed.

2004 saw the Macs planning a move to Darwin up in the Nothern Territory some 3,500 km or 2,000-odd miles north-west of Brisbane which has a sub-tropical climate to a continental one whereas the Top End, as it is called of the Nothern Territory, is purely tropical with the odd cyclone which flattened the city of some 100,000 people in 1974 in turn has become phoenix-like and is now the fastest growing city in Australia. Darwin is home to the prawn trawlers also a cultutred pearl industry. The Top End has a lot to offer: a constant climate of 25 to 30°C degrees perennially which hopefully should alleviate Mac's chronic arthritis and he may be able to indulge in one of his favourite pastimes, another disease called golf.

Nearby is the Kakadu National Park a world tourist attraction with Aboriginal cave drawings, salt and fresh water crocs and the wild cape buffalo. There are also numerous cattle properties along with the delicious barra (barramundi), a fresh and salt water fish, not forgetting to throw in a few cray tails.

Shelley, his daughter, is busy raising grandson William Jack (3) and Richard, his son, has his hands full with granddaughters Catlin (10) who has a musical gift and Olivia (6), as the name suggests, the possibility of an acting career.

Memsabih Ronnie warns Mac to forget breeding Rotties as Stafford the Staffordshire is a wee jealous woof a bit tottery on his pins at a human 98 years.

Mac threatens to write a golf book as no amateur seems to have climbed that mountain. Already he is designing a bungalow with a pool and spa in the middle, surrounded by a cyclone-proofed house of galvanised metal frame, reinforced concrete blocks rendered, and semi-circle type colour bond roof.

This now brings forward another phase in their lives; as the prophet says, 'You can't keep a good dog down.'

Presidential Palace, Santiago, Chile, 1997

Port Villa, Vanuatu, 1998

Appendices

Appendix A
Chronology – Korea 1950–53

1905	Russia/Japan
1910	Korea – Japanese Colony
1943	Cairo Conference US/GB
1945	Independence
1948	Soviet Alignment
1948	Dr Sygman Rhee President
1949	UN Recognise Republic of Korea
1950	Elections – North Korea Demands One Country
25.06.50	North Korean Army crossed the 38th Parallel
30.06.50	Seoul Fell
04.07.50	Suwon US Action
14.07.50	US Reinforcements: Taejon, 90 Miles South of Seoul
05.07.50	Naval – UK, Australia, New Zealand
02.07.50	77th Australian Mustangs Squadron, Iwakuni
25.07.50	Turkish Offer
26.07.50	UK Brigade, UK, NZ and Australia
03.08.50	Naktong Pusan Bridgehead. General Walton Walker, 8th Army

29.08.50	Arrival 1st Middlesex and 1st A & SH per HMSS *Unicorn* and *Ceylon*
01.09.50	Naktong breached 17 places
05.09.50	27 Brigade 11,000 yds Naktong SW Taegu
15.09.50	Counter-attack Taegu
15.09.50	1st Marine 7th Infantry Inchon
16.09.50	24th Division Counter-attack
22.09.50	'B' Coy Middlesex, Plum Pudding Hill, Pt 325 Middlesex Hill
23.09.50	'B' Coy 282 'C' Coy 388 A & SH
28.09.50	Taejon Recaptured. Arrival 3rd RAR
10.10.50	Kaesong
17.10.50	'A' Coy & 'B' Coy Sariwon
20.10.50	Pyongyang
21.10.50	Sukchon Turks 187th RCT 82nd Airborne Division
23.10.50	Sinuiju
27.10.50	8th Army halted by Chinese Peoples Liberation Army (Volunteers)
08.11.50	Air Battle, SINUIJI
05.12.50	Withdrawal, Pyongyang
27.12.50	General Ridgeway in Command Korea
08.01.51	PLA & NK Armies held Wonju
15.03.51	2 months Counter-attacks Seoul re-taken
11.04.51	Gen MacArthur relieved
22–25.04.51	Kapyong 3 RAR
25.04.51	1st A & SH depart Korea

25.04.51	IMJIM River Battle
10.07.51	Ceasefire discussions, Panmunjom
26.10.52–28.05.53	THE HOOK
27.07.53	Armistice

Appendix B
Korea 1950–51

NAMES	ACTIONS	VISITATIONS
Boswell	Anju	Changhowon-Ni
Boyde	Ichon	Chonju
Bristow	Inchon	Chongchon river
Buchannan, D	Kumchon	Chorwon
Buchannan, N	Kunu-Ri	Chungdong
Clark	Naktong I, II & III	Chunju
Clarke	Pakchon I & II	Han river
Craig	Pyongyang	Iwakuni
Collett	Sariwon I & II	Kaesong
Delaney	Sibyon-Ni	Kure
Docherty	Sonju	Pusan
Gordon-Ingram	Suchon	Pyongtaek
Kinnear	Uyijongbu	Sasebo
Mackellar	Yongdu-Ri	Seoul
Mitchell		Sinuiju
Muir		Suchon
Murray		Suwon
O'sullivan		Taedong

Peet

Penman

Slim

Sloane

Sweeney

Syme

Wilson, D

Whittington

Taegu

Toju

Waegwan

Wonju

Yalu

Yondong-po

Yongyu

Appendix C
Armour and Artillery

RUSSIAN T34

Weight:	36 tonnes (35.4 tons)
Length:	9.02 (29 ft 7 in.)
Height:	2.68m (8 ft 9½ in.)
Armament:	1 x 100mm gun, 2 x 7.62mm and 1 x 12.7mm machine guns.
Ammunition Carried:	42 rounds of APHE, HEAT and HE, 3,000 rounds for 7.62mm, 500 rounds for 12.7mm.

BRITISH CENTURION V

Weight:	51.8 tonnes (51 tons)
Length:	9.85m (32 ft 4 in.)
Height:	3m (9 ft 10½ in.)
Armament:	1 x 105mm gun, 2 x 7.62mm and 1 x 12.7mm machine guns.
Ammunition Carried:	64 rounds APDS and HESH, 4,250 rounds for 7.62mm, 700 rounds 12.7mm.

RUSSIAN Y34/85

Weight:	32 tonnes (31.5 tons)
Length:	7.5m (24 ft 6 in.)
Height:	2.38m (7 ft 10 in.)
Armament:	1 x 85mm gun, 2 x 7.72mm machine guns.
Ammunition Carried:	56 rounds for 85mm, 2,745 rounds for machine guns.

USA SHERMAN M443

Weight: 31.5 tonnes (31 tons)
Length: 7.53m (24 ft 9 in.)
Height: 2.93m (9 ft 7 in.)
Armament: 1 x 76mm gun, 2 x 0.30 in. machine guns,
                           1 x 0.50 in. machine .300 gun.
Ammunition Carried: 89 rounds for 76mm, 7,750 rounds for
                           0.30, 6,250 rounds for 0.50.

ARTILLERY

105mm 4-inch Howitzer 12,500yds 33 lbs US
155mm 6-inch
Self-Propelled Anti-Tank SU 76 RUSSIAN
25 Pounder BRITISH
122mm 5-inch RUSSIAN
8-inch Howitzer 'Persuader' US

Appendix D
Weapons (Small Arms)

MAKE	TYPE	CALIBRE	NATIONALITY	MAGAZINE
Mauser	Pistol	7.63mm	German	10
Luger	Pistol	9mm	German	8
Walther	Pistol	9mm	German	8
Beretta	Pistol	9mm	Italy	7
Arisaka	Rifle	6.5	Japanese	5
Woodpecker	Med. to Light Machine Gun	6.5	Japanese	30
Webley and Scott Mark VI	Revolver	.45	British	6
Enfield	Revolver	.3	British	6
Browning	Pistol	9mm	British	13
SMLE	No. 1 Rifle	.303"	British	10
SMLE	No. 4 Rifle	.303"	British	10
SMLE	No. 5 Rifle (Carbine)	.303"	British	10

Sten Gun	Machine Carbine	9mm	British	32
Lewis Gun	Light Machine Gun	.303	British	97
Bren Gun	Light Machine Gun	.303	British	30
Vickers	Med. Machine Gun (air or water cooled)	.303	British	Belt-Fed 250
Mosin Nagant	Rifle	7.62mm	Russian	5
Brup Gun	Sub-machine Gun	7.62mm	Russian	35 or Drum 71
Shpagina DP28	Light Machine Gun	7.72	Russian	47
Maxim	Med. Machine Gun	7.62	Russian	250 Belt
Colt 45	Pistol	.45	USA	7
Smith & Wesson	Revolver	.45	USA	6
Springfield	Rifle	.300	USA	5
Garand	Self-loading Rifle	.30	USA	8
M1	Carbine	.30	USA	15 OR 30
Thompson	Sub-machine Gun	.45	USA	20 OR 30

Grease Gun	Sub-machine Gun or Machine Pistol	.45	USA	30
Browning Bar	Light Machine Gun	.30	USA	20
Browning	Med. Machine Gun, Water Cooled	.30	USA	250
Browning	Med. Machine Gun, Water Cooled	.30	USA	230
Browning	Heavy Machine Gun, Metal Link Belt	.50	USA	110

Appendix E
Glossary: Ranks and Formations

Private (Trooper, Sapper, Gunner, Guardsman, Marine)

Lance Corporal (L/Bombardier) 1/2 Section 5 ORs

Corporal Bombardier Lance Sgt 10 Section

Sergeant 35 Platoon

Colour Sergeant Company

(Quartermaster Sgt, Staff Sgt) Quartermaster

Sgt Maj (Warrant Officer 2nd Class WO 11) 135 Company

Regt Sgt Maj (Warrant Officer 1st Class WO 1) 1,000 Battalion

2nd Lt/1st Lt (Subaltern 2nd Lt) 35 Platoon

Captain 135 2i/c Company

Major 135 OC Company

Lt-Col 1,000 CO Battalion

Colonel 2,000 CO Demi Brigade

Brigadier General 4,000 BC Brigade

Major General 15,000 Division

Lt-General 30,000 Corps

General 100,000 Army

Field Marshal 300,000 Army Corps/Army Group

Appendix F
Commonwealth Casualties, Korea 1950–53

	Killed in Action		Wounded in Action		Missing★		TOTAL	
	Off	OR	Off	OR	Off	OR	Off	OR
Aust	9	252	40	994	4	33	53	1,279
Can	11	283	59	1,143	2	45	72	1,471
Ind	--	--	--	4	--	--	--	4
NZ	2	20	15	64	1	--	18	84
RSA	--	--	--	--	1	--	1	--
UK	71	616	187	2,311	52	1,050	310	3,976
TOT	93	1,170	301	4,516	60	1,128	454	6,814

TOTAL: 7,268

Off – Officers
OR – Other Ranks

Appendix G
Commonwealth Decorations, Korea 1950–53

Award	Australia	Canada	New Zealand	United Kingdom	TOTAL
Victoria Cross	--	--	--	4	4
George Cross	--	--	--	2	2
KBE	--	--	--	1	1
CB	--	1	1	--	2
CBE	1	3	--	4	8
OBE	12	17	--	29	58
MBE	14	58	9	80	161
BEM	2	21	3	30	56
DSO	6	19	4	37	56
MC	26	33	11	113	183
GM	1	1	--	3	5
DCM	5	8	1	15	31
MM	40	52	7	111	209
Mentioned in Dispatches	84	247	45	571	947
Foreign Decorations	17	--	4	77	98

Appendix H
Formations and Units, 1950–51

27th British Commonwealth Brigade (The Cinderella, Woolworth, Fire Brigade)

INFANTRY

1 Bn The Middlesex Rgt Aug. 1950–May 1951

1 Bn The Argyll & Sutherland Highlanders Aug. 1950–Apr. 1951

3 Bn The Royal Australian Rgt Sep. 1950—

2 Bn Princess Patricia's Canadian Light Infantry Feb. 1951—

60th Indian Field Ambulance (Parachute) AMC Jul. 1950—

16th Field Rgt Royal New Zealand Artillery 1951—

41st (Independent) Commando Royal Marines Aug. 1950–Mar. 1951

29th Brigade Group

INFANTRY

1st Bn Royal Northumberland Fusiliers Nov. 1950–Oct. 1951

1st Bn Gloucestershire Rgt Nov. 1950–Nov. 1951

1st Bn Royal Ulster Rifles Nov. 1950–Oct. 1951

ARMOUR

8 King's Royal Irish Hussars Nov. 1950–Dec. 1951

'C' Squadron 7th Royal Tank Rgt Nov. 1950–Oct. 1951

ROYAL ARTILLERY

45 Field Rgt Nov. 1950–Nov. 1951

11 (Sphinx) Independent Light AA Battery Nov. 1950–Nov. 1951

(4.2 Mortars June '51)

170 Independent Mortar Battery Nov. 1950–Oct. 1951

14 Field Rgt Nov. 1950–Dec. 1951

ROYAL ENGINEERS

55 Field Squadron Nov. 1950–Jul. 1951

ROYAL ARMY MEDICAL CORPS

26 Field Ambulance Dec. 1950–1954

29th Commonwealth General Hospital KURE

Queen Alexandra's Royal Military Nursing Corps

Queen Alexandra's Royal Naval Nursing Corps

Royal Army Nurses Corps

CORPS

Royal Electrical and Mechanical Engineers

Royal Army Ordnance Corps

Intelligence Corps

Royal Military Police

Royal Army Pay Corps

Navy, Army, Air Force Institutes

ROYAL AIR FORCE

Royal Australian Air Force No. 77 Squadron

Royal Canadian Air Force No. 426 (Thunderbird) Transport Squadron

South African Air Force No. 2 Squadron (Flying Cheetahs)

ROYAL NAVY

HMS *Unicorn*, Aircraft Carrier 1950–1953

HMS *Ceylon*, Cruiser 1950–1952

Royal Fleet Auxiliary (Numerous)

HMHS Marine Hospital Ship 1950–1953

ROYAL AUSTRALIAN NAVY

HMAS *Bataan*, Destroyer 1950—

HMAS *Warramunga*, Destroyer 1950—

AMERICAN UNITS

24th (Taro Leaf) Infantry Division USA

1st Cavalry Division USA (5th, 7th and 8th Regiments)

1st US Marines Division

2nd (Indian Head) Mechanised Infantry Division USA

3rd Infantry Division USA

82nd Airborne Division USA (187th Regimental Combat Team)

MASH (Mobile Army Surgical Hospital)

USS (Troop Transport) *Montrose* USN

Appendix I
Organisational Chart,
Royal Papua New Guinea Constabulary 1981

All British Commonwealth Police Forces were set up on the same principles. These were originally based on military formations. Another strong influence was the Royal Irish Constabulary, when dealing with unrest. Both UK and Dominion Forces have the same concepts, likewise Colonial Forces which had a more regular exchange of ideas due to internal transfers. Training methods and the law were similar throughout.

RPNGC Establishment/Strength		
Commands	Officers	Rank & File
PHQ	Commissioner 1	7,000
	Deputy 2	
	Assistant 6	
	Chief Supt 2	
Regions/Divisions	ACP 3	2,000–1,000
(7)	CSP 4	600–300
Provinces (20)	SSP/SP/CI 1	300–150
Stations (51)	SP/CI/IP 1	150–50
Substations (12)	IP/SI 1	50–25
NCOs Attached	Members on Parade	
Sen/Sgt Major	500–1,000	Region/Division
Sgt/Major	100–200	Province
S/Sgt	50–100	Station
Sgt	25–50	Substation
Cpl/S/Cons	5–10	Section
L/Cpl/Cons1/c	1–5	Subsection
Constable		

PHQ (Port Moresby) CP					
CSP SO1				CSP PR	
DCP Admin		Civil Sec		DCP Ops	
ACP P&T	Accounts/ Pay	ACP Logs	ACP Ops	ACP Crime/Pros	ACP Traffic & Transport
Band/ Legal/ Records/ Postings/ Recruits/ College		R&D/ QM			

Regions/Divisions ACP NCD (Port Moresby)		
SP POM	SSP Boroko	SP Gerehu

SP Enga P	SP Southern HP	ACP Highlands (Mt Hagen) SSP Western HP	SP Chimbu P
CI Wabag	CI Mendi	SP Hagen	CI Kundiawa
IP Laigam	SGT Pangia	IP Banzj	IP Kerowagi
IP Porgera		IP Minj	Sgt Nondugl
IP Wape- namanda		SI Anglimp	
		SI Muglamp	

ACP NG Mainland (Lae)				
CI West Sepik P	SP East Sepik P	SSP Morobe P	SP Madang P	SP Eastern HP
IP Vanimo	CI Wewak	SP Lae	CI Madang	CI Goroka

SI Wutung	SI Angoram	SI Mumeng		SI Yonki
	IP Maprik	IP Finschhafen		IP Kainantu
		SI Wau		IP Henganfoi
		IP Bulolo		CI Highway Patrol
				Sgt Wabatung

CSP Islands Division (Rabaul)			
CI West New Britain P	SSP East New Britain P	CI New Ireland P	CI Manus P
IP Kimbe SI Hoskins Sgt Talasea	SP Rabaul IP Kokopo SI Kerevat	SI Konos IP Kavieng IP Namatanai	IP Lorengau

CSP Bougainville Division (Kieta)		
IP Loloho	CI Kieta	IP Panguna

CSP Papua Division (Port Moresby)				
CI Western P	IP Gulf P	CI Central P	CI Northern P	CI Milne Bay P
IP Daru	IP Kerema	IP Berina SI Sogeri SI Kopiano	IP Popendetta	IP Alotau SI Samarai

CSP Mobile Force (Riot Paramilitary)			
SP Islands	SP Highlands	CI NG Mainland	CI National Capital
IP Tomaringa 2 Training 2	IP Kundiawa IP Mt Hagen 3 IP Mendi IP Wabag	IP Goroka IP Lae	IP Port Moresby 3

Provincial Police Stations				
		SP/CI		
Shift IP 4 Duty Officer 4	IP CIB	IP Prosecutions	SI Transport	IP Barracks
IP Traffic	IP Process Warrants & Summons	IP Dog Sec	SI Firearms	Station Clerk

RAPID ACTION TEAM (RATS 1, 2, 3, 4)
40–60 Saturation Policing in area of high crime incidence
CI
Commands four sections of:
IP
Cpl
CIB/Prosecutions
Traffic
Police woman
Dog handler
Photographic
SI
Sgt
Gas Gunner 2
Shot Gunner 2
Driver Tip Truck
Driver Land Cruiser 2

(A section can operate as two subunits as the complement of Officers and NCOs is beefed up to provide separate actions.)

The Field Constabulary

This was governed by the Administration Department. The Regular Constabulary policed the cities, towns and settled areas. The Field Constabulary policed the remote and unsettled areas. Each Province had a Provincial Commissioner, his sub-provinces were controlled by an Assistant Provincial Commissioner, who in turn had the support of

Provincial Officers and Patrol Officers operating Patrol Posts along with cadets. Regular Constabulary were seconded in strengths of 5 to 15 rank and file. PNG had some 80 Sub-Provinces and approximately 60 Patrol Posts. Each Province had around about 5–8 such Detachments. They had the ability to call in Regular Constabulary if needed. The 'Kiap' was well educated and a dedicated person.

Police on the ground were in a ratio of 1:500 or 1:1,000 dependent on different variables such as incidence of crime, distance, terrain, communication, transport and funding.

The Chain of Command was on a ratio of 1:3 or 1:5.

Maps

KOREA, SHOWING LINES OF ADVANCE, 1950 TO 1953

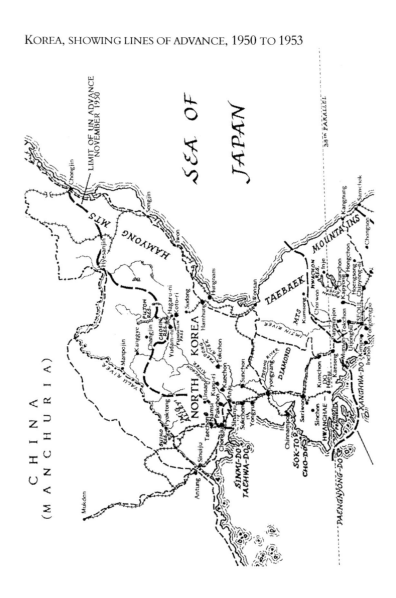

398

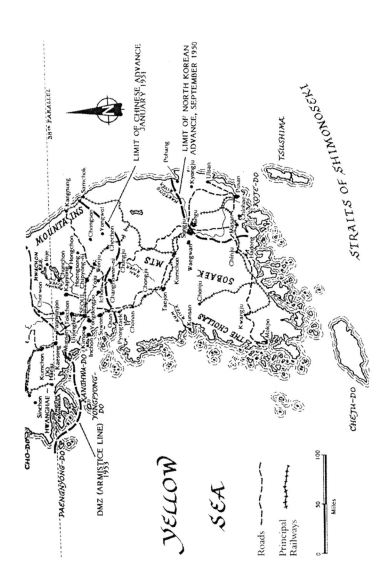

38th PARALLEL

LIMIT OF CHINESE ADVANCE JANUARY 1951

LIMIT OF NORTH KOREAN ADVANCE, SEPTEMBER 1950

N

TSUSHIMA

STRAITS OF SHIMONOSEKI

Pohang

Kangnung

Samchok

Inje

MOUNTAINS

HWACHON KYE

Chongson

Chongwol

Chunchon

Chorwon

Kapyong

Heongsong

Hongchon

Hwachon

DAEDONG

Kyongju

Ulsan

Pusan

KOJE-DO

Yongju

Yoju

Chechon

Songju

Taegu

Milyang

Kimhae

MTS

Wonju

Chungju

Changhowon-ni

Ichon

Waegwan

Chinju

SEOUL

Osan

Pyongtaek

Chonan

Taejon

Kumchon

Chongju

SOBAEK

Suwon

Uijongbu

NAKTONG MTS

Songhwan

Kunsan

Kwangju

THE CHOLLAS

Chonju

Imjin

Panmunjom

Munsan

Tokchon

Inchon

Kaesong

Masong

Haeju

KANGHWA-DO

Kumchon

Sinchon

HWANGHAE DO

Mokpo

Masan

Chinhae

YONGPYONG-DO

CHO-DO

PAENGNYONG-DO

DMZ (ARMISTICE LINE) 1953

YELLOW

SEA

CHEJU-DO

Roads ---

Principal Railways +++

Miles

0   50   100

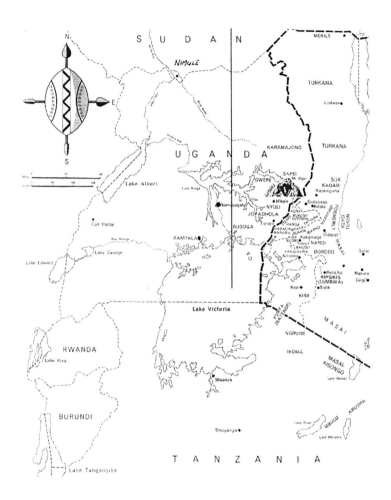

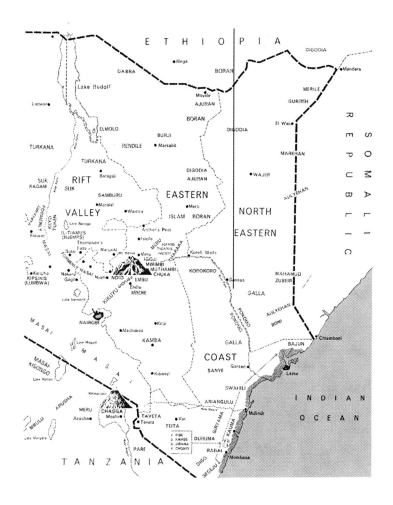

ETHIOPIA

DIGODIA

GABRA   BORAN   Mandera

•Mega

Lake Rudolf   Moyale   MERILE
                   AJURAN   GURREH
Lodwar•   El Wak•
          ELMOLO   BORAN
                               DIGODIA   MAREHAN
TURKANA   SURJI
          RENDILE   •Marsabit   •WAJIR   AULYEHAN

          TURKANA   Baragui   DIGODIA
SUK   AJURAN
KADAM   SUK   SAMBURU
RIFT   •Maralal   EASTERN   NORTH
VALLEY   •Wamba   Meru•
                    ISLAM BORAN   EASTERN
          Lake Baringo   Archer's Post
EL-TIAMUS   Korch Wells   MAHAMUD
(NJEMPS)   Thompson's   •Isiolo   MERU   ZUBEIR
          Nanyuki•   Mt Kenya   Meru IGEMBE
Eldoret•   Kitale   Mt Kenya   Mbeu TIGANIA KOROKORO
                    IGOJI MWENZI
KIPSIKIS   Nakuru•   Nyeri• NDIO MWIMBI   •Garissa   GALLA
(LUMBWA)   Gilgil•   EMBU MUTHAMBI CHUKA
          Lake Naivasha   KIKUYU MBERE   POKOMO
MASAI   NAIROBI•   AULYEHAN
          Lake Magadi   •Machakos   •Kitui   BONI
MASAI   KAMBA   GALLA   BAJUN   Chiamboni•
MASAI
KISONGO   COAST   Garsan•   Lamu•
          •Kibwezi   SANYE   INDIAN
ARUSHA   SWAHILI
MBULU   MERU   CHAGGA •Voi ARIANGULU   OCEAN
     •Arusha Moshi• TAVETA TEITA GIRYAMA Malindi•
Lake Manyara   •Taveta   1 RIBE DURUMA
                    2 KAMBE RABAI• Mombasa•
          PARE   4 CHONYI
T A N Z A N I A   DIGO

S O M A L I   R E P U B L I C

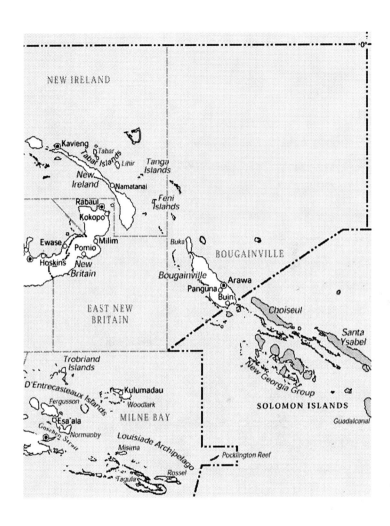

NEW IRELAND

Kavieng
Tabar
Tabar Islands
Lihir
Tanga Islands
New Ireland
Namatanai
Feni Islands
Rabaul
Kokopo
Ewase
Milim
Buka
BOUGAINVILLE
Pomio
Hoskins
New Britain
Bougainville
Panguna
Arawa
Buin
EAST NEW BRITAIN
Choiseul
Santa Ysabel
Trobriand Islands
D'Entrecasteaux Islands
Kulumadau
Woodlark
New Georgia Group
Fergusson
SOLOMON ISLANDS
Esa'ala
MILNE BAY
Guadalcanal
Goschen Strait
Normanby
Louisiade Archipelago
Misima
Pocklington Reef
Tagula
Rossel

0°

Bibiliography

PART I: KOREA

Our Men In Korea by Eric Linklater, 1952

The Korean War by Tim Carew, 1967

Fortune Favours The Brave by A J Buker, 1976

The Korean War by Max Hastings, 1987

About Face by Col David H Hackworth & Julie Sherman, 1989

Korea – The Forgotten War by John Hooker, 1989

At War In Korea by George Forty, 1997

The Korean War by Michael Hickey, 1999

PART II: GLASGOW POLICE 1951–1955, 1964–1966

The Big Men by Joe Pieri

PART III: KENYA POLICE

The Sorcerer's Apprentice by Elspeth Huxley, 1951

A Thing To Have by Elspeth Huxley, 1954

Isle of Cloves by F D Ommannery, 1955

Leopard in my Lap by Michaela Denis, 1955

Lightest Africa by F Spencer Chapman DSO, 1955

Something of Value by Robert Ruark, 1955

The Flame Trees of Thika by Elspeth Huxley, 1959

Born Free by Joy Adamson, 1960

The Kenya Police 1887–1960 by W Robert Foran, 1962

Bwana Game by George Adamson, 1968

Animals of East Africa by Louis S B Leakey, 1969

The Peoples of Kenya by Joy Adamson, 1975

Tales of Kenya by J W Ord, 1997

Kenya Cowboy by Peter Hewitt, 1999

HABARI (KPA) *Magazine*, by Mike Hudson & Former Officers of Kenya Police, 2002

INTERLUDE ONE: AUSSIE – TASSIE 1966–67

The Book Of Australia by The Watermark Press, 1998

PART IV: PAPUA NEW GUINEA 1947–82

Neo-Melanesia by Rev. Francis Mihalic SVD, BA, 1957

Patrol Into Yesterday by J K McCarthy, 1967

New Guinea by James L Andersen Donald Hogg, 1969

Battleground South Pacific by Bruce Adams/Robert Howlett, 1970

Isles of the South Pacific by Maurce Shadbolt/Olaf Ruhen, 1971

Encyclopaedia of PNG by Peter Ryan, 1972

Port Moresby by Ian Streaty, 1973

Village Directory by Govt Printer, 1973

PNG by PNG Govt Gazette, 1975

Paradise by Air Niugini In Flight, 1977

Orchids PNG by Andee Millar, 1978

The Best of Grass Roots by Wayne L Grant, 1980–81

PART IV: NEW ZEALAND

Beyond Skippers Road by Terri MacNichol, 1965

High Country Four Seasons by Gordon Roberts/Brian Turner, 1985

PART V: CHILE, CANADA

Short History of Chile by Sergio R Villalobos, 1996

Canadian History by Ann Douglas, 1997

Printed in the United States
113484LV00001B/10/A

9 781844 014217